WALKING THE VIA FRANCIGENA PILGRIM ROUTE – PART 4

ROME TO MONTE SANT'ANGELO, BARI, BRINDISI AND SANTA MARIA DI LEUCA

by Sandy Brown and Nicole Bukaty

JUNIPER HOUSE, MURLEY MOSS,
OXENHOLME ROAD, KENDAL, CUMBRIA LA9 7RL
www.cicerone.co.uk

First edition 2025
ISBN: 978 1 78631 249 5
eISBN: 978 1 78765 192 0

Printed in Singapore by KHL Printing on responsibly sourced paper.
A catalogue record for this book is available from the British Library.
All photographs are by Sandy Brown unless otherwise stated.

Route mapping by Lovell Johns www.lovelljohns.com

Contains OpenStreetMap.org data © OpenStreetMap contributors, CC-BY-SA. NASA relief data courtesy of ESRI

Cicerone's EU representative for GPSR compliance is Easy Access System Europe, Mustamäe tee 50, 10621 Tallinn, Estonia. Email gpsr.requests@easproject.com.

Updates to this guide

While every effort is made by our authors to ensure the accuracy of guidebooks as they go to print, changes can occur during the lifetime of an edition. Any updates that we know of for this guide will be on the Cicerone website (www.cicerone.co.uk/1249/updates), so please check before planning your trip. We also advise that you check information about such things as transport, accommodation and shops locally. Even rights of way can be altered over time.

The route maps in this guide are derived from publicly available data, databases and crowd-sourced data. As such they have not been through the detailed checking procedures that would generally be applied to a published map from an official mapping agency, although naturally we have reviewed them closely in the light of local knowledge as part of the preparation of this guide.

We are always grateful for information about any discrepancies between a guidebook and the facts on the ground, sent by email to updates@cicerone.co.uk.

Register your book: To sign up to receive free updates, special offers and GPX files where available, create a Cicerone account and register your purchase via the 'My Account' tab at www.cicerone.co.uk.

Front cover: The route to Santa Maria di Leuca can be combined with a pilgrimage to Monte Sant'Angelo before walking the Adriatic coastline (photo: Nicole Bukaty)

ROUTE SUMMARY TABLES

Stage	Start/finish	Distance	Total ascent	Total descent	Duration	Page
1	Rome to Castel Gandolfo	26.2km	552m	145m	7hr	45
2	Castel Gandolfo to Velletri	21.5km	481m	582m	5¾hr	53
3	Velletri to Cori	18.9km	344m	266m	5hr	58
4	Cori to Sermoneta	20.3km	534m	708m	5½hr	62
5	Sermoneta to Sezze	11.0km	307m	240m	3hr	66
6	Sezze to Abbazia di Fossanova	20.9km	241m	513m	5½hr	69
7	Abbazia di Fossanova to Terracina	20.6km	130m	104m	5¼hr	74
8	Terracina to Fondi	22.0km	378m	407m	6hr	83
9	Fondi to Itri	15.1km	336m	170m	4¼hr	88
10	Itri to Formia	21.1km	358m	516m	5½hr	91
11	Formia to Marina di Minturno	19.8km	100m	115m	5hr	95
12	Marina di Minturno to Sessa Aurunca	24.2km	372m	170m	6½hr	100
13	Sessa Aurunca to Teano	15.4km	314m	312m	4¼hr	107
14	Teano to Roccaromana	20.6km	114m	164m	5¼hr	111
15	Roccaromana to Alife	21.4km	302m	347m	5½hr	115
16	Alife to Faicchio	19.3km	325m	252m	5¼hr	119
17	Faicchio to Telese Terme	12.6km	255m	370m	3½hr	123
18	Telese Terme to Vitulano	16.6km	796m	398m	5½hr	127
19	Vitulano to Benevento	17.1km	187m	493m	4½hr	131
20	Benevento to Buonalbergo	23.3km	766m	357m	6½hr	136
21	Buonalbergo to Celle di San Vito	29.0km	873m	708m	8hr	141
22	Celle di San Vito to Troia	17.4km	314m	599m	4¾hr	151
23	Troia to Castelluccio dei Sauri	23.7km	184m	343m	6¼hr	154
24	Castelluccio dei Sauri to Ordona	20.0km	137m	297m	5¼hr	158
25	Ordona to Stornara	20.3km	141m	148m	5¼hr	162
26	Stornara to Cerignola	17.9km	97m	84m	4½hr	166
27	Cerignola to Canosa di Puglia	19.3km	99m	110m	5hr	169
28	Canosa di Puglia to Andria	24.1km	267m	221m	6¼hr	173
29	Andria to Corato	13.9km	113m	38m	3½hr	176
30	Corato to Ruvo di Puglia	12.2km	126m	96m	3¼hr	179
31	Ruvo di Puglia to Bitonto	18.4km	13m	154m	4¾hr	182
32	Bitonto to Bari	23.7km	211m	302m	6¼hr	185
33	Bari to Mola di Bari	23.6km	98m	102m	6hr	190

Stage	Start/finish	Distance	Total ascent	Total descent	Duration	Page
34	Mola di Bari to Monopoli	29.1km	203m	207m	7½hr	194
35	Monopoli to Savelletri	21.4km	137m	136m	5½hr	200
36	Savelletri to Torre Canne	8.9km	37m	37m	2¼hr	204
37	Torre Canne to Torre Santa Sabina	30.1km	140m	142m	7¾hr	206
38	Torre Santa Sabina to Brindisi	31.0km	148m	143m	8hr	211
39	Brindisi to Torchiarolo	25.2km	184m	163m	6½hr	261
40	Torchiarolo to Lecce	22.5km	144m	117m	5¾hr	266
41	Lecce to Martano	30.9km	194m	174m	8hr	273
42	Martano to Otranto	30.5km	205m	266m	8hr	278
43	Otranto to Vignacastrisi	23.9km	216m	138m	6¼hr	286
44	Vignacastrisi to Tricase	14.3km	127m	119m	3¾hr	292
45	Tricase to Santa Maria di Leuca	18.0km	119m	164m	4¾hr	296
Total		**937.2km**	**11,719m**	**11,637m**	**247hr**	

MONTE SANT'ANGELO VARIANT AND VIA LITORANEA CONNECTION

Stage	Name	Distance	Ascent	Descent	Duration	Page
MSA23	Troia to Lucera	21.7km	122m	340m	5½hr	219
MSA24	Lucera to San Severo	24.2km	115m	246m	6¼hr	223
MSA25	San Severo to Stignano	21.3km	447m	283m	5¾hr	227
MSA26	Stignano to San Giovanni Rotondo	19.7km	885m	503m	6hr	231
MSA27	San Giovanni Rotondo to Monte Sant'Angelo	24.2km	533m	342m	6½hr	237
Total		**111.1km**	**2102m**	**1714m**	**30hr**	
VLC	Monte Sant'Angelo to Bari	143km	597m	1344m	33hr	246

Dedications

From Sandy Brown

To Rocky Brown-Nieblas who no one guessed would move from sister to collaborator to business partner. Her empathy and attention to detail are legendary, and her friendship over many decades is priceless.

From Nicole Bukaty

To my mother who teaches me courage in the face of adversity, and my father who gave me his love for all things big and, importantly, small.

Acknowledgments

Nicole Bukaty researched and wrote the historical, artistic, architectural, and cultural information in this book, researched lodgings, and summarized the walking stages from Monte Sant'Angelo to Bari. Sandy Brown walked and cycled the rest, took photographs, wrote captions, edited maps, wrote the primary walking directions, and compiled statistics. Together, they wrote the Introduction. This book wouldn't have happened without the leadership of Angelofabio Attolico of the EAVF and Region of Puglia. In addition to his stewardship of the route, his excellent guidebook was always a handy reference in our work. Jonathan Williams joined a research expedition to Lazio, and his photos, walking directions, and companionship are always a treasure. Eric Partika was a welcome walking companion on the same route and became an invaluable communicator with local service providers. An unexpected gift was to be accompanied by the Gruppo dei Dodici, volunteers who were inspired by the late Alberto Alberti, longtime friend and advocate of the Via Francigena in the South. We especially thank Roberto, Giancarlo, Mario, Michele, Herta, Carmine, Luigi, Giuseppe, Vincenzo, Antoniella, Lucia, Emilia, and other Dodici members who accompanied us from Rome as far as Sessa Aurunca. Indispensable in Troia were Michele and Antonio. Although an injury kept him from the main research trip, Giovanni Ramaccioni was invaluable as our trusted guide to Italy in general and Puglia in particular. For co-author Sandy Brown, his wife Theresa Elliott is a constant source of strength and inspiration. Nicole Bukaty's fellow pilgrim and sister Patrycja Bukaty shared the scenic and culinary delights of the Puglian coast and contributed to parts of this guide.

CONTENTS

Symbols used on maps

start point
finish point
start/finish point
11.1 distance marker
3.2 alt distance marker
main route/alternative route
main route (alternative stage)
alternative route (alternative stage)
international/regional boundary
railway station
woodland
urban areas

summit
pass
bridge
building
P parking
castle
cemetery
church/cathedral/monastery
viewpoint
lighthouse
point of interest
other feature

FACILITIES

groceries
ATM
rest/picnic area
toilet
drinking water
pharmacy
hospital
medical clinic
tourist/pilgrim information
bus station
tram stop
ferry
airport

accommodation
- hostel, religious or private hospitality
- hotel
- B&B
- camere/ guest rooms
- apartment
- agriturismo
- camping

catering
- café
- restaurant
- bakery
- bar

Relief
in metres

1000–1200
800–1000
600–800
400–600
200–400
0–200

MAP SCALES

Route maps at 1:100,000
Town maps at 1:25,000 unless otherwise stated (see scale bar)

SCALE: 1:100,000
0 kilometres 1 2
0 miles 1

SCALE: 1:25,000
0 kilometres 0.25 0.5
0 miles 0.25

GPX files for all routes can be downloaded free at www.cicerone.co.uk/1249/GPX.

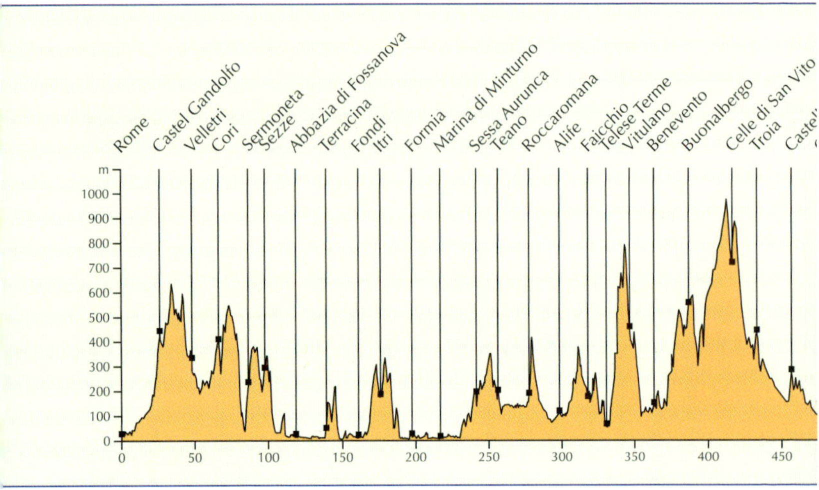

The city of Troia is obscured by trees at the top of the far hill in this springtime view (Stage 22)

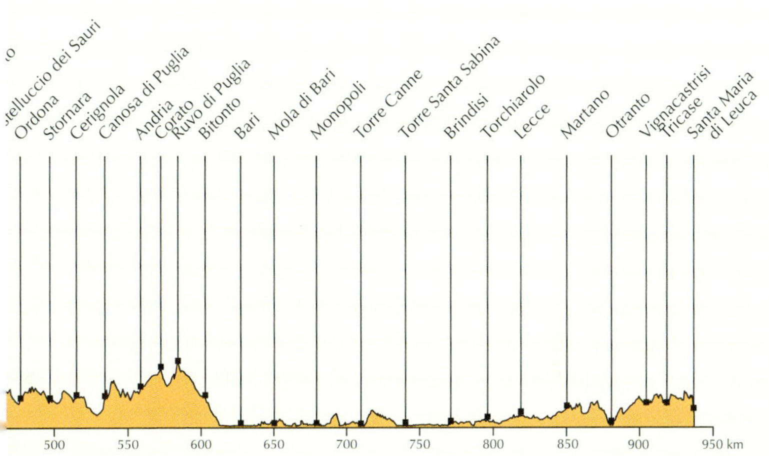

...o
...telluccio dei Sauri
Ordona
Stornara
Cerignola
Canosa di Puglia
Andria
Corato
Ruvo di Puglia
Bitonto
Bari
Mola di Bari
Monopoli
Torre Canne
Torre Santa Sabina
Brindisi
Torchiarolo
Lecce
Martano
Otranto
Vignacastrisi
Tricase
Santa Maria di Leuca
500
550
600
650
700
750
800
850
900
950 km

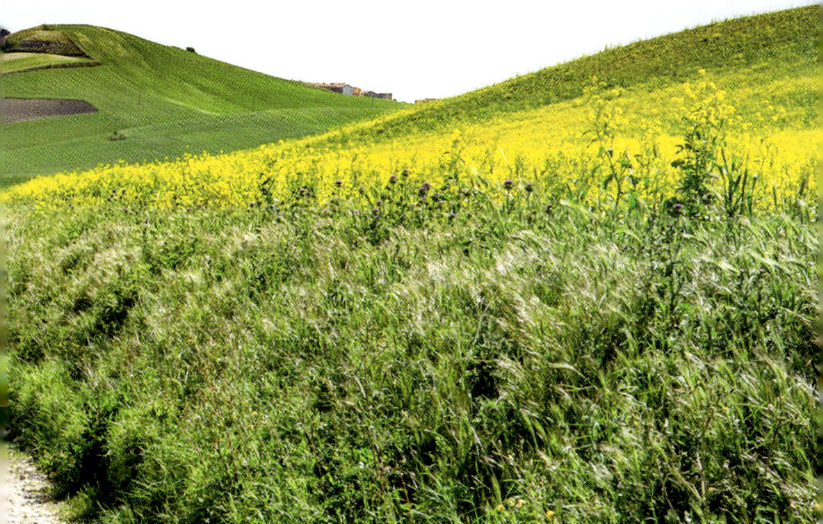

FOREWORDS

The Via Francigena – The Road to Rome – is a Cultural Route of the Council of Europe. The European Association of the Via Francigena ways (EAVF) is a voluntary association of regions and local authorities of England, France, Switzerland, and Italy and currently accounts for more than 240 members. It was established on April 7, 2001, in Fidenza (Emilia-Romagna, Italy) to promote the Via Francigena – a 3200km pilgrim route from Canterbury to Santa Maria di Leuca. The route starts from Canterbury and travels through France and Switzerland to Rome and continues to the south of Italy, heading toward Jerusalem. It passes through 16 European Regions (Kent, Hauts-de-France, Grand Est, Bourgogne-Franche-Comté, Vaud, Valais, Valle d'Aosta, Piedmont, Lombardy, Emilia-Romagna, Liguria, Tuscany, Lazio, Campania, Basilicata, Puglia) in 5 countries (England, France, Switzerland, Italy, and Vatican City). The association carries out activities to enhance and promote the route at all institutional levels: local, regional, national, and European.

In 2007 the Council of Europe declared the association the 'carrier network' of the Via Francigena, appointing it the official body for safeguarding, protecting, promoting, and developing the Via in Europe.

This guide of the route from the eternal city of Rome to Santa Maria di Leuca is the result of collaboration between the EAVF, the involved regions, Cicerone Press, and local associations. It is intended for walkers and pilgrims who want to discover the beauty of the Via Francigena in the South: a spectacular voyage along ancient roads that takes in archeological sites, castles aplenty, and nature's wonders amid boundless horizons where land, sky, and sea blend together.

We wish you all a good journey! *Buon cammino*!

Francesco Ferrari
President, European Association of the Via Francigena ways
For all information, visit www.viefrancigene.org or follow us on our social media:
Facebook: @ViaFrancigenaEU; Instagram: Viafrancigena_eu

The publication of this guide represents an important moment in the technical and interpretative extension of an itinerary that is as complex as it is fascinating. The journey of the Via Francigena in southern Italy has been long and not without difficulties. It has been more than 10 years since the first meeting on this topic in Luxembourg between the EAVF president, Massimo Tedeschi, and the director of the European Institute for Cultural Routes of the Council of Europe, Penelope Denu.

To achieve the goal of developing the route south of Rome, the Regions of Lazio, Campania and Puglia coordinated together with the aim of redesigning the Via Francigena. Determination of the actual route led to a feasibility study that then gave rise to a timetable of actions necessary to guarantee the usability of the itinerary. A major project of safety and signage works, for instance, was carried out with

A fanciful sign, painted by a local Francigena volunteer, on the route near Giulianello (Stage 3)

autonomous regional funds, integrated this year by the Ministry of Culture and the Ministry of Tourism.

With the awareness that a path cannot function without an infrastructure of services, each region has also secured the availability of religious accommodations, B&Bs, agriturismos and hostels that themselves have taken up the challenge of contributing to a development model which will become an important driving force precisely in those areas of the south that are suffering from depopulation and economic depression.

But all this is not enough. To have lasting results over time, this process could not ignore the participation of local administrations and communities. While the Via Francigena was being built, many municipalities in the center-south joined EAVF, achieving the dual objective of finding a concrete space for dialogue with European partners and of promoting their heritage at an international level. Furthermore, a third sector, organized with the model of 'community committees', has become a point of reference not only for travelers, but for the locals themselves, starting helpful processes within the territory that are leading to new modes of active citizenship.

From this perspective, the certification of the southern Via Francigena could only be a logical consequence. In Bari, on October 18, 2019, the delegates of the EAVF unanimously voted to extend the

Via Francigena to the south, a decision that was subsequently ratified by the Council of Europe the following year.

The pandemic that followed did not slow down the project. Significantly, 'The Road to Rome,' the international exhibition event that celebrated the twentieth anniversary of the EAVF, concluded in Leuca on October 18, 2021. The event demonstrated that the Via Francigena was becoming a point of reference for a new generation of leaders wanting to invest in a different model of tourism, a model more culturally integrated and environmentally sustainable.

The years between 2022 and 2024 confirmed this trend, supported by a significant increase in foreign pilgrims who increasingly see the southern route as a way to get to know a part of Europe previously known only for its coastline. Unfortunately this period was also marked by the death of EAVF founder Massimo Tedeschi, but the appointment of Francesco Ferrari as president is certain to continue the trend of growth and development.

A single Via Francigena from Canterbury to Leuca is the result: no longer a Via Francigena of the South but Via Francigena in the South, meaning – in this simple geographical determination – a fully European route, an integral part of the identity of its territories and citizens.

The journey has just begun.

Aldo Patruno
Director of the Department of Tourism, Economy of Culture and Territorial Development, Puglia Region
Vice President, EAVF

When, in 2018, the late president of the EAVF, Massimo Tedeschi, entrusted me with the task of reconstructing the Via Francigena in the South, the goal of creating a route of international interest still seemed very far away. In previous years the itinerary had been fragmented for political reasons into an infinite number of local segments, which had caused the overall identity of the oldest pilgrimage route known in Europe to be lost.

The technical work we had ahead of us was therefore very arduous and involved difficult choices. On the one hand, it was necessary to recover the historical and architectural testimonies of the journeys to Rome and Jerusalem. On the other, we had a duty to guarantee the modern traveler safety and essential services. Clearly, in the six centuries since the end of the pilgrimage era in the Middle Ages, the landscape has inevitably changed and it was not always possible to slavishly follow the ancient routes (assuming that archaeological research had actually identified them). The physical barriers to use of ancient routes included the growing population, the invasion of asphalt, the multiplication of high-speed rail lines, hydrogeological instability, and legislation that in Italy does not allow transit on private paths. Fragments of the ancient routes appear only as relics of a pedestrian world largely erased by mechanization.

And yet, as often happens on paths, somehow the solution presented itself spontaneously by listening to the local communities and traveling the territories slowly, as pilgrims, before as technicians. I, Claudio Focarazzo, and Lorenzo Lozito travelled all 900km of the Via Francigena in the South several times and in different seasons of the year. Now the entire route has been set, digitally mapped, divided into stages and organized for accommodations.

The ancient road system was a guide for us, an orientation that allowed us to choose the best possible route, taking care to save from oblivion the true soul of this journey: the material and spiritual heritage linked to the stories of men and women who, in times less comfortable than ours, risked their lives to reach the dream of the Holy Land.

Thanks to the work of the Ministry of Tourism, the Regions of Lazio, Campania and Puglia, the EAVF, the communities, and many volunteers – all of whom worked many years to develop the infrastructure of this route – I am happy that we are able to support the creation of this guide, a guide that I am sure will help the international public appreciate the beauty and historical depth of central-southern Italy.

Buon cammino.
Angelofabio Attolico, Ph.D.
Coordinator of the Committee of the Caminos, Cultural Itineraries and Cycle Tourism, Puglia Region
Technical Manager of the Via Francigena in the South, EAVF

A Francigena pilgrim walks on the ancient pavers of the Via Appia south of Rome (Stage 1)

INTRODUCTION: ROME TO MONTE SANT'ANGELO, BARI, BRINDISI AND SANTA MARIA DI LEUCA

Before anyone ever dreamed of making a pilgrimage to Santiago de Compostela in the far west of Europe, the pilgrim route south of Rome was already centuries old. Rome itself, of course, was an ancient pilgrimage destination of immense importance, and many would walk to Rome and return to their homes well satisfied with their journey. Beyond Rome, though, across the sea, in a storied and holy land, lay the crown jewels of Christian pilgrimage: Bethlehem, Galilee, the Mount of Olives, Gethsemane, and in Jerusalem the holiest of sepulchers, the tomb that could not hold the Son of God. For European pilgrims, between their homes and the Holy Land lay the mountains, valleys, plains, and seaports of Southern Italy.

Ancient and medieval pilgrims walked beyond Rome on the former empire's crumbling and timeworn roads, thoroughfares that had already begun their slow descent from road to lane to pathway to forest and mire and meadow. The pilgrims came from their cities and villages, from their convents and monasteries, from their hovels and castles. They came on foot or on horseback or alongside a donkey. They spent months under hot sun or shivering in cold rain, and fell asleep after too much wine, with pilgrim songs echoing in their ears. They were monks and noblewomen, soldiers and priests, beggars and farmers, and adventurers. From Rome, in a vast and timeless procession, they slowly made their way to the Adriatic ports of Bari, Brindisi, and Otranto, and then were carried by the wind to other seaports and trails in faraway lands where, with luck and grace, they would land in front of the object of their dreams.

To walk the Via Francigena in the South (VFS) is to join the same unending stream of pilgrims who passed along the same Roman roads, climbed the same green mountains, walked across the

Signs of many kinds welcome Via Francigena pilgrims south of Rome (Stage 8)

same vast fields, and stood looking with misty eyes at Europe behind them and the endless sea ahead.

As we walk in this new millennium, we experience parts of today's Italy where tourists seldom venture, and for our efforts we come to know an entrancing land of great geographical and cultural beauty. The route touches the coastlines of three seas – the Tyrrhenian, Adriatic, and Ionian. It crosses from the volcanic lakes and ridges of Lazio to the forested limestone mountains of Campania. In Puglia it transits broad grain fields on the Tavoliere and, if a pilgrim chooses, climbs the white stones of the Gargano to look down on the sweeping curve of the Gulf of Manfredonia. In the cultural mosaic that is Southern Italy, French is spoken in the heights between Campania and Puglia, Greek is spoken in Salento, and Italian itself knows at least four distinct Pugliese accents. South of Gaeta, across the old border with the Papal States, there is lingering affection for the Bourbon dynasty of old and a keen nostalgia for what was lost in forming the new state of Italy. The Via Francigena south of Rome is a treasure chest of history, culture, geography, and nature, and to walk these ancient paths is to open the lid to its wonders and be forever transformed.

Built by the Romans in AD114–117, the Arch of Trajan in Benevento celebrates completion of the Via Traiana, connecting the Via Appia from Benevento to Brindisi (Stages 19 and 20)

ORIGINS OF THE VIA FRANCIGENA IN THE SOUTH

Just as the 990 walk of Sigeric was the historical benchmark for the Via Francigena north of Rome, the records of an anonymous pilgrim in the years AD333–334 are the most historic and well-documented template for the Via Francigena in the South. Often called the Bordeaux Pilgrim, since his route began in Bordeaux (modern France), this ancient wayfarer made his way on Roman roads across Europe to Constantinople and from there via Antioch to Jerusalem. He returned by way of Constantinople and took a route across the Balkan Peninsula, sailing from Valona (modern Albania) to arrive at Otranto on the Italian Peninsula. Retracing that route (see Appendix D) it is quite clear he took the Via Appia-Calabra north from Otranto then the Via Appia Traiana from Brindisi to Rome.

The Via Appia was commissioned by Appio Claudio in 312BC. Its purpose was to link the empire's capital with crucial coastal gateways to the Balkan Peninsula and the Eastern Mediterranean, facilitating trade, political alliances, and military exploits. It became the most vital of the 400,000km of consular roads striking out of Rome, and it is no wonder, therefore, that outside the city and along the route, countless Roman and early Christian sites were built, such as mausoleums, temples, crypts, and catacombs. Although the cobblestone paving and much of the route itself has been obliterated by modern roads and tracks, the VFS creates a walkable itinerary that keeps as close as possible to the original track, with impressive evidence of Roman post stops, camps, temples, bridges, aqueducts, mile markers, and municipalities sprinkled along the way.

In addition to the Bordeaux Pilgrim, many other noble and humble pilgrims trod the same path, including St. Winnebald (701–787), likely of Wessex, who walked to Rome in 722 with his father (who died on the journey, in Lucca) and his brother, St. Willibald (700–787). Winnebald continued from Jerusalem in 724 and returned to become a monk at Montecassino and eventually bishop at Eichstätt.

Along this pilgrim way, there are additional destinations that have themselves been the object of devotion by local, national, and international travelers. The relics of St. Nicholas of Myra, template for the modern Santa Claus, have long been a destination of reverence at Bari. For centuries, Marian devotion has compelled people to visit the Basilica of Santa Maria di Leuca, and the shrine devoted to the Archangel Michael at Monte Sant'Angelo has been the destination for thousands, including St. Francis of Assisi, who walked here in 1216.

In October 2019, the EAVF approved a walkable route that closely follows the Bordeaux Pilgrim's itinerary between Rome and Otranto, extending it an additional 56km to include the historic pilgrimage site at Santa Maria di Leuca at the southern tip of Italy. It also added a 252km variant that allows pilgrims to walk to Monte Sant'Angelo, with connections to the main route at Troia in the west and Bari in the east. By combining this route with the Canterbury–Rome portion of the Via Francigena, the EAVF has created one of the greatest pilgrimage walking routes of the world: an international, cultural, historic, and geographic escapade spanning 3200km from the UK through France and Switzerland to the most southerly tip of mainland Italy.

A ROUTE STEEPED IN HISTORY

The Via Francigena in the South is an odyssey brimming with ancient relics, monuments, and art, bringing to life this venerable land's historical and mythical past. It is possible to group together six different historical periods on the Italian Peninsula south of Rome: prehistoric, pre-Roman, Roman, the Middle Ages, early modern, and modern.

The prehistoric period (46,000–1000BC)

There is ample historical evidence of Neanderthal populations in the Italian Peninsula, and *Homo sapiens* appeared in the area as early as 46,000BC. In the Copper, Bronze, and Iron Ages of prehistory, they developed into the populations we know of today by evidence gained mostly from dolmens, menhirs, and pottery found in archeological excavations. Dolmens are chambers or tombs usually consisting of a flat rock held up by two or more tall, thin rocks. Menhirs are upright, usually pointed, standing stones that perhaps stood as territorial or religious markers. Dolmens and menhirs can be found in many places along the Francigena, particularly around Otranto.

The pre-Roman period (1000–272BC)

Written history describes several political and linguistic groupings at the dawn of the 1st millennium BC. Etruscans and Latins populated the area around Rome, the Umbri and Samnites lived further south, Oscan peoples lived in modern-day Campania and northern Puglia, while Lucani, Mesapi, and Greek colonists lived in the coastal areas of the south. Rome was founded in 753BC and by 272BC had achieved hegemony over the southern Italian Peninsula. In 312BC the Via Appia was initiated and ran from Rome to Benevento, then on the frontier of Roman territory.

Small boats shelter at the Santo Spirito harbor near Bari (Stage 32)

The Roman period (272BC–AD476)

With most of Italy under its control, Rome turned its focus toward its domination of the Mediterranean basin. After Carthage and other Mediterranean powers were subdued, the Roman Empire paved the way for a 200-year period of relative peace and prosperity, the Pax Romana (27BC–AD180), which left a legacy of monuments, works of art and literature, and a network of roads stretching throughout the Mediterranean area and beyond. The Via Appia was extended from Benevento to Brindisi by Emperor Trajan, and today the Via Appia Traiana is a UNESCO World Heritage Site. The style of the art and architecture from this period is referred to as classical, and the Pantheon and Colosseum in Rome are fine examples.

The Middle Ages (476–1130)

While the Eastern Roman Empire of Byzantium, headquartered in Constantinople, would continue for another 1000 years, the Western Roman Empire ultimately fell to Odoacer of the Danube area in 472. Byzantine armies fought to return control to Rome, but ultimately Odoacer was replaced by the Ostrogoths and then the Lombards (Longobardi, in Italian). With support from the Papacy, the Franks, under Charlemagne, declared a new Holy Roman Empire in 814. Over the following centuries, the Saracens would make incursions into Southern Italy, while the Normans would unite much of the south into the Kingdom of Sicily. With the constant threat of invasion after the fall of Rome, urban areas that had not needed fortifications during the Roman period were moved to more defensible hilltops and surrounded by thick walls. Architecture from this period is sometimes lumped into a grouping called, in Italian, Longobardo. The Norman period left architectural treasures, mostly in fortifications, while church architecture late in this period would be considered Romanesque.

Kingdom of Sicily (1130–1861)

Northern and Central Italy became leaders in the Renaissance and Counter-Reformation, but focus shifted from the Central Mediterranean to the Atlantic Ocean as European powers colonized the Americas. The Kingdom of Sicily became a possession of Spain and Austria in the Bourbon dynasty, which ended when Napoleon established the Kingdom of Italy in 1805. A period of turmoil and rebellion occurred before and after 1861, when the army of the Kingdom of the Two Sicilies was defeated at Calatafimi by a Northern Italian army under Giuseppe Garibaldi on May 13, 1861. The latter part of this period saw the flowering of the ornate baroque style of architecture, followed by the (slightly) more restrained neoclassical style.

The modern era

Many Southern Italians trace the end of the Kingdom of the Two Sicilies to the beginning of the 'Piedmontization' of the south. The subsequent economic deterioration would lead to a diaspora of impoverished Southern Italians looking for better lives, particularly in the

The hilltop town of Sonnino basks in spring sunshine (Stage 7–8A; photo: Jonathan Williams)

Americas. Today, Italy's south is differentiated culturally and economically from the rest of Italy, with more agriculture, less industrialization, fewer governmental services, and a more traditional and religious culture. Increasingly, Puglia is seen in Italy as a region that has been spared industrialization, and one that continues to attract a tourist clientele that appreciates its spectacular scenery, outstanding gastronomy, and vibrant culture.

LANDSCAPES

Southern Italy's nuanced landscapes and cultures do not cease to impress travelers, who are absorbed into Italian life on an intimate scale. The route passes through the three regions of Lazio, Campania, and Puglia and their nine provinces: Roma, Latina, Caserta, Benevento, Foggia (the third-biggest province in Italy), Barletta-Andria-Trani, Bari, Brindisi, and Lecce.

Lazio is a land of contrasts, where ancient forest and volcanic lakes have inspired artists and poets who visited the hilltop towns, and where the Tyrrhenian Sea became the inspiration for the epic tales of Homer's *The Odyssey*. The sections through Campania remain largely unexplored by visitors; silence permeates the green mountains, where caves served as hideouts and shrines, and every rounded corner reveals another sweeping view. To reach Puglia is to arrive at sun-baked, colorful fishing towns with castles and cathedrals bathed in an ivory light. Anyone with a fleet has invaded this land where the Adriatic Sea meets the Ionian Sea and, being the longest coastline in Italy, it boasts meadows of wildflowers above sea caves ideal for snorkeling. Inland, the thin soil of the region's gently rolling hills is dense with olive groves, with a web of *tratturi* (drove roads) easing the way.

LANGUAGES

While on the trail, you will need basic Italian to communicate with the locals, except in some of the major cities. Accommodation hosts may or may not speak English.

THE PILGRIM EXPERIENCE

Overall, the VFS is an easy route, although some stages are challenging. Above all, accommodation arrangements need forward planning and advance reservation. As the pilgrimage is still in development, with minimal pilgrim-related infrastructure, be prepared for a possibly solitary walk, unlike other popular routes. Although pilgrims may be few, you will find the locals friendly and helpful. Their joy at meeting pilgrims is contagious and do not be surprised by invitations for drinks or meals. They may even accompany you on a stage! There are several helpful local associations that aid pilgrims, and a list of useful contacts and sources of information is provided in Appendix B.

The credenziale (pilgrim passport)

The *credenziale* is a pilgrim's identity card; it is a booklet that can be stamped with a *timbro* (stamp) to record the journey. For religious or donation-based accommodation, it is important to show your credenziale to prove your authenticity as a pilgrim, and you can also receive pilgrim discounts where these are offered. Although not all are official Via Francigena stamps, you can get them from lodgings, eateries, churches, and cathedrals. The credenziale must be presented in order for you to receive your completion certificate (Testimonium), should you wish (see below for further details on the Testimonium). Pilgrim discounts, upon presentation of the credenziale, may apply to meals and drinks, as well as a 10% discount on Trenitalia and Trenord trains (www.viefrancigene.org/en/trenitalia-en) and Flixbus coaches in low season (www.viefrancigene.org/en/partners/flixbus).

To purchase your credenziale (usually €8 in cash), all locations and contact details are listed in Appendix B. Updates can be found at www.viefrancigene.org/it/punti-di-distribuzione.

The Testimonium (certificate of completion)

On the VFS, even if you don't attempt it all in one go, and as long as you have walked the last 100km or cycled the last 200km, you are eligible to receive a *Testimonium* (certificate of completion) from Brindisi, Monte Sant'Angelo, Rome/Vatican City, and Santa Maria di Leuca. The Testimonium is an exquisite scroll – an excellent reward for your undertaking. To qualify for a Testimonium, it is essential to gather two stamps a day, at least on the final 100km for walkers and final 200km for cyclists.

For a Testimonium from St. Peter's Basilica in the Vatican, you must have walked from Priverno (coming from the south along the VFS). The basilica is open daily 07.00–19.10. You can skip the long security queues on St. Peter's Square and go straight to the first metal detector under the colonnade. Show the security guard your credenziale and they will direct you to the metal detector at the front of the queue. You will need to remove restricted items and put your backpack through the scanner. Then, with your pack, go to the cloakroom to the right of the steps that lead to the basilica. Here at the booth a volunteer will greet you, stamp your credenziale, and fill out your Testimonium. Don't forget to store your backpack in the cloakroom to enjoy your explorations!

For a Testimonium in Monte Sant'Angelo, the rules have recently

Exterior of Abbazia di San Magno (Stage 8; photo: Jonathan Williams)

De immensa sua benignitate, Matris Sanctissimae
cor misericordia ita erga peccatores instanter plenum
disposuit Deus, ut christifideles semper
et ubique implorarent praesidium.
Quam porro peregrini etiam ex universo orbe
per Via Francigena
in extrema hac Salentinorum terra portam Orientis,
utriusque maris pharum, pulchrum arcum aetheri ac populo
peregrinanti certae spei et solacii documentum venerantur, ut
fulgida Mediterranei stella
indeficiens lumen convertat hunc in locum transitus,
commercii et quandoque conflictus.
Quapropter,

Rector insignis Basilicae Pontificiae
Minoris Deo in honorem
Beatae Mariae Virginis
de finibus terrae dicatae

intra fines
Dioecesis Uxentinae - Sanctae Mariae Leucadensis,
ut omnibus peregrinis authenticum visitationis
propter devotionis affectum vel voti solutionem
ad haec Sanctissimae Matris Dei limina patratae
praebeat testimonium,
omnibus et singulis inspecturis notum facit

Sanford Webster Brown

hoc sacratissimum devote visitasse templum
pacis implorandae ibique Beatissimae
Deiparae rogavit auxilium.
Cuius splendoris increati luminis intercessione,
Dominus omnipotens tibi per Verbum receptum
et sacramenta celebrata concedat vitam immutare atque
ad bonum fratrum efficiendum ac magnalia
Dei verbo et opere referre nuntianda.

Datum ex aedibus Basilicae Beatae
Mariae Virginis de finibus terrae,

die 24 mensis Marzo anno Domini 2024

Rector Basilicae Pontificiae

Editio MMXXI - Iubilaeum MMXXV

A Testimonium issued at Santa Maria di Leuca (Stage 45), for which pilgrims must walk from at least Lecce (Stage 41)

changed (as of early 2025). Formerly testimonia were given to all who walked one day to the sanctuary there, yet now a minimum of 100km is required, meaning a walk from Troia is necessary to receive the certificate. Head directly to the Basilica Santuario di San Michele Arcangelo's main entrance reception and ask one of the nuns either there or at mass. It is open July to September 07.30–19.30, April to June and October 07.30–12.30 and 14.30–19.00, and November to March 07.30–12.30 and 14.30–17.00.

For a Testimonium in Brindisi, you must have walked at least from Bari (coming from the north) or Vignacastrisi (coming from the south). It is essential to notify and book your request two days in advance by emailing br.antichestrade@gmail.com or sending a WhatsApp to Antonio Melore on tel 388 113 0368. The pick-up point is at the Accademia degli Erranti, the Statio Peregrinorum of the Via Francigena (information center for pilgrims), located at Via Giovanni Tarantini 35 (Ex Convento delle Scuole Pie). It is open Monday to Saturday 10.00–12.00 and 16.00–20.00.

For a Testimonium from Santa Maria di Leuca, you must have covered the route at least from Lecce. You can collect it at the sacristy within the Basilica of Santa Maria de Finibus Terrae, open daily 06.00–22.00. You can pre-request it by emailing testimonium@camminidileuca.it, attaching a copy of your ID and credenziale. Alternatively, you can complete the form on this website: www.camminidileuca.it/testimonium. You must still present your ID and credenziale at the sacristy.

ROUTE AND SCHEDULE OPTIONS

Selecting your starting point and the best schedule for you depends entirely on your own circumstances. In addition, the VFS can easily be completed in sections, with public transport facilitating different starting and end points.

For ease, the best starting points are major train transport hubs, such as Rome, Benevento, Lucera or San Severo (on the Monte Sant'Angelo variant), Bari, Brindisi, and Lecce. Excellent bus connections also allow pilgrims to consider other starting locations, such as Troia, for example.

The most popular section is from Lecce southbound (totaling just over 100km and allowing a pilgrim to receive their Testimonium in Santa Maria di

Leuca), yet many commence in Bari, opting to solely complete the 13-day Puglian coastline route.

In brief, Rome to Benevento takes 19 days, Benevento to Troia 3 days, Troia to Monte Sant'Angelo 5 days, Monte Sant'Angelo to Bari 6 days, and Troia to Bari 10 days. The overall walking distance to Santa Maria di Leuca is 60.6km more via Monte Sant'Angelo and the Via Litoranea Connection.

Once you reach Troia, you have two options: to continue on a direct inland route to Bari via Canosa di Puglia, or to veer toward the coast through Monte Sant'Angelo. Some pilgrims also choose to walk to Monte Sant'Angelo and then return by public transport to Troia to continue along the inland route.

The second option from Troia is the pilgrimage via Monte Sant'Angelo within the high hills of the sublime Gargano National Park. After 110km on flat then steep uphill roads and paths, you reach the grotto of the Archangel Michael, having also passed through San Giovanni Rotondo, which houses the remains of Padre Pío, a most venerated religious figure in the Puglia region, and beyond. From here, the coastal route leads to Bari, where you reconnect with the inland route. This waymarked variant is known as the Via Litoranea (the littoral route). Although there are recommendations to bus ahead along a couple of stages owing to dangerous road walking, this option also passes through the glorious cities of Barletta and Trani, taking in historical remains in Manfredonia, as well as other incredibly picturesque coastal fishing villages and towns. In total the Monte Sant'Angelo (MSA) and Via Litoranea Connection (VLC) variants combined take around 11 days to complete. Therefore, this option totals 46 days from Rome to Santa Maria di Leuca, one day more than the direct inland route.

The coastal variant is split as follows: Troia to Monte Sant'Angelo is 111.1km and the Via Litoranea Connection from Monte Sant'Angelo to Bari is 143km, thus totaling 254.1km. The direct route from Troia to Bari is 193.5km. Therefore, the overall walking distance to Santa Maria di Leuca is 60.6km more via Monte Sant'Angelo and the Via Litoranea Connection.

GETTING THERE AND BACK

For journeys around Italy, see www.trenitalia.com/it.html for trains and www.viefrancigene.org/en/partners/flixbus for coaches to/from major cities. There are three international airports close to the VFS: Roma–Fiumicino Leonardo da Vinci Airport (FCO), Naples International Airport (NAP), and Bari Karol Wojtyła Airport (BRI). Brindisi Airport (BDS) and Foggia Gino Lisa Airport (FOG) offer national flights, although Foggia does not connect with Rome or Naples.

You will need to catch trains or coaches if starting anywhere other than at one of the airport cities on the waymarked route. Journey duration times provided below are the minimum to be expected. Note that coaches can get booked up quickly during national and school holidays, especially in high season. High-speed trains can also be busy, so book ahead. Flixbus coach stops on the VFS are located in Roma, Nemi, Benevento, San Severo, San Giovanni Rotondo, Manfredonia,

Barletta, Andria, Corato, Ruvo di Puglia, Bari, Mola di Bari, Polignano a Mare, Monopoli, Brindisi, Lecce, Otranto, and Santa Maria di Leuca. Remember that upon presentation of the credenziale, there are discounts on Trenitalia and Trenord trains (www.viefrancigene.org/en/trenitalia-en) and Flixbus coaches in low season (www.viefrancigene.org/en/partners/flixbus).

Getting to Vatican City

Train and airport shuttle services run regularly from the airport to the center of Rome (¾hr). Within the city, several buses operate from the different train stations to the Vatican, and, of course, walking is an option.

Getting to Benevento

Fly into Rome airport, take the train to Roma Termini train station then change to take the train to Benevento (2hr). From Naples airport, take the airport shuttle to Roma Termini train station then two trains, changing in Caserta (40min then 40min).

Getting to Troia

From Rome, take the train to Foggia (3hr) then a local coach (¾hr) of the Ferrovie del Gargano (www.ferroviedelgargano.

Much of the Via Francigena in the South follows remote Adriatic coastline (Stage 34)

com). From Naples, take a Flixbus to Foggia (3hr) then the local coach to Troia (¾hr). From Bari airport, you can take two coaches, changing in Foggia (1½hr then ¾hr), or get a bus into the center (20min) then a train from Bari to Foggia (1¼hr) and, finally, the Foggia–Troia coach (45min). You can also walk (2.9km) from Bari airport to Bari Stazione di Palese train station, outside of the center, and catch the train to Foggia from there.

Getting to Monte Sant'Angelo

From Foggia (linked by train or coach from Rome, Naples, and Bari airports), take a local coach with Ferrovie del Gargano. There are direct coaches (1¾hr), or you may have to change in Manfredonia (1hr then ¾hr plus waiting time).

Getting to Bari

From Bari airport, you can walk along the old waymarked route for 11.9km, skirting around the airport (see the Stage 32 map with the old route). Alternatively, take a bus from the airport (1hr), which runs every hour. There is also a metro (underground/subway) stop, Bari Europa, with regular connections to the center – it is located 1.8km from the airport. From Rome, direct trains to Bari Centrale train station take 4hr 25min, and from Naples, Flixbus runs a coach service (3hr 5min).

Getting to Brindisi

From Bari, there are regular trains (1hr). Walking the 4.3km from Brindisi Airport to the city center takes approximately 1hr and follows the Francigena waymarked route that circumnavigates the airport (see Stage 38 for walking directions). There are buses, but it takes half an hour to get to the bus stop. Direct trains operate from Rome (5hr 20min). From Naples get the Flixbus to Bari first (3hr 5min). Alternatively, fly from Rome (1¼hr).

Getting to Lecce

From Rome, take a train (5hr 33min). From Naples take a coach via Taranto (5hr 47min), or two trains, changing in Caserta (49min then 4¼hr). Trains also run from Bari (1hr 20min) and Brindisi (25min).

Getting to Santa Maria di Leuca

You have to go through Lecce. From there, you can take a direct coach (2¼hr) or a train to Tricase (1hr 50min), followed by a coach (25min). Coaches from Brindisi will take you as far as Gagliano del Capo (1hr 46min), and from there take a bus (8min). From Gagliano you can walk on the Francigena waymarked route for 6km to the lighthouse, or 7.5km into town, mostly downhill (see Stage 45 for walking directions).

Leaving Santa Maria di Leuca

For bus times visit www.cotrap.it/salento-in-bus. You must go through Lecce by either taking bus 105 to Tricase (25min) and then a train to Lecce (1hr 50min) or bus 107 or 108 to Lecce (2¼hr). You can also walk (6.5km) or take bus 105 or 107 to Gagliano del Capo (8min), where Gagliano Leuca train station connects to other towns and cities.

Brindisi's National Monument of the Italian Sailor (Stage 38)

WHEN TO GO

There are several points to consider regarding the best time to walk.

For budget planning and accommodation, winter is less costly, whereas in summer, expenses can more than double and last-minute accommodation can be hard to find, especially along the crowded coasts.

Generally, the further south you go, the warmer it gets at all points of the year (based on 2023 data). November to March between Rome and Monte Sant'Angelo sees average temperatures of 8°C to 12°C, with lows of -4°C. From Bari to Santa Maria di Leuca average temperatures vary between 8°C and 14°C, with lows reaching 1°C. In these months, temperatures can attain 24°C. Note that in winter there can be snow between Benevento and Monte Sant'Angelo.

During April, May, September, and October, average temperatures across the route range between 13°C and 24°C, with Puglia remaining warmer. Average temperatures between June and August fluctuate between 19°C and 29°C, and they can soar to 40°C degrees, particularly in July and August.

October, November, January, and March–May are the rainiest months in Rome, Benevento, Troia, and Monte Sant'Angelo. South of Troia remains relatively dry throughout the year, with more rain in January, April, May, and November.

Overall, the best months for walking are mid to end of September, October, May, and June. Puglia is also lovely in March and April.

PLANNING YOUR DAY TO DAY

Unlike some pilgrimage routes, the VFS calls for essential advance stage preparation to get the most out of your trip, meet your daily budget, and, importantly, ensure the certainty of a place to sleep.

STAGE PLANNING

The guidebook is organized to average a walking distance of 20–25km per day. Some distances are unavoidable to reach a lodging, and others have been arranged to offer walkers an opportunity to stay at recommended municipalities. Before every stage, inspect the distances, ascent and descent, and the availability of provisions.

Provisions along the stage

It is beneficial to plan ahead for the following day: calculate pit-stops and make advance food and drink purchases if needed. If a drinking fountain or service is not mentioned in the route description, assume there isn't one.

Provisions at stage end

Stages have been organized with access to provisions in mind. Note that on variant Stage MSA25, you should carry snacks (that don't require cooking) for your evening meal and for the next day if you plan to stay at the monastery in Stignano, although alternative accommodation is available.

Lodging options

Details of accommodation are included in each listing and stage end at municipalities, with at least one lodging option that is usually open year-round.

LODGINGS

There are different types of accommodation along the route, but the majority are hotels and B&Bs, since many towns do not yet have pilgrim-specific lodgings. The VFS is perfectly walkable, but the infrastructure of inexpensive or donation-based lodgings will take some time to become fully developed (writing in 2024). It is wise to always check and book ahead on this trail because many options can be booked out, including those listed and verified in this guidebook. Check www.booking.com and other online sources for the most up-to-date availability and pricing, and although it is nice to switch off from the web, not having a place to stay can quickly become frustrating when relying

White buildings cling to the cliffs above Lama Monachile and Grotta Piana at Polignano a Mare (Stage 34)

Two pilgrims drink from the Fontana della Gorgone in Nemi (Stage 2), designed and donated by local artist Luciano Mastrolorenzi (b. 1929)

on last-minute decision making. Note that most hotels will expect advance reservations either online or by paying a deposit by bank transfer.

Also note that several places are difficult to contact in advance, in particular, religious accommodation and local parishes. Therefore, many pilgrims just turn up and knock on the church door, and this is what the churches expect. Do not be surprised if you cannot get hold of them beforehand. In addition, these options are usually open all year and only lodge pilgrims (not other tourists).

This book lists pilgrim-specific lodgings if available, and some hotel/B&B options. A list of accommodations in the book, plus additional verified lodgings, can be downloaded at www.cicerone.co.uk/1249/downloads. The EAVF also maintains a directory at www.viefrancigene.org/en/accommodations-facilities, while the Dodici Group maintains a list for Lazio at www.gruppodeidodici.eu.

Hostels

With low-cost accommodation in dorms (usually in bunk beds), hostels can be found in bigger cities, such as Rome and Bari. Prices can vary seasonally.

Religious accommodation

Several parish churches, seminaries, and monasteries provide shelter for pilgrims; these are called Accoglienza Religiosa (religious hospitality). Often donation based, they offer basic beds or floor space to pilgrims. There are nearly always showers but at times there may be no hot water. No bedding is provided, there is seldom heating, and few have kitchens or washing machines. No food is provided. Even so, to keep these running, donations are essential. Note that where details of cost and the number of beds are not provided in this guidebook, the best idea is to send a WhatsApp text a day or two before, expressing your imminent need for a bed, and simply show up at the door and knock if they have not responded to your text. Do consider planning ahead and investigate alternative accommodation in your chosen town for the night should the church be unresponsive.

People's homes

In a select few municipalities, locals have opened their doors to pilgrims to provide welcoming *accoglienza* (hospitality). Sleeping arrangements tend to involve the host offering you a spare room in their house and use of the shower. At times these are donation based or have a set cost for dinner, bed, and breakfast. To keep these running, donations are essential and sometimes required.

Hotels, B&Bs, and other lodging establishments

There are various types of lodgings with private rooms: hotel ; B&B (bed and breakfast) ; *affitacamere* (guest room) ; *alloggio turistico/casa per ferie/casa vacanza* (holiday home) or ;and *agriturismo* (farm/rural hotels) . Nearly all these forms of accommodation offer breakfast, and many have deals with local restaurants for breakfast, lunch, and dinner. All these lodgings prefer and expect advance bookings from pilgrims, often online or with a bank transfer. Very few of these lodgings have kitchens that pilgrims can use, and note that prices listed in this guidebook are indicative and the minimum to be expected: they should be confirmed and agreed upon directly with the establishment. Prices also vary significantly depending on the time of year.

Apartments

Some pilgrims opt to share a self-catered apartment for the night to avoid the cost of eating out. Often, no contact details are available online, and hosts expect advance bookings made on hotel booking websites. Where direct contact details have been confirmed with hosts, they are included in the lodging listings within this guidebook.

Camping

Campsites along the route are indicated in the guidebook, although they are seasonal and tend to open only between April and September inclusive. Wild camping is not permitted in Italy, but there are several coves and beaches where you are likely to see locals and tourists pitching overnight in the summer. Outdoors fires should not be lit under any circumstances and there should be minimum impact on the surroundings.

FOOD

If you have eaten in Italy before, it may be the reason you're back. Italian cooking is earthy, hearty, local, and fresh. The Francigena travels through lesser-known lands where exquisite food is plated up for locals and visitors alike, with little risk of a disappointing meal.

Colazione (breakfast) tends to be a pastry, such as *un cornetto* (a croissant). Snacks available throughout the day include pizza, *insalata* (salad),

Pasta e fagioli *(pasta and beans) is a hearty example of Pugliese cuisine*

panino/focaccia (sandwich), and *gelato* (ice cream).

Eating out in an *osteria*, *trattoria*, or *ristorante* (all translating as 'restaurant,' with varying degrees of formality) may feel like a puzzle at first. The classic menu involves four courses: starting with the antipasti (nibbles – usually olives, anchovies, cured meats) then *primi* (first courses – pasta or soup), *secondi* (main course – usually meat or fish) with *contorni* (side vegetable dishes, ordered separately), and finishing with *dolci* (desserts). All are served with *bevande* (beverages) and *caffè* (coffee) as a relaxing option to finish your meal. You may discover that restaurants are open from 19.30 and that in small towns and villages there is no place serving a noon meal. On these occasions, it is best to have shopped at a grocery store so you can enjoy a picnic in the park while local residents are dining at home.

There are some delicious specialties to try on your way, and pasta appears in all forms. In Lazio, spaghetti, *bucatini*, and *tonnarelli* shapes are plated *alla carbonara*, *alla gricia*, and *all'amatriciana*, which all include cheese and pork. For vegetarians, the *cacio e pepe* removes the bacon and flavors it with pepper. For the adventurous, offal is popular, such as *coda alla vaccinara*, a tomato and celery oxtail stew, or one of the various roast lamb dishes, including the melt-in-your-mouth *abbacchio* smothered in garlic, rosemary, and sage. *Carciofi* (artichokes) and *fiori di zucca* (courgette flowers) are served in a variety of scrumptious ways. Along the way, stop at an *agriturismo* or *masseria* for incredible cheeses, cured meats, local and organic meat, home-grown vegetables, and juicy fruit.

As the route reaches Puglia, meat continues to feature, and you may find game, goat, and even horse on the menu. Some also love *gnummeridde*: lamb gut stuffed with offal, garlic, and herbs, resembling Scottish haggis. What is certain is that you will not escape the enticing seafood along the coast, caught the same day, such as oysters, octopus, mussels, lobster, and unbattered calamari. Popular vegetables include *cardoncello* mushrooms, *piselli* (peas), *cavolo* (cabbage), *fagioli* (beans), *ceci* (chickpeas), and *cime di rapa* (turnip tops). Eating fruit in Italy is heavenly and feels like you're consuming all of the sun's vitamin D. Inevitably, Puglia's culinary highlights also include olives from majestic, age-old trees; almonds (especially around Cerignola); the small, ear-shaped *orecchiette* pasta; and the protected *burrata* cream of mozzarella. Dishes are doused in Puglian *olio d'oliva* (olive oil): the region produces more 'liquid gold' than the rest of the country put together.

BUDGET PLANNING

The VFS is substantially more expensive than walking a Camino in Spain. Accommodation is available at prices ranging from donation based to inevitable hotel stays, with prices varying immensely at different times of the year. Walking solo becomes costly, as most hotels will charge the same price for one or two people. Eating out can be affordable, especially if you choose a pizza and share a salad, and Italian portions are generous.

Expect a daily budget of anywhere from €15–150 or more per day, depending on accommodation, self-catered options, and appetite.

PREPARATION AND TRAINING

Few sections require any technical skills but, because of the high percentage of paved walking and the distances between services along much of the route, it is important to get your body and feet ready. It is wise to break in the shoes and backpack that you plan to use. Absolutely essential is blister prevention, so try to purchase your walking shoes, including spares, six months in advance and wear them as often as possible. The following is an ideal program to start at least three months before departure:

A sign in Itri advertises Italian foods, including panini (sandwiches), prodotti tipici *(local products), cheese, olives,* tielle *(stuffed bread), and fruits and vegetables (Stage 9)*

- Wear your main shoes and socks as often as possible
- Start walking at least 10–15km two or three times per week
- Start walking two days in a row with a packed backpack + 2 liters of water
- Try to fit in a 25–30km walk once a week (ideally carrying your backpack)

For more useful advice, see the following helpful articles: www.cicerone.co.uk/how-to-get-hill-fit-and-train-for-long-distance-walking and www.cicerone.co.uk/how-to-walk-a-camino-without-blistering-pain.

WHAT TO PACK

Generally, the aim is to ensure that your bag weighs a maximum of 10% of your bodyweight, including provisions. Variations on this depend on the season, region, and a pilgrim's size or experience. Always bear in mind that you will need to leave space for water and snacks. Essential items include:

- 40-liter-capacity backpack
- Rain cover for your pack
- Poncho/waterproof jacket
- Waterproof and/or quick-dry trousers
- Walking shoes (lightweight trail for summer, waterproof trail for winter) and hiking sandals for switching into and for evenings
- Clothes: two quick-dry T-shirts, a long-sleeved jacket or sweater layer (light for summer, fleece and/or thermal for winter), two pairs of shorts, one pair of trousers, underwear, and three pairs of socks. A warm jacket, hat, gloves, and neck buff are recommended in the colder months
- Bedding: in summer, a light two-season sleeping bag is largely sufficient; in winter, take a bag that goes down to at least 0°C. For a pillow, either bring a pillowcase into which you can stuff clothes or use one of your T-shirts. A sleeping mat will also help the hardy pilgrims who choose to stay in some of the very basic accommodation options available. If you plan to stay only in hotels and B&Bs, you

do not need to carry a sleeping bag or make a pillow

- Reusable water bottles, preferably with an insulation system to keep your water cool: at least one 1.5 liter bottle in summer is advisable to quench your thirst and to soak your hat or hair. In hot weather, 1 liter of water per 10km is a minimum
- Protection: summer or winter hat, sunscreen, and sunglasses
- Insect repellent
- Basic first-aid kit, including blister plasters
- Quick-dry lightweight towel. If you are staying in B&Bs, this will not be necessary, except for after dips in the sea!
- Toiletries: take shampoo that works as body wash and for hand-washing clothes
- Some toilet paper/tissues with a few small plastic bags, for when nature calls
- Hiking poles, if you prefer walking with them
- Parasol or umbrella, if you prefer walking with one
- Phone (and camera) and chargers with European adaptors
- Debit/Credit cards and cash (available at ATMs. Most religious lodgings accept only cash)
- Travel/Identity documents (originals and photocopies) in a plastic wallet/ ziplock sandwich bag
- Head torch if you plan early-morning starts
- Earplugs
- Credenziale (pilgrim passport)
- Whistle (for remote sections, to signal your presence and, potentially, to deter dogs)
- For picnicking pilgrims: a knife, fork, spoon, and plastic container can come in handy

BAGGAGE AND STORAGE SERVICES

Except in Lazio, the VFS does not have a luggage-transfer service for pilgrims, which emphasizes the importance of packing light. Local taxi services will charge their usual passenger rates rather than a luggage-transfer rate.

Two luggage-transfer options exist for Lazio:

- For the stages between Rome and Minturno, your contact is Corrado (who also hosts pilgrims in Velletri), tel 328 3864047 or email corradobisini1959@gmail.com. He charges €50 per stage, and the cost remains the same for one or five pieces of luggage. He can take a maximum of eight backpacks/suitcases, depending on size. Bookings for individual stages must be made at least two days in advance, but, for ease, he suggests organizing all of the stages at the same time via email or WhatsApp. He is happy to receive requests in English.
- For the stages between Rome and Teano, your contact is Juri (who also taxis pilgrims to and from Rome's FCO airport for €70 per car and up to €100 for a minivan), tel 347 628 7383 or email greencoppoladriver@gmail.com. He charges €50 per stage and can take four

backpacks/suitcases. He can organize more cars to transport more luggage. Bookings for individual stages must be made at least two days in advance, but, for ease, he suggests organizing all of the stages at the same time via email or WhatsApp. He speaks good English.

LOCAL FACILITIES AND PRACTICAL INFORMATION

Getting to know the ins and outs of Italy's services helps you to plan ahead, particularly regarding access to drinking water and food.

A gentle way to introduce yourself to the Via Francigena in the South is to contact the Gruppo dei Dodici (Group of Twelve) with any queries on your stages from Rome to Teano. Volunteers from the group are prepared to help locate lodgings and food and, with advance notice, will even accompany you on your walk; see www.gruppodeidodici.eu.

Important to remember is the *pausa*, an afternoon nap or rest period during which kitchens and businesses close before reopening for the evening.

Drinking water is available at fountains, except where marked as *non potabile* (undrinkable) or can be purchased in all towns marked with [restaurant symbol] or [shop symbol] symbols. Drinking fountains are also noted in the text and on maps.

Shops, supermarkets, and pharmacies open in the mornings from 08.00 or 10.00 until 13.00. Small shops close for the afternoon and reopen between 16.30 and 19.00.

Afternoons can feel like a food desert, when shops and restaurants outside of tourist areas are closed. So, it is a very good idea to pack your own lunch, even if you will be passing through a village. Streets then come alive at about 16.30, when you may wonder where all these people suddenly came from. Hotel breakfast is usually available from 07.00 or 08.00, while cafés are often open all day for a drink or snack. Lunch service is spotty in small towns outside tourist areas and runs between 12.00 and 14.00. Restaurants begin opening at 19.30 and end their service by 22.00. A handy trick for those who like their coffee/tea and/or breakfast before setting out is to purchase it the night before as a takeaway, especially if your lodging has a microwave.

Public transport and taxis can be used along this route and, if required, your lodging or local bar will have the most up-to-date details. They will be able to advise you which bus services are available, even though they may not always be listed online or appear on your phone's map. Note that local bus tickets must be purchased in advance at a local café/bar near the bus stop. Many locations are well serviced by coaches and even trains and are represented in municipal information boxes (see Figure 1 in 'How to use this guide').

Cash is almost always the preferred and only payment method in parish and home lodgings along the way, while credit cards work in hotels and many B&Bs. Larger markets and almost all cafés, bars, restaurants, and grocery shops accept credit cards. ATMs for cash withdrawals are indicated by a € symbol in municipal information boxes (see Figure 1 in 'How to use this guide'), so plan accordingly.

In addition to being useful in emergencies, mobile phones are also useful for accessing digital maps and the GPX files available with this guidebook and with the official Via Francigena app. Mobile-data access and phone reception are very strong, except in the mountainous terrain of Campania.

Taking your dog

Taking your dog is not recommended due to the lengthy asphalt sections and weather patterns. To add to this, if you have a dog with you, local dogs and livestock could feel provoked and may react. Importantly, most accommodation options do not accept dogs.

WAYMARKING

The route is quite well signed in many areas with the Via Francigena monk icon and painted red and white blazes, sometimes with Gerusalemme (Jerusalem) indicated on stickers as the destination (rather than Santa Maria di Leuca). Other posters and some waymarking bollards (especially in Puglia)

A pasture on the way to Monte Sant'Angelo looks down toward the Gulf of Manfredonia on the Adriatic Sea (Stage MSA27)

also guide the way. On many occasions, the route follows SP roads, which stands for *strada provinciale* (provincial road), comparable to B roads in the UK. In Campania the route is sometimes shared with CAI (Club Alpino Italiano, meaning Italian Alpine Club) waymarked trails.

Overall, Puglia and Lazio are better signed than Campania, with the latter missing about 40% of its waymarks, although the other two regions can also lack signage at times. Therefore, you will find yourself rigorously checking your guidebook directions, particularly upon entering and leaving towns and cities. At the time of writing (summer 2024), local stewards of the Francigena are continuing to extend the waymarking along the entire route and variants, so signage is continually improving.

SAFETY AND HEALTH

For all emergencies in Italy, dial 112.

Crime

In the unlikely event of witnessing or experiencing violence or crime, report it immediately to the police (tel 112).

Animals

It is essential to always leave a gate as you find it, since the route passes through farms with livestock. The creatures you will come across most often will be dogs and cattle – and the occasional legendary dragon, if you're lucky. The large sheepdogs (usually the Maremma breed) tend to bark and sometimes are not tied up, which can feel uncomfortable. Absolutely ignore them, steer clear, and continue on your way: they are simply sending out a warning while guarding their herds. There are also some errant dogs that are very distrustful of humans. Avoid eye contact with dogs, but if you feel an attack is imminent, point a walking stick or umbrella directly in the dog's eyes as a warning. If you bend down and pick up a rock, you will likely see the dog quickly give you a wide berth. Carrying a dog-deterrent whistle may also prove helpful. Do not approach any cattle or sheep as they are not household pets and could attack if they feel threatened. Wild animals include boars and snakes, yet they have not been known to be problematic for walkers. Never approach a boar as they are near-sighted, wary of predators, and can be dangerous if they attack. Boars depend on smelling and hearing their predators, so if you see paths recently disturbed by rutting behavior, a precautionary strategy is to make noise.

Avoiding injuries

The trail has few technical sections requiring scrambling or climbing and no specialist equipment is required at any time. To avoid complications, prepare yourself by using shoes suitable for either dirt trail or asphalt surfaces; stay hydrated; walk in single file on busy roads, always facing traffic; prevent blisters by covering hot spots before blisters develop; and take your time on steep hills until your body is used to the cardio challenge.

Via Francigena signs most commonly are red and white blazes, but there are many variations, often with the profile of the pilgrim in yellow, taken from the façade of Fidenza Cathedral

Figure 1: Example of stage description and municipal information

In seven blocks come to the tall **Monumento al Marinaio d'Italia**. The 54m-high boat-rudder-shaped monument was inaugurated in 1933 to commemorate those fallen at sea during war. It is engraved with more than 36,000 names of deceased sailors. Visits cost €5. Climb onto the pedestal of the tower to find stairways down to a right-hand turn onto the lungomare, which leads to the second pedestrian ferry dock, **Banchina Villaggio Pescatori**. You can pay the €1.10 ferry ticket in cash or by card on board or follow the instructions on the sign to download the MooneyGo app. Ferries leave about every 20min, taking you across the harbor to **Banchina Montenegro** in the city center.

Dock, turn left onto the lungomare, and go up the wide right-hand steps to the Roman column marking the end of the Via Appia Traiana (**2.4km**). Keep straight past the monument for the pilgrim's office on **Via Giovanni Tarantini** in a weathered building called La Corte degli Artigiani. The main shopping street is on Corso Umberto I.

distance between intermediate points

elevation population distance remaining to Santa Maria di Leuca

total distance from previous municipality

infrastructure

27.1KM BRINDISI (ELEV 19M, POP 87,820) (165.3KM)

Brindisi, with its Eastern Mediterranean flavor, has forever been a bridge between Italy and lands across the water. To this day, it is the favorite embarkation point for Greece. Throughout the late Middle Ages, pilgrims and crusading knights set sail from the docks, and the city has many stories to tell. Here ends the Via Appia Traiana. At the top of the Scalinata Virgiliana (Virgil's steps), two columns once stood, serving as navigation tools for incoming vessels. One 18.7m column remains with its ornate capital, while the other was moved to Lecce (Stage 40). Brindisi is also home to the remains of one of Frederick's beloved Norman-Swabian castles and the everlasting Cattedrale di San Giovanni Battista, built in the 11th century, which has survived seven earthquakes. The Museo Archeologico Francesco Ribezzo is cherished for its Punta del Serrone 3rd-century BC bronzes, discovered in Brindisi's waters. Two more stand-out churches are the 12th-century Chiesa di Santa Lucia and the Chiesa e Chiostro di San Benedetto (1090). Don't forget to pop into the Accademia degli Erranti (Academy of the Wanderers and now the Brindisi pilgrim office) for your Testimonium (see Introduction).

place description

Parrocchia Cattedrale €Donation, Piazza Duomo, tel 0831 521 157, cattedralebrindisi@gmail.com. Very basic sleeping arrangements on the floor; no mattress or bedding provided.

B&B Mare Nostrum Brindisi 5/18, €-/30–35/60/75/100/110, Via Armengol 47–49, tel 328 861 6413, bandbmarenostrum@libero.it, www.facebook.com/BBMareNostrumBrindisi/?locale=it_IT. Breakfast included; €25 per person for groups of five or more people.

facilities

Infrastructure symbols

HOW TO USE THIS GUIDE

The aim of this guidebook is to provide thorough descriptions, maps, accommodation listings, and stage suggestions that enable pilgrims to find exact locations and feel reassured along what is a solitary route. Appendix A supplies a planning grid to help you determine your own stages. In addition, some **historical background** is included.

Stage starts and finishes are at specific locations in the centers of towns of interest and are calculated using the official EAVF tracks.

Distance statistics are rounded to 0.1km and slight discrepancies naturally occur when these rounded numbers are added together.

Ascent and descent figures are cumulative and should be examined in conjunction with elevation profiles. Data was gathered using Gaia GPS, NASA, and other elevation sources available through www.gpsvisualizer.com, and totals will not be equivalent to statistics gathered with recreational GPS units and other software calculations.

The **difficulty** of each stage is rated as easy, moderate, hard, or very hard, taking into account length, steepness, terrain, and frequency of services.

The **duration** excludes breaks and is calculated using a formula based on 4km per hour. For every 100m of ascent, 10min are added.

Approximate percentages of **paved surfaces** are given, since paved and asphalted surfaces can be harder on your feet and may determine your shoe selection. Percentages are crowd-sourced through www.RideWithGPS.com and are based on the official EAVF GPS tracks.

Distances to **accommodation** options are rounded to the nearest 0.1km, so there may be slight variations between stage totals and cumulative intermediate distances. For readers who prefer longer stages, accommodation options into the next stage are provided up to about 32km from each stage's starting point.

A **stage overview** gives an overall description and tips with regard to provisions and the type of terrain covered.

Within the walking directions, **intermediary distances** between specific features are often provided when helpful to aid with planning.

Accommodation listings are accurate as of summer 2024. Hotel prices may vary from those listed, which are the minimum rates to be expected in low season. Note that rates tend to increase every year.

Telephone numbers are provided in their local form. If you are calling from outside Italy or with a non-Italian SIM card, use the international access code for the country you are calling from, followed by the country code for Italy (39) and then the number provided. For example, to call 333 455 577 from the UK, dial 0039333455577. You can also use +39333455577 if your dialing pad is supplied with the '+' symbol.

GPX DOWNLOADS

Free GPX tracks for the routes in this guidebook are available to download at www.cicerone.co.uk/1249/GPX.

ESSENTIAL FOREIGN TERMS

anfiteatro amphitheatre
agriturismo farm hotel
anfiteatro ampitheater
casedda (*casedde*) round stone hut(s)
cattedrale cathedral
chiesa church
concattedrale co-cathedral (a secondary cathedral within a diocese)
contrada/via street/road
credenziale pilgrim passport
duomo cathedral
lungomare beach promenade
masseria (*masserie*) walled farm complex(es)
municipio town hall
parrocchia parish church
piazza square
palazzo palace/mansion

SECTION 1: LAZIO

Pilgrims walk the ancient pavement of the Via Appia Antica south of Rome (Stage 1)

Much of the Via Appia in Latium (modern Lazio) was built in the flood-prone lowlands along the Tyrrhenian Sea, so its post-empire successor was forced to hug the area's volcanic hillsides and ridges. Following the later route, the Francigena in Lazio crisply undulates between mountaintops and beaches, rewarding the walker with both dramatic mountaintop views and calming seaside promenades.

STAGE 1

Rome to Castel Gandolfo

Start	Piazza San Pietro, Vatican City, Rome
Finish	Piazza della Libertà, Castel Gandolfo
Duration	7hr
Distance	26.2km
Total ascent	552m
Total descent	145m
Difficulty	Moderately hard due to footing, duration, and climb at the end
Percentage paved	86%
Lodgings	Castel Gandolfo 26.2km, Albano Laziale 28.3km

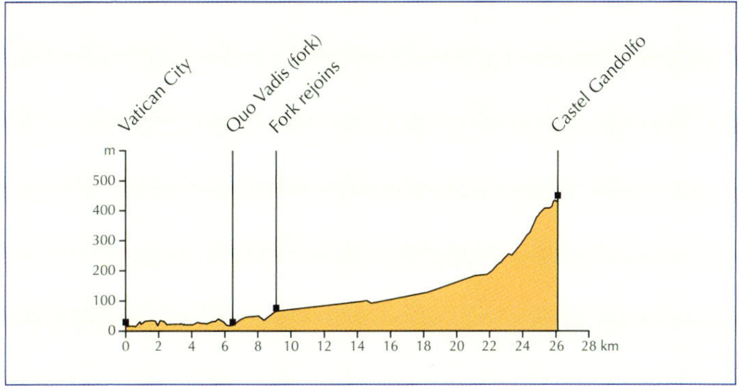

To put it simply, the first stage of the Via Francigena travels from the Pope's office to his summer home. Starting at the premier church of Western Christianity, it touches on spectacular Roman ruins, transits a famous 2000-year-old thoroughfare dotted with centuries-old tombs, and ends at a quaint village on the rim of a volcanic crater set above a sparkling lake. Maybe the best description is the Italian word *indimenticabile*, meaning 'unforgettable.' Cafés placed at regular intervals make a light snack and a refillable water bottle sufficient for the day.

0KM ROME (ELEV 21M, POP 2,900,000) (937.1KM)

Center of the Roman Empire and home to the Papacy for most of 2000 years, Rome is a wondrous outdoor museum and festival of modern Italian culture and gastronomy. Discovering Rome's treasures brings to light over 2000 years of history in an extravaganza of innumerous architectural and artistic styles that reappear along the pilgrimage. Architect/artist rivals Borromini and Bernini, both wanting space and attention, have blessed the city with an overarching baroque gloss that sometimes obscures its more ancient roots.

Graciously, the VFS potters by many celebrated monuments as pilgrims set off, but to appease your desire to see it all now, head to the flamboyant Trevi Fountain (1762) with its plethora of cream-colored mythological protagonists and beasts. As per traditional lore, to guarantee your return to Rome, you must toss a coin over your right shoulder into the waters.

Your tour of Rome (on this occasion) can be organized as follows:

North-east Rome

Furthest from our route, North-east Rome is very trendy. Among designer shops and pastel-colored buildings lies Piazza di Spagna, where the Spanish Steps (1723) lead to the 16th-century French Trinità dei Monti Church, recalling both Spanish and French hold over Italian soil. Close by, within Rome's largest public park, the Villa Borghese, sits the Galleria Borghese, built in the 17th century and home to masterpieces by Raphael, Bernini, and Caravaggio, to name a few.

Medieval highlights

Next up, diagonally opposite, on the west bank of the Tiber River, the authentic Trastevere neighborhood recalls Rome's medieval quarter and offers an abundance of fashionable eateries, bars, hotels, and boutiques. It boasts two stand-out churches: the Chiesa di San Francesco a Ripa remembers St. Francis of Assis's visit, and the beautiful Santa Maria displays magnificent 12th-century golden mosaics on its facade.

The historical center

Rome's Centro Storico (historical center) is the location of the city's ancient jewels. It runs south and south-east, starting from vibrant Piazza Navona, which owes its elliptical shape to Emperor Domitian's racetrack, built in AD86. Bernini's vivacious Fontana dei Quattro Fiumi is the square's centerpiece. Head 450m east to locate the Roman Empire's best-preserved marvel of engineering: the Pantheon. This massive temple to the gods became a church in the 7th century and has thus withstood the test of time. It boasts the world's biggest unreinforced concrete dome with an exposed oculus at its core. Across from here stands the

Gothic Basilica di Santa Maria sopra Minerva; fashioned in 1280 by Florentine Dominican monks in distinguishable layers of colored marble, it is home to relics of St. Catherine of Siena. Next to it stands Bernini's charming elephant bearing Rome's smallest obelisk. Further afield, by Termini train station, the Basilica Papale di Santa Maria Maggiore, the city's most magnificent early Christian basilica, contains a grandiose interior and mosaics and the tallest bell tower in Rome (1377). Make a stop at the Campo de' Fiori, where inns housed pilgrims.

Roman monuments

A definitive symbol of the Roman Empire is the 1st-century AD Colosseum in which 55,000 people would enter through the 80 arches to witness bloody spectacles. The adjacent Roman Forum offers a fascinating glimpse into Imperial Rome and is best viewed on a tour of its own. Here was the start point of the Via Appia, which initially connected Rome with the outer reaches of its growing empire at Benevento; under Emperor Trajan, it was extended to Brindisi.

The Vatican

Set apart from Rome proper is the Vatican, the world's smallest state with the world's biggest church: St. Peter's Basilica. Set on foundations created around AD326 by the Roman Emperor Constantine, it is said to hold the remains of St. Peter, martyred in AD64. Consecrated in 1626, the current interior was carefully crafted to interweave grandeur with intimate piety by the hands of the most renowned Renaissance and baroque artists, including Bramante, Raphael, Michelangelo, and Bernini. On Wednesdays, beginning at 09.00, when the Pope is in town, a Papal Audience is held in St. Peter's Square (for information on tickets, see www.papalaudience.org). Discover the sumptuous interior of the church and admire Michelangelo's graceful *Pietà*, the dramatic dome, and the right foot of the bronze statue of St. Peter, which has been adoringly caressed by pilgrims. Finally, visit one of the richest collections of art in the world within the Vatican Museums, where you can view Michelangelo's priceless frescoes on the ceiling of the Sistine Chapel.

Spedale della Provvidenza di San Giacomo e San Benedetto Labre O Do Br Dr W S 2/27, €Donation, Via dei Genovesi 11/B, tel 353 428 6139 or 327 231 9312, info@pellegriniaroma.it, www.pellegriniaroma.com. Register between 15.00 and 17.00, sleeping bags required.

Casa per ferie Santa Maria alle Fornaci O Pr R Br Cr S Z 54/108, €-/80/110/180/-, Piazza Santa Maria alle Fornaci 27, tel 06 9604 4811 and 06 9604 4812, info@santamariafornaci.it. Religious accommodation with hotel rooms.

Roma

1 Spedale della Divina Provvidenza di San Giacomo e Benedetto Labre

2 Monastero Santa Chiara

3 Casa per Ferie Santa Maria alle Fornaci

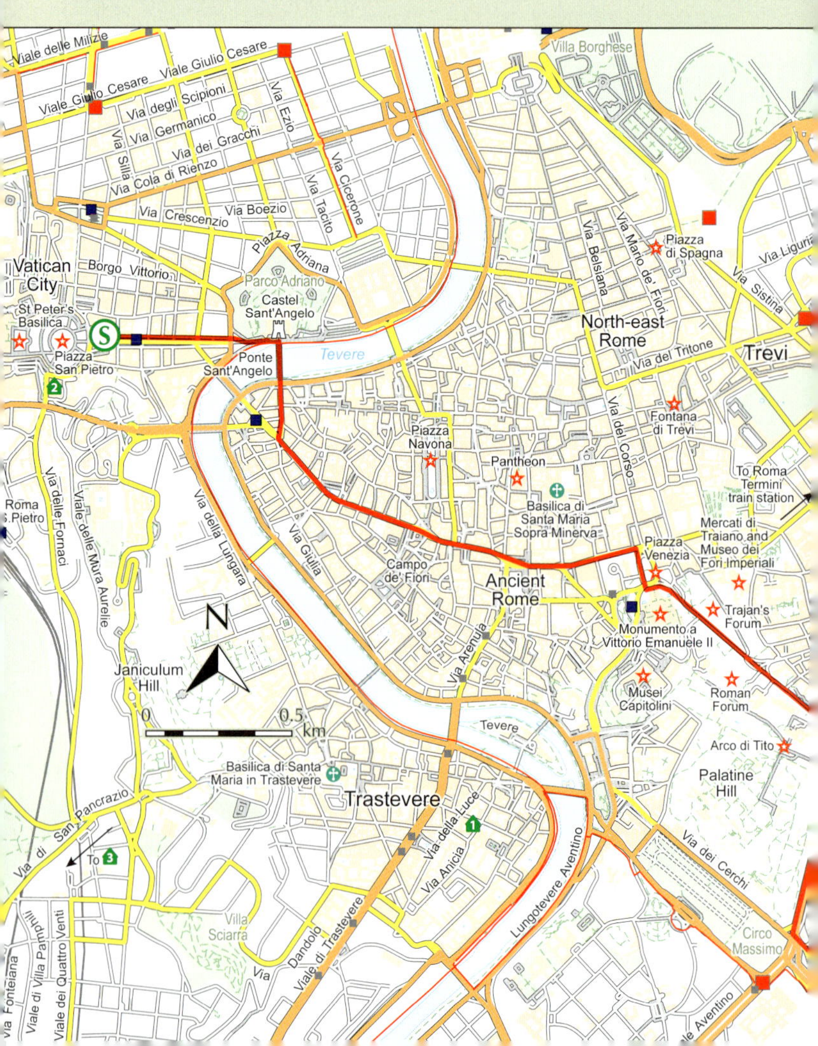

With St. Peter's Basilica behind you, go straight onto Via della Conciliazione to the hulking walls of **Castel Sant'Angelo**. Initially Emperor Hadrian's mausoleum, it served as a fortress and prison before becoming a residence for popes in turbulent times. When Pope Saint Gregory the Great was praying despairingly to end the city-wide plague, the warlike St. Michael Archangel appeared before him. The castle was named after the saint, and his statue stands before this medieval citadel, pointing pilgrims to the Archangel's shrine in Gargano National Park. Turn right and cross the Tiber River on Ponte Sant'Angelo. In four blocks turn left onto busy Corso Vittorio Emanuele II and continue to **Piazza Venezia** with its Monumento Nazionale a Vittorio Emanuele II. Locally nicknamed the 'wedding cake' or the 'typewriter,' this rather spectacular pile of neoclassical finery celebrates the creation of the Italian state.

Basilica San Pietro, the largest church in the world, is the starting point of the Via Francigena south of Rome

Keeping the monument on your right, continue past Rome's ancient treasures – Trajan's Forum, the Roman Forum, and Arco di Tito – then turn right just before the **Colosseum** onto your first worn paving stones of the Via Appia, alongside Via di San Gregorio. After the park, turn left at the stoplight and follow the wide boulevard Viale delle Terme di Caracalla to soon spot your first signage for the Via Francigena and to then cross onto the cobblestones of **Via di Porta San Sebastiano**. Go through the medieval and Renaissance gates of the Roman walls to then walk against traffic on a narrow sidewalk. Pass under the railway to reach the **Quo Vadis Church** (**6.5km**). This

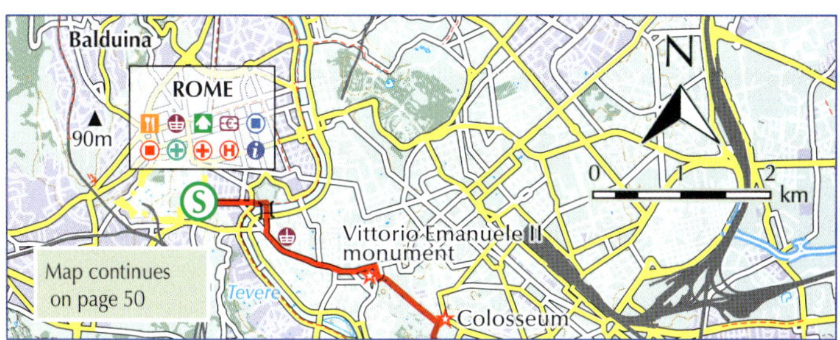

quaint 17th-century church holds a stone replica foot imprint of where Jesus is said to have appeared before St. Peter, who was fleeing martyrdom in Rome. Peter enquired, 'Domine Quo Vadis?' (Lord, where are you going?).

Come to two options designed to keep you off the most nerve-wracking automobile-dominated portion of the Via Appia.

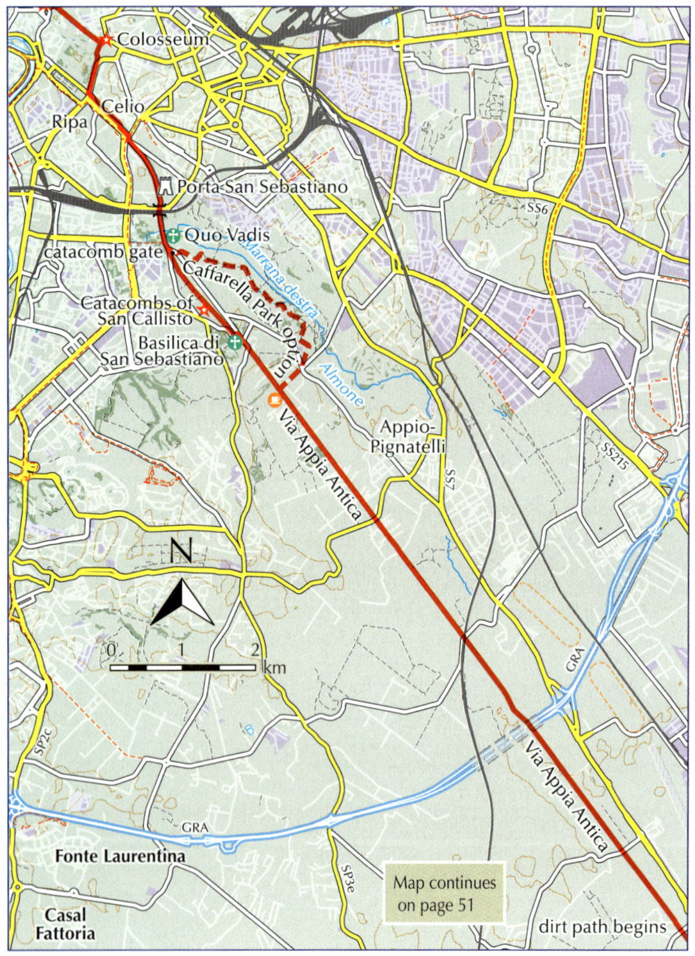

Callisto main route: First check the park's opening hours at www.catacombesancallisto.it since the gates close after hours. At Quo Vadis Church, follow signs to the right through the gates and up and into the park surrounding the **Catacombs of San Callisto**. The complex includes a 12-mile network of tunnels on four levels, with some as deep as 20m. In total, 10 martyrs, 16 popes, and many early Christians are buried here.

Caffarella option: If the gates to Callisto are closed, follow signs left into the quiet **Caffarella Park**, where shaded paths lead joggers, walkers, and cyclists through one of Rome's larger public green spaces.

Both options arrive at a quieter portion of the Via Appia, at the doorstep of the **Basilica di San Sebastiano** with its own set of catacombs and the traditional location of the remains of St. Sebastian. Here begins the **Via Appia Antica**, one of the most interesting and historic walks you can take anywhere in the world. Ancient roads lead out of the Roman Empire's capital in each and every direction, yet none are more important than the Via Appia, heading to the Adriatic ports and the East. The road was awarded a UNESCO World Heritage title in 2024. The route continues for at least 12km in an arrow-straight trajectory across ancient paving stones marked with deep grooves from centuries of cart traffic, and past the many Roman mausoleums that appear in succession under the shadows of immense umbrella pines. Near its end, in **Santa Maria delle Mole** (food, groceries, train, bus), the route becomes a narrow dirt path (with ancient pavers still hidden underneath) and then finally ends (**14.5km**) at a street lined with parked cars.

Turn left, following signs at the next stoplight then, oddly, double back through a McDonald's restaurant parking lot. The mystery of the waymarks is solved when a sign directs you down a metal staircase under the fast-food restaurant, where you find a perfectly restored stretch of ancient roadway that once branched toward the region of Abruzzo. Turn right afterward and pass the **Abbazia del Nostra Signora del Santissimo Sacramento**, a residence of Trappist monks who sell their own olive oil and other local monastic delicacies.

Signs now lead you up through neighborhoods to the rim of the volcanic crater to arrive at the SP216/Via Bruno Buozzi, where you turn right (**Fabiola B&B** and **B&B Ai Glicini Castelli Romani**). Following more signs, after 700m, fork left, climbing with lovely lake views into the heart of **Castel Gandolfo** at the Piazza della Libertà sitting in the shadow of the Papal Palace (**5.2km**).

26.2KM CASTEL GANDOLFO (ELEV 426M, POP 8971) (910.9KM)

Castel Gandolfo is one of 16 towns making up the Castelli Romani territory, all nestled within the Colli Albani hills. Today, they are holiday destinations for Romans escaping the city heat. The Papal Palace, built in the 13th century by the Gandolfo family, was, until recently, the Pope's summer residence. It is now a museum incorporating the elegant gardens and papal helipad! The Lago Albano, below town, is formed from a crater of the extinct Vulcano Laziale. The surrounding rich volcanic soil is ideal for vineyards for the popular Velletri, Frascati, and Marino wines.

- **Atlantis inn** O Pr R Br Cr S Z 12/46, €-/50/100/150/-/-, Via Santa Lucia Filippini 11, tel 335 625 9562 or 345 212 1521, info@atlantisinn.it. Reservations preferred; price includes breakfast; some apartments have washing machines.

- **Il Raduno** O Pr R W S 1/3, €-/50/60/80/-/-, Corso della Repubblica 31, tel 338 735 1803, info@ilradunocastelgandolfo.it.

The Apostolic Palace at Castel Gandolfo was purchased by the papacy in 1596. It served as a refugee center in World War II, when the town housed 12,000 people who fled the fighting around Rome

STAGE 2

Castel Gandolfo to Velletri

Start	Piazza della Libertà, Castel Gandolfo
Finish	Municipio, Velletri
Duration	5¾hr
Distance	21.5km
Total ascent	481m
Total descent	582m
Difficulty	Moderately hard (due to footing on trails and several slopes)
Percentage paved	50%
Lodgings	Albano Laziale 2.1km, Nemi 10.5km, Velletri 21.5km

Today is a walk through shady forests along ancient volcanoes, interrupted by the delightful presence of medieval Nemi, a perfect halfway point for lunch. You are presented with a choice immediately: to take the official route down to the interesting town of Albano Laziale or to take a shortcut along the crater rim on the auto-centric SP71b, which saves 1.1km. After Nemi, more long walks through a hilly, new-growth forest recovering from intermittent logging operations lead to Velletri, a large, historic, and diverse city with sweeping views of the coastal plain.

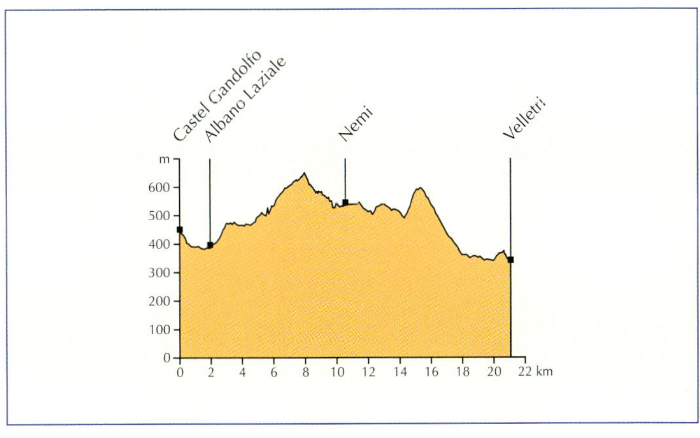

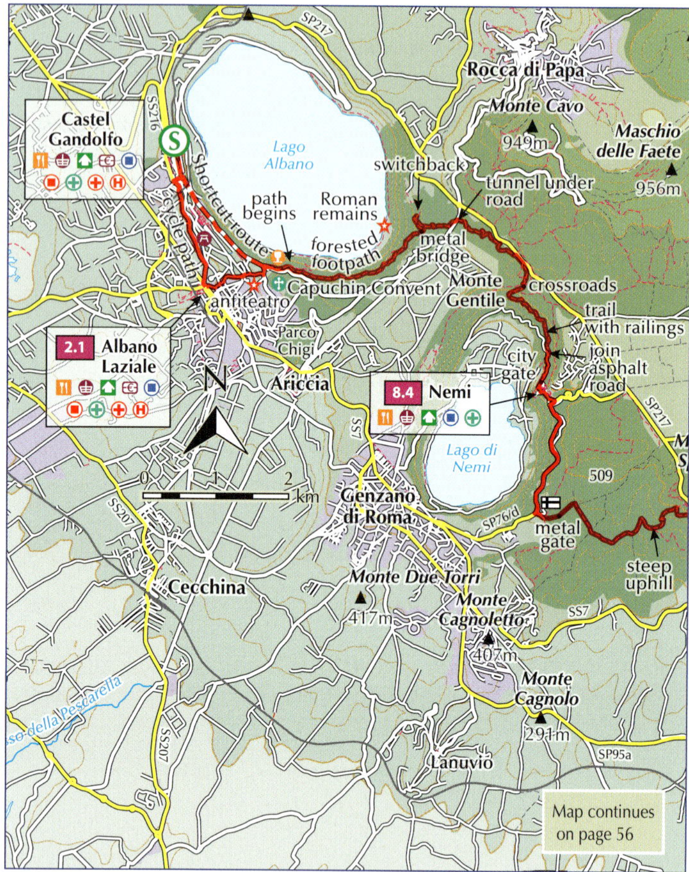

With the Papal Palace behind you, head straight downhill on Corso della Repubblica. In Piazza Cavallotti, almost at the end, head down the stairs then take a second staircase past a parking lot to turn right. Shortcut: continue on the narrow Via Carlo Rosselli, past Chiesa di Santa Maria Assunta, and meet the other route at the Capuchin Convent). Pass through the city gate, cross the street, and pick up the **cycle path** below Viale Giovanni Paolo II. When it ends, continue on a sidewalk to Piazza Mazzini in **Albano Laziale**.

2.1KM ALBANO LAZIALE (ELEV 406M, POP 41,654) (908.8KM)

Discover the ancient amphitheater, the Tomb of Horatii and Curiatii (who, according to myth, battled for the town's dominion), the Baths of Caracalla, the cisterns, and the aristocratic villa of Pompey the Great. In 946 the city was among the growing fiefdoms of the Savelli family, becoming the region's capital until the Unification of Italy. In the year 1000, the Santuario di Santa Maria della Rotonda was built on top of a Roman nymphaeum. The Cattedrale di San Pancrazio originates from the 9th century.

Seminario Vescovile Do Piazza san Paolo 5, tel 06 932 0021, seminario@diocesidialbano.it and curia@diocesidialbano.it, www.diocesidialbano.it.

Villa Altieri Hotel O Pr R Br Dr Cr Z 26/70, €-/65/85/111/-/- Via Appia Nuova 1, tel 06 932 0562, info@villaaltieri.it, www.villaaltieri.it.

Fork uphill before the piazza (square) onto Via Cairoli, and on Piazza Pia, turn right to find the cathedral entrance (food). Continue on this street, passing the Bishop's Palace and the Roman ruins of Porta Praetoria. Turn left uphill onto Via Aurelio Saffi, spotting Santa Maria della Rotondo on the left, with its centuries-old frescoes and Roman mosaic entry, and reach the ancient Cisternoni on the right. These Roman cisterns are believed to be the only ones in the world still functioning.

Near the top of the climb, veer left past Santuario di San Gaspari (containing paintings from the Caravaggio school) then turn right onto Via Anfiteatro to the ancient **anfiteatro** (ampitheater) after which signs lead uphill to join the shortcut route on Via Carlo Rosselli at the **Capuchin Convent**. Across the street find a bar and to its right take a path forking left downhill. Keeping straight ahead on the road for 750m leads to **Miralago**. The path widens, becoming a tranquil, well-marked, shaded, and scenic traverse of the crater wall with its occasional caves. After the path crosses a **metal bridge**, it begins to climb steeply, reaching a trail bed of bedrock. Afterward, switchback right, still climbing up the crater wall, where mountain bikers are common on weekends. Pass through a **tunnel** under the main road, cross an old asphalt road, and keep uphill on the path. Pass the Fontana Tempesta, whose waters are supposedly restorative for walkers. As you descend, come to a **crossroads** of paths and follow signs for 'Nemi 30' to descend on a rocky trail with glimpses of Lago di Nemi on the right.

Soon the trail has **railings** on the lakeside, a sign you are nearing Nemi. Merge with a road then a surface of cobblestones. An off-route right turn leads to the remains of the Tempio di Diana Nemorense (a detour of 2km with 262m ascent one way). Within this (now overgrown and ruined) temple, Romulus was born, according to legend. Fantastic views of the lake accompany you as you enter town. Go through a **city gate**, turn left, and pass under the *palazzo* (palace/mansion) archway to find the main piazza in **Nemi** (**8.4km**).

8.4KM NEMI (ELEV 528M, POP 1910) (900.4KM)

The town's name stems from the Latin *nemus*, meaning 'forest,' and its inhabitants are proud of the wild strawberries, mushrooms, and flowers that grow in the local woods. The strawberry festival takes place yearly on the first Sunday of June. Overlooking its namesake volcanic lake, the 10th-century Palazzo Ruspoli is the oldest palace in the vicinity. Artists, musicians, and writers drew inspiration from Nemi, including Hans Christian Andersen, Goethe, Stendhal, and D'Annunzio. Remarkably, Charles Gounod composed his 'Ave Maria' while contemplating the moonlit lake, and Lord Byron included Nemi in his poem *Childe Harold's Pilgrimage*. The Belvedere Terrace in Piazza Roma is dedicated to the English poet.

Locanda Lo Specchio di Diana O Pr R Cr S 5/14, €-/60/70/115/115/-, Corso Vittorio Emanuele 11, tel 06 936 8714, info@specchiodidiana.it, www.specchiodidiana.it. Restaurant on site.

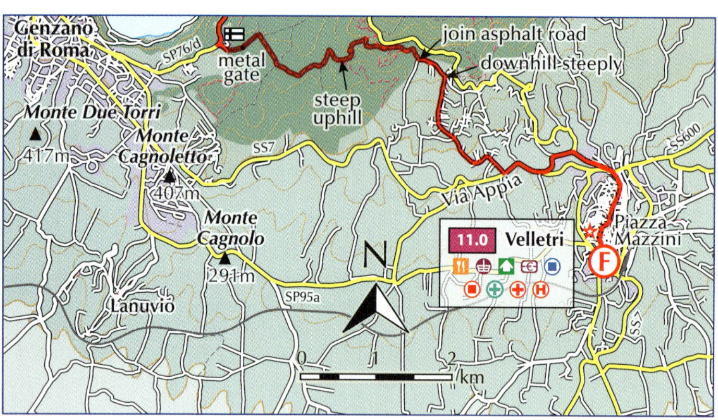

As you leave town, enter the Church of the Crucifixion and see the somewhat gory and curiously carved crucifix. Peering at the face of Christ on the cross, move from one side of the chancel to the other to see the odd illusion that the face sees you from both sides. Now follow the main road out of town, with lovely views. Watch for signs to go left onto an uphill cobblestone road, passing Nemi cemetery (**2.0km**), then, after a **metal gate**, fork right onto a dirt road through a forest recovering from recent

A central Nemi side-street full of Italy's warm, historic, urban colors

logging. Excellent waymarking on forest paths leads to a pulse-quickening climb up **Monte Spina**. Before the summit, fork right and, thankfully, traverse more gently to eventually curve left, joining a downhill path that leads to a house and a road. Soon fork right, heading steeply downhill with distant views of the sea and on a series of well-marked downhill roads, arrive at the now-mechanized **Via Appia** after which a left turn leads to a double roundabout and fountain in modern **Velletri**. The road climbs into the old town, passing the 14th-century Torre del Trivio to arrive at the *municipio* (town hall) and Bishop's Palace (**8.9km**).

11KM VELLETRI (ELEV 367M, POP 53,365) (889.4KM)

The Roman Velitrae (Velletri) has an imposing entrance through the Porta Napoletana, which dates from 1511–1519. Initially resembling a castle stronghold rather than a church, the Basilica Cattedrale di San Clemente was constructed on Roman foundations. Its structure dates from the 12th century, yet it retains original Roman columns. The underground chapel holds frescoes depicting the translation of the relics of two saints: Saint Pontianus and Saint Eleutherius.

Taberna Velitrae/Accoglienza with Corrado O Pr Do R Br Dr S 1/2, €-/35/-/-/-/-, Via Guido Nati 5, tel 328 386 4047, corradobisini1959@gmail.com. Price includes bed, dinner and breakfast. Your hosts are Corrado and Viviana.

A Casa di Ciccio da'mmonte O Pr R S 3/7, €-/30/60/90/-/-, Via Paolina 150, tel 333 815 9466 or 347 812 3667, francesca.nardini90@gmail.com. Maximum two bikes.

STAGE 3

Velletri to Cori

Start	Municipio, Velletri
Finish	Temple of Hercules, Cori
Duration	5hr
Distance	18.9km
Total ascent	344m
Total descent	266m
Difficulty	Moderate due to elevation changes
Percentage paved	77%
Lodgings	Cori 18.9km, Norma 31.3km

After a couple of demanding stages, today's shorter distance will feel like a relief. Two nerve-wracking roadside walks are balanced with a tranquil stroll through the green Giulianello Reserve. Wide vistas precede your arrival in Cori, a town of surprising historical treasures. Lake Giulianello's waterfront park is a restful lunch spot, or you can continue on to the cafés in the town itself.

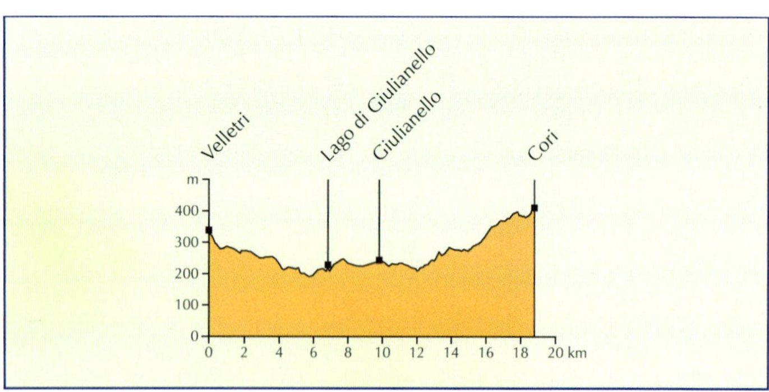

Go behind the left side of the municipio and head down stairs through Piazza Mazzini, once an amphitheater (services). Pass through the Porta Napolitana, looking back toward its most historic and photogenic side. Following waymarks, keep downhill, pass a train depot and **Via Francigena info point** then fork left gently uphill onto Via

Ferruccio Parri at the gas station. After the *liceo* (school), where the sidewalk ends, fork left downhill. Pass a recycling center, heading uphill on a narrow lane, then join the highway to the left (I Ciliegi) for one block before crossing it (food) and arriving at **Le Meraviglie** farm shop (closed Mondays). On the left, find **I Sapori dei Castelli Romani**, restaurant open every evening and for Sunday lunch.

Continue by plots of olives, kiwis, grapes, and artichokes. The custom of planting fava (broad) beans among vines introduces a favorite local dish of fava with pecorino cheese and wine. At the crossroads and end of the road, keep straight onto a wide gravel road, which soon becomes a path leading down into a terrain of fields interspersed with woods in the Giulianello Reserve. At the bottom, cross over a seasonal stream, pass below a sheepfold, follow a grassy trail under power lines, and cross another stream at the Velletri-Cori municipality boundary. On the hilltop on the right, the ruins of a Roman villa are testimony to the agriculture that supported the empire's capital. Head down to the waterfront park by **Lago di Giulianello** (**7km**).

The **Giulianello Reserve**, declared a Natural Monument in 2007, is the result of a long litigation against the noble family that had dominated the property for years. The struggle finally resulted in the award of the property to the community of *cittadini* (citizens) who had long tended the fields. Rather than divide up the property, they kept the farmland as a single legal entity, owning it as a cooperative. The result is a vast fertile organic oasis preserving a working farm and park.

Green crops fill the roadsides along the valley to Giulianello

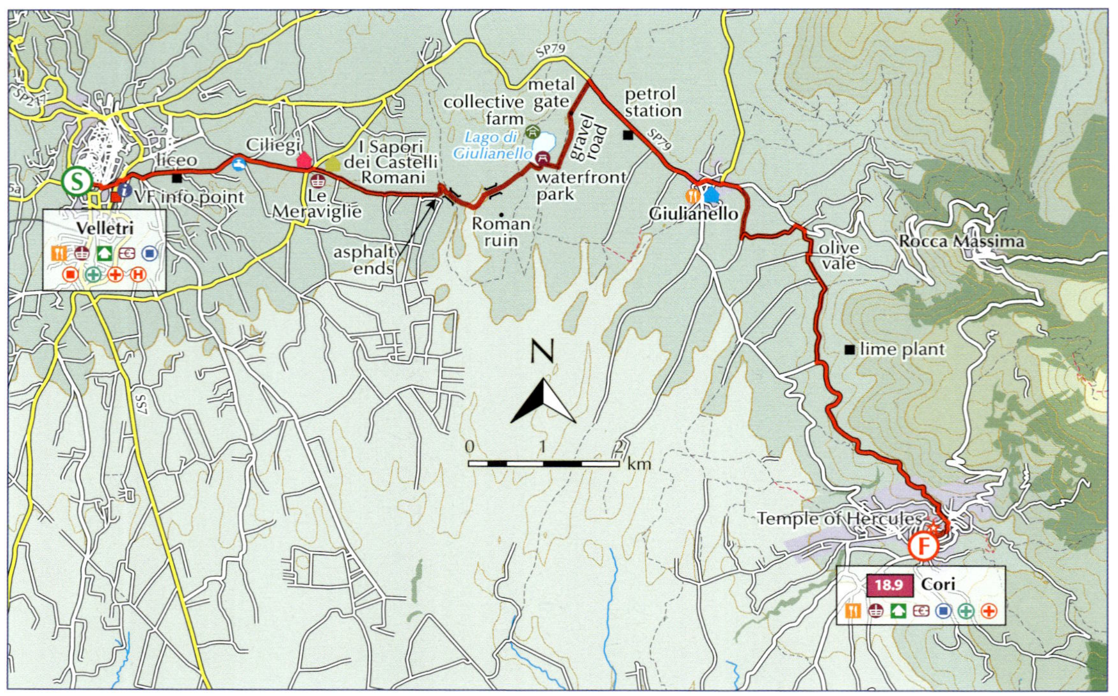
SP79
metal gate
collective farm
petrol station
Lago di Giulianello
gravel road
Ciliegi
I Sapori dei Castelli Romani
liceo
S
VF info point
waterfront park
Le Meraviglie
Giulianello
Roman ruin
Velletri
asphalt ends
olive vale
Rocca Massima
lime plant
N
0
1
2
km
SS7
Temple of Hercules
F
18.9
Cori

After joining an uphill path, reach a gravel road dotted with historical narratives about the lake. Pass through a **metal gate** where the road widens and upon reaching the highway, turn right initially on a pathway running inside the fence along the highway but soon joining it after a gas station (food) until you arrive at **Giulianello** itself (**3.7km** food, www.qcmgiulianello.it). The Chiesa di San Giovanni Battista houses a 16th-century statue of Baby Jesus, said to have been carved from trees of the Garden of Gethsemane. At the roundabout in town, turn left onto a tree-lined promenade and fork right at a pizzeria with views of the spectacularly high village of Rocca Massima. Follow signs onto a gravel road between two walled industrial properties then onto a pleasant two-track road among olive groves and a seasonal creek. After a series of asphalt roads toward the left, keep to a road heading around the foot of the tree-covered mountain. Where the road ends at a **lime plant**, turn left onto an uphill road into **Cori**, continuing to hug the slope, with views of the coastal plain emerging. Arrive in town by a play area then follow signs uphill, reaching the ruins of the **Temple of Hercules**.

18.9KM CORI (ELEV 403M, POP 10,456) (870.5KM)

Within what once was Roman Cora, now a very picturesque hilltop town, archeological remains from the 6th–1st centuries BC include the old polygonal cyclopean walls, the acropolis with its Temple of Hercules, the bridge, and the three surviving towering columns of the Temple of Castor and Pollux (Tempio dei Dioscuri). The majority of present-day Cori dates back to the 7th century. It blossomed in the 11th and 15th centuries under the jurisdiction of the Papal States and the Senate of Rome, as evidenced in the beautiful Oratorio della SS Annunziata with its fantastically preserved frescoes. Construction began in 1411, ordered by the Spanish Cardinal Pedro Fernández de Frías. The Latin inscription on the portal reads 'De Spagna fuit qui me legerit dicat unu(m) pater n(oste)r p(ro) a(n)i(m)a mea,' meaning 'He was from Spain. Whoever reads me, say an Our Father for my soul.'

Il Circo della Farfalla (ex Convento San Francesco) O Do R K S Z 19/50, €Donation, Piazza San Francesco d'Assisi, tel 388 622 3905, accoglienza@ilcircodellafarfalla.com.

STAGE 4

Cori to Sermoneta

Start	Temple of Hercules, Cori
Finish	Piazza del Popolo, Sermoneta
Duration	5½hr
Distance	20.3km
Total ascent	534m
Total descent	708m
Difficulty	Moderately Hard due to climbs/descents
Percentage paved	73%
Lodgings	Norma 12.5km, Sermoneta 20.3km, Sezze 31.3km

Dramatic scenery defines this stage, with vistas of lofty hilltop towns and distant cities below in the plain. The UNESCO archeological site at Norba offers a chance to imagine a pre-Roman era behind colossal stone walls, with services nearby at Norma. The climb to Sermoneta at the end of the day gets the heart pumping, but that is quickly forgotten while enjoying the charms of this village left unchanged for centuries.

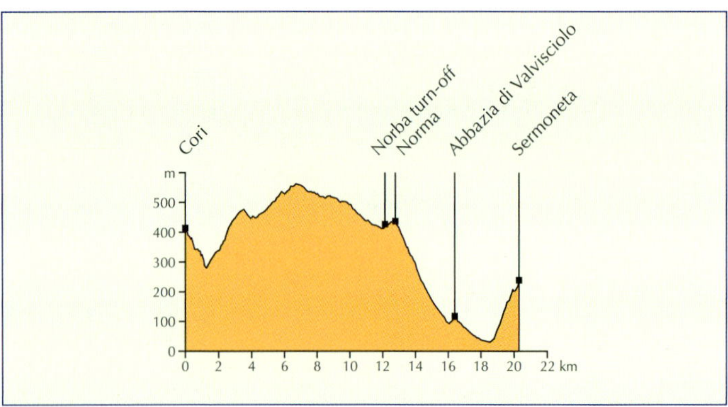

Although GPS tracks send you around the park, instead continue downhill from the Temple of Hercules, following plentiful signs in a labyrinth of stairs and archways ending in a covered stairwell/gallery extending 100m down the hillside. Note the largest stones set at the lower layers of the walls. They were built by the Volsci Italic people, and locals still call them by their traditional name of 'cyclopean' – the stones were so large they were believed to have been placed by the mythical, one-eyed giant. At the bottom of Upper Cori, cross a **stone bridge** and turn left to steeply climb on Via Le Case, which switches at times to gravel, with dramatic views to the plain and back to Cori and to the green Lepini Mountains as you travel through olive groves and horse pastures.

At the road end, turn right and immediately right again then left 200m later onto a wider road, slowly climbing the slopes of Monte Arrestino as panorama after panorama unfolds. This Via Passeggiata San Giovanni makes a hard right turn at **Via Malerba** and in 1km arrives at the turn-off to the Archeological Park of Ancient Norba (300m off route).

Said to be founded by Hercules himself, the 38-hectare stronghold of **Norba** fell into complete ruin by 81BC. The inhabitants favored Marius in his struggles with Silla, and rather than risking it falling into enemy hands, they burned their city down, thus ensuring Silla's army gained nothing. Fortunately, the immutable walls are some of the best preserved of any Roman city in the world.

Return to the route and turn right to head back onto Via Passeggiata San Giovanni to the center of **Norma**.

12.5KM NORMA (ELEV 438M, POP 3623) (858.1KM)

In addition to visiting the archeological park, three churches are recommended: the 16th-century Chiesa della Santissima Annunziata, which sits on 12th-century foundations; the unusual terracotta-colored Oratorio di San Rocco (18th century); and the 19th-century Chiesa della Madonna del Carmine. Curiously, Norma is also home to the Chocolate Museum, where a visit includes a tasting and an insight into chocolate-making utensils.

Antica Norma Alloggio Turistico O Pr R Br 4/8, €-/-/50/-/-, Via Nazionale 27, tel 333 313 4800 or 338 848 1094, anticanorma@libero.it ,www.anticanorma.it. €150 for a group of 8 people.

Pass the Madonna del Carmine Church and 100m later fork left downhill onto Via Delle Svolte. The road ends and becomes a steep descent on a rough gravel path that crosses a **wooden bridge** and reaches the narrow and busy Via Norbana. Turn left onto it briefly and at the first switchback follow signs straight onto a gravel road (water) that shortcuts the road's long curve. Promptly fork right, go straight at a crossroads, take a bridge, and follow signs that lead straight to the **Abbazia di Valvisciolo**. Dedicated to Saints Peter and Stephen, the abbey was built between 1150 and 1170 and includes a museum that displays 50 engravings, drawings, and woodcuts by famous artists, including Albrecht Dürer.

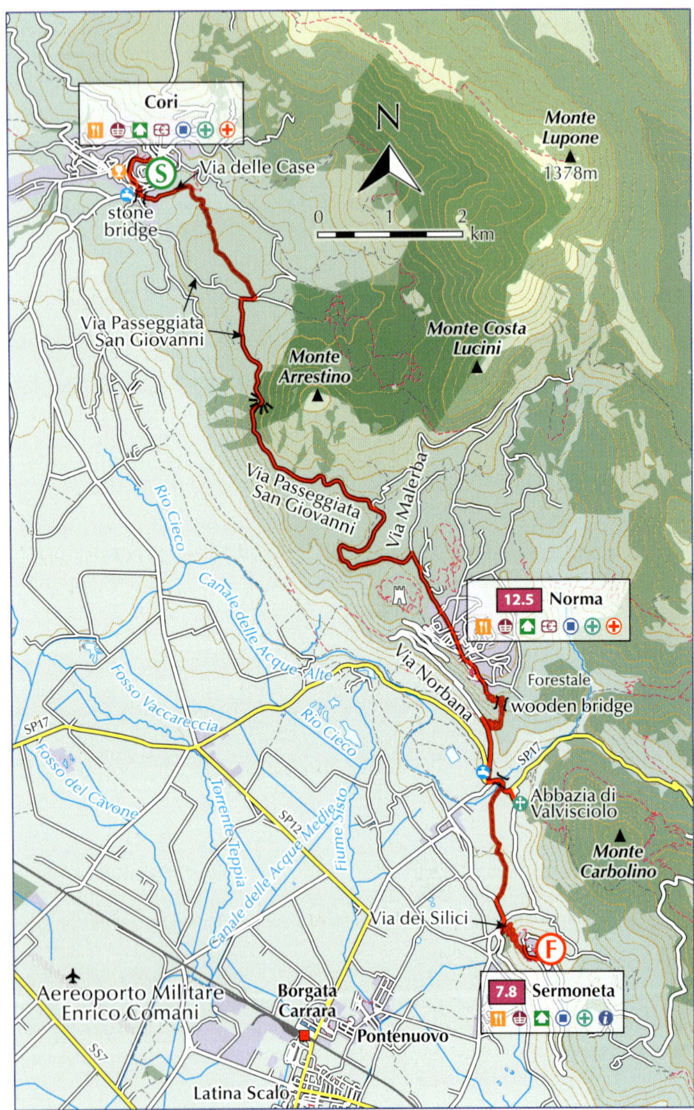
Cori
S
Via delle Case
stone bridge
N
0 1 2 km
Monte Lupone
1378m
Via Passeggiata San Giovanni
Monte Arrestino
Monte Costa Lucini
Via Passeggiata San Giovanni
Via Malerba
Rio Cieco
Canale delle Acque Alte
12.5 Norma
Via Norbana
Forestale
wooden bridge
Fosso Vaccareccia
Rio Cieco
SP17
SP17
Fosso del Cavone
Torrente Teppia
SP12
Canale delle Acque Medie
Fiume Sisto
Abbazia di Valvisciolo
Monte Carbolino
Via dei Silici
F
7.8 Sermoneta
Aereoporto Militare Enrico Comani
Borgata Carrara
Pontenuovo
SS7
Latina Scalo

After your visit, retrace your steps and on the abbey side of the bridge, waymarks lead onto a downhill lane through small fields and olive groves. Join a larger road, then at the intersection, look across for signs onto a steep gravel path, **Via dei Silici**. It sends you down 300m in eight switchbacks to reach a flagstone walkway and a left fork up to an opening in the city walls of **Sermoneta**. Then turn right uphill, following signs to the Piazza del Popolo.

7.8KM SERMONETA (ELEV 254M, POP 10,037) (850.2KM)

Sermoneta is perched fantastically, overseeing the Pontine Plain, and arriving here is a leap back in time to the town's medieval origins. Archeological excavations unearthed an Iron Age necropolis composed of 76 inhumation tombs and 19 incineration tombs. The Cattedrale di Santa Maria Assunta in Cielo and its tower were built in a Romanesque style in the 12th century on the ruins of a temple dedicated to the goddess Cybele. The bell tower and other 13th-century additions were likely thanks to interventions by the Cistercian monks of Fossanova Abbey (Stage 6), and they transformed much of its appearance into the solemn Gothic style. The Chiesa di Santa Maria delle Grazie (1591) displays another pretty Romanesque cathedral tower. Most majestic are the tower and counter-tower of the now-destroyed Castello Caetani, built by the Annibaldi lords in the early 13th century. Additions and modifications were mainly undertaken in the 15th century by the Borgia family, giving it its current alluring air. Notable guests included Frederick III in 1452, Charles V in 1536, and Pope Alexander VI's daughter, Lucrezia Borgia.

La Tana del Coniglio O Pr Do R Br Dr 2/4, €-/30/30/-/-/-, Via San Francesco 3, tel 339 276 9739. Two wooden bungalows with two beds at €30 each, camping €20 per tent, prices include dinner and breakfast.

Sermoneta stands on the hillside with the Agro Pontino plain below and Monte Circeo (541m) beyond

STAGE 5

Sermoneta to Sezze

Start	Piazza del Popolo, Sermoneta
Finish	Basilica Concattedrale di Santa Maria, Sezze
Duration	3hr
Distance	11.0km
Total ascent	307m
Total descent	240m
Difficulty	Moderate due to uneven footing
Percentage paved	55%
Lodgings	Sezze 11km, Priverno 24.3km, Abbazia di Fossanova 31.9km

Gorgeous scenery accompanies you on this very short stage, although in wet weather it could be a time-consuming morass of muddy dirt roads. The route stays at moderate elevation, crossing a saddle between two mountains that separate Sermoneta and Sezze. Sermoneta is a tourist favorite, while Sezze, which was partly destroyed in World War 2, is a more workaday town. The stage length requires little need for much food, and there is no water source for about 9km between the towns.

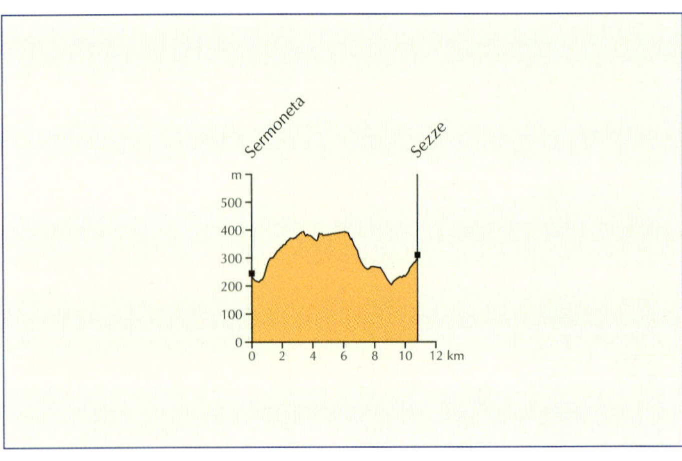

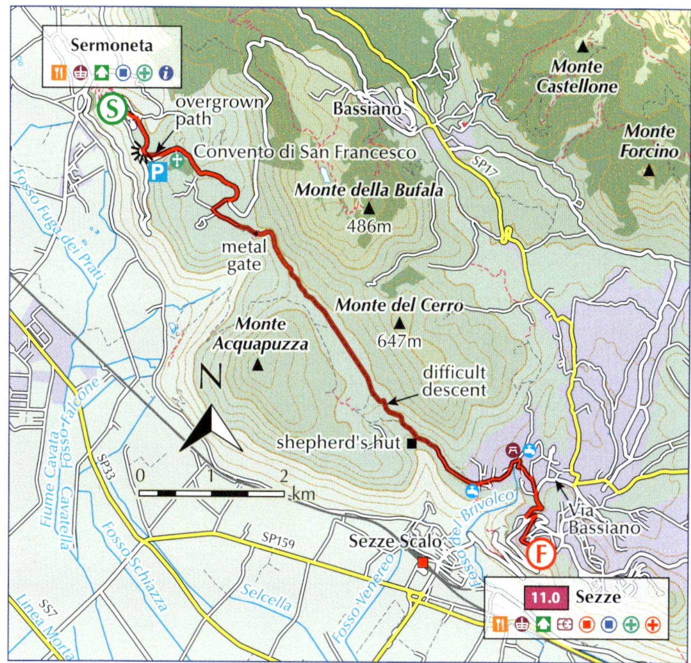

Follow signs downhill from Piazza del Popolo and, passing through Porta del Pozzo, look out from inside the medieval battlements. Continue straight along the road between the Lepini Mountains and olive groves. Turn left before the **overlook** and take the overgrown path forking immediately left away from the road. Beware, this path may be overgrown and dewy, so sometimes it may be best to remain on the asphalt. Pass the **Convento di San Francesco** and its very old chapel (usually closed) and an oak tree planted by the Franciscans in 1495. Continue uphill and at the end of the road turn left uphill, with the Lepini Mountains on the left, soon reaching a summit among pastures. Go through a left-hand **metal gate** onto a dirt track to be immersed in scenic woodland, traversing the mountainside and the saddle between Monte della Bufala and Monte del Cerro, with expansive views toward Latina and the sea. Surrounded by cyclamen and other wildflowers (in season), you will hear the bells of grazing Maremma cows nearby.

Soon encounter remnants of a Bourbon gate with two posts of stone: a tax-collection post for travelers between Sermoneta and Sezze. The path then widens to a farm track that becomes muddy and sticky in damp weather, leading to a change in territory in the form of lupine (*Lupinus*) fields, pastures, and vineyards. When the road turns to the right, the route instead heads down a somewhat treacherous, ankle-challenging descent with Sezze ahead below Monte Trevi, all in the shadow of Monte Semprevisa (1536m), the tallest of the Lepini Mountains.

When you pass a **shepherd's hut**, the road, blessedly, turns to asphalt and climbs then descends into Sezze's neighborhoods. At the bottom (water), a hairpin bend leads over a bridge then uphill to a T-junction and a right turn uphill onto Via Bassiano to the center of **Sezze**. Turn left at a crossroads onto Via Madonna della Pace by the now-abandoned 16th-century Madonna della Pace Church, built to remember the end of 300 years of hostilities between the people of Sermoneta and Sezze. Climb the steps at the end of the road, cross the street and head uphill onto Via del Mattatoio, turn left at a parking lot, and reach the understated facade of the *duomo* (cathedral).

After a 17th-century fire, the main entry to the 14th-century cathedral of Santa Maria in Sezze was reversed to its apse, while high over the altar (not shown) is a rose window over the former entrance

11KM SEZZE (ELEV 317M, POP 23,697) (839.3KM)

According to legend, Setia (Sezze) was founded by Hercules in 382BC. Remains of grand villas tell of Roman Imperial prosperity. In the Middle Ages trouble arose due to Sezze's geographical location on the Via Pedemontana, a commercially crucial road linking north and south. Although under free jurisdiction, Sezze adhered to papal administration and popes regularly visited. Its position was attacked throughout its history, first by opponents to the Pope then by the Caetani family and, finally, in 1407 by Ladislaus, King of Naples. It endured further suffering during the 1656 plague, followed by looting from Spanish and Austrian troops. The most notable church is the 13th-century Cattedrale di Santa Maria. (Note: the train serving Sezze is 3km away in Sezze Scalo.)

B&B Casa Papona Pr R K Br W S 3/8, €-/-/60/-/100/-, Via Piagge Marine 221, tel 335 789 8004, casa.papona@gmail.com.

B&B Casa Salvi Pr R K Br S 3/6, €-/30–35/60–70/-/-/-, Via Sedia del Papa 43, tel 0773 888488 or 333 870 7898, casasalvi.bandb@gmail.com.

Agriturismo Barbitto Pr R Br Dr Cr S 11/22, €-/45/70/90/-/-, Via Colli 47, tel 0773 888 523, ristorantebarbitto@tiscali.it or deangelisivan@libero.it. Closed at Christmas.

STAGE 6

Sezze to Abbazia di Fossanova

Start	Basilica Concattedrale di Santa Maria, Sezze
Finish	Abbey Church, Abbazia di Fossanova
Duration	5½hr
Distance	20.9km
Total ascent	241m
Total descent	513m
Difficulty	Moderate
Percentage paved	47%
Lodgings	Priverno 13.3km, Abbazia di Fossanova 20.9km

Vast views of the Agro Pontino plain and the distant Tyrrenhian Sea mark this stage of two distinct halves: a mountainous descent and a flat canal-side walk. The stage ends at Abbazia di Fossanova, an oasis of calm steeped in history. The medieval town of Priverno offers mid-stage refreshment but scant lodging options.

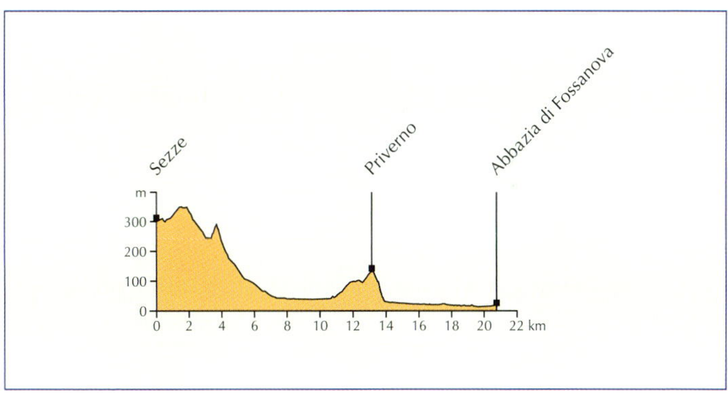

Pass the duomo on its left side and follow the curving road through the old town. At a roundabout, take the second right onto uphill Via Piagge Marine, passing the pharmacy, fruit store, and café. Pass the turn-off to the anfiteatro, turn right at the next roundabout with an old olive oil mill wheel in its center, continue uphill then follow signs lightly downhill to go through a **gate/door** on the right. Walk downhill on grass, with spectacular views of mountains and sea.

Map continues on page 71

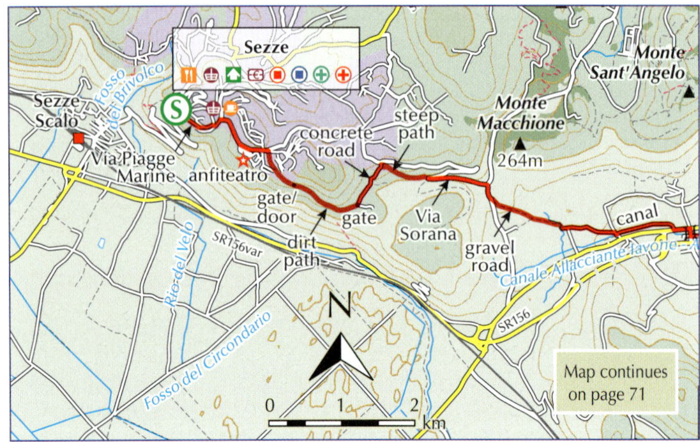

As you cross the **Agro Pontino (Pontine Plain)**, idyllic views toward the Pontine Islands in the Tyrrhenian Sea narrate Homeric myths. The land is named 'Terre di Ulisse' (land of Odysseus) and here the Greek King of Ithaca had many of the most recounted adventures of *The Odyssey*, most famously that of his romance with Circe. Some say that the epic also portrays the cliffs above the Tyrrhenian Sea as the dwelling place of Aeolus and his four winds.

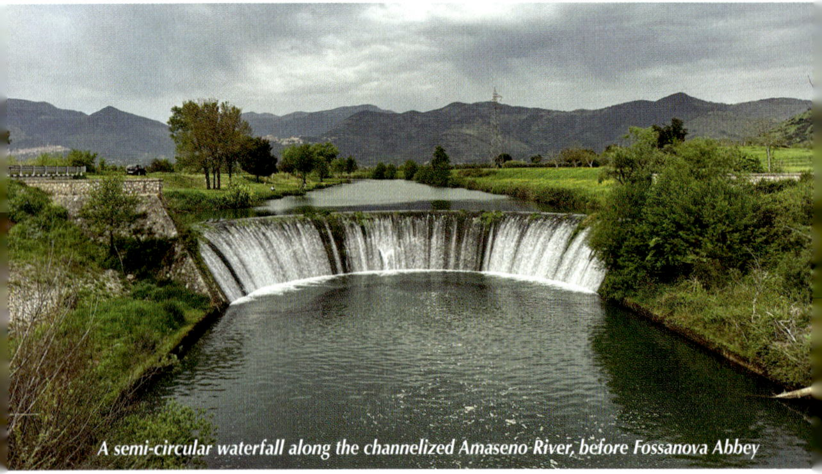

A semi-circular waterfall along the channelized Amaseno River, before Fossanova Abbey

13.3KM PRIVERNO (ELEV 127M, POP 13,735) (826KM)
Roman Privernum was first founded by the Volsci people, who lived in the valley of the upper Liris River in the 5th century BC. The town was destroyed, rebuilt, renamed several times, moved, and returned to its original location, and then finally named Priverno in 1927. The charming old town is set around the 12th–13th century Piazza Giovanni XXIII, and, most importantly, the Cattedrale di Santa Maria Annunziata houses the skull of the philosopher and theologian St. Thomas Aquinas.

Accoglienza with Gloria Pr Do R K 1/2, €Donation, Via Principe Amedeo 27, tel 328 092 3193, gloria.aresu@gmail.com. Gloria welcomes pilgrims into her home, offering a double sofa bed in her living room. Reservations required to ensure availability.

Fork right onto a dirt path and away from the descending road to continue the traverse. Clinging to the mountainside, with a thin rope for security, the path may test the sensitivities of anyone with acrophobia but, in reality, is safe. At the end of the path, turn left onto a gravel road by a **gate**. Climb steeply on concrete and near the top, turn right under an olive tree to a descent on a driveway. When it comes to an end, continue on a steep, grassy path, which can be slippery for the first 100m, before

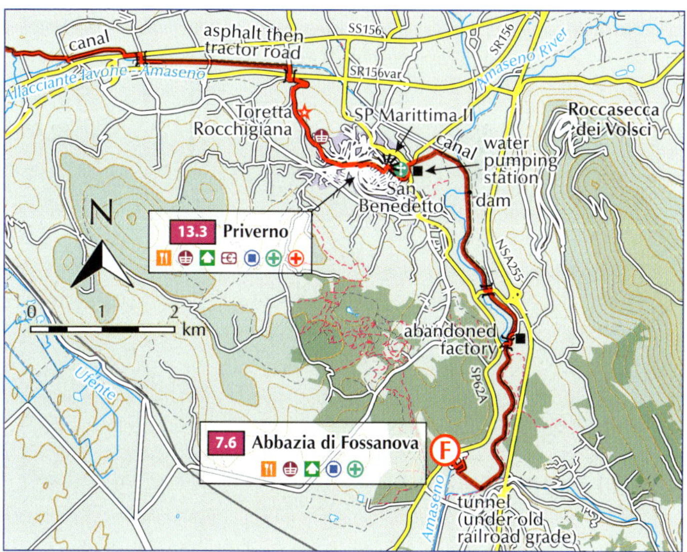

it eases to reach **Via Sorana**. Turn right downhill, with views onto Priverno across the valley, then reaching fields near the valley floor, ensure you fork left onto a **gravel road**.

When the gravel road ends, continue on a narrow road toward town. As the road curves, turn left just before a **bridge** to walk by the grassy channel. At the end of the road, head along the SS156 highway for 150m then turn right across the canal and immediately left, following the road then a dirt track for about 2km.

Upon reaching a road, Via Torretta Rocchigiana, turn right onto it over the busy **SR156var** and curve uphill, passing the town's medieval watchtower, **Torretta Rocchigiana**, a grocery store, and, at a roundabout, the historic Church of San Antonio Abate (stamp). Continue uphill and at Piazza XX Settembre, turn left, finding cobblestones beneath your feet: a one-time Roman Via Consolare. Arrive at Piazza Vittorio Emanuele with its town hall, cathedral, and archeological museum.

Turn left at the Museo Archeologico onto Via San Giorgio, descending on cobblestone steps. Set within the Palazzo Antonelli, with its pleasing amaranth and gray Renaissance facade, the museum contains a collection of more than 1000 historical objects. Turn right at the next street (or continue straight for a panoramic viewpoint from the old city walls). The two options rejoin 100m later at the 13th-century Church of **San Benedetto**. Go through the parking lot and descend on steps or along the steep street. Cross the SP Marittima II, continue downhill on steps, and keep ahead on the road by a **water pumping station**. After 75m, fork right onto a white gravel road, back alongside the canal encountered previously.

The canal spills into the Amaseno River, which leads to Abbazia di Fossanova. Pass a semi-circular **dam**, cross an auto bridge then keep following the river on a pleasant, flat footpath. Join a road just before an **abandoned factory** after which, turn right, back over the river, on another auto bridge, picking up a flat gravel road, which eventually reveals views of the abbey's tall cupola. Pass under the railway through a **tunnel**, leaving the river, then turn right and follow signs around the abbey boundary to the piazza at its front door.

7.6KM ABBAZIA DI FOSSANOVA (ELEV 24M, POP 102) (818.3KM)

In 1874, the Abbey of Fossanova was declared a National Monument, and its quaint surrounding village offers glimpses of the past. Built by Benedictine monks, it was home to Pope Gregory IV prior to his election in 827. The Abbey's name *fossa nova* means 'new ditch/channel,' as it lay in a marshy location. The Cistercians labored to channel the swamps of the overflowing Amaseno River. St. Thomas Aquinas, the greatest theologian of the 13th century and author of *Summa Theologica*, rode along the Via Appia on his donkey, having been called by Pope Gregory X to attend the Second Council of Lyon, a conference with the aim of reuniting the Catholic and Orthodox Churches (in response to the Great Schism of 1054). Alas, disaster struck when a branch hit him. Recuperating at the Abbey, he died here on March 7, 1274. The Abbey upholds continuous prayer between 08.30 and 18.30, and daily mass is held at 17.00.

Casette rosse nel borgo di Fossanova O Pr R K Cr W S 4/12, €-/110/130/140/150/160, Via dell'Abbazia, tel 349 804 7398, info@fossanova.it, www.fossanova.it/fossanova-home-eng. Minimum three nights' stay in August.

Consecrated in 1208, the Abbey at Fossanova is an important example of the Gothic style, imported to Italy by the French Cistercian monks who built it

STAGE 7

Abbazia di Fossanova to Terracina

Start	Abbey Church, Abbazia di Fossanova
Finish	Cattedrale, Terracina
Duration	5¼hr
Distance	20.6km
Total ascent	130m
Total descent	104m
Difficulty	Moderate due to hard surfaces and lack of shade
Percentage paved	95%
Lodgings	Terracina 20.6km, Monte San Biagio 33.7km

After the sublime scenery of previous stages, there is some disappointment with this flat, plain one, and, although within sight, the salty sea waters lie 30min off the trail. In the meantime, the central piazza of Terracina is a surprise treat, with Roman ruins and a venerable cathedral. Midway on the stage are a bar and grocery, but there is scant shade. The next two stages form two sides of a triangle, while a mountainous option (Stage 7–8A Variant) forms the third and cuts off a day at the price of a stiff but scenic climb.

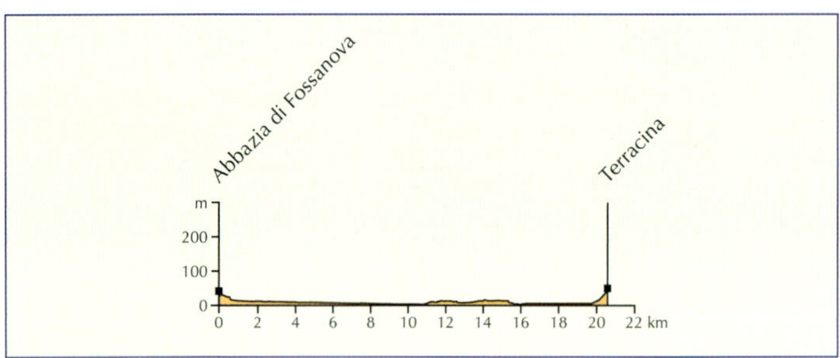

Pass through the abbey's main gate and turn left to walk on the SP62A Via Marittima II for about 400m. Take the first left onto SP Sonninese, cross the **Amaseno River bridge**, and turn right onto Via Argine Amaseno (**0.9km**) alongside the river. Continue straight to take the Stage 7–8A Variant. This road and its sibling on the other side of the river will be your thoroughfare throughout the day.

Pass under the **train bridge** and come to an intersection with the Strada Longitundinale A1 highway whose lanes are divided by a 1.2m concrete barrier, which

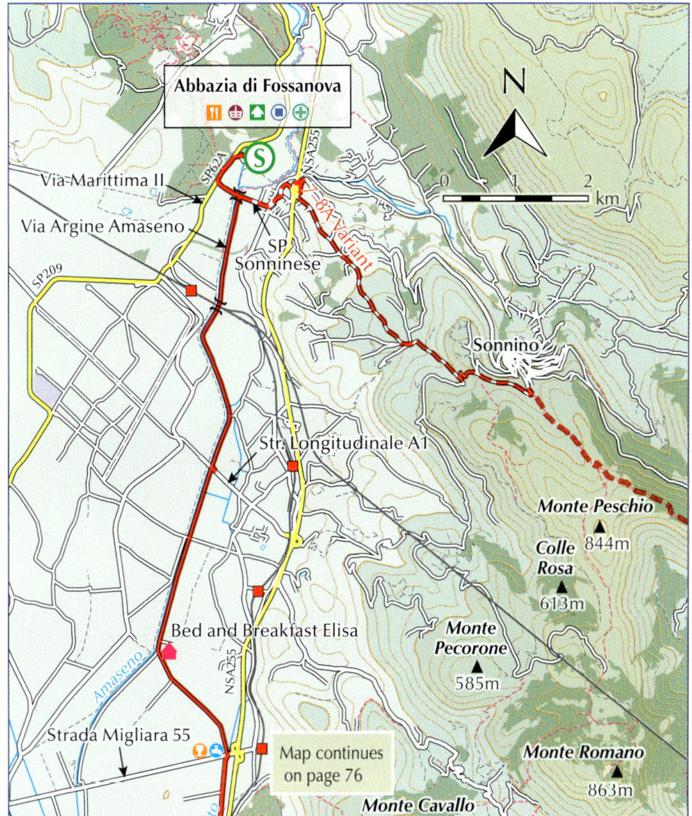

you can either climb over or go around by turning left. Once you have surmounted the barrier, continue on the same riverside road as before, now on dirt. Fork left away from the river in about 2.5km (on the left is Bed and Breakfast Elisa) and at an intersection with the **Strada Migliara 55** come to a crossroads with a bar and water (**8.4km**).

Due to a landslide and construction works, the route detours from the signage and at the Jesus statue, instead of turning left to cross under the highway alongside the railway, continue straight. About 2km later pass under the highway bridge (**3.7km**, groceries, water) to continue on the quiet Via Piedamontagna (a medieval replacement for the Via Appia). Pass an area of freshwater springs with a modern flour mill and the somewhat sparse ruins of the ancient **Temple of Feronia**.

If you ask at the office of the flour mill, the owner will let you visit the **temple ruins** and see the large resident fish in the clear water spring. The temple itself was devoted to Feronia, goddess of wild nature, adopted by the Romans from Etruscan and Sabine religions. A story recounts how a fire destroyed Feronia's forest: when the locals decided to flee with all their adoration objects, the woods suddenly flourished into the most vibrant green.

Come to the first houses of Terracina, noting the Roman mausoleums familiar from Stage 1 along the Via Appia Antica. Pass the train station then a roundabout, go through the **Porta Romana**, and in a few blocks come to the Piazza Municipio, the duomo, and other wonderful monuments, all with a lovely view toward the Tyrrhenian Sea.

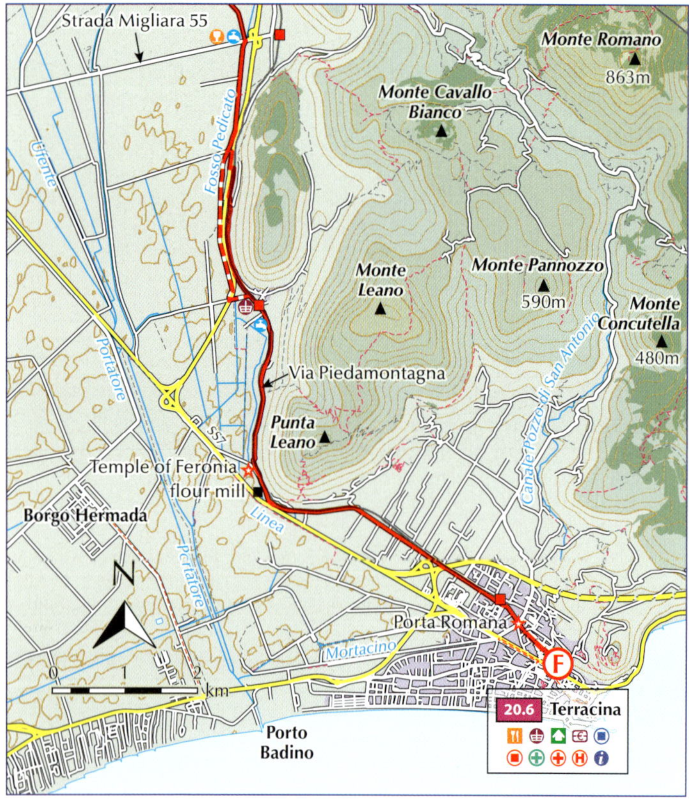

Ruins of the ancient Temple of Feronia, goddess of wild nature, alongside the Via Appia route before Terracina

20.6KM TERRACINA (ELEV 40M, POP 44,720) (797.7KM)

The seaside town of Terracina, or Roman Anxur, beckons with its Roman remains and myths. In Homer's *The Odyssey*, Odysseus disembarks upon its shores; dedicated to Circe, the legendary Monte Circeo National Park is where Ithaca's king met the sorceress (bus ride 20min, timetables at https://cotralspa.it). In town, Roman highlights include the main square, Piazza Municipio (the adjacent ancient Roman Forum retains its original steps), medieval walls, the four-faced honorary arch, and the impressive theater. Terracina also boasts an alluring duomo, representative of its varied history with its 5th–6th century origins and its later alterations. Notable churches include the Chiesa di San Domenico (16th century), the Spanish baroque Chiesa del Purgatorio, the ruins of Chiesa della Madonna delle Grazie (13th century), and the Italian neoclassical Chiesa del Santissimo Salvatore.

Parrocchia San Domenico Savio O Do R S Z 1/4, €Donation, Piazza Alfredo Fiorini 1, tel 339 496 8602, lillycapasso@gmail.com.

STAGE 7–8A VARIANT

Abbazia di Fossanova to Monte San Biagio

Start	Abbey Church, Abbazia di Fossanova
Finish	Via Europa, Monte San Biagio (0.5km after town)
Duration	7½hr
Distance	23.1km
Total ascent	1030m
Total descent	1020m
Difficulty	Hard due to climbs, descents, and footing
Percentage paved	64%
Lodgings	Sonnino 7.4km, Monte San Biagio 22.5km, Abbazia di San Magno, 26.9km, Fondi 31.5km

This mountainous stage is very different from the route so far. Nearly 9km of sometimes steep and stony mountain paths provide a centerpiece for the day. There are several other trails over the hills, and the route is unclear in a couple of places. In poor weather, navigation is harder and the coastal route is recommended. A little mud and slippery limestone in the wet might lead to a slower crossing. On hot days, take plenty of water between Sonnino and Monte San Biagio. An extra hour on this already long and challenging day takes you to the Monastery of San Magno, a fitting finish if you can make it.

Note: walking directions contributed by Jonathan Williams.

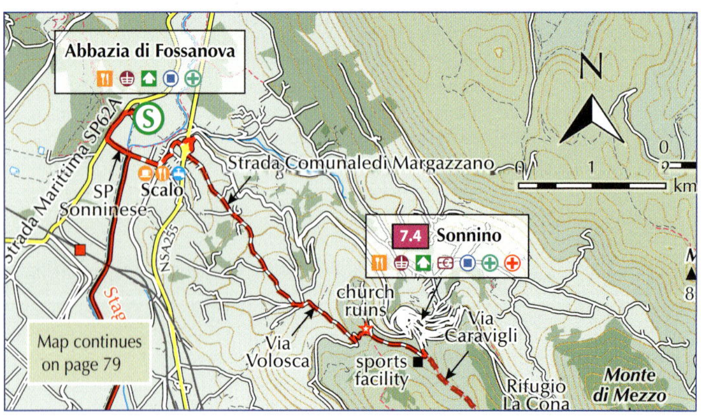

Map continues on page 79

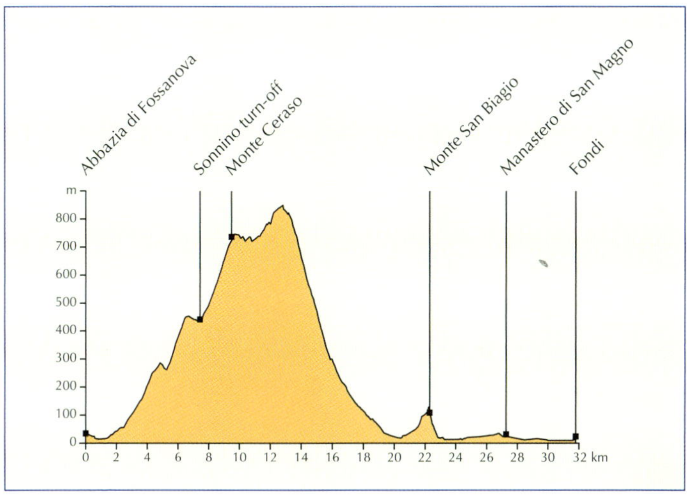

From the Abbey, go past the café to leave the complex and turn left carefully along the narrow and busy Strada Marittima. After 500m turn left by a factory onto the **SP Sonninese**, toward the mountains ahead. The main route to Terracina turns right alongside the Amaseno River onto Via Argine Amaseno (**0.9km**), but on this variant instead go straight to a T-junction in the hamlet of **Scalo** (food, groceries, water). Turn left at the junction, following a road snaking over an interchange, then immediately almost double back and take the quiet **Strada Comunale di Morgazzano**, which leads much of the way to Sonnino.

Climb increasingly steeply between olive and orange groves, houses, and farmsteads. After 5km the road drops to a junction. Turn left and after 150m, turn right steeply uphill on **Via Volosca**, named after the Volsci, and pass the ruins of the Chiesa della Madonna della Pietà. Quite abruptly come to a play area with spectacular views over Sonnino then drop down to the uppermost houses of town by a small **sports facility**. Here climb uphill on Via San Marco (continue straight for 1km for the town's services).

7.4KM SONINNO (ELEV 410M, POP 7352) (792.3KM)

The hilltop town's name stems from the Latin *sommum*, meaning 'summit.' Its current urban layout dates from the Middle Ages, when those fleeing the Saracens sought refuge in the hills. Both the Chiesa di San Michele Arcangelo and the Chiesa San Francesco are of medieval origin. Although in a ruinous state, the castle dates from the 9th century, the tower from the end of the 14th century. It is a town well regarded for the quality of its award-winning olive oil, and its 5000 ancient trees grow organically on dry-stone wall terraces.

Parrocchia San Michele Arcangelo Do Via Vittorio Emanuele II 1, tel 0773 809 851.

Bed and Breakfast Seba & Paola O Pr R Br Cr W S 1/2, €-/40/60/-/-/-, Via Merlot 1, tel 329 379 2974, beb.sebaepaola@gmail.com. Reservations required; breakfast included.

A view of the lowlands and mountains from Monte San Biagio (photo: Jonathan Williams)

Alloggio del Grand Tour O Pr R K Cr S 3/13, €-/45/85/120/150/185/220, Via Vittorio Emanuele II, tel 328 422 1418, grotti.a@libero.it. Reservations through www.booking.com preferred; one single room and two six-person apartments available.

After 100m on Via San Marco, turn right onto Via Caravigli and 100m later, when the tarmac ends, continue on a narrow path alongside a wooden fence. Here the Via Francigena shares the path with a local hiking trail, the CAI 534, which helps guide the way. Note that CAI trails will reappear in the next few stages; CAI stands for 'Club Alpino Italiano' (the Italian Alpine Club). Climb steadily on the good but stony path and after about 30–40min, pass the mountain hut of **Rifugio La Cona** (**1.5km**). Set at the foot of Monte Ceraso (818m) and Monte Peschio (844m), the refuge provides shelter in case of a storm.

Continue on a path, only lightly etched into the hillside, up a broad ridge before breaking left and into woods, again with a wooden fence alongside you. Staying in woods, cross the ridge gradually downhill. After a traverse, ensure you ignore the descending path marked 534A. The Via Francigena soon reappears and continues traversing to a saddle between Monte di Mezzo (808m) and Monte Tavanese (944m). These hills within the Ausoni mountain range are named after the 8th-century BC Italic people known as the Ausones in Greek, some of the first Greek settlers in Italy.

Follow signs carefully in the limestone wilderness, first right uphill then bearing left to lead to a second saddle marked with a large power line and a **junction of many paths** (**4.8km**). Thankfully, the Via Francigena is clearly marked downhill. After descending for 10min, pass above a farm building and start a steep descent down a

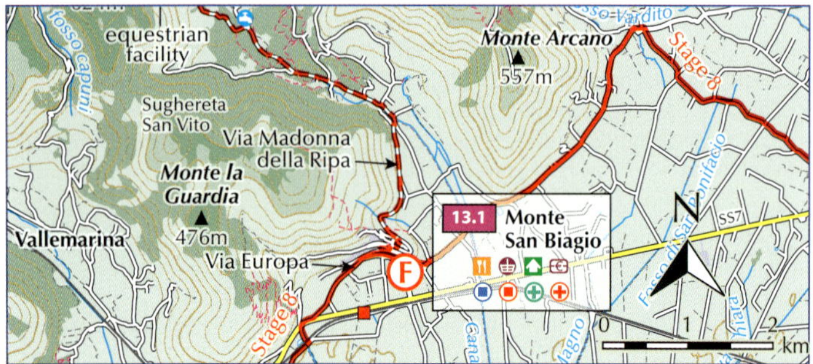

rough path. Cross the impressive Pozzo delle Cutine limestone slab and descend more steep paths to reach a road at the hamlet of **Vetica** (**2.3km**, no services).

Turn right down the road for 5.5km. Pass an **equestrian holiday center** and the San Vito cork oak forest: its 300 hectares making it the largest of its kind in mainland Italy. The road levels and passes a water source (drinkability unclear). Just after a bridge, turn right up **Via Madonna della Ripa** and, climbing toward Monte San Biagio, keep right on Via Monticelli. Entering town, turn sharp right up Via Ferdinando II to follow an intricate route of ups and downs, and below buildings, emerging at the town hall on Viale Littoria (**6.5km**).

15.1KM MONTE SAN BIAGIO (ELEV 105M, POP 6044) (799.7KM)

This well-preserved summit town, first documented in 1099, was initially named Monticelli. The Lombard castle was built on Roman ruins in the 7th century and was a stronghold of the Duchy of Gaeta (867–906) and later of Fondi (934). Although humble in its remains, the triangular tower is one of few remaining in Europe. The new name of Monte San Biagio followed the Unification of Italy. The town's patron, Saint Biagio, is worshipped as an otolaryngologist.

B&B Virginia O Pr R Br Cr S 4/12, €-/50/70/-/100/-, Via Portella Inferiore 17, tel 333 105 8631.

Alloggio Turistico L'Ulivo O Pr R K Br W S Z 12/36, €-/50/60/-/100/-, Via Mola Vecchia 3, tel 335 537 9154.

To now connect with the route from Terracina, turn left downhill, shortcutting long loops of Viale Europa. The route is not well marked but unfolds as you find each series of steps to reach **Via Europa**, rejoining the main route where it intersects at the bottom of Via Madonna Della Mercede (**0.5km**).

STAGE 8

Terracina to Fondi

Start	Cattedrale, Terracina
Finish	Piazza Unità d'Italia, Fondi
Duration	6hr
Distance	22km
Total ascent	378m
Total descent	407m
Difficulty	Hard due to uneven footing and climbs/descents
Percentage paved	72%
Lodgings	Monte San Biagio 13.1km, Abbazia di San Magno 17.4km, Fondi 22km

Bidding adieu to sea views, the Francigena veers inland, hugging the mountainsides, finding Fondi and Itri on its way back to the coast at Gaeta. In the process, this day offers some of the most beautiful vistas on the entire Via Francigena and also some of its most challenging footing on trails that can be daunting and best avoided in inclement weather. After you have conquered the climb and then a walk along the highway, the hike up to Monte San Biagio may feel like an extreme exertion, so an overnight at Monte San Magno or Fondi makes more sense.

Note: walking directions from Monte San Biagio to Fondi contributed by Jonathan Williams.

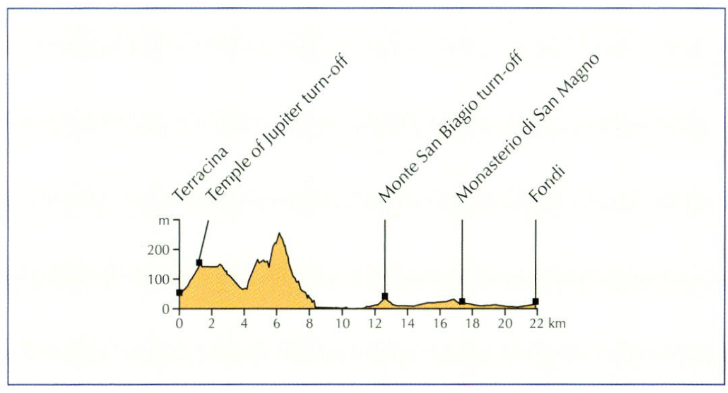

The long Gulf of Gaeta coastline after Terracina, with Gaeta on the distant point

In the Piazza Municipio, retrace your steps and, under the arch next to the duomo, turn right and up the stairway alongside the Capitolium ruins. Head through the opening in the city wall and turn right uphill toward the top of the city. Come to the turn-off to the Tempio di Giove (Temple of Jupiter, 1.1km away); congratulations on completing the day's first climb. Although the round trip is discouraging, the remains of the 1st-century BC temple are impressive and the site has spectacular views of the Tyrrhenian Sea.

After the driveway, fork right and begin a brief descent on narrow **Via Piazza Palatina**. As you look ahead, you can now see your next climbing opportunity, above a quarry that has taken away part of the mountainside. As you ascend again, enjoy views of the bay to the right and reach a summit and gravel road with vistas over the open Tyrrhenian Sea, a plain of lakes, Monte San Biagio on the mountainside, and Fondi beyond. After the last home, turn left, go through a gate, and begin the steepest and rockiest climb of the day on a path. After a barbed-wire fence, a descent leads to a road momentarily before you turn left and go through a **gate** to climb on a rocky trail surrounded by shrubs, particularly Scotch broom, with evidence of diverse wildlife, including livestock and wild animals (boar, wolves, lizards, and yes, snakes). Before the summit, shade is offered by olive trees and after a photo opportunity at the top, start the tricky descent, following signs.

The path here makes several turns so ensure you look for red and white blazes reassuringly guiding your way. Soon arrive at a wood of small mature trees then reach a widening of the path, which seems to head directly toward the lake below. Instead, switchback twice and, at a third switchback, go straight onto a downhill path. Soon hear the sounds of cars from the road below and pass on the uphill side of a galvanized steel **avalanche fence**. The path then surprises by heading back up the mountain briefly to the top of a precipitous 5m stone embankment. Very carefully descend on this treacherous obstacle, and the slippery path that follows, to promptly arrive at a gravel road with a wooden fence. Turn right to be greeted by a shady picnic area next to a 7m stone monument welcoming people into the kingdom at the border of the Papal States – also warning that bad behavior will be countered by good laws within this peaceful land.

Now continue alongside the **SS7 Via Appia highway** for 1.5km, keeping the mountains on your left. On the left, deep in the trees, is the ancient Mausoleo di Galba. Just before the first curve, fork right to a road running parallel below the highway and then alongside the railway. Cross a **bridge** then immediately turn left onto a canal-side road. Later, turn left at the concrete bridge over the canal, go under the railway and the highway, then follow the highway for a brief 50m before turning left onto the next road, **Via Portella Inferiore**, with Monte San Biagio gloriously appearing above. The tower across to the left was the old gateway to the town and the Kingdom of the Two Sicilies. It welcomed many notable people to Monte San Biagio, including Mozart, who visited on May 11, 1770. At the end of the road, climb a stairway and turn left uphill on Via Europa into town, or turn right to skirt along the foot of it on Viale Europa, joining the Stage 7–8A Variant 300m later at the edge of upper **Monte San Biagio** (**12km**).

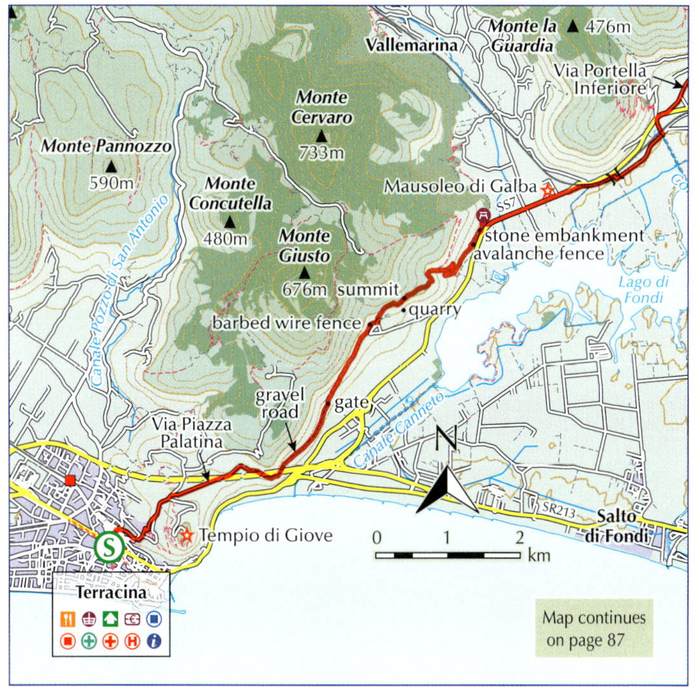

13.1KM MONTE SAN BIAGIO (ELEV 109M, POP 6044) (784.6KM)

See description in Stage 7–8A Variant.

If visiting Monte San Biagio, take the steps at Via Madonna della Mercede and climb into the town, crossing several roads on an intricate route, looking out carefully for the limited Via Francigena signage.

To continue to Fondi, go straight ahead and after 130m keep left on Via Vecchia. After a restaurant, keep left again onto **Via Provinciale San Magno**. Pass a water fountain then a grocery and fork left as the road becomes **Via Rene**. Small farms, olive groves, and citrus orchards lead you for an hour to the turn-off for Abbazia di San Magno, 200m off route on the left. Head through parking lots and climb to a gangway to reach the church.

4.3KM ABBAZIA DI SAN MAGNO (ELEV 29M, POP UNKNOWN.) (780.3KM)

The 3rd-century martyr San Magno was born Magnus of Anagni, and this abbey was built in his honor by Saint Honoratus in the 6th century. Soon after construction, it became home to Benedictine monks and depended on Montecassino. The original medieval church contains 11th-century frescoes depicting Saint Benedict's life.

Monastero di San Magno O Pr Do R K W S 10/20 & 1/8, €Donation, Via Valle Vigna, tel 379 212 2700 or 379 155 2095, viandanti@monasterosanmagno.it, www.monasterosanmagno.it/index.htm. Reservations preferred; two bikes maximum; no bedding.

To continue to Fondi, turn right just after the monastery turn-off and continue on **Via San Magno**, past farms and groves. After 1¾hr, keep right at a junction and turn immediately left onto the SS7/Via Roma/Appian Way. Continue into the outskirts of Fondi, bear right at a small roundabout onto **Via Corso Appio Claudio**, and pass shops to the castle at Piazza Unità d'Italia.

4.6KM FONDI (ELEV 14M, POP 39,550) (775.7KM)

The 14th-century castle that dominates the center of Fondi stands as a symbol of the tumult that this strategically located settlement experienced on the Via Appia at the frontier between the Kingdom of Sicily and the Papal States. An acquisition by violence or marriage to the Lombards, Byzantines, Saracens, Gaetans,

Caetani barons, French, Holy Roman Empire, and Di Sangro family, the town today has found prosperity in its original purpose: as hub of the Plain of Fondi agricultural district. During France's rule, Prospero Colonna was granted the city for his services during the Franco-Spanish conflicts. His son, Vespasiano, married the countess Giulia Gonzaga, famed for her intelligence and beauty. Upon her husband's death, she transformed the palace into a cultural center, attracting many illustrious Renaissance figures, including the infamous corsair Barbarossa. On August 8, 1534, Barbarossa attacked the city to kidnap and gift her to Sultan Suleiman II, yet the abduction failed. In his rage, he set the city aflame and slaughtered its inhabitants. Of note are the Castello Caetani, now home to the Museo Civico, the Chiesa di San Francisco (14th century), the Chiesa/Cattedrale di San Pietro (13th century), and the Jewish Museum.

- **Al Centro** O Pr R S 3/6, €-/40/60–80/-/-/-, Via Benedetto Croce 20, tel 320 181 1249.
- **A Casa d'Antonella** O Pr R K Br Cr S 5/17, €-/40–50/60–80/80–100/90–120/100–140, Via Paolo Borsellino 25, tel 338 156 2398, bebacasadantonella@tiscali.it, https://it-it.facebook.com/people/A-casa-d-Antonella/100063565090663.
- **Casa Fusco** O Pr R Br Dr Cr W S 3/6, €-/50/50/-/-/-, Via Daniela Manin 15, tel 380 474 1609.

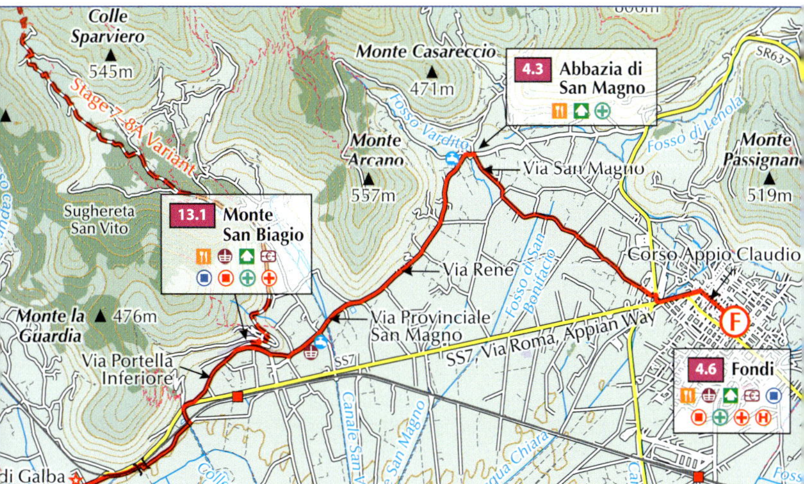

STAGE 9

Fondi to Itri

Start	Piazza Unità d'Italia, Fondi
Finish	Piazza Incoronazione, Itri
Duration	4¼hr
Distance	15.1km
Total ascent	336m
Total descent	170m
Difficulty	Moderate due to climbs and highway walking
Percentage paved	67%
Lodgings	Itri 15.1km, Gaeta 29.4km

A long walk along the Roman paving of the Via Appia Antica is a highlight of this short stage that crosses the ridge of the Monti Aurunci between Fondi and Itri. With little shade, an early start would beat the heat on a sunny day, and with no trustworthy water source, plan an ample supply.

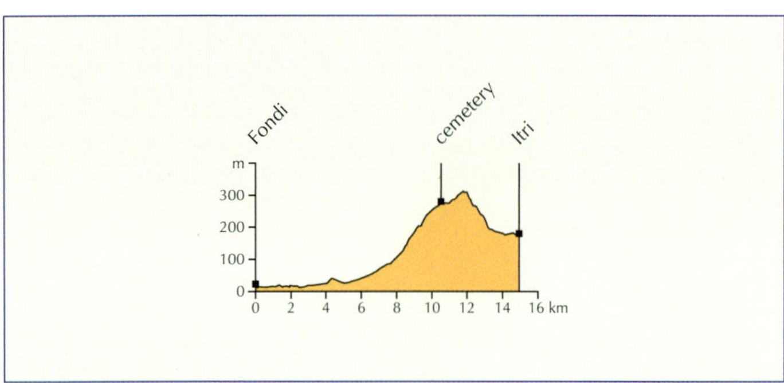

From Piazza Unità d'Italia, head down Viale Vittorio Emanuele and, just before the San Francesco Church, jog right onto Via Antonio Gramsci. Pass the municipio and at the stop sign turn left onto Via Arnale Rosso. In three blocks go right on **Via Fucito**, curving through the outskirts, where the road becomes a canal-side dirt path alongside. At the path end, turn right onto Via Vetrine, skirting left around the hillside, which contains the Parco Regionale Monti Ausoni e Lago di Fondi (groceries). Curve around onto **Via Gegni** alongside a drainage channel then among houses to head toward the next hill.

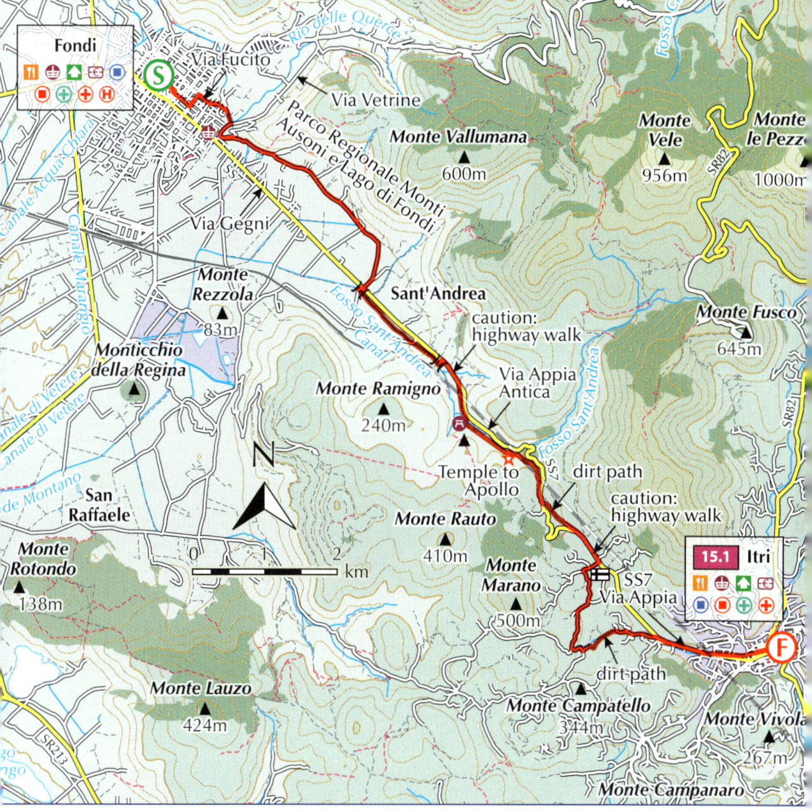

After turning south, carefully cross the SS7 highway (**5.1km**) to pick up a road, then cross the **Fosso Sant'Andrea Canal** and turn left alongside it, climbing as the waterway cascades. Follow signs to turn left across the canal and then to turn right onto a 400m walk on the highway itself (facing traffic!).

Fork right onto a dirt road at an information board of the Monti Aurunci Nature Park to now walk on the original cobblestone of the **Via Appia**. This stretch of the Via Appia has paving, a bridge, and Roman mile marker 56 among other construction from three main eras: Roman (3rd century BC), Renaissance (16th century), and Bourbonic (18th century). Midway come to several ruined walls that once held a 4th-century BC **Temple to Apollo**, followed by the Church/Fort of Sant'Andrea. Remarkably, the fort is not in smithereens following innumerable battles for the dominion of the Kingdom of Naples since the 16th century by many nations as well as hostility from Neapolitan troops, Papal troops, and famous brigands, such as the bandit Marco Sciarra, Rome's very own Robin Hood.

Cross a bridge over the canal then carefully cross the **SS7** onto a dirt path, with further remains of the ancient roadway, before returning to the highway for 500m of careful roadside walking. Pass the **cemetery** by turning right uphill among olive trees with peekaboo views of Itri. Near the top of the hill turn left and descend steeply to catch a narrow path ahead downhill. Continue on black paving stones on a now wider path then join a downhill dirt road to meet an asphalt road. At the road end, join the modern **Via Appia**, with sidewalks soon thankfully emerging. Watch for a left fork onto Corso Appio Claudio to enter **Itri** and reach Piazza Incoronazione, with the medieval old town above you.

The 13th-century bell tower of Itri's Church of Santa Maria, which was destroyed in World War 2 (photo: Jonathan Williams)

15.1KM ITRI (ELEV 175M, POP 10,357) (760.5KM)

The town's name is often linked to the Latin *iter*, meaning 'journey,' referencing its position on the Roman road as it runs across the Pontine Plain, although the first mention of the town was not until 914. Its iconic castle, dating from 882, was built to overlook the surrounding urban dwellings and inhabitants. Built under the order of the Duke of Gaeta Docibile I, the castle took several centuries to construct. Later, his nephew added a tower named 'of the crocodile,' as its prisoners were fed to the snapping animals swimming below. The oldest church is the beautiful Chiesa di San Michele Arcangelo (11th century) with a bell tower and roof testifying to Arab-Norman design, a rare example of this blend in Lazio. The snake on the city's coat of arms gave rise to the legend that the city was founded by Amyclae inhabitants (present-day Gaeta) who fled the shores due to an invasion of snakes. The dog represented alongside the snake refers to a different story in which a dog saved Itri from a snake invasion.

Il Fiore in una Stanza O Pr R Br Cr S Z 6/12, €-/35–45/60–70/-/-/-, Via Cesare Battisti 1, tel 0771 721 1423 or 333 722 6567, info@ilfioreinunastanza.it, www.ilfioreinunastanza.it. Breakfast included.

Casa Ileana O Pr R K Cr W S 1/4, €-/35–40/50–60/90–120/120–160/-, Via Giuseppe Mazzini 3, tel 389 817 6997, casaileanaitri@gmail.com. Reservations required.

STAGE 10

Itri to Formia

Start	Piazza Incoronazione, Itri
Finish	Municipio, Formia
Duration	5½hr
Distance	21.1km
Total ascent	358m
Total descent	516m
Difficulty	Moderate due to road walking and hills
Percentage paved	100%
Lodgings	Gaeta 14.3km, Formia 21.1km, Gianola 26.4km, Scauri 30.6km

Stunning vistas over hills to the sea and pleasant walks along sandy beaches form the memorable part of this stage, which also includes some noisy, truck-filled roadsides through industrial areas. The Francigena route skips the scenic old city of Gaeta and misses some of the historic sights of Formia, including the impressive Roman cistern and the supposed Tomb of Cicero, so plan extra time for a little off-piste exploration. Take food and water for the first 12km after which ample services mean you'll be fine.

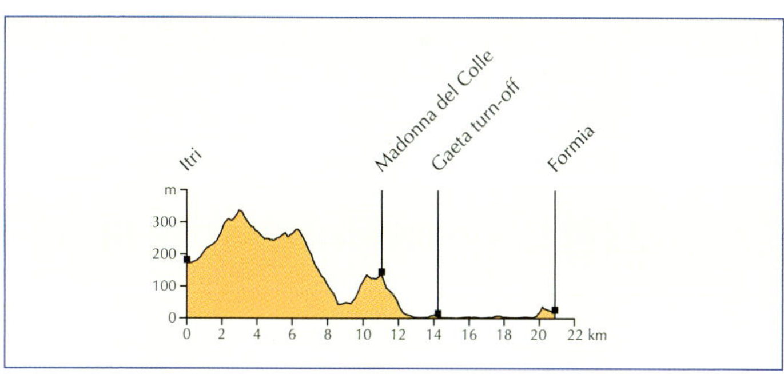

Turn right to head back to the Via Appia, curving around a fountain onto a sidewalk out of town. Cross the street and take the second of two left turns uphill on the **SP105 Via Aurelio Padovani**. In about 1.5km, fork left off the highway, climbing steeply up **Monte Campanaro**, with views back toward Itri and to the coast. Arrive at the summit

Green hills give way to open sea before Gaeta

among centuries-old olive trees to begin the descent among vistas to terraced hillsides and the Tyrrhenian Sea.

This quiet **Via delle Vignole** becomes a curvy and scenic descent, eventually reaching a T-junction where a left turn takes you along the busy **SP138 Via Sant'Agostino**. After it makes a hard right turn, watch for a left turn onto the much-quieter Via del Colle, which climbs steeply to a summit and the 17th-century **Cappellina Marinara Rurale Madonna del Colle**.

Now descend steeply between stone walls, entering **Gaeta**. Cross a highway and pass a cemetery to turn right onto **Via Bologna** and, after a few blocks, reach your first beach! In the most southern promontory of Lazio, the Riviera di Ulisse Regional Park lies at the foot of the Aurunci Mountains, which cascade toward the crystal-clear sea where nature and Homeric myths intertwine. Turn left, joining the built-up *lungomare* (beach promenade), aiming for a green headland ahead with its belt of fortress walls. When the sidewalk ends, turn left before a series of tall hotels after which take a wide sidewalk downhill to the marina, ignoring the uphill road. Turn left at the roundabout and continue by the **marina** on any of the sidewalks through these modern parts of town. For the old town, detour right at the roundabout.

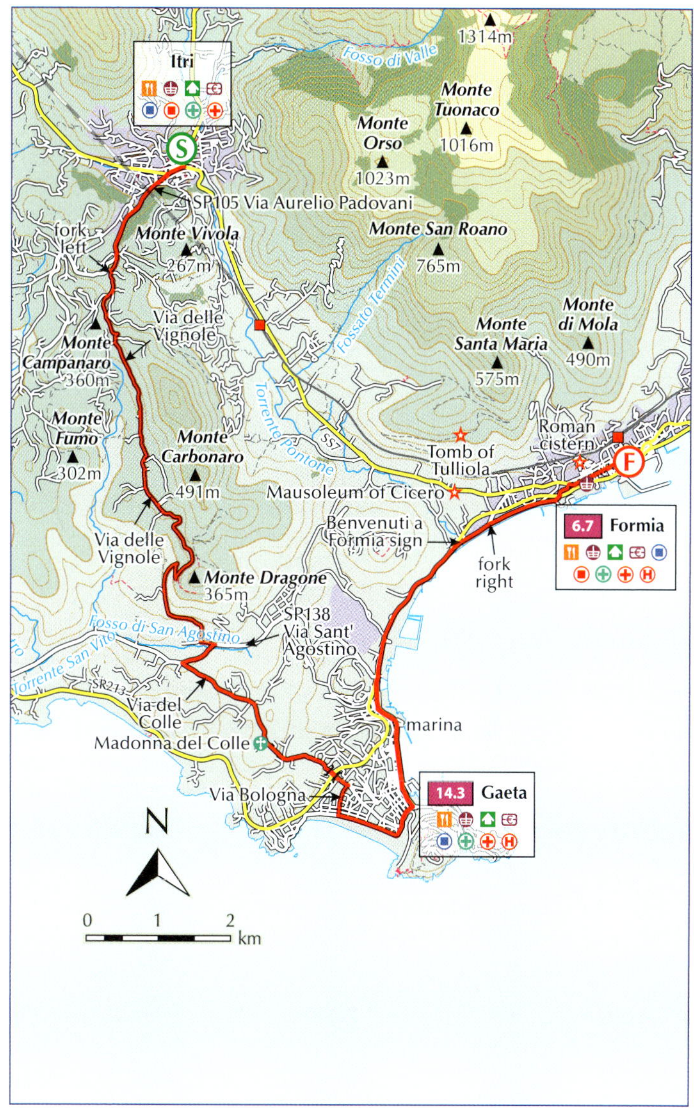

1314m
Fosso di Valle
Itri
Monte Tuonaco
1016m
Monte Orso
1023m
SP105 Via Aurelio Padovani
Monte San Roano
765m
fork left
Monte Vivola
267m
Fossato Termini
Via delle Vignole
Monte Campanaro
360m
Monte di Mola
490m
Monte Santa Maria
575m
Torrente Pontone
Monte Fumo
302m
Monte Carbonaro
491m
SS7
Roman cistern
Tomb of Tulliola
Mausoleum of Cicero
Benvenuti a Formia sign
6.7 Formia
Via delle Vignole
fork right
Monte Dragone
365m
Fosso di San Agostino
SP138 Via Sant' Agostino
Torrente San Vito
SR213
Via del Colle
Madonna del Colle
marina
Via Bologna
14.3 Gaeta
N
0
1
2
km

14.3KM GAETA (ELEV 2M, POP 19,423) (746.2KM)

An ancient town, Gaeta was favored by Roman senators and emperors as a holiday destination. In the 9th century, Gaeta became an autonomous maritime republic that rivaled Genoa, Venice, and Pisa, standing up to Saracen fleets. However, it was conquered by the Normans and later the Angevins and the Aragonese, as evidenced by the castle. Nicknamed 'the city of 100 churches,' the town still has no less than 21, of which 3 stand out. The Basilica Cattedrale di Santa Maria Assunta e dei Santi Erasmo e Marciano (11th century) has a 57m-high Moorish bell tower. The Santuario della SS. Annunziata-Gaeta and adjoining hospital dates from the early 13th century, with baroque features dating from the 17th century. The Tempio di San Francesco d'Assisi was constructed by Charles II of Anjou (14th century) on the foundations of a chapel supposedly built by Saint Francis himself.

- **Parrocchia San Carlo Borromeo** O Do R W S 1/2, €Donation, Piazza San Carlo, tel 348 859 1154, parrocchiasancarlogaeta@gmail.com.
- **Casetta del Camminatore – Accoglienza with Chiara**, tel 320 089 3257, ec.cirella@gmail.com.

Continue along the pleasant marina, past a succession of shops and restaurants, reaching a sidewalk through a busy industrial area. At the **Benvenuti a Formia** sign, fork right off the busy road onto a quieter beachside walk then, watching for signs, keep right, remaining on the lungomare. After a park with sweeping views back to Gaeta, fork left uphill and under the main road. Here turning left then right onto the SS7 leads after 1.4km to the imposing yet damaged tomb of the 1st-century BC political philosopher Cicero. His daughter, Tulliola, is said to be buried on the hill opposite (no access). Take the first right onto the long, straight SS7 leading to the municipio in **Formia**. Continuing ahead leads to the town's services.

6.7KM FORMIA (ELEV 12M, POP 37,136) (739.5KM)

Legend says that the city was founded by the Laestrygonians, the blood-curdling cannibal giants who menaced Odysseus and who destroyed nearly all of the hero's ships. Ancient and Roman remains include the polygonal walls, large villas, an amphitheater, and a theater. Formia's ancient Tomb of Cicero has long been associated with the Roman statesman (106–43BC), whether or not Cicero is buried there, and the town's Roman cisterns are said to be the biggest in the world (bring a flashlight; for info on both sites see www.formiae.it).

- **Villaggio Don Bosco** O Do R S 7/40, €Donation, Via Appia Lato Napoli 86, tel 349 286 0771, donmariano@gmail.com, www.donboscoformia.it. Check ahead for availability; use of the kitchen may be possible. Located 2.5km past Formia, on the next stage.

STAGE 11

Formia to Marina di Minturno

Start	Municipio, Formia
Finish	Minturnae Archeological Park, Marina di Minturno
Duration	5hr
Distance	19.8km
Total ascent	100m
Total descent	115m
Difficulty	Moderate due to hard surfaces
Percentage paved	89%
Lodgings	Gianola 5.3km, Scauri 9.5km, Marina di Minturno 19.8km, Castelforte 28.3km

This is the last full stage in Lazio, and from this point the route leaves the shores of the Tyrrhenian Sea, bearing east to the mountains and the Adriatic. You may remember this stage for the sound of waves on the sandy beach or for the fascinating archeological site at Marina di Minturno. Ample beach bars and cafés provide refreshments. Save an hour or two of energy to visit the archeological park and museum, as well as the British war cemetery, the Bourbonic chain bridge, and the aqueduct.

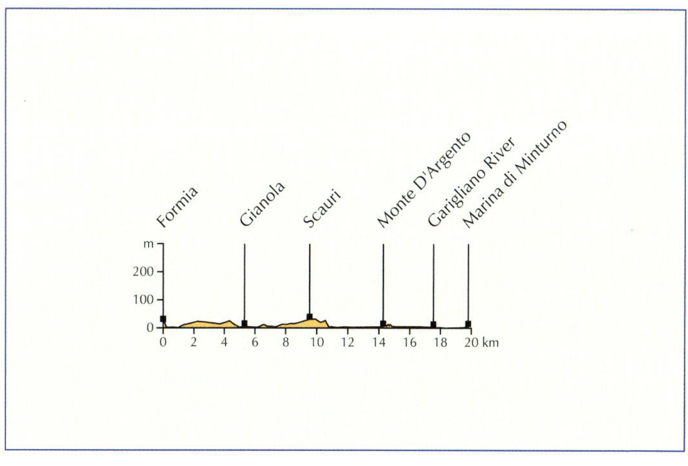

From the municipio continue on the busy, modern **Via Appia/SS7** and soon take a recommended right-hand fork onto Via Tullia toward the well-preserved neighborhood of Mola.

> Constructed under the orders or Charles II of Anjou in 1289, the 27m-high **Torre di Mola** is a small castle/fortress built on top of Roman baths, with a chapel devoted to the Archangel Michael. The tower was destroyed in World War 2 but painstakingly restored post-war and now houses the city archives.

Keep straight to return to the Via Appia/SS7 and proceed straight across the roundabout toward the coast, soon passing the posh landmark **Grande Albergo Miramare** then **Villaggio Don Bosco Oratorio** (see lodging information for Formia). As the train tracks near on the left, turn right onto **Via Santo Janni**, pass a grocery store, and reach the beaches of **Gianola**.

5.3KM GIANOLA (ELEV 5M, POP 3420) (734.2KM)

Most outstanding in Gianola are the remains of Villa di Mamurra, a luxurious Roman home belonging to the knight Lucio Mamurra, friend of Gaius Julius Caesar. The knight accompanied Caesar to Gaul as the *praefectus fabrum* (prefect of engineers), and from his immense financial acquisitions he built his home, as well as the Porticciolo Romano pool, used for fish farming.

Hotel Tirreno Formia O Pr R Br Dr Cr S 10/28, €-/35/45/55/65/-, Lungomare Città di Ferrara 7, tel 0771 1978 133 or 348 146 6497.

Turn left onto the enjoyable seaside Lungomare Città di Ferrara, passing seasonal cafés and restaurants, with views back to Gaeta and Formia. After 1km the lungomare curves left, avoiding the wooded headland of Monte Scauri and Monte d'Oro first on **Via Foce** then **Via delle Vigne**. See the map for a worthy variant: a verdant interlude from the asphalt that follows the trail system of Monte Scauri across to Via Pirae.

4.2KM SCAURI (ELEV 29M, POP 7259 INCLUDING FORMIA AND GIANOLA) (730KM)

According to scholars, the toponym Scauri derives from Marcus Aemilius Scauruse, consul then *princeps senatus* from 115BC, to whom is accredited the construction of the Ponte Milvio in Rome, as well as Roman roads across Italy. The 16th-century coastal defense tower on the Monte d'Oro headland goes both by 'Quadrata' (squared) and 'dei Cavallari' (of the knights).

Hotel Ristorante La Rosetta Pr R K Br Dr Cr W S Z 20/40, €-/35/40/54/-/-, Via Lungomare Nazario Sauro 104, tel 0771 614 952, info@larosettascauri.it, www.larosettascauri.it. Closed December 23 to end of February inclusive.

B&B A casa di Antonella O Pr R K Cr S 4/16, €-/49/49/59/69/-, Via Appia Trav. D'Acunto 13, tel 347 056 1168.

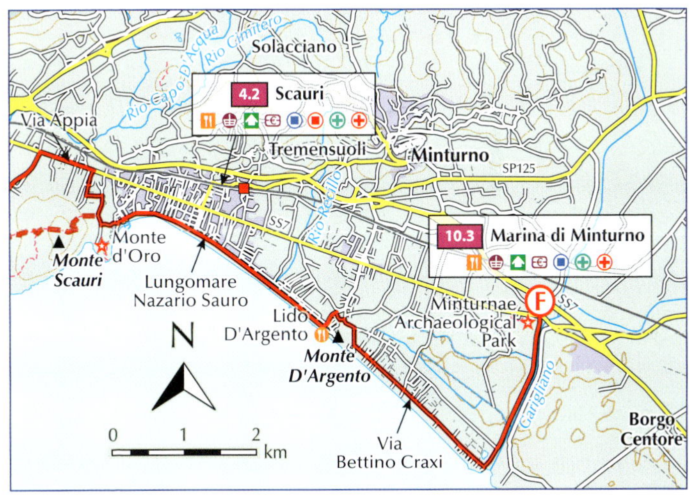

Roman engineers built this 11km-long aqueduct to bring fresh mountain water to the ancient city of Minturnae

Founded in 1987, the hilly regional park of **Gianola e Monte di Scauri** is set on Mesozoic limestone reliefs and combines nature and history in a magnificent setting. Among the prevalent cork oak trees dwell night birds, migratory birds, and a variety of gulls, as well as shyer mammals, such as foxes and voles. It is also home to seahorses, lizards, snakes, and the precious, rare loggerhead turtle.

Turn right onto a quieter 800m stretch of the SS7 at the entrance of **Scauri**.

Before entering Scauri proper, follow signs right and downhill on Via Monte di Scauri, where zigzags bring you to **Lungomare Nazario Sauro** and a lovely 4km of beachside walking past seasonal bars and restaurants. Turn left after the **Lido D'Argento** beach restaurant, following signs around Monte D'Argento, then turn right onto Via Antonio Paduano and curve left for a 2.5km walk on the straight and quiet **Via Bettino Craxi**. The road ends at the Garigliano River; you have reached the far southern border of Lazio and can look across the river to the region of Campania. The river was said to be the home of the water nymph Marica, who represents the shimmer of the sun on the water.

Turn left here onto Via Foce Garigliano and continue alongside the river for 2.5km, spotting the high suspension towers and cables of the modern SS7 bridge, the metal truss work of the prior SS7 bridge, and, as you near it, the low metal chains of the Bourbonic Via Appia bridge. A left turn brings you to the entrance of the **Minturnae Archeological Park and Museum**.

10.3KM MARINA DI MINTURNO (ELEV 5M, POP 20,276 INCLUDING INLAND MINTURNO) (719.7KM)

The ancient port of Minturnae, the southernmost city in Lazio, is the last on our route before we cross into Campania tomorrow. Within the archeological Roman complex are outstanding remains of the theater, the Republican and Imperial forums, temples, the market, the baths, the *tabernae* (shop/stall), and parts of the aqueduct and Via Appia cobblestone. The lower city was destroyed by the Lombards, forcing the locals to move uphill in the late 6th century. The city became part of the first Duchy of Gaeta and later belonged to the Abbey of Montecassino.

- **Parrocchia San Biagio V.M.** O Do R S Z 1/4, €Donation, Via Simonelli, 9, tel 0771 680 137, parrocchia.sanbiagio@gmail.com. Reservations preferred.

- **Albergo Teatro Romano** O Pr R Br Dr Cr Z 14/25, €-/40–60/, Via Appia Km 156, tel 0771 614 928 or 328 253 1944, info@albergoteatroromano.com, www.albergoteatroromano.com. One room has wheelchair access and must be reserved well in advance; three-course pilgrim menu €20.

The archaeological park at Minturnae includes this colonnade along the ancient city's forum

STAGE 12

Marina di Minturno to Sessa Aurunca

Start	Minturnae Archeological Park, Marina di Minturno
Finish	Duomo, Sessa Aurunca
Duration	6½hr
Distance	24.2km
Total ascent	372m
Total descent	170m
Difficulty	Moderate due to length
Percentage paved	53%
Lodgings	Castelforte 8.5km, Sessa Aurunca 24.2km, Corbara 27.5km

The route soon leaves main roads and crafts a passage through farms and villages to reach Castelforte before crossing the Garigliano River into Campania. Note immediately that waymarks become less common in Campania, and you will be forced to rely more on written directions and maps (GPX files are also available to download). **Note**: walking directions from Marina di Minturno to Castelforte contributed by Jonathan Williams.

An alternate route to Sessa Aurunca, not yet implemented, makes an immediate crossing of the Garigliano River on the SS7 bridge and heads in a somewhat more direct trajectory to Sessa Aurunca.

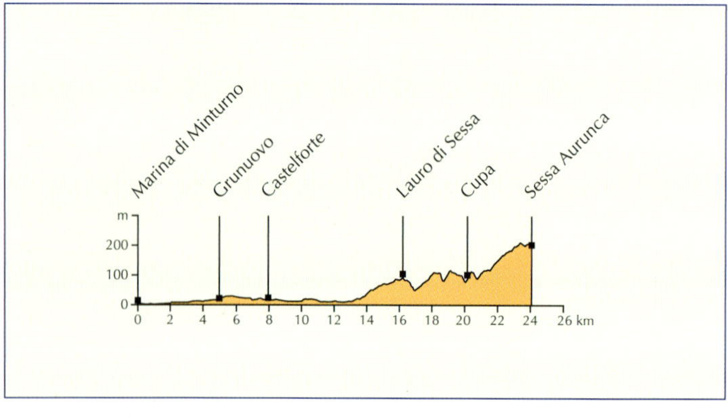

From the gate of the Minturnae Archeological Park, continue to the Fernando II bridge.

The **Ponte Real Ferdinando II di Borbone** was built in 1832 by its namesake king and was the first suspension bridge in continental Europe, a prized showpiece of the power of the Kingdom of the Two Sicilies. It was reconstructed following its destruction in World War 2.

Carefully cross the right-hand side of the interchange then pass under the autoroute and railway on **Via Porto Galeo**. Keep right at the first bend and, after 1.3km, turn left onto Via Pantaniello, a country lane that switches between dirt track and asphalt. Cross Via Stradone to join Via Volpara and, at the next junction, turn left onto the first **Via Campanili I Trav.** (there will be three!) (**3.7km**). After 300m, turn right onto II Trav Campanili and, after a further 400m, turn left at a junction with Via III Trav. Campanile. Take the next right, Via ex Ferrovia, and, after 400m, bear left then immediately right past a pizzeria and school. At the end of the road, turn left then right onto Via Francesco Baracca, the main road into **Grunuovo** (**5.1km**, groceries, food, ATM). Pass through the straggling village and, after an electrical store, bear right on **Traversa Luigi Rizzo**, leaving on a country lane reminiscent of England with its tunnel of deciduous trees.

Cross a junction and bear left at the next fork, keeping to Tr. Luigi Rizzo, and turn right at the end. At the next fork veer left past a football pitch onto a narrow, asphalted path then turn first right to cross the SP Vellote onto a gravel track. At its end, turn left onto the SP308 to head into **Castelforte**, or go right to continue on your way.

8.5KM CASTELFORTE (ELEV 128M, POP 4303) (711.2KM)

The hilly town retains buildings of the medieval bourgeoisie and has two notable churches: the 17th-century San Giovanni Battista and Santa Maria del Buon Rimedio (1996). Most interestingly, the Polish national hero General Dąbrowski, who had joined Napoléon's Army, quelled the revolt against the French in Castelforte on a night known as the 'Bloody Easter' in 1799. The Polish national anthem is dedicated to him. During World War 2, the town suffered tremendously with much destruction and afterwards was awarded the Gold Medal for Civil Valor by the Italian government.

- **Casa Plotino** O Do R K Br W Z 3/6, €Donation, Via Palombaia 8, tel 346 642 5585, eremoaquilaepriscilla@gmail.com. Your host is Vicenzo.
- **Accoglienza with Emilia** O Pr R K W S Z 3/8, €30, Via Luigi Rizzo 125E, tel 347 461 7319. Check ahead for availability.
- **B&B Sykelgrima** O Pr Dr R Br Cr S 8/21, €-/55/65/75/-/-, Via Contrada Viaro 9, tel 347 840 1887 or 347 924 6659, bandbsykelgrima@gmail.com. Breakfast included; three-course dinner and drink €18.

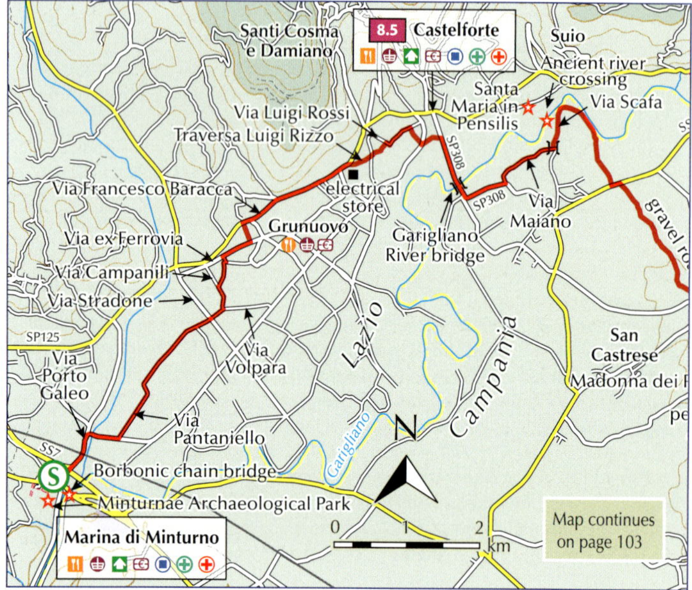

Turn right, walking on the SP308, and take the **Garigliano River bridge** into the region of Campania (**0.7km**). Of the 20 administrative regions of Italy, Campania is ranked third for population size, with 5.5 million inhabitants concentrated mainly around its capital, Naples. It also boasts 10 UNESCO World Heritage Sites.

Immediately, you will notice a change in crops, including soft fruits such as apricots and peaches. Turn left onto **Via Maiano**, at an orange wall surrounding a farm, to soon find yourself on a (potentially muddy) dirt road among peach orchards. Cross a bridge over a sometimes-dry canal, ignoring the path alongside it, and immediately turn left onto **Via Scafa**, a tranquil, flattish **gravel road** among farms, following the riverbank on your left. As the route heads north, you pass the ancient crossing of the Garigliano River where it is thought the 3rd-century philosopher Plotinus died. Having crossed a canal, turn left onto the Ex-SS430 and take the first right-hand gravel road through fields and orchards. Turn left onto the SP312 and reach the Church of Santa Maria delle Grazie in **Lauro di Sessa** (**6.7km**, food, groceries, pharmacy). Take the second right after the church, descending out of town on Via Astricelli, keeping to the cobblestone. After the tiny Chiesa Sant'Antonio (bench), turn right (water) onto Via Madonna dei Pozzi, which leads, 700m later, to the peach-colored **church** of the same name.

Originally dedicated to the Archangel Michael, the 11th-century church and cave of **Santuario Madonna dei Pozzi** (Madonna of the wells) was once named Madonna della Cava (of the cave) after a blind shepherdess witnessed an apparition of the Virgin Mary.

Turn left at the church to start climbing, with noticeably improved waymarks. After a peach orchard the road becomes an uphill grassy slope with vast views as far back as Minturno. Veer left at a **derelict building** after which watch for an unmarked right turn to a two-track road. Turn left at the next fork then promptly descend on an overgrown and rutted road. Cross a creek and ascend on a grassy road, passing a stone farmhouse and crossing a gravel road to glimpse the tiny hamlet of Cupa on the opposite hill. Pass an old **stone church** then a farmhouse, continuing on a tractor road and crossing a left-hand fence line. At a sunken road, turn left downhill then turn left uphill at a T-junction on another sunken road into **Cupa** (**4.6km**, water).

Pass a church on your left (water) then fork right steeply downhill over a creek. Turn left uphill onto gravel around the forested base of Monte Ofelio then pass through the archway of the tall stone **Chiesa di Monte Ofelio**, which once had a pilgrim hospital caring for travelers to and from Rome. Turn left uphill onto Via Monte Ofelio, soon coming to the first houses of **Sessa Aurunca**. Merge with the main road, Via XXI Luglio, and, before the ducal castle, turn left into the old city. Turn right to the Fontana dell'Ercole, where a right turn leads to signs bearing left onto Via Garibaldi then right to the duomo (**3.8km**).

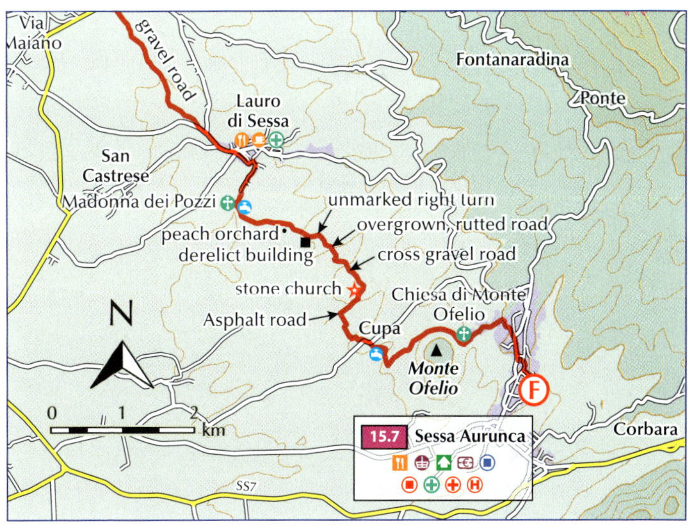

15.7KM SESSA AURUNCA (ELEV 205M, POP 20,209) (695.4KM)

Before the Roman conquest in the 4th century BC, Sinuessa or Suessa, which was its Roman name, was part of the Aurunca Pentapolis and became the capital of the region when Aurunca was destroyed in 337BC by the Romans. The city prospered in the Imperial Age, with monuments financed by Vibia Matidia, a relative of Emperor Trajan, including the aqueduct, the library, the theater, and works of art now within the town's museum. The town claims to be home to the most prized of all Roman wines: Falerno. Following decline after the fall of the Roman Empire, Sessa Aurunca saw glory return in the 12th century with the building of the cathedral in a beautifully clear Romanesque style using pre-existing Roman foundations and materials.

Sede Legambiente di Sessa Aurunca O Do R K Br W S 2/13, €10, Via Taddeo de Matricio 55, 388 421 6292, info@legambientesessa.it. Breakfast in the adjacent bar included.

B&B Monte Ofelio Pr Dr R Br W 4/14, €-/20/40/-/-/-, Via Monte Ofelio 2, tel 327 825 6270, bandbsykelgrima@gmail.com. Reservations preferred; closed November 15 to January 31 inclusive; camping and shower possible for €7; breakfast €7 from 08.00, dinner €20.

Sessa's Roman amphitheater

SECTION 2: CAMPANIA

Evening sunlight catches homes on a canal in Telese Terme (Stage 17)

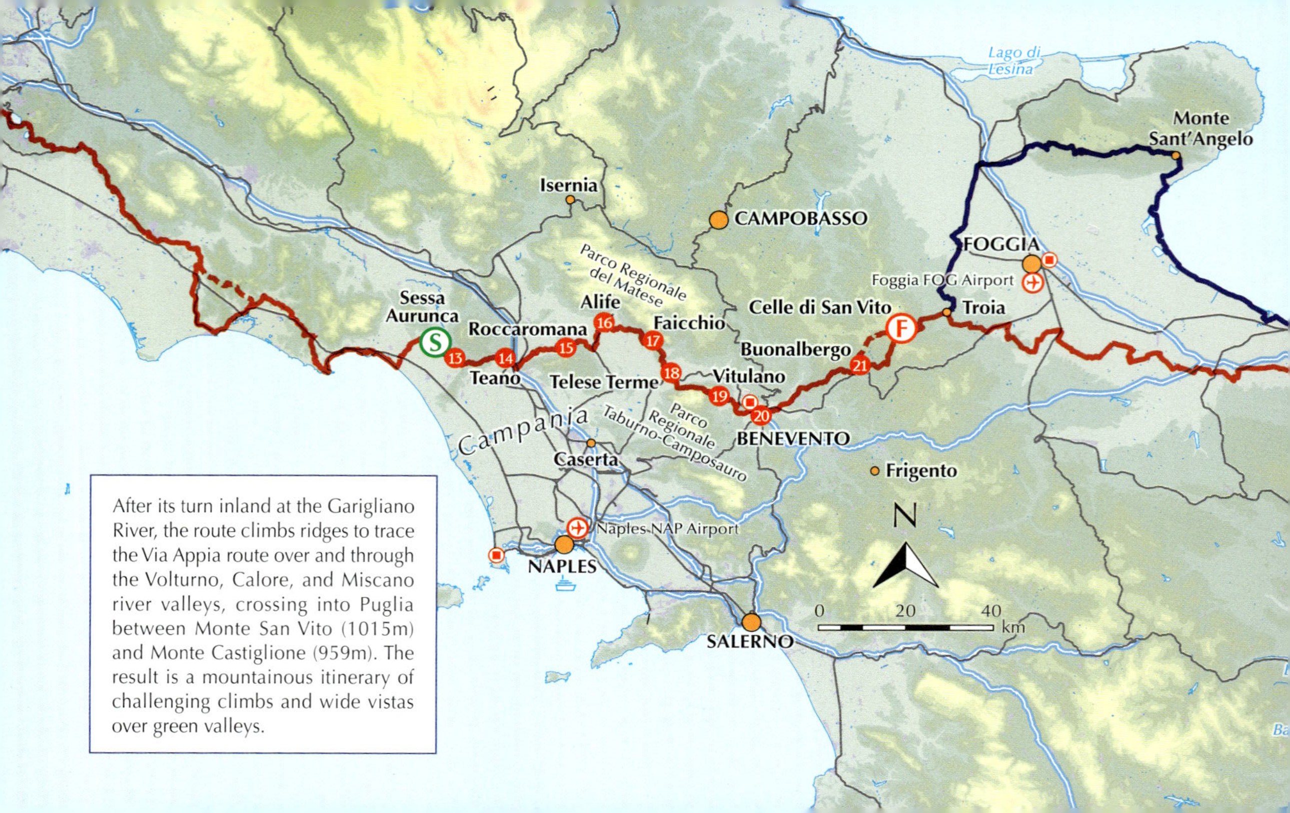

After its turn inland at the Garigliano River, the route climbs ridges to trace the Via Appia route over and through the Volturno, Calore, and Miscano river valleys, crossing into Puglia between Monte San Vito (1015m) and Monte Castiglione (959m). The result is a mountainous itinerary of challenging climbs and wide vistas over green valleys.

STAGE 13

Sessa Aurunca to Teano

Start	Duomo, Sessa Aurunca
Finish	Piazza del Duomo, Teano
Duration	4¼hr
Distance	15.4km
Total ascent	314m
Total descent	312m
Difficulty	Moderate
Percentage paved	67%
Lodgings	Corbara 3.2km, Teano 15.4km, Pietramelara 32.5km

This is a pleasant and short stage with dark forests and tufa stone cliffs offering much shade. The centerpiece of the walk is a mountainous woodland traverse on a pathway between Fontanelle and Casamostra. A small grocery in Fontanelle offers the only option for mid-stage sustenance, although a few water sources allow for refills.

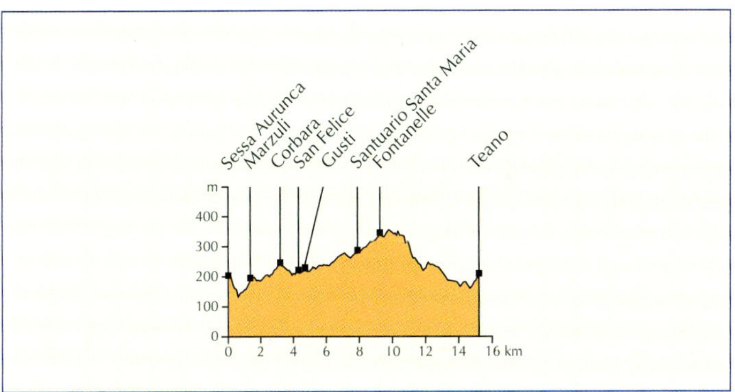

After visiting the duomo, retrace your steps on Via San Nicola and turn right in one block. Pass the narrow Via Marconi then immediately turn right after the water faucet. Take a lane down wide steps and turn left in 50m to continue downhill, between stone walls, toward forested mountains. At the end of the walkway, turn left onto a rough path downhill that leads to a descent on a concrete road. At the end of the road, by a sheer stone cliff, pick up a path again to cross over a seasonal creek where a climb begins, leading to a right turn onto a gravel road. Pass the haunting **Madonna del Ponte** abandoned church and, still heading uphill, look for a curious face carved into the tufa stone of the cliffs. The uphill gravel road turns to asphalt and passes through an archway under a villa. Come to an intersection in the village of **Marzuli** (no services, except Chiesa di Santa Maria delle Grazie ahead) and turn right, reaching a T-junction with the Via Corbara-Marzuli. Turn left onto it (road sign for Corbara), heading up a ridge between two river valleys to reach the main piazza of **Corbara** with its white, one-domed church tower festooned with blue and yellow tiles.

3.2KM CORBARA (ELEV 237M, POP 2478) (692.3KM)

The hamlet's patron saints are Saint Bartholomew, to whom the parish church is dedicated, and Saint Erasmus, who is celebrated annually in July. During the festivity, a person descends from the roof of the church dressed as an angel, to depict how the saint was saved from martyrdom.

Accoglienza with Angelo Pr Do R K €Donation, tel 329 579 2087. Call to check ahead and get directions. If Angelo has no availability, he will contact a local B&B.

Fork left after the tower to continue on streets decorated with colorful murals. As the homes thin out, fork right downhill toward a creek and the now-familiar cliffs, where a right turn leads to a shaded road descent. Cross another creek and reach the chapel of **Madonna del Latte**, a relic with no door but often with candles lit on its altar. Climb steeply on broken asphalt through woods, pass under the SP209, and veer right into the hamlet of **San Felice** (**1.1km**, no services). Continue straight, merging with the quiet SP209 to leave the village, above the outskirts of Cascano on the right (food, groceries, **B&B La Casa di Viola**). At the end of the road, turn left onto the SP31 at the outskirts of Gusti (**0.4km**). Pass a piazza (food) and a soccer pitch among olive, hazelnut, pine, fig, and eucalyptus trees. Start descending between hills, pass **Cascine e Dintorni Hotel**, and come to a first summit at an olive grove and a vineyard then fork left after a cherry orchard.

Climb the road and fork right just before the boundary of Cappelle di Teano (no services), toward the **Santuario Santa Maria delle Grazie** of Cappelle, where Stations of the Cross on tile designs appear on the right. You may suffer a little disappointment when you arrive here and notice that weeds choke the grounds of this large, nondescript, yellow stucco building. Pass the sanctuary on a narrow road alongside a small cherry orchard to descend again. Ignore signs for the Cascata delle Corriole waterfall (which is often dry and unimpressive), keep uphill, and enter **Fontanelle** (**4.7km**, groceries, water). As the road curves right, walk past modern homes and take the first left, Via Cantinella, uphill to narrow streets in an older neighborhood. The climb crosses a narrow road onto a shaded track to reach the highest summit of the day and a cliffside path

across a scenic mountain traverse. Come to an enormous orange **Big Bench** (**1.1km**), seemingly plopped here from out of the sky. In 2010, Chris Bangle built the first Big Bench and since then this community-building project has spread around the globe. This bench is the 350th of over 450 erected so far (www.big-benchcommunityproject.org).

The path begins a descent, occasionally on rounded stone pavers: a section of the Roman Via Adriana honoring Emperor Hadrian. Fork right, descending steeply on more pavers, pass a water tap, and reach the fringes of **Casamostra** (no services), leaving by a hulking ruin. Begin a brief climb leading to a tall **stone villa** and its well-manicured grounds after which turn right onto a lane that leads onto a gravel road on the left where you double back then promptly turn right, aiming for a straight course toward Teano.

The Church of Sant'Eustachio in Fontanelle basks in the midday sun

As Teano's steeple appears ahead, find yourself on a 1km stretch of pavers of the Via Adriatica **Roman road**, complete with cart grooves. After passing a well-tended **Ave Maria chapel**, begin a shaded, sunken road climb then, with Teano more visible, fork right downhill and over a stream to conquer the stage's final climb. The road merges toward the right with the SP329. After a tall stone wall, turn left on a stone staircase to follow a switchback road leading to the Piazza del Duomo (**4.9km**).

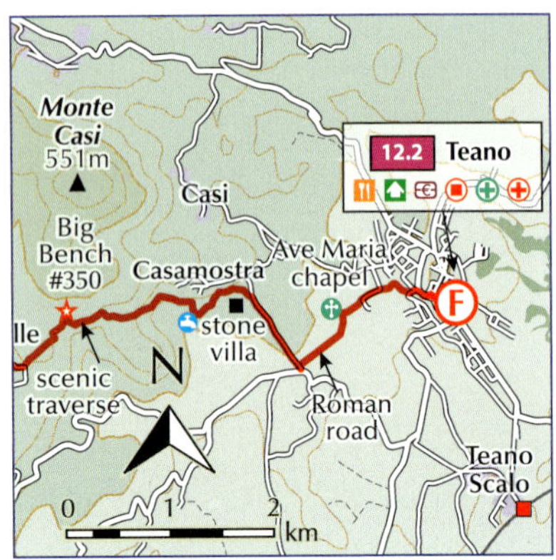

12.2KM TEANO (ELEV 202M, POP 11,289) (680KM)

The area was once the capital of the Sidicini Italic people, and remnants of fortifications and a necropolis have been uncovered. Roman Teanum Sidicinum developed thanks to its strategic position at the intersection of the Via Latina and the Via Appia, and you can visit many monuments from the time. The town prospered during the Imperial Age and expanded in the Lombard era with the construction of the defensive castle and walls. Teano is best known for being the location of the meeting between Italian nationalist fighter Giuseppe Garibaldi (who had defeated in battle the Kingdom of the Two Sicilies) and Vittorio Emanuele II, the King of Sardinia on October 26, 1860. While the handshake mollified certain factions among Italian city-states, it also ambivalently established unified Italy as a kingdom. The city's previous cathedral, now the Chiesa di San Pietro in Aquariis, is dedicated to the town's patron saint, who, stories tell, killed a threatening dragon in the 4th century. The current cathedral, the Cattedrale di San Clemente, was initially completed by the 12th century but was rebuilt in neo-Romanesque style after the 1943 Allied bombings.

B&B La casa di Anna O Pr R Br S 3/7, €30, Via Nicola Gigli 13, tel 327 624 2098, bblacasadianna7@gmail.com, www.facebook.com/housesw. Price indicated upon presentation of the credenziale.

Il Moro Bianco O Pr R K Br Cr W S 3/9, €30, Via Cavone 6, tel 339 398 6809 or 0823 885 775, info@ilmorobianco.it, www.ilmorobianco.it.

STAGE 14

Teano to Roccaromana

Start	Piazza del Duomo, Teano
Finish	Park/Piazza, Roccaromana
Duration	5¼hr
Distance	20.6km
Total ascent	114m
Total descent	164m
Difficulty	Moderately hard due to stressful highway walking
Percentage paved	91%
Lodgings	Pietramelara 17.1km, Roccaromana 20.6km, Dragoni 32.1km

This is a well-serviced stage of gentle undulations among fields and hill towns, although it is almost completely on asphalt. A long and dangerous highway walk along the SP112 is one of the most stress-inducing passages of the entire Via Francigena, and it is followed by a narrower walk on the SS6. The one shortcut offering some respite from the highway is an overgrown, isolated pathway. Otherwise, the hill towns of Riardo and Pietramelara offer picturesque opportunities for exploration, while a truck stop adds an additional chance to refuel and relax.

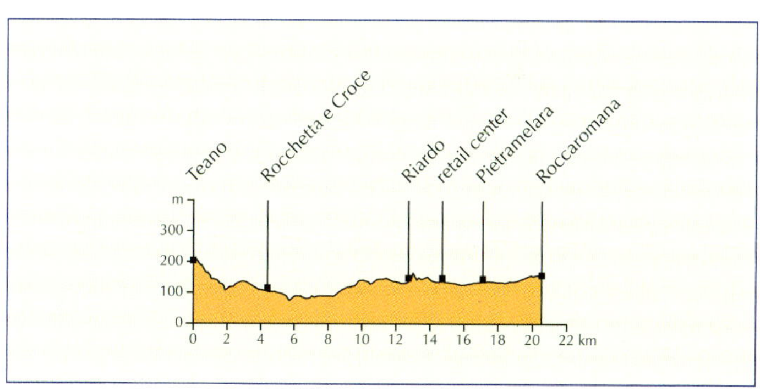

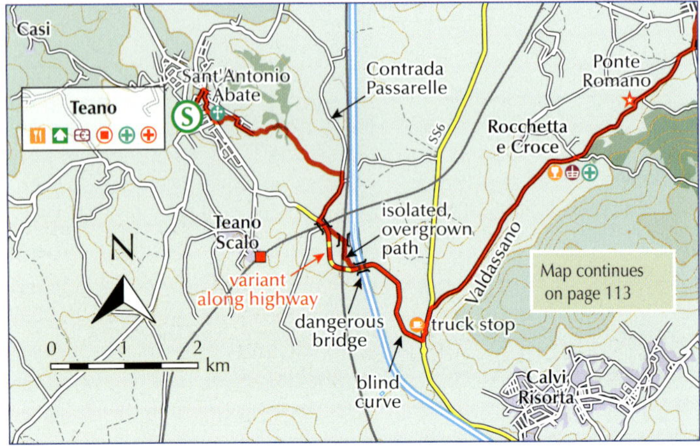

With the duomo behind you, turn left onto Corso Vittorio Emanuele and, in three long blocks, turn right down Via Nicola Gigli then keep right to stay on the same road and pass through the Porta Napoli city gate. In 150m, fork left at **Chiesa di Sant'Antonio Abate** and then left again to reach the 2nd–1st-century BC anfiteatro and impressive boneyard of marble and granite columns and capitals. Continue downhill on the pavers then asphalt, passing hazelnut trees and a Roman milestone of the Constantinian era, which measured the distance from Teanum Sidicinum to Rome. Descend steeply, cross a stream, and start gently climbing on a shaded road at the end of which turn right onto the wider **Contrada Passerelle**. Turn next right then left onto the very busy SP112, go over the railway, and immediately turn left under it. Variant: stay on the SP112 to avoid the isolated, overgrown path.

The road becomes a very disused, overgrown path with brambles between the railway and a large metal fence. Keep left as it becomes asphalt along the end of the fence and, at the end, turn left to join the SP112 and cross over the motorway on a **dangerous narrow bridge**. Keep on this perilous SP112 and, at its end, turn left onto the even busier **SS6**, where a hard shoulder can help you dodge cars and trucks. After a roundabout come to a **truck stop** (**6.5km**, food) then fork right downhill (signs to Valdassano) on a blessedly wider and quieter road. A gentle uphill stretch passes a pharmacy, bar, and grocery shops in **Rocchetta e Croce** (**2.9km**).

The road skirts the right-hand steep hill, aiming for a passage between a ridge on the right and a lonely hill in the valley on the left. Pass signs for the Ponte Romano di Val d'Assano (obscured by vegetation) and swiftly climb toward Riardo, turning left by a **derelict building** then right onto **Via San Leonardo** to the village's medieval castle (**3.3km**, food, groceries, train 2.5km away, pharmacy). The medieval hamlet has been known for its mineral waters since Roman times.

Turn right at the peach-colored Church of San Leonardo, left at the piazza (bar), and take uphill cobblestones. Turn right downhill under an archway and down steps (water) after which turn left onto Via Madonna della Stella, which weaves to the blockish **Santa Maria della Stella Church**, opposite the Fiera del Mobile exhibition center. The church preserves original 11th-century frescoes depicting the Virgin and Baby Jesus, the Archangel Michael, and other saints. Turn left afterward to reach the **retail center** Parco Commerciale Alice Riardo (food, groceries, ATM, WC) then shortcut through the parking lot, turn right out of the center, and immediately turn left onto quiet Via Pescara. This leads through fields to Pietramelara, with views to the mountaintop fortress of Torre di Roccaromana. Arrive in town, cross through the outdoor market grounds onto Via San Giovanni, keep to the basalt pavers of Viale Europa, and turn right onto Via San Pasquale to Pietramelara's municipio (**4.5km**).

Riardo's 9th-century Longobard castle dominates the skyline

17.1KM PIETRAMELARA (ELEV 139M, POP 4495) (662.9KM)
Founded by the Lombard princes Landolfo and Atenolfo, Pietramelara suffered several attacks, leaving it in an abandoned state. The first, in 1496, followed an Aragonist assault where only seven families were spared. They rebuilt the city, including the understated Palazzo Ducale, which still preserves its original interior decorative wall and murals. Following more devastation during the World War 2 Allied bombings, it was rebuilt and repopulated, and its original maze-like medieval layout has been lovingly preserved.

A casa nostra O Pr R K Br S 2/5, €-/30/60/70/80/90, Via Mancini 143, tel 333 411 6514.

Pass the municipio and at the next fork, despite the Via Francigena sign pointing left, head right toward the Church of the Annunciation. Crossing the piazza and Via Marconi, keep the **church** on your left and follow **Via Sant'Antonio Abate** out of town. At an unmarked fork, go left onto **Via Cinquevie**, with views to Torre di Roccaromana. Keep ahead on Via Sapienza through **Santa Croce** (no services), veer left after its church, and keep left to **Roccaromana** ahead, arriving at its parklike piazza.

3.5KM ROCCAROMANA (ELEV 150M, POP 820) (659.4KM)
The small medieval town of ancient origin became part of the Duchy of Benevento in AD700. Famous for its mouth-watering, pan-fried, handmade gnocchi (potato pasta), the town celebrates the dish every July.

Il Giardino Segreto di Roccaromana O Pr Do R K Br W S 4/19, €20/20+/20+/-/-/-, Via Peluso 3, tel 347 523 4383, giardinosegreto.roccaromana@gmail.com, www.giardinosegretoroccaromana.wordpress.com/accoglienza/. Reservations preferred; breakfast included; additional donation requested for single and double occupancy.

STAGE 15

Roccaromana to Alife

Start	Park/Piazza, Roccaromana
Finish	Cathedral of Santa Maria Assunta, Alife
Duration	5½hr
Distance	21.4km
Total ascent	302m
Total descent	347m
Difficulty	Moderately hard due to steep climb
Percentage paved	82%
Lodgings	Dragoni 11.5km, Alife 21.4km

The hilltop Torre di Roccaromana is one of the scenic highlights of the Via Francigena and well worth the climb, although an official alternate route through Pietravairano (not marked on the ground and not described here) offers a way around. The roadside walk on the very quiet SP67 to Baia e Latina is easy and scenic, but after a diversion to Dragoni to find a walkable route, the track puts you onto the perilous SS328 to enter Alife. Instead, with a little advance planning you can take the easy, quick, and direct train from Dragoni to Alife station. This stage-end town has ample evidence of its Roman roots and, despite the diminutive size of its buildings, is an important regional hub. Refreshments are available in Statigliano, Baia e Latina, Dragoni, and Alife.

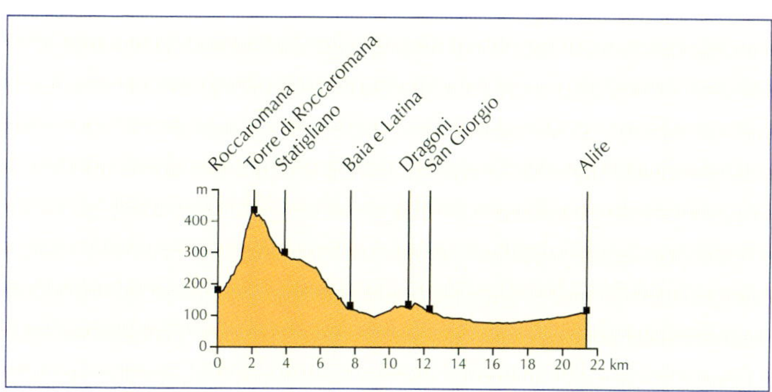

After the park, head uphill on Via Roma and pass the municipio, the neoclassical Church of San Cataldo, a stairway (water), and a terrace parking lot with glorious views to arrive at a fork and two options. Cyclists can go left downhill, circling Monte Castello, otherwise walkers should bear right uphill on switchbacks on the shaded **SP67**, passing the small shrine of the **Madonna di Carmelo**. To visit the tower, take the second right-hand trailhead steeply uphill, following red and yellow blazes, then head up a concrete road to the piazza of the **Torre di Roccaromana** (**2.2km**).

> In spite of its name, **Torre di Roccaromana** was built by Normans between the 11th and 12th centuries and was strengthened in the following two centuries. With breathtaking views toward the surrounding mountains, it has retained its chapel, fireplace, cistern, and spiral staircase.

After visiting, backtrack down the road past the trailhead, cross over or under the **auto gate**, pass luxurious wedding venue Tenuta Donna Fausta, and arrive in **Statigliano** at an intersection with the SP67 you left at the trailhead. Turn right onto it downhill through town (**1.9km**, food, water, groceries). Fork left after the yellow Church of Santa Margherita to stay on the tranquil **SP67 Roccaromana-Baia e Latina**, which descends alongside a stream in a lovely narrow valley, a true highlight of the day.

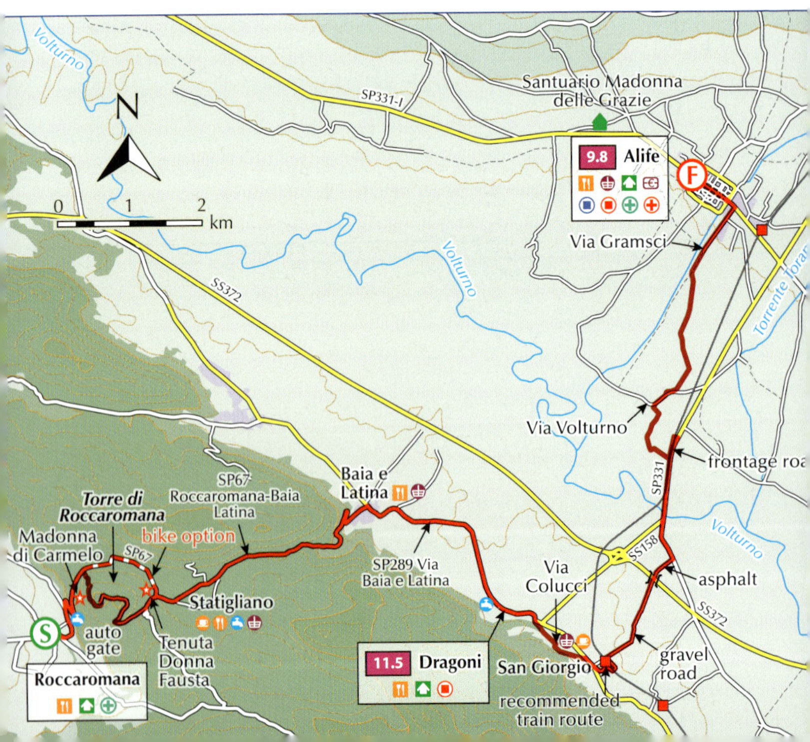

The view from the base of Torre di Roccaromana

At a T-junction, turn right onto Via Annunziata through the center of **Baia e Latina** (**3.7km**, food, fruit). This road soon becomes the **SP289 Via Baia e Latina**, which heads counter-intuitively south-east with glimpses of Alife (north-east) on the left, at the foot of a quarry in the Monti Trebulani. A cave dedicated to the Archangel Michael is located there. Arrive at the first buildings (water) of **Dragoni** then ensure you fork right to head uphill on cobblestone **Via Colucci** (take the next left for a bar) to an archway (water). After a piazza turn right then immediately left onto Via Municipio.

11.5KM DRAGONI (ELEV 116M, POP 1924) (647.9KM)

Dragoni was built on the ashes of the ancient 4th-century BC Samnite city of Cubulteria, destroyed by Quintus Fabius Maximus Verrucosus during the Second Punic War. Two legends surround the origins of the name: One version tells of a cave-dwelling dragon on Monte Melanico who threatened the city, insisting that every year a girl be sacrificed. The heroic Archangel Michael killed the dragon and freed the town. In the second account, it was Saint George who defeated the creature, a saint associated with both dragons and snakes. This tale tells of many snakes that lay in circles on what once was San Giorgio square. The dragon descended from the hills to feast on the snakes and was killed by Saint George, liberating the town of both menaces.

L'Alcova Del Conte O Pr R K Br W S 2/5, €-/80–90/90-100/120-130/140-150/160-170, Via Castagnola 16, tel 342 528 5078. Reservations required via www.booking.com.

Don Ciccio Rest & Ride Pr 19/19, €5, Via Casa Sparse, tel 342 528 5078, 339 766 1051 or +41 78 955 9698, donciccioreststride@gmail.com, www.spots.roadsurfer.com/en-gb/shop/don-ciccio-rest-ride~p969524. Bathroom with cold shower only.

This street descends to the highway at the Annunziata Church, where you turn right (food, groceries). After some shops in neighboring **San Giorgio**, fork left downhill to begin crossing the valley. Pass yellow apartments, curve right, and come to the railway tracks, with the Dragoni station just to the right. Recommended: To avoid walking on the busy and dangerous SS372, instead take the EAV train for Alife in the direction of Piedimonte Matese, an 11-minute ride that saves frayed nerves and perhaps your well-being (for the schedule go to https://planner.eavsrl.it). If you must walk, cross the tracks and turn right then left onto a gravel road. Cross over the **SS372** (which leads to Benevento in 1hr), turn next left into an industrial area, merge with the busy left-hand SS158 (no sidewalk), and cross the **Volturno River** as cars speed by you. The railway emerges on the left. Soon turn left off the highway to the frontage road across the tracks and bend left alongside them for 310m. Turn right, away from the tracks, onto the road, perpendicular to the highway, and follow a succession of roads through these river bottomlands where waymarking is scant. First turn right onto a two-track gravel road then left at the end onto a lane (Via Juncere) and right onto the deserted **Via Volturno**. After 180m, fork left and, at the T-junction (520m later), turn left through more farmland for 1.4km and, at the end of the road, turn right onto to merge with **Via Antonio Gramsci**. At Piazza della Liberazione, turn left through the city gates to Alife's cathedral.

9.8KM ALIFE (ELEV 110M, POP 7376) (638.1KM)

The town of Samnite origin was conquered by the Romans in 326BC, becoming Allifae. The current layout is testament to the Roman presence, with orthogonal road axes within gated walls. Remains include the amphitheater, the cryptoporticus, the forum, epigraphs, and sarcophagi. The Chiesa Madonna della Grazie was built by the Normans on top of a Roman mausoleum and transformed in the Middle Ages by the order of Saint John of Jerusalem. The Cattedrale di Santa Maria Assunta has a 12th-century Romanesque crypt, and the Chiesa di Santa Caterina d'Alessandria (14th century) was restored following the earthquake of 1688.

Raja Rooms B&B O Pr R K Br S Z 2/6, €-/55/60/80/100/-, Viale Caduti sul Lavoro 86, tel 347 256 9763 or 349 582 0853, alife.rajarooms@gmail.com, www.facebook.com/p/Raja-Rooms-BB-100057227238664. Total cost of €150 for six people.

Santuario Madonna delle Grazie O Do S 2/4, €Donation, Via Provinciale Vergini (SP 150), tel 348 735 7865 or 0823 918 459 comitatomadonnadellagrazia@gmail.com. Your host is Marisa Corrado. Located 2.5km out of town: keeping the cathedral facade to your left, head north-west on Via Napoli-Roma and through the Roman arch to take the SP158. After 2.1km, turn right onto Via Provinciale Vergini (SP150) and reach the yellow 20th-century church on your left 400m later.

STAGE 16

Alife to Faicchio

Start	Cathedral of Santa Maria Assunta, Alife
Finish	Church of San Rocco, Faicchio
Duration	5¼hr
Distance	19.3km
Total ascent	325m
Total descent	252m
Difficulty	Moderate due to one strenuous climb
Percentage paved	80%
Lodgings	Faicchio 19.3km, Telese Terme 31.9km

This pleasant stage in two halves takes in farmland on the valley floor at the start and mountains and forests at the end. In between is a stiff climb, but when it's done you find yourself on a scenic roadway with non-stop vistas onto the expanses of the valley below. The stage end is the historic mountainside town of Faicchio, set among lofty green peaks. A bar in Gioia Sannitica offers the sole refreshment along the way, except for a water faucet in Auduni.

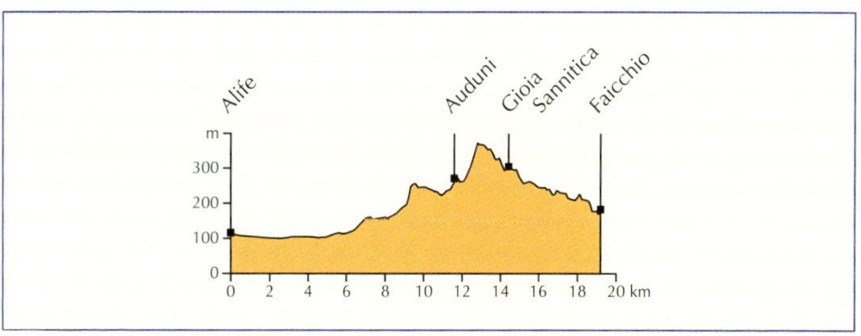

Keep the cathedral on your right and retrace your steps through the old city, out under the Porta Napoli. Cross the bridge, pass the municipio and mausoleum where, next to a service yard, a peek through locked gates shows the 1st-century BC **Roman ampitheater**. Cross over a roundabout (groceries) onto a quiet road and fork left onto the SP151 toward Totari, among scattered homes and crops. Turn left in 400m and find waymarks directing you right onto a **gravel road**, which can get muddy. At the end of the road jog right onto the SP66 for 150m, picking up a new road on the left to keep

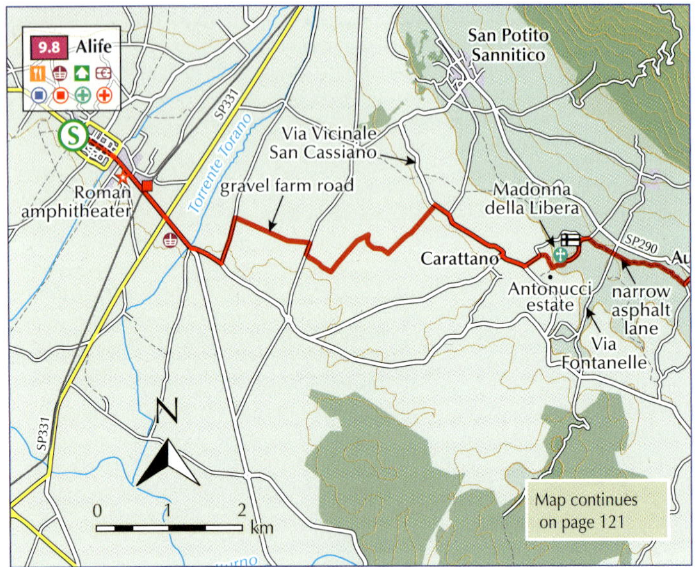

in the same south-east direction. Soon the road heads left but keep to a gravel road for 50m then turn right onto asphalt, with left-hand views of green mountains.

The road bends left twice before heading uphill by farmsteads. Arrive at a right turn onto the busier **Strada Vicinale della Rena**, climbing closer to the mountains. Descend over a stream and, once across, go immediately left uphill into the hamlet of **Carattano** (**8.3km**, no services). Keep uphill on the road, following signs to fork left and right toward the green hilltop, passing an old wash house (bench). Turn left before the gates of the Antonucci estate onto wide cobblestones and then head uphill steps in the shade. Pass the yellow chapel of **Madonna della Libera** (benches), climbing to the cemetery at the summit, where Stations of the Cross on tiles lead downhill.

Come to the curve in another road and follow the road to the right for 30m before turning right on a narrow lane that follows the trajectory of the busier SP290. After crossing **Via Fontanelle**, descend steeply to a stream, enjoying views of Mazzucchella (1371m) and Monte Erbano (1385m) ahead. At an unmarked fork, in sight of the clock tower of Auduni, go right then take the next left up to **Auduni** (water). Cross the SP290, turn right before the **yellow church** (benches) to descend and cross a creek then ascend the slope of Monte Monaco di Gioia (1332m) in the Matese massif, home to eagles, roe deer, wolves, and its highest peak, Monte Miletto (2050m). Descend over another creek bed and begin the day's first steep 120m road climb among fields and woods, reaching the stage's highest point at 373m.

Turn first right onto a road that undulates along the mountainside with beautiful views to the valley floor and the nearby town of Gioia Sannitica. Soon, after a brief traverse, begin a descent which continues to the end of the stage. Turn left at an unmarked fork by a stone wall. The road on the right leads to a (hard, 1.6km, 244m ascent) detour to a barely visible 10th-century fortification.

The **fortification** was the location of the tragic story of Erbanina. Accused of being a witch by her husband, the lord of this castle, she was thrown to her death from the ramparts. At the time, so-called *janaras* (witches) were vastly persecuted; however, a minority idolized them, creating much controversy. These tales have inspired writers and musicians, including Paganini and Laurence Sterne. The nearby Monte Erbano is named after Erbanina.

Follow signs to go next right downhill, spotting the yellow onion dome of Gioia Sannitica's church. Reach a piazza with an enormous hollow tree (benches), head left toward a yellow palazzo marked 'Il Borgo Antico,' and curve downhill after the yellow Chiesa di San Felice you saw from above, which contains a statue of Saint Michael the Archangel, the town's patron, who is celebrated yearly. Soon climb toward a yellow palazzo, pass along its right side, and, at the end of the road, turn right directly downhill. Carefully turn left onto Via Roma **SP83** (a right turn leads to food, groceries, pharmacy) and, as you near the town of **Annunziata**, watch for signs to fork left off the highway onto a parallel quiet lane.

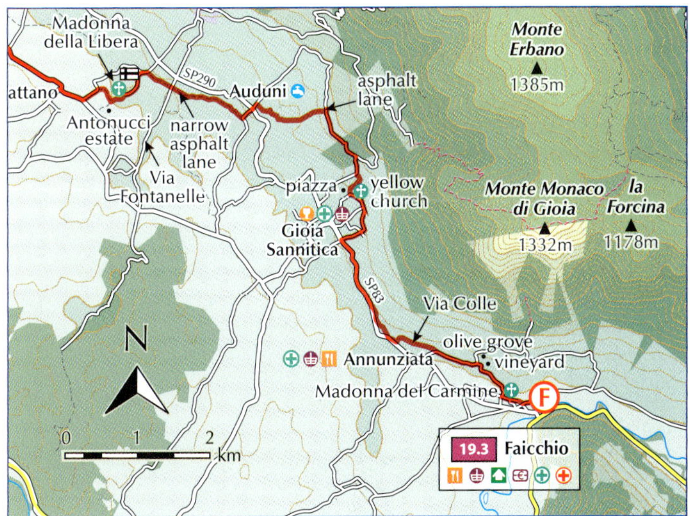

Faicchio's church of Ave Gratia Plena sits on the slopes of Monte Monaco di Gioia, overlooking the Volturno Valley

Briefly touch the SP83 again before turning left onto **Via Colle** and, as you cross Via Russi, pass another gleaming yellow onion dome steeple, this time of the 18th-century Parrocchia Ave Gratia Plena. The road itself turns right at an **olive grove** then immediately left at a **vineyard**, and left again to descend as the stone dome of the Madonna del Carmine convent appears ahead. At the end of the road, turn left downhill, now in **Faicchio**, and pass a post office (ATM) and the driveway of the Chiesa di Santa Maria del Carmelo. Merge left onto Via Regina Elena and arrive at the Church of San Rocco, above on the left (water), and the ducal palace on the right (**4.1km**).

19.3KM FAICCHIO (ELEV 170M, POP 3347) (618.7KM)

Faicchio's history is demonstrably ancient, with Neolithic remains located in the vicinity, as well as signs of a Samnite civilization in the ruins of megalithic walls above the town. A popular excursion and local pilgrimage leads up to a cave (699m) devoted to the Archangel Michael, which holds frescoes of Byzantine influence. In town, the Palazzo Ducale dates from the 12th century, with towers from the 16th century. Faicchio also boasts five churches, including the Renaissance Parrocchia Santa Maria Assunta.

- **Parrocchia S. Maria Assunta** O Do S Z 1/3, €Donation, Via Collegiata 8, tel 347 661 0155, www.facebook.com/parrocchiasmafaicchio.

STAGE 17

Faicchio to Telese Terme

Start	Church of San Rocco, Faicchio
Finish	Main baths, Telese Terme
Duration	3½hr
Distance	12.6km
Total ascent	255m
Total descent	370m
Difficulty	Moderate due to climbs
Percentage paved	72%
Lodgings	Telese Terme 12.6km, Solopaca 17.1km

The route now begins a transit of the Telesina Valley, on its way to the mountains separating it from Benevento. Three mountains stand in the way of you arriving at the valley floor, and this short stage on mountainsides offers a lovely quick walk with frequent vistas from shaded paths. Afterward, there is time left over for a relaxing visit to the thermal baths, bars, and restaurants of Telese Terme. An overgrown trail before Massa is the lowlight, while a groomed forest path on Monte Pugliano is a highlight. There are no services, so bring adequate supplies.

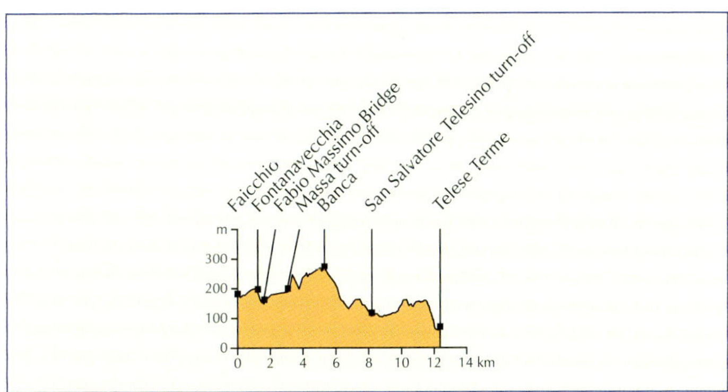

Continue uphill on **Via Fabio Massimo**, passing the fortress-like walls of the Church of Santa Lucia, with views to the left of the granite bluffs of the Matese ridge. The road curves left over a **bridge**, entering Fontanavecchia (La Carrozza sul Titerno). Pass a church on

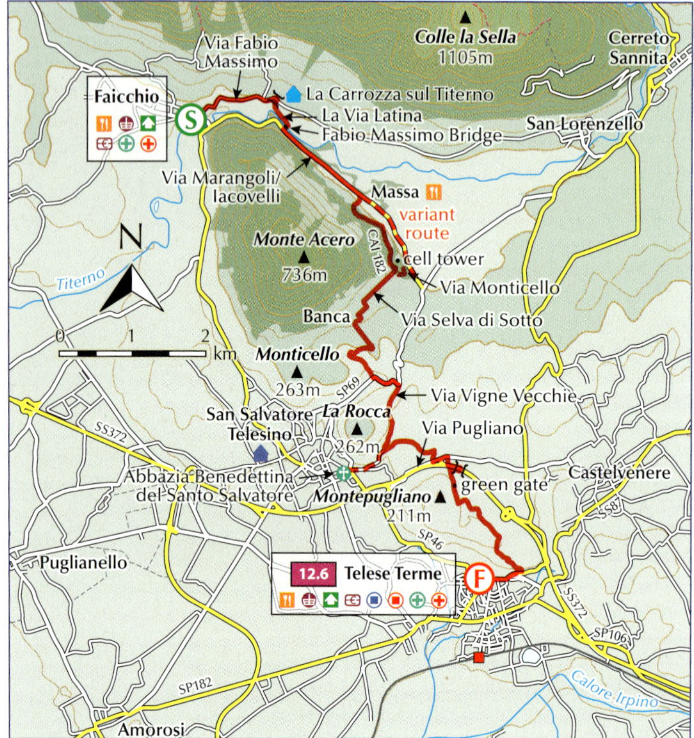

the left and take the first hard right promptly to descend steeply on a concrete drive signed 'La Via Latina,' which follows the Titerno River. Soon the path turns right onto the beautiful **Fabio Massimo Bridge**, constructed during the 3rd century. It is held that Titus, son of Fabius Maximus, drowned in the Titerno River during a battle against the Samnites.

Once across, turn left onto **Via Iacovelli**, climbing gradually along the contours of Monte Acero (736m) and passing hayfields and vineyards, with mountain views in all directions. After a small hazelnut grove, about 200m before the roundabout at the edge of **Massa** (200m away, food), signs direct you right onto an overgrown, hilly two-track road (**3km**). An alternate, easier, and less overgrown option is to remain on the road through the roundabout and then head uphill on Via Monticello to connect with Via Selva Palatina di Sotto. The steep ascent takes you to a left turn downhill on a gravel road among undergrowth and scattered trees. At the end, turn right steeply uphill onto an asphalt road, following **CAI182** signs. In 30m fork right onto a steep and rocky path and, near the summit, leave the CAI182 to regain the overgrown path that soon descends. Turn right onto an unmarked and nearly impassable trail leading uphill under birch trees. Turn left at an overgrown road that soon meets the green mast of a **cell tower**, here a welcome outpost of civilization. Just beyond take an asphalt driveway by Villa Muntruano then turn right onto **Via Selva Palatina di Sotto** (**1.5km**), which leads through olive and soft fruit orchards. At the end, turn right then left into **Banca** (no services).

Descend with views of the three low hills of the day: from right to left, Monticello, La Rocca (holding a fortress), and Montepugliano, beyond which lies Telese Terme in the wide valley. The shaded road steeply descends, curving near the face of Monticello, reaching the SP69 on the outskirts of **San Salvatore Telesino**. Turn left onto the SP69 then follow signs pointing right onto narrow **Via Vigne Vecchie** which immediately curves right toward La Rocca. At the end of this lane, turn left onto another lane (**3.8km**). A right turn here brings you in 1km to the Abbazia Benedettina in San Salvatore Telesino, and further on, **Locanda della Pacchiana**.

A long downhill road leads to Telese Terme, with the Taburno Camposauro massif in the distance

San Salvatore Telesino grew in the 13th century around the 10th-century Benedictine Abbazia del Santo Salvatore on which it depended until the 16th century and from which it gained its name. In 1098, Saint Anselm of Canterbury completed his *Cur Deus Homo* here.

Descend along a creek then turn right onto a road between olives and vines to cross it. On top of the hill lie ruins of the 13th-century Rocca di San Salvatore Telesino defensive tower and 16th-century church. This road ends at **Via Pugliano**, where a left turn onto it passes over an interchange with the busy SS372. Turn right 200m later onto a narrow lane alongside then continue over the highway and start curving along the base of Montepugliano, soon on gravel. Go around or under the **green forest gate** on the right at a fork and head uphill, then turn left downhill on a wide pleasant path by the 'Parco Naturalistico I Puri' sign, through moss-covered stones. Go right at an unmarked fork to climb slightly on a path that narrows at a concrete plaza and climbs up through forest, among large rocks, before descending and merging with a wide downhill path that switchbacks to sounds of the city below. Soon the red tile roofs of Telese Terme appear. At the bottom, turn right onto the SP15 Via Bagni Vecchi, coming to the gates of the main baths of **Telese Terme** (**4.3km**). Turn left onto the boulevard for services.

12.6KM TELESE TERME (ELEV 57M, POP 7613) (606.2KM)
Ancient Telesia is known for its thermal spa (www.termeditelese.it, open June to September), owing to the sulfur springs flowing from Montepugliano (211m), with its many cast sinkholes called Puri. The springs appeared after the great earthquake of 1349, and the bubbling waters provide excellent respite for a weary body. The earthquake, however, eradicated all signs of the original cathedral in Telese Terme, although some remains are preserved in the Parrocchia Santo Stefano, where the bell tower is now used as a dovecote.

Magico Riposo O Pr R K Br Cr S 3/6, €-/35/60/-/-/-, Via Roma 9, tel 328 654 4468 or 328 573 2457, www.dormireincampania.it.

Telese Terme as seen from Montepugliano

STAGE 18

Telese Terme to Vitulano

Start	Main baths, Telese Terme
Finish	Piazza San Menna, Vitulano
Duration	5½hr
Distance	16.6km
Total ascent	796m
Total descent	398m
Difficulty	Hard due to uneven footing and climbs/descents
Percentage paved	48%
Lodgings	Solopaca 4.5km, Vitulano 16.6km, Benevento 33.7km

As it makes its way east, the route must surmount the Taburno Camposauro massif, which separates the Telesina Valley from the Calore and Sabato. The result is the toughest 16.6km of the Francigena since Rome, but the reward is a series of spectacular views back to the Telesino and toward Benevento. The very tall climb is made harder by untended, barely passable trails, but fortunately the road offers an alternative, although it costs an additional 3.2km in distance. If you choose to walk the trail and it is overgrown, you have two remaining trail segments you can avoid by taking the road. If you insist on walking the trail, wear long pants and bring garden gloves and snips. Even if the trail is fine, wear shoes with optimal traction for the very steep and slippery paths. Solopaca offers the only services, so bring plenty of food and water to fuel your demanding day.

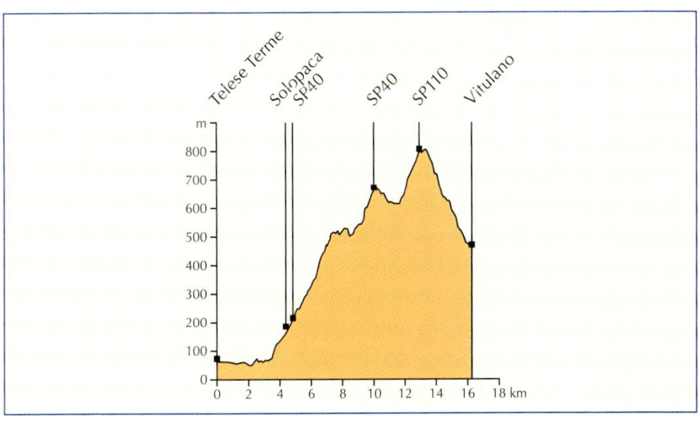

A view back toward Telese Terme and Faicchio from Lago di Telese

With the gates of Telese Terme on your left, begin to retrace yesterday's path along Viale Europa, but turn right immediately onto **Via Caio Ponzio Telesino**, spotting the challenging mountains for the day. From right to left are two ridges, followed by two conical peaks. These together are the Taburno Camposauro, and you will make your way between the ridge and the first of the conical peaks, Monte Pèntime (1168m). Cross over the railway, turn next left, and pass **Lago di Telese** (benches), a popular fishing spot. At the end of the lake make a sharp right over the Calore Irpino River and, 600m after the bridge, follow signs onto a left-hand narrow lane (a direct shortcut on the road is possible). Fork left before an estate onto a gravel road then fork right uphill before a vineyard onto **Via Taverna del Duca**, which turns to asphalt, climbing steeply by farmhouses. Now in **Solopaca**, cross a road, pass a cemetery, cross a roundabout (food), and reach the peach-colored tower with green onion dome of the **Chiesa del Santissimo Corpo di Cristo** on Via Roma.

4.5KM SOLOPACA (ELEV 182M, POP 3797) (601.7KM)

As a fiefdom of great Neapolitan noble families from the mid-15th century, Solopaca thrived greatly in the 17th and 18th centuries, testified by its splendid Palazzo Ducale, with its original geometric and floral facade, and the Chiesa del Santissimo Corpo di Cristo and intricate baroque belltower. Traces remain of its entwined Samnite and Roman origins, along with evidence of the city's birth in the Middle Ages, but little remains of the Norman castle (1100).

Palazzo Cusani Pr R Br W S 4/10, €-/40/70/90/120/-, Via Roma 5, tel 338 381 2065, palazzocusanisolopaca@gmail.com, https://palazzocusani.wixsite.com/palazzocusani. Closed November to February inclusive.

Turn right at the church (water) then turn immediately left onto Via Iannone, where red and white blazes finally return, and follow alpine route CAI200. If you opt for the road across the ridge, turn left here and follow the SP44/SP110 or fork to several steeper asphalt variants that lead to switchbacks up the mountain. Begin the first big climb, through town then among olive trees, and cross over **Via degli Ulivi**. Fork left

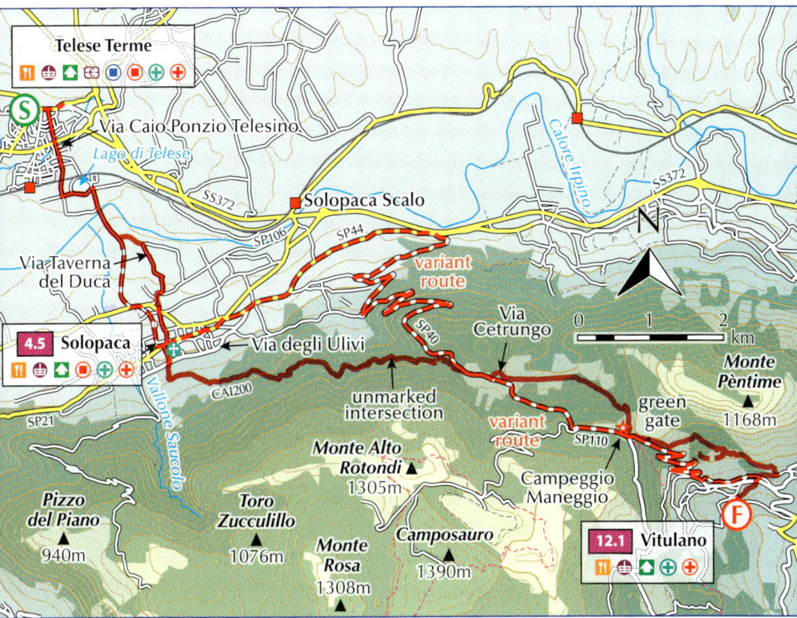

uphill after an olive grove, looking back to views of Telese Terme, soon enjoying the shade under a canopy of young trees. After the gate of a property, where the asphalt transitions to gravel, you enter the Parco Regionale del Taburno-Camposauro, which extends over 12,370 hectares, with Monte Camposauro (1390m) its highest peak. With glimpses to Monte La Pizzuta (1214m) across the valley on the left, the route varies between a wide forest trail and a passage of former roadway hidden under long sunny meadows of flowers and butterflies. At an **unmarked intersection (518m)**, turn right uphill, following CAI blazes and occasional Francigena signs. The wide trail dissipates momentarily into a steep uphill mountain trail for 30m then returns before a sign points off onto a very steep and slippery uphill path (to avoid it, stay on the wider path). End up at another wide path where signs point left to the original road/path, where you turn right (wondering why you were on the steep path!).

Keep uphill onto the **SP40 dei Salici** (**5.6km**) and, after a bald Pizzo del Tesoro mountain appears on the left, come to a decision-making point. If trail maintenance was good on the prior path, it might also be the case on this roadway which soon becomes a path. If not, it is best to take the SP40. To choose the path, turn left and descend on Via Cetrungo (**0.2km**), otherwise continue on the SP40 roadway. On the main route, having chosen the path, follow a wooden fence on the left then continue after a dirt landslide to climb alongside the fence where soon you are on a wide path covered in tall grass, ferns, and brambles. Finally, turn left onto the Madonna del Grotto road – done with overgrown roads for a bit. Head uphill to the Campeggio Maneggio church horse-riding grounds.

Turn left at the road just beyond, arriving at the road's summit. A meadow to the right reveals vast views to the south-east, including to Vitulano far below. Back on the road, immediately fork left (**0.2km**), climbing on gravel at first. If trail conditions have been poor, it is also best to take the road here, which, now in the Benevento province, bears a new name – the SP110. Just after the path's summit, fork right at the **green gate**, with fantastic views of Vitulano, and keep steeply downhill on the trail then the concrete path, where you greet the familiar half-broken wooden fence on your left, and start carefully threading down on this overgrown trail. Pass a series of (sometimes concealed) concrete benches then take the concrete steps to a narrow downhill road. Turn right downhill to the town and, at the Church of San Giuseppe, turn right, descending on flagstones to cross the SP110 (**2.8km**) directly into the old town (avoiding long switchbacks). Pass the Church of Santa Maria and its enormous plane tree and turn left onto Via Roma to reach Piazza San Menna (**0.6km**).

12.1KM VITULANO (ELEV 463M, POP 2732) (589.5KM)

Although Vitulano is an ancient city, the oldest remaining building is the 15th-century Convento della Santissima Annunziata. Despite being subjected to several earthquakes, the Franciscan convent still preserves some original features, such as the wooden ceiling of the oratory dedicated to San Rocco, built after the plague of 1656, which retains its structural and pictorial form. The town is famed for its marble, used in the grand staircase of the Italian city of Caserta and, fascinatingly, in the spires of the Moscow Kremlin in Russia. The hub of Vitulano is the MorisCafè and Restaurant, owned by Anna Sisto, who also operates the town's pilgrim lodging, about 1.2km from the center.

B&B da Anna Pr R Br Dr Cr W S 2/4, €-/25/40/-/80/-, Via Santissima Trinità 1, tel 324 879 6458 or 368 302 9603, anna.di.sisto@gmail.com. Bed, breakfast, and dinner €45 per person.

STAGE 19

Vitulano to Benevento

Start	Piazza San Menna, Vitulano
Finish	Arch of Trajan, Benevento
Duration	4½hr
Distance	17.1km
Total ascent	187m
Total descent	493m
Difficulty	Moderate due to hills
Percentage paved	97%
Lodgings	Benevento 17.1km

Today the mountain passage over the Taburno Camposauro massif ends by descending to the Calore Irpino valley. After a mountainside traverse from Vitulano, the route climbs above Contrada Palazzo, descends to the Calore River, then takes a flat and easy pedestrian/cycle trail almost to the gates of Benevento, leaving plenty of time to explore the town. Foglianise has a café and bakery, but after that the route is without services until Benevento, one of the largest cities between Rome and Bari.

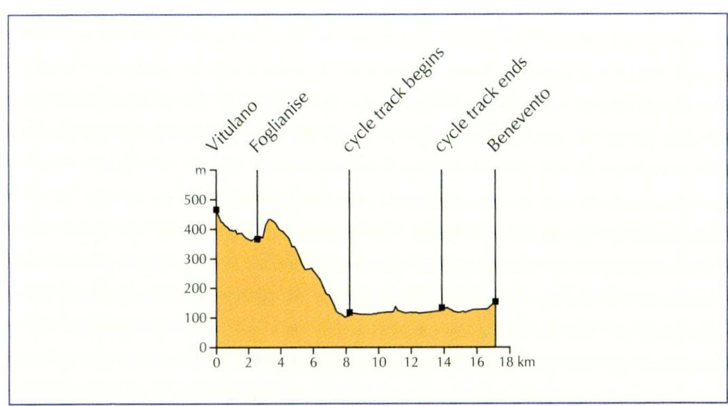

From the piazza, head downhill on **Viale San Pietro**, passing the municipio on your left. Head straight through the roundabout (keeping the Church of San Pietro on your right) onto the quiet SP4. Pass through the hamlet of **Sirignano** (no services), enjoying

beautiful views to your right, and soon come to the SP109 in **Foglianise** (**2.5km**, food, bakery). The town is dominated by the soaring Monte Caruso (834m) from which it quarried the stone so prevalent along its Lombard alleys. Just before a commercial center, fork left uphill on Via Palazzo, arriving on cobblestone **Contrada Palazzo** in the upper town. About 50m before the cobblestones end, turn left steeply uphill, first on a stone sidewalk then on steps at the top of which, by a yellow church, turn right, still uphill, and soon come to **Via Acquara-Barassano**. Hiking signs point to a lightly discernable left uphill track that leads to the Eremo di San Michele (a steep detour of 1km with 249m ascent one way), a cave (658m) devoted to Archangel Michael, situated partway up Monte Caruso.

The road becomes a lonely farm track with lovely views and reaches a summit before descending among olives. After crossing **Via Acquara** at a diagonal, fork right downhill and immediately left at the next fork onto an overgrown and **washed-out asphalt road**. At the end, turn right onto the SP109 for 150m then turn left downhill onto a narrow drive among large modern homes. At the end of this road, turn left downhill onto **Via Comunale Trescine**, among more olives and grapes with views now toward the north-west. Pass a 20th-century chapel and piazza, descending in earnest toward the river valley and rolling farmland beyond. Soon make out your trajectory to Benevento – along the winding river at the feet of the hills and toward a tall peak in the distance.

At the valley floor, turn left onto the SP71, which runs parallel to the Fondo Valle Vitulanese autostrada (motorway). Pass the motorway access marked 'Benevento,' cross the **Calore Irpino River**, and fork right onto Via Sant'Angelo. Pass under the freeway bridge and turn right onto the pink **pedestrian/cycle track** (**5.7km**).

Local residents take an evening stroll toward the Campanile di Santa Sofia on Benevento's Corso Garibaldi

Named the **Oasis Lipu**, and protected since 2008, the 'Beneventan Wetlands' extend over 886 hectares. Within its three types of woods, you will encounter spectacular aquatic birds, as well as birds of prey, owls, woodpeckers, swallows, cranes, passerines, treecreepers, doves, and hoopoes.

Cross Via Sant'Angelo then pass through a dark 250m **tunnel** (or take the right-hand lane around the bluff). On the hill above are ruins of the 10th-century Chiesa di Sant'Angelo a Piesco from the Lombard era. After a time, you will see Benevento's buildings on the right. Cross **Via Pantano** onto a shaded road, pass the Malevento Sport Club (a relaxing stop with a pool and café, 10.00–18.00, €10, reservations advised, tel 347 1439132), and, at the end of the cycle path, continue straight on. At the end of the road, turn left then right and right again onto **Via Vitulanese**, a busy arterial that heads over the railway to a right turn at a roundabout. Pass a gas station (food) and either cross Viale Virgilio at a gap in the guardrails to the train station and nearby services or continue straight on Viale Virgilio along the river. With the former choice, turn right to pass under two railway bridges then make an immediate left onto Via Campagna to **Benevento's train station**. After the station, fork right onto Via Principe di Napoli, which heads over the Calore Irpino River, connecting with the riverside option. Once across the river, turn left uphill on Via del Pomerio and, 0.5km later, reach Trajan's Arch (**8.8km**).

17.1KM BENEVENTO (ELEV 147M, POP 56,201) (572.4KM)

Roman period

Roman Beneventum was founded following the defeat of Pyrrhus of Epirus (late 3rd century BC) and being the furthest point from Rome in that period, it became a crucial city for Roman dominion. Emperors Trajan, Nero, and Septimius Severus all stopped at this midway location along the Via Appia Traiana. The triumphal Arco di Traiano guarded the entrance to the city, boasting the emperor's virtues, and Hadrian's Teatro Romano (AD126) could hold 15,000 spectators. Hellenic and Roman finds can also be admired in the Museo del Sannio, situated in the cloister of the 8th-century Chiesa di Santa Sofia, a UNESCO World Heritage Site. Within this lovely church with its Moorish exterior, the miniscule Beneventan script was born and used in Italy's south for five centuries.

The Lombards

In the 4th century, Benevento became a bishopric and in 663 it was an important Lombard Duchy to which the city owes its Rocca dei Rettori castle and the reconstructed Cattedrale di Santa Maria de Episcopio, which still has its original features. In Benevento, an aura of legend surrounds the Lombard conversion to Christian worship, which has inspired authors, musicians, and painters, as well as the strong, local, herbal liquor Strega (*strega* means 'witch'), which, according to folklore, forever unites a couple. The label depicts dancing maidens linking arms around a walnut tree. They were the *janaras* (a term also used to describe witches) who lived by a sumptuous walnut tree where Benevento's Lombard rulers partook in rituals.

Parrocchia Beato Moscati O Do R K W S 2/4, €15, Via Nicola Ciletti 1, tel 082 453 479, parrocchiamoscati@virgilio.it.

Hostel Le Stanze del Sogno O Pr Do R K Br Dr Cr W S Z 7/22, €25/35/60/75/100/125, Piazzetta de Martini 3, tel 3272 818 783, lestanzedelsogno@gmail.com, www.lestanzedelsogno.com. Reservations required; some rooms have kitchens.

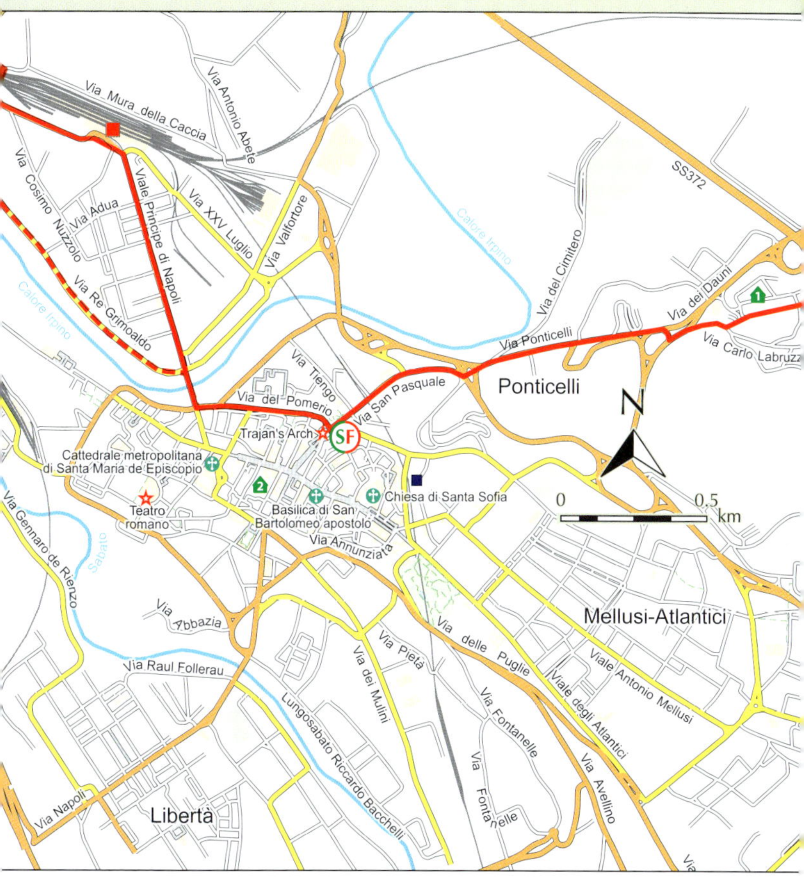
Benevento
1 Parrocchia Beato Moscati
2 Hostel Le Stanze del Sogno
Via Mura della Caccia
Via Antonio Abete
Via Cosimo Nuzzolo
Via Adua
Viale Principe di Napoli
Via XXV Luglio
Via Valfortore
Calore Irpino
SS372
Via del Cimitero
Via dei Dauni
Via Re Grimoaldo
Via Ponticelli
Via Carlo Labruzz
Via Tiengo
Via San Pasquale
Ponticelli
Via del Pomerio
Trajan's Arch
SF
Cattedrale metropolitana di Santa Maria de Episcopio
Chiesa di Santa Sofia
Teatro romano
Basilica di San Bartolomeo apostolo
Via Annunziata
0
0.5 km
Via Gennaro de Rienzo
Sabato
Via Abbazia
Mellusi-Atlantici
Via Pietà
Via delle Puglie
Via dei Mulini
Via Raul Follerau
Viale Antonio Mellusi
Viale degli Atlantici
Via Fontanelle
Lungosabato Riccardo Bacchelli
Via Avellino
Via Napoli
Libertà

STAGE 20

Benevento to Buonalbergo

Start	Arch of Trajan, Benevento
Finish	Piazza Garibaldi, Buonalbergo
Duration	6½hr
Distance	23.3km
Total ascent	766m
Total descent	357m
Difficulty	Hard due to ascents and uneven walking surfaces
Percentage paved	78%
Lodgings	Buonalbergo 23.3km, Casalbore 26.2km

The route generally follows the trajectory of the SS90bis, climbing a ridge between the Tammaro and Miscano valleys to arrive at the mountain village of Buonalbergo. A few relentless climbs on this stage are compensated by tranquil vistas of green hills and mountains. Mud in low places on the dirt roads requires extra care in wet weather. With no intermediate services, and considering the total ascent and distance, bring plenty of water and food.

Possible alternate route (not mapped): watch for signs that direct you north of the Carlore-Irpino River onto a new, less urban route planned between Benevento and Contrada Valentino.

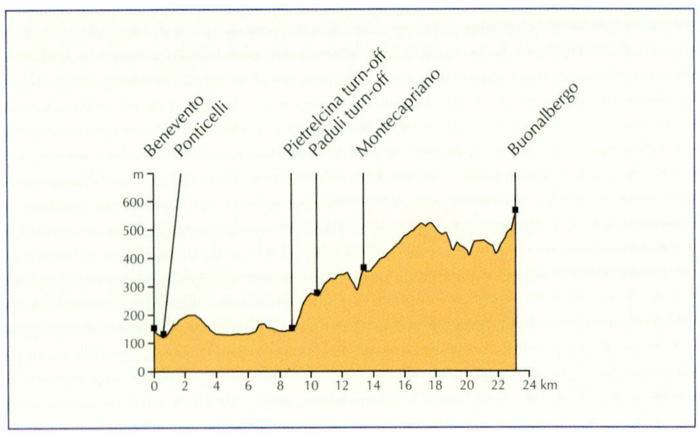

With the downhill side of Trajan's Arch behind you, go straight, winding down **Via San Pasquale** to cross over a complex intersection of roads and a stream on a wide sidewalk into the Ponticelli neighborhood (bakery). Fork right uphill onto **Via Ponticelli**, beginning the day's first climb.

Pass the modern Church of **San Giuseppe Moscati** (with its unique rocket ship steeple) on its right side, and promptly fork left uphill onto Via N. Ciletti to cross over the SS372 and continue ahead on Via Beccaria Cesare. Pass the fire command center then a large grocery store and, at the T-junction, cross onto a quiet, narrow lane with a **prison** facility on your right then head downhill. Carefully cross the **SS90bis**. Soon the lane becomes a gravel two-track road then, depending on the quality of its recent maintenance, it may become the bed of a seasonal stream, with water flowing on one, the other, or both tracks.

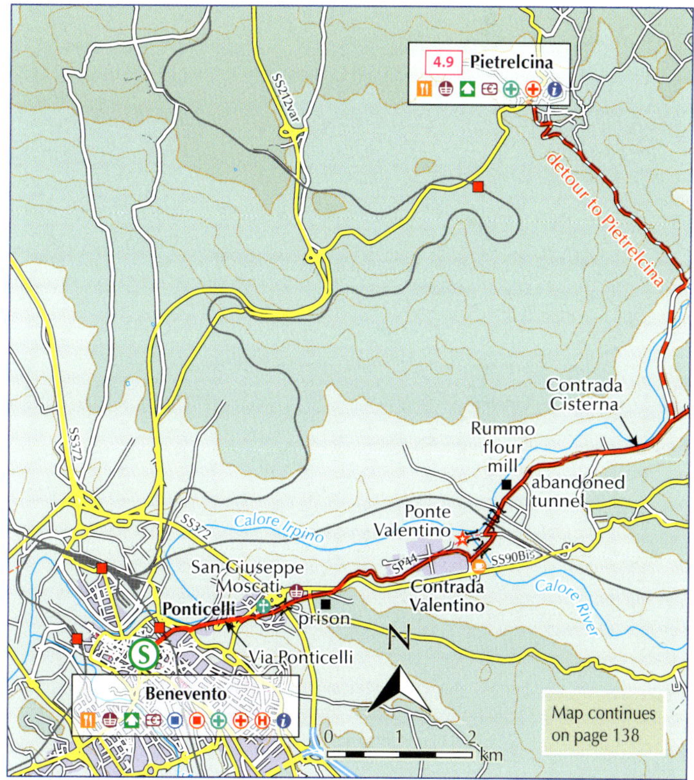

Arrive at the **Contrada Valentino** industrial area, called Ponte Valentino, at the valley floor and, when the lane ends at a T-junction, keep on grass for a block then turn right onto the wide **SP44** through this working zone. Notice two bridges spanning the Calore River, which the route avoids: the brick Ponte Valentino (commissioned by 2nd-century Emperor Flavius Valens) and a deserted metal bridge. Instead, curve right with the road and, just before the gas station (**5km**, food), turn left to cross over the river. Once across, turn left, greeting the metal bridge, then curve right along the road through the industrial zone. Pass under two bridges and, after the **Rummo flour mill**, instead of curving right with the road, keep straight to climb on a narrow road alongside the large concrete retaining wall and walk through an apparently disused, **abandoned tunnel**. Exiting, see the towns of Paduli and Torre Monte, which you will walk below.

The now gravel road descends to find in wet weather a frog pond where the road should be. Carefully work your way around it to then climb back on asphalt and merge with the **Contrada Cisterna** road (**2.7km**), on which you remain for the next hour alongside fields. After passing a farm on the left, fork right onto a road heading

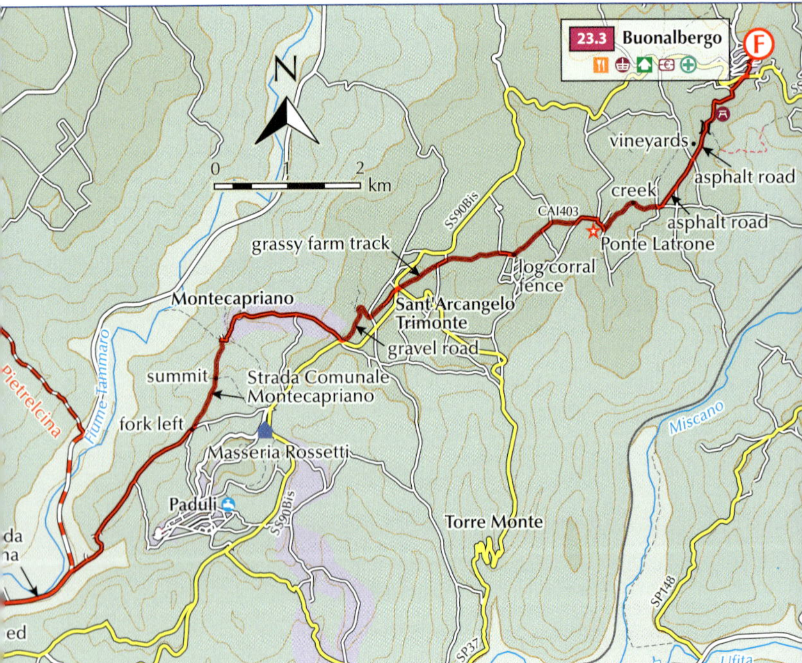

strenuously uphill in the direction of Paduli. A left fork here leads to Pietrelcina (food, groceries, accommodation, ATM, pharmacy, clinic, information), birthplace of Saint Pio (Padre Pio), a roundtrip of around 10km **Dimora Forgione B&B**. Pausing to catch your breath, enjoy views back to Benevento. Descend briefly, passing the road to Paduli (water).

The town's **Chiesa di San Bartolomeo Apostolo** (18th century) is accessed through a square bell tower. Its unusual facade is a remnant of a previous Romanesque church and it still accommodates two original Roman limestone slabs.

Ascend again and fork left ahead onto the **Strada Comunale Montecapriano** (**3.9km**) still uphill. A right turn and 1.5km lead to **Casa Turistica Masseria Rossetti.** Come to a summit with wide views ahead then descend and at the bottom, after a couple of bends, begin a brutal ascent to **Montecapriano** (no services).

Before the road merges with the SS90bis, take a **gravel road** on the left, which will be your main route, in several incarnations, for the next 5km. Climb gradually, making a loop away from and back to the road, cross a narrow lane, and, climbing more steeply, pass among farm buildings. Soon cross the SS90bis at a sign welcoming you to **Sant'Arcangelo Trimonte**. Keep to the same road, still climbing, and ignore a right-hand driveway to continue now on what has become a (sometimes overgrown) **grassy farm track**. Briefly join an asphalt lane but continue straight when that road turns left. Cross a shallow valley with vistas toward the Miscano Valley and Buonalbergo to the left. Touch down on asphalt briefly at a **log corral fence** and kiosk then follow signs directing back to the grass. Watch carefully for a sign to go right back onto a grassy track, the CAI403 (a very bumpy, uneven, and treacherous track between a horse paddock and cow pasture). Use extreme caution on this slippery and downhill track, particularly in wet weather. Finally, turn left onto a narrow lane and turn left again. Pass a sign for the municipality of Buonalbergo and the ruins of the Roman bridge Ponte

The track leads through rolling, green hills between Benevento and Buonalbergo

A look back while climbing steps in Buonalbergo

Ladrone (bridge of the thieves), and head steeply uphill between fields. At the end of the lane, turn right downhill then, following signs, turn left downhill on another poorly maintained and muddy grassy track pointing straight at Buonalbergo, reaching a Via Francigena kiosk. Just before the information board, take the road on the right to make a detour to the Roman bridge of Ponte delle Chianche (1km with 10m ascent one way).

Ford a **creek** before being rewarded with another brutal climb to turn right onto a driveway and then immediately left onto a road where distant hills appear under a carpet of green. Soon fork left onto a road among vineyards, climbing as Buonalbergo comes into focus. Dive down onto a red-railing **bridge** over a stream, and then attack the last ordeal: climb very steeply into town. The road ends at the SS90bis Via Rodolfo Scrocco, just right of the yellow Chiesa del Carmine. Tackle the 67 steps and another seriously steep climb to arrive at Piazza Garibaldi (**11.7km**).

23.3KM BUONALBERGO (ELEV 552M, POP 1525) (549.1KM)

This very hilly town, full of stone steps, has always welcomed travelers and as early as the Norman era had already gained its rightful name of Buonalbergo (translating as 'good inn'). Well placed along the Via Traiana and also the Pescasseroli-Candela drove road, it is no wonder that the hosting custom grew, the town even welcoming Henry VI, Holy Roman Emperor. Destroyed recurrently by earthquakes then by Charles VIII and finally and fatally by a landslide, the town was rebuilt in 1525. Important buildings include the 17th-century Palazzo Spinelli and the 20th-century Chiesa de San Carlo Borromeo.

Casa del Pellegrino O Pr Do R Br Dr W S 2/5, €25/25/50/-/-/-, Via Rodolfo Scrocco 46, tel 377 244 8073, mennittodonatella@gmail.com. Dinner and breakfast included; located at the bottom of the town.

STAGE 21

Buonalbergo to Celle di San Vito

Start	Piazza Garibaldi, Buonalbergo
Finish	Church of Santa Caterina, Celle di San Vito
Duration	8hr (8hr wet weather option)
Distance	29km (29.1km wet weather option)
Total ascent	873m (861m wet weather option)
Total descent	708m (641m wet weather option)
Difficulty	Hard due to length and long climbs/descents
Percentage paved	58% (78% wet weather option)
Lodgings	Main route: Casalbore 2.9km, Celle di San Vito 29km Wet weather route: Casalbore 2.9km, Castelfranco 18.3km, Faeto 26.5km, Celle di San Vito 29.1km

Although this long but beautiful stage marks the transition from Campania to Puglia, the scenery and topography remain distinctly Campanese – mountainous and forested. You are also faced with an important decision: whether to choose the main route and adhere most closely to the Via Traiana or to select the wet weather route to avoid a potentially hazardous fording. Both are tough, and it's best to let the weather decide for you. Prior to the option are the bakery at Casalbore and the interesting Santa Maria dei Bossi shrine and rest area.

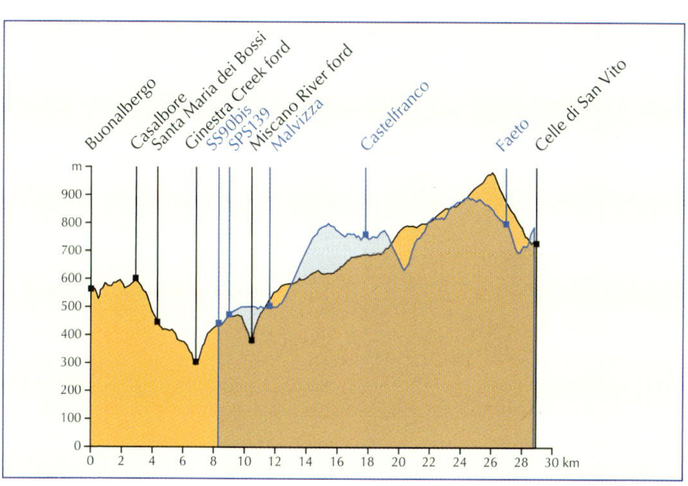

Facing the church in Piazza Garibaldi, go left uphill, turn right onto Via Lombardo, descending to the old wash house of **Fontana del Lombardo** and crossing the Torrente Santo Spirito. Climb steeply on a path along a wooden fence, turn right onto a gravel driveway uphill then turn first left onto a road downhill among wheat fields. After a **farmhouse fence**, turn left onto gravel, which soon turns to grass through fields then back to asphalt to pass a garbage depot. Go downhill to take a left at a roundabout and head up into **Casalbore**.

2.9KM CASALBORE (ELEV 592M, POP 1574) (546.1KM)

The village developed in the Middle Ages as is evidenced by its 12th-century Norman fortress tower, still standing strong and made of local gray stone.

Parrocchia Santi Pietro e Paolo O Do S €Donation, Via Papa Giovanni XXIII 4, tel 0825 849 164. Very basic accommodation with mattresses on the floor and no showers.

Aia di Lazzaro O Pr R Br Dr Cr W S Z 3/10, €-/35/-/-/-, Contrada Sant'Elia, tel 0825 849 288 or 339 791 9231, info@aiadilazzaro.it, www.aiadilazzaro.it. Bed, breakfast, and dinner €50. The host hopes to open a pilgrim hostel so check for updates (writing in summer 2024).

The Church of Santa Maria dei Bossi near Casalbore

Pass a pilgrim-friendly bakery and bar then turn right at the roundabout. Head downhill, passing a **sports complex** (soccer field) and, before the tennis courts, veer left onto a downhill driveway. At its end use a sidewalk beside a concrete retaining wall then take the narrow path that leads onto a road. Pass a Via Francigena kiosk, turn right, and take the path on the left that leads to downhill steps and a stone marked as the imprint of Santa Maria dei Bossi. Follow right on grass, which soon turns to asphalt, downhill to the **Santa Maria dei Bossi chapel** (**1.5km**), first mentioned in the 5th century and built on the site of a Roman mausoleum. An uphill gravel path takes you to the statue and viewpoint (benches).

After your visit, continue toward the road below to find a St. Michael Archangel statue, where a golden plaque wishes pilgrims protection along the Via Micaelica to Monte Sant'Angelo. Turn left onto the **SS90bis**, heading downhill among fields to arrive, in 20min, at a fork with the SPS139 (**1.2km**) and an important choice. Francigena signs point you to the right, the summer (official) route, an option you can confidently take when you are sure the river level will allow you a safe fording. The unmarked wet weather route (recommended) avoids the uncertainties of fording an unsafe river with high water levels, adding 2.1km to the stage's total distance. While the official route includes some Via Appia ruins and softer walking surfaces, the wet weather route has fewer potential challenges and offers intermediate stops at Castelfranco and Faeto.

Summer (official) option

At the SPS139, fork right, descending on pavement, then fork left onto gravel near the confluence of the Ginestra Creek and the Miscano River. Carefully gauge the level of water in the Ginestra and, if safe, cross to the other bank. Notice a fragment of the ancient Roman **Ponte di Santo Spirito**, also known as 'Ponte del Diavolo,' of the Via Appia Traiana. Note that you can skip this descent, the fording, and the 100m climb by staying on the SS90bis where the summer route rejoins the wet weather option. Return to the SS90bis, cross it, and join an uphill path to the SP273. Fork right (**2.6km**) while the wet weather route continues straight. Descend for a second fording, this time of the **Miscano River** (**2.3km**), in warm weather barely a creek. Once across, begin a long 14km climb, first along the SP54 for 1.3km then left at the first two-track dirt road, mostly among wild fields of hay. Continue through the dispersed farm community of **Tre Fontane** (no services). Excitingly, cross into Puglia just before joining the SP125, which leads to the holiday town of Villaggio San Leonardo (**12.9km**, no services).

Ruins of the 2nd-century Ponte Santo Spirito, once part of the Via Traiana, sit near a modern railway bridge across the Miscano River

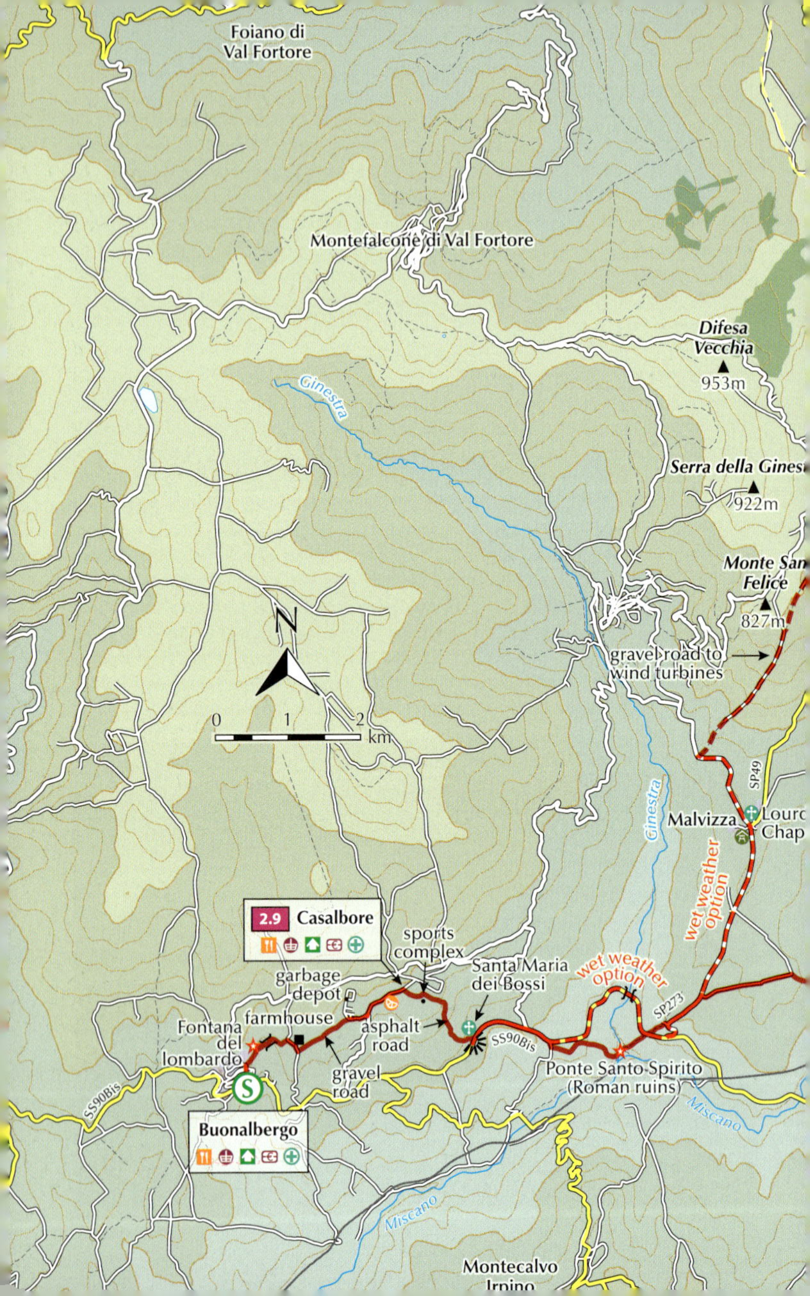
Foiano di
Val Fortore
Montefalcone di Val Fortore
Difesa
Vecchia
953m
Ginestra
Serra della Ginest
922m
Monte San
Felice
827m
N
0
1
2
km
gravel road to
wind turbines
SP49
Malvizza
Lourd
Chap
Ginestra
wet weather
option
2.9 Casalbore
sports
complex
garbage
depot
Santa Maria
dei Bossi
wet weather
option
SP273
farmhouse
asphalt
road
Fontana
del
lombardo
SS90Bis
gravel
road
Ponte Santo Spirito
(Roman ruins)
Miscano
SS90Bis
Buonalbergo
Miscano
Montecalvo
Irpino

Castelluccio Valmaggiore
Monte Vento 1056m
Monte San Chirico 991m
29.0
2.5
Celle di San Vito
Torrente Celone
8.7
Faeto
Monte Tufaro 918m
Difesa 1060m
F
Colle Servigliuccio 897m
ford stream
12.2
Castelfranco in Miscano
derelict house and tower
Monte Buccolo 852m
Monte San Vito 1015m
gravel road
Padre Pio Statue
Campania
Puglia
SP126
Castiglione 959m
Villaggio San Leonardo Faeto
SP125
Monte Calvello 921m
Monte del Niglio 919m
Tre Fontane
gravel road
Greci
SP54
2-track dirt road
SS90
pathways
Torrente Cervaro
iscano
er ford
Savignano Irpino
SS90Bis
SS90

To your right is **Monte Castiglione** (959m) upon which stood the Crepacore castle, inhabited in the 12th century by Charles of Anjou's Provençal militia. The following century would see part of this French-speaking community seek safety and better weather among the churches and monasteries of Faeto and Celle di San Vito.

Fork right onto the SP126 and then turn left in about 2km onto a gravel road below wind turbines (water). Reach the high point of the stage on the slopes of Monte San Vito (**3.4km**, 1015m) after which descend to join the wet weather option in the woods with a right turn (**1.3km**) just before **Celle di San Vito** (**0.9km**).

Wet weather option

In wet weather continue on the SS90bis to avoid a fording of the potentially dangerous Ginestra River and cross said river on a scenic **bridge** among speeding cars and trucks. Cross the summer route (or simply turn left to take it for 350m until the routes rejoin briefly) just before the fragmented **Ponte di Santo Spirito** then fork left uphill, on the SP273 road, toward Castelfranco. On the way uphill, the summer route rejoins and then forks right at the first road, heading toward another fording. Pass an abandoned gas station before the right-hand turn-off to Castelfranco and soon arrive at the Chapel to Our Lady of Lourdes (bench) in **Malvizza** (**5.8km**, no services).

Across the fields on the right are the **Bolle della Malvizza**, a large cluster of mud volcanoes. The emissions of bubbles are particularly distinguishable after rainfall. The town is crossed by a transhumance road known as the Via della Lana (road of wool), used by shepherds and their Abruzzo sheep.

Continue straight on the SP125, which winds like a ribbon, then at a tight right curve, turn right onto a steep gravel road heading up the mighty **Monte San Felice** (827m) toward wind turbines. Near the top, fork right onto a gentle uphill lane and, at the brow of the hill, see Castelfranco in Miscano ahead. At the entrance to town turn left onto Via Nino Bixio to the center (**12.5km**).

18.3KM CASTELFRANCO IN MISCANO (ELEV 758M, POP 794) (540.9KM)

The city was first documented in the late 12th century. In the Aragonese era, its importance was considerable: King Fernando himself arrived there to review his troops.

Affittacamere Casa Paoletta O Pr R Z 5/12, €-/30/-/-/-/-, Contrada Sant'Elia, tel 338 214 3871, www.facebook.com/p/Casa-Paoletta-affittacamere-100045947095892. Check ahead for availability.

Keep the church on your left and wind downhill through town on Via Capitano Antinozzi, cross over the river, turn left onto Traverso Largario, and turn left again in one block before a soccer pitch. Fork right before the statue of **Padre Pio**, returning to the countryside, with more wind turbines along the ridges. Descending, take note of the white road climbing the arm of Monte Difesa (1060m), your next challenge. Turn right onto a broken asphalt road then turn left onto a lane along the valley. In 100m turn left again for the second major steep climb of the day, up the mountain. The road ends near the summit (901m). Fork right with the whoosh of the surrounding wind turbines, entering Puglia! At a **derelict house and tower** begin gradually downhill, soon sighting Castelluccio Valmaggiore's rooftops below and the Tavoliere plains beyond. The road bends downhill toward **Faeto** then passes the gas station to the center of town.

8.7KM FAETO (ELEV 798M, POP 616) (528.3KM)

As the highest village in the Daunia Mountains and second-highest municipality on the route (excepting Monte Sant'Angelo on the variant), Faeto came to life after Charles of Anjou's mercenary Provençal soldiers descended from the fortress of Crepacore on the Castiglione hill, where they had been strategically hiding from the dangerous threats of the Angevins, Durazzeschi, and Aragonese. They came from the Burgundy and Savoy regions of France, where the Provençal dialect was spoken. To this day, both Italian and Franco-Provençal are spoken here. Recommended visits include the Casa del Capitano (15th century), the ethnographic Museum of the Franco-Provençal civilization, and the civic museum of the territory. The neighboring forest of Faeto covers 150 hectares and is home to wolves, wild cats, badgers, and woodpeckers.

Parrocchia SS Salvatore O Do R K S 6/9, €15–25, Via Roma 8, tel 347 017 8780, donantoniovalentinousa@gmail.com. Your host is Don Antonio.

A lonely ruin looks out over the wide, green territory on the wet-weather route to Celle San Vito

Turn right at a small piazza (benches) to descend, passing a covered bench and kiosk then a wastewater treatment plant as the shaded road becomes impossibly steep on lumps of unsmoothed concrete waste. Ford a **small stream** and climb the scrappie, rocky hill serving as a roadway where, near the top, the summer official route rejoins by the spring gate of an electric fence (**1.7km**).

Combined route

Near the top of the hill arrive at the first homes of **Celle di San Vito**, loop through the quiet woods, turn left after a large terrace overlooking a soccer pitch, and, now on Via Roma, pass a viewpoint then the municipio to reach the Chiesa di Santa Caterina (**2.6km**).

2.5/26KM CELLE DI SAN VITO (ELEV 723M, POP 148) (520.1KM)

Standing over the Celone Valley, with the all-important role of controlling the Via Traiana and the Camporeale–Foggia drove road, Celle di San Vito is the tiniest town in Puglia to be a provincial capital, and it is the only place, other than Faeto, with a Franco-Provençal minority in Puglia. A small convent, now in ruins and dedicated to San Nicola, sheltered pilgrims on their arduous journeys, and by the end of the 13th century, it also housed the Provençal mercenaries of Charles of Anjou in the monastic cells, hence the name *celle* (cells).

B&B Le Fontanellas O Pr R Br Dr Cr S 3/8, €-/25/-/-/-/-, Via Fontanelle, tel 329 315 3008 or 329 973 5621, casadellefontanelle@gmail.com, www.facebook.com/lefontanellecelle. Reservations preferred; discounts for groups and pilgrims using their own sleeping bags. If the B&B is closed, they will help find other lodgings.

SECTION 3: PUGLIA – CELLE DI SAN VITO TO BRINDISI

Exterior detail of Bitonto's Cathedral of Santa Maria Assunta (Stage 31)

The route makes a gradual descent to the Adriatic coast, first through Tavoliere fields and then through vast olive groves once overseen from behind protective *masserie* walls. Medieval city centers hold Romanesque architectural jewels both inland and along the coast, where whitewashed buildings are set beside clear, blue-green seas.

STAGE 22

Celle di San Vito to Troia

Start	Church of Santa Caterina, Celle di San Vito
Finish	Concattedrale, Troia
Duration	4¾hr
Distance	17.4km
Total ascent	314m
Total descent	599m
Difficulty	Moderate due to climbs/descents
Percentage paved	59%
Lodgings	Troia 17.4km, Giardinetto Vecchio 30.5km

Transitioning from the forested mountains and pastures of Campania to the rolling prairies of the Tavoliere, today you feel your arrival in Puglia. Beginning with a long and shaded climb up Monte Buccolo (852m), you then descend nearly 500m, mostly on asphalt, to tracks along wheat fields. After a last 100m climb to Troia, prepare to enjoy a surprisingly prosperous agricultural town with a rich history. The town is an important option point: Monte Sant'Angelo to the north or Bari to the east. While there are no intermediate services, the route is short and not difficult.

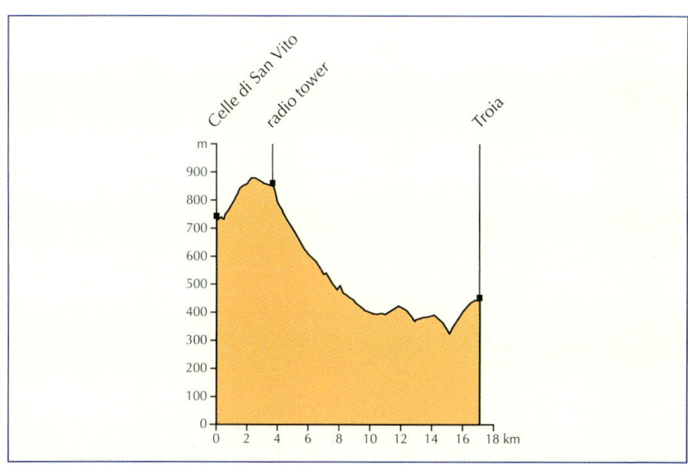

Retrace your steps from the Church of Santa Caterina and return uphill on Via Roma, passing the municipio, the viewpoint, and the large piazza. Continue straight on the road, descending through woods. At a fork by a roadside water fountain, turn right steeply uphill, and turn left at the T-junction, ascending to the **SC Ignazia/SP126** to turn left toward Troia.

With most of the climbing accomplished, enjoy vistas to lush valleys and towns passed yesterday. At the end of the ridge, with the wind-turbine-studded Monte Buccolo (852m) on your right and the forested Colle Serviglíuccio (897m) on your left, descend on switchbacks. From this vantage point, observe the sweep of the Tavoliere before you, with Troia on a low hill, Lucera on the left, and fields sprinkled with wind turbines. To the left are the hills of the Gargano region, home to Monte Sant'Angelo. You can either take the roadway downhill or, just after the **radio tower** (**3.9km**), take a grassy track, shortcutting three of the six switchbacks then joining the road for the remaining three.

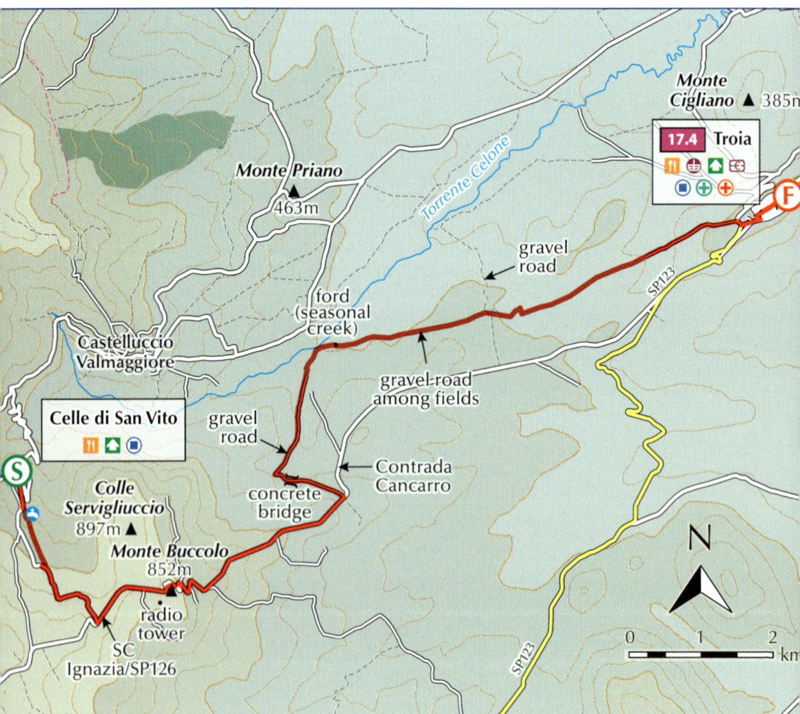

Partway downhill, keep straight, ignoring the right-hand fork and, near the bottom at a crossroads, follow signs straight onto the SP123, which heads to Troia, but instead turn left onto a track for a more friendly entrance into town. Head downhill, cross a **concrete bridge**, and climb, then, in 100m, turn right onto a **gravel road** descending under utility lines. At the bottom, fork right among fields then ford a **seasonal creek** and climb gradually to the top of a ridge, with Troia ahead. Jog right at a gravel road, directly toward the town hidden in the trees on a hilltop. Arriving at Via Circonvollazione, turn right and come to Piazza d'Ungheria (services) where a right onto pedestrianized Via Regina Margherita reaches the Concattedrale della Beata Vergine Maria Assunta in Cielo (**13.5km**).

The elaborate rose window and bronze doors of Troia's Cattedrale di Santa Maria Assunta are considered some of Puglia's finest medieval artworks

17.4KM TROIA (ELEV 424M, POP 6689) (502.7KM/563.4KM)

Designated its Greek name of Aecae by the Bordeaux Pilgrim in their document of 1024, Troia was reborn in 1017 as a Byzantine fortress against the Lombards, who named it Troia after the famous city in Asia Minor. It fell into Norman hands in 1066 then was destroyed by Frederick II in 1229. Medieval buildings include the 10th-century Church of San Vincenzo Martire and the 11th-century Basilica of San Basilio Magno, perhaps of early Christian origin. Taking 30 years to build, the co-cathedral is an excellent example of the fusion of cultures in medieval Puglia, blending Byzantine, Puglian Romanesque, and Saracen influences, notably in the rose window. Three original medieval scrolls of the Exultet are found inside.

Hospital del Cammino O Do R S Z 2/40, €Donation, Via Regina Margherita 4, tel 393 891 7725.

STAGE 23

Troia to Castelluccio dei Sauri

Start	Concattedrale, Troia
Finish	Chiesa del Santissimo Salvatore, Castelluccio dei Sauri
Duration	6¼hr
Distance	23.7km
Total ascent	184m
Total descent	343m
Difficulty	Moderate due to distance and low hills
Percentage paved	97%
Lodgings	Giardinetto 13.1km, Castelluccio dei Sauri 23.7km

At Troia the mountains end and you are introduced to the wide Tavoliere plain stretching toward the Adriatic Sea. This stage comes immediately after an important choice: to fork left toward the Gargano hills and Monte Sant'Angelo (Stages MSA23 to MSA27) or to fork right more directly toward Bari (this stage and all subsequent stages in this section). The terrain is fairly flat, except that both Troia and Castelluccio dei Sauri are perched on tables, meaning a descent and climb bookend the stage. In between are quiet asphalt roads, wide fields of crops, active and abandoned farms, and clusters of wind turbines and solar farms, resulting in a meditative day.

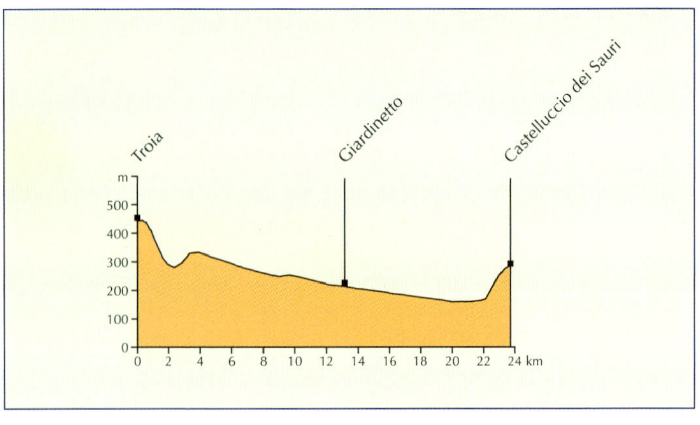

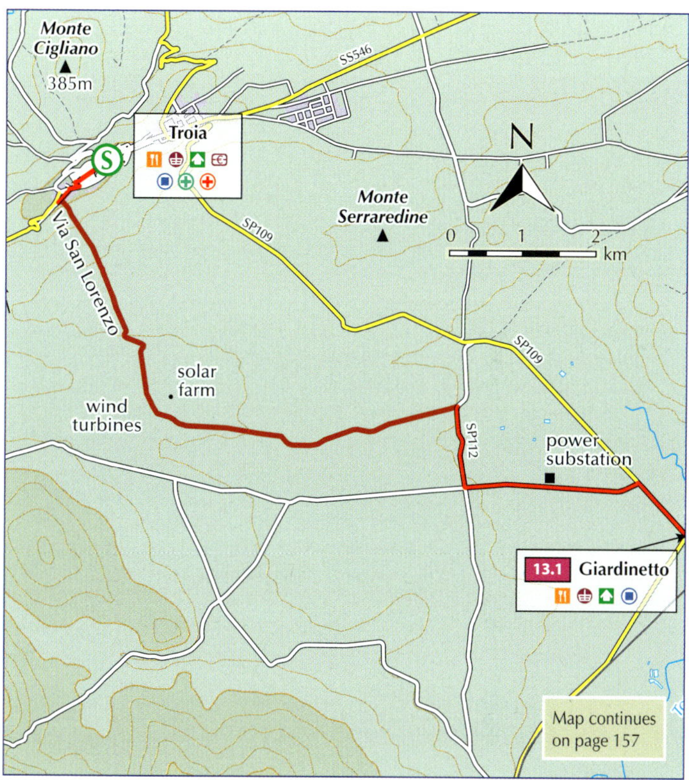

With your back to the concattedrale, go left, retracing your steps to the start of Via Regina Margherita. Turn left downhill, turn right in one block onto Via Alfonso Tredenari, and, after one long block, turn left then fork right down Via Sansone Verona, away from yesterday's route. After a hairpin bend, turn right down **Via San Lorenzo** and out of town to the farmland, hills, and wind turbines of the Tavoliere ahead.

The **Tavoliere** (tableland plains) makes it clear why Puglia is known as 'the breadbasket of Italy.' Indeed, 80% of Europe's pasta comes from this region, and it is also the country's largest alluvial plain. The grid-like wheat and grain fields, stretching for 4500km^2 between the Apennines and the Gargano Peninsula, were cultivated by the Romans, and to this day are the soil that gives birth to the famous *orecchiette* pasta.

Pass a **solar farm** and join a quiet road through a valley and over a low ridge of wind turbines. Just over the brow of a hill, pass a shooting range and turn left onto gravel. Pass a vast solar farm and merge right on gravel. Reach a farm, turn right onto the **SP112**, and pass the D'Alessandro farm. Turn left at the next intersection, pass a **power substation**, and turn right onto the SP109, which reaches **Giardinetto** at the next crossroads.

13.1KM GIARDINETTO (ELEV 213M, POP 16) (489.7KM)

The town is a small cluster of new homes and farm buildings initially constructed in 1941 when American troops were stationed along the Gustav Line. At an intersection of two highways, the town's café/grocery (WC) is a hub for truckers transiting the surrounding flatlands.

Agriturismo Posta Guevara O Pr R Br Dr Cr W S Z 35/70, €-/40/60/80/95/-, Strada Statale 90 – Pod. 1, tel 0881 976880, 342 780 6551 or 3412 780 4714, info@postaguevara.com, www.postaguevara.com.

The road stretches across rolling plains covered in crops on the Tavoliere after Troia

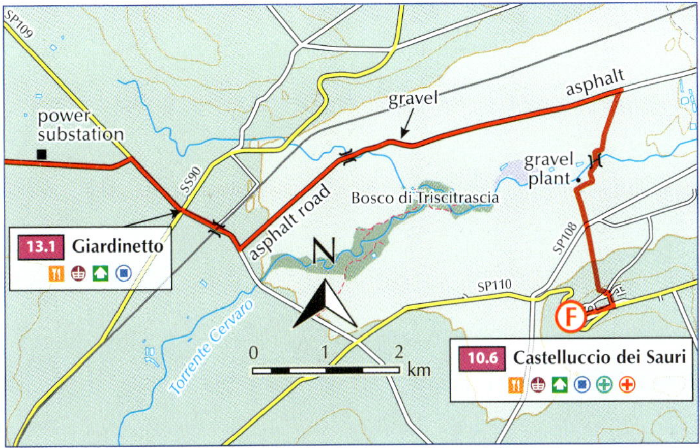

With Castelluccio dei Sauri just visible on the hill ahead, go right then through an intersection. Cross the **railway**, take the first left onto an asphalt road following the trajectory of the tracks (lying 300m to the left), and cross over a **drainage canal**. The road turns to gravel and after it returns to asphalt, turn right toward the hill. Cross over the Torrente Cervaro, turn left at a **gravel plant**, cross the SP108, and ascend on asphalt to **Castelluccio dei Sauri**. At the end of this road, now in town, turn left onto Via Circonvallazione and immediately turn right, arriving in four blocks on the town's main street, Via Roma. Turn right then fork right after Piazza Cesare Battisti onto Via IV Novembre to reach the plain white Chiesa del Santissimo Salvatore.

10.6KM CASTELLUCCIO DEI SAURI (ELEV 279M, POP 2024) (479KM)

Castelluccio, a rural town committed to agriculture, witnesses constant depopulation. Its modern, trim, and straightforward layout is a result of the devastating earthquake of 1980. In its hey-day as a Byzantine settlement, the Eastern Emperor Leo III, known as the Isaurian (hence the addendum 'dei Sauri') installed one of his cavalry units in the territory. Today, the local hippodrome is home to horse racing at a national level. The town is quiet, with the main services centered around the modest Madonna delle Grazie Church.

Parrocchia SS. Salvatore O Pr R S Z 2/2, €Donation, Via Basilio Leone, 43, tel 324 699 6268. Reservations required; call or WhatsApp priest Don Dafridus.

STAGE 24

Castelluccio dei Sauri to Ordona

Start	Chiesa del Santissimo Salvatore, Castelluccio dei Sauri
Finish	Church of San Leone Vescovo, Ordona
Duration	5¼hr
Distance	20km
Total ascent	137m
Total descent	297m
Difficulty	Easy
Percentage paved	85%
Lodgings	Ordona 20km

An easy, though unshaded, day of walking through immense farms under the Tavoliere's wide-open skies, accompanied by the music of wind turbines. Ordona's Herdonia archeological site (just a few hundred meters into tomorrow's stage) is worth a visit if you are willing to brave the lack of signage, tour guides, descriptions, and services. The related museum requires advance reservations. There are no intermediate services, so plan enough food and water.

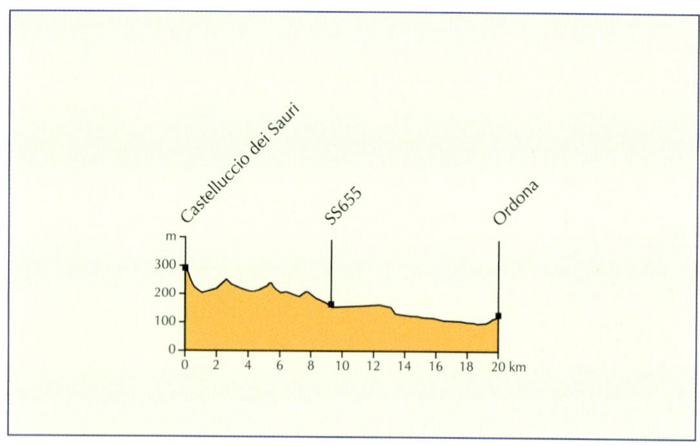

From the church, keep downhill one block, passing the municipio on your right, and reach a viewpoint over dozens of wind turbines spinning in the constant Tavoliere

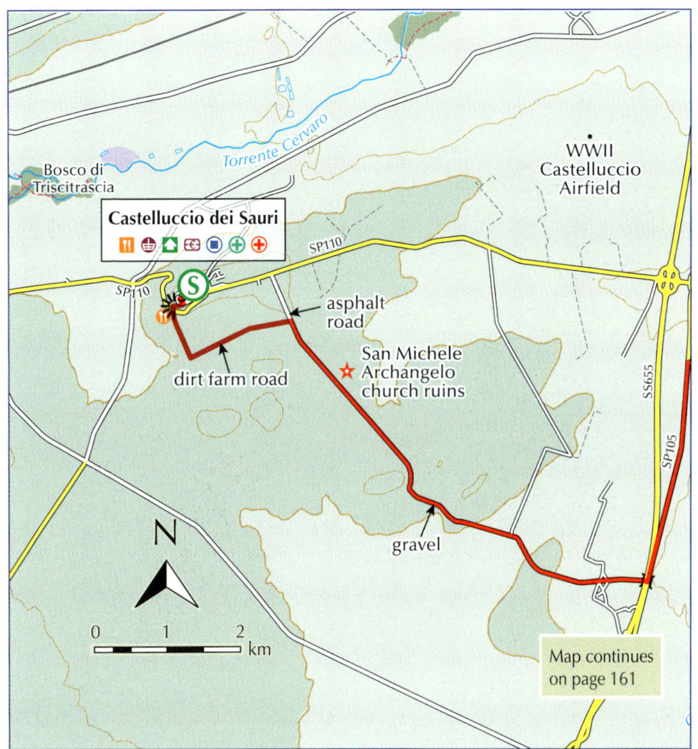

breeze. Go left onto Via Circonvallazione and, after a hairpin right turn, find a wide downhill sidewalk. Cross the **SP110**, keep the restaurant on your right, and take a downhill gravel road. At the bottom, turn left onto a dirt farm road (muddy in wet weather) and climb a low rise. Turn right onto an asphalt road and pass the abandoned **Church of San Michele Archangelo** then fields and properties.

Climb a gentle hill to what becomes a paradise of solitude, soon seeing the town of Ascoli Satriano on the far ridge to the right. The road ascends and descends among olive groves, giving a first glimpse of Ordona to the left in the far distance. Pass under the **SS655 Bradanica** (**9.2km**) and turn left onto the **SP105**, a former highway where the odd car still zooms by. Toward the top of a hill, watch carefully for signs to turn right onto an asphalt road then immediately turn left onto a gravel road toward wind turbines. Zigzag past a farmhouse, cross fields, cross the **SP110**, and take a wide gravel road. The SP110 also leads to Ordona.

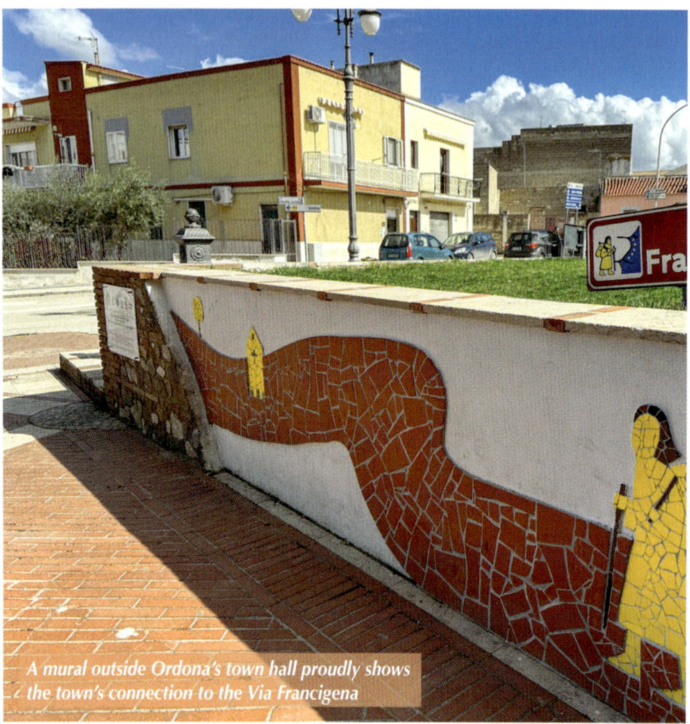

A mural outside Ordona's town hall proudly shows the town's connection to the Via Francigena

Toward the left, across the highways, was the World War 2 **Castelluccio Airfield**, which, from 1944, was the base of the 451st Bombardment Group (Heavy) of the US 15th Air Force.

Soon turn right at the wind turbine, but then immediately fork left on an initially imperceptible then otherwise unmarked gravel road around the hill. In the fields on the left lie the ruins of Ponte Romano di Herdonia. A lonely metal sign leads to a right turn toward Ordona, lying on the low ridge ahead. After bisecting the fields on a dirt track, turn left under a **rusted pipeline bridge** then immediately turn right over a stream and turn left onto gravel and cross the railway (train 100m further). Turn left uphill onto Viale Stazione to pass the modern, yellow Municipio di Ordona and head along Via d'Aloia to the Church of San Leone Vescovo (**10.7km**).

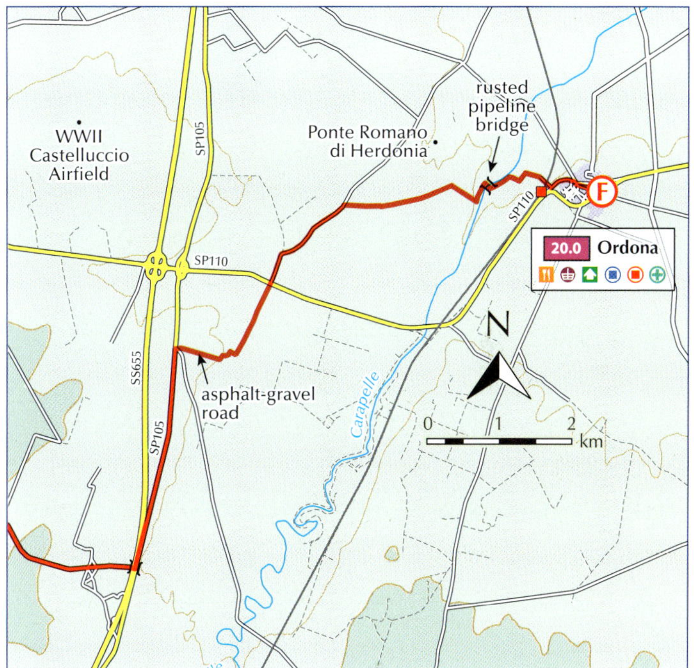

20KM ORDONA (ELEV 117M, POP 2805) (459.1KM)

Another agricultural town and key stopover for legions, exiles, and wanderers along the Via Traiana, the old Herdonia thrived following Norman and Swabian rule until conquered by the Aragonese in 1484, who demolished the ancient site for good. The 'new' town of Ordona, in its current location, was born as one of the five royal towns established by the Bourbons in a process of repopulating the Tavoliere.

- **B&B Corbo Francesca** Pr R K Br Cr W Z 2/3, €-/25/50/-/-/-, Via Raffaello 7, tel 339 789 3631, corbo.fra@tiscali.it. Closed November 1 to March 18 inclusive.

- **La Casa di Nonna Lina** O Pr R Br W S 2/4, €-/35/50/80/90/-, Via Irpinia 3/A, tel 335 825 4553, lacasadinonnalina@gmail.com. Breakfast included.

STAGE 25

Ordona to Stornara

Start	Church of San Leone Vescovo, Ordona
Finish	Church of San Rocco, Stornara
Duration	5¼hr
Distance	20.3km
Total ascent	141m
Total descent	148m
Difficulty	Easy
Percentage paved	81%
Lodgings	Stornara 20.3km, Cerignola 34.7km

The elevation changes of today's route afford wide views toward the Gargano headland. The stage includes welcome and convenient refreshments at Stornarella, 15.3km into the day. Take time in Stornara to enjoy the colorful murals in what is otherwise a plain agricultural town.

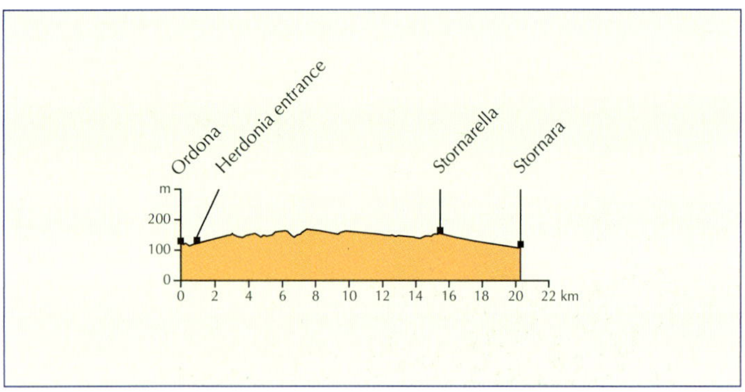

On Via d'Aloia, with the church to your right, go straight then turn left a block before the municipio, threading south-west through town on Via Soldato Leone Sinigaglia. At its end, cross the **SP110** onto a gravel farm road then take the first quiet, arrow-straight asphalt road out of town to arrive,100m later, at the unmarked entrance to the **Scavi Archeologici di Herdonia** (**0.9km**).

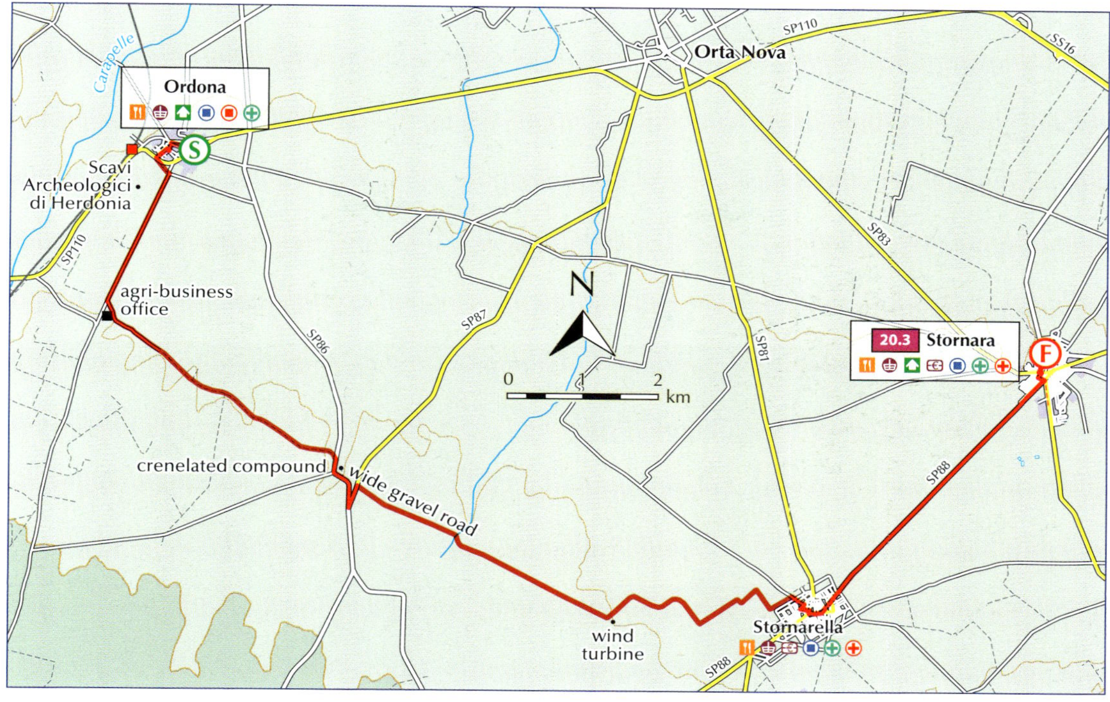

Carapelle
Ordona
Scavi
Archeologici
di Herdonia
SP110
Orta Nova
SP110
SS16
SP83
agri-business
office
SP86
SP87
N
0
1
2
km
SP81
20.3
Stornara
crenelated compound
wide gravel road
SP88
wind
turbine
Stornarella
SP88

A statue of San Rocco, pilgrim saint, is illuminated against one of the many Stornara murals

To visit this undeveloped and underappreciated site, enter the gate, where it feels like you are entering a private farm. Head toward the large, white palazzo, 200m onward, and veer to its right on a narrow path. Follow the path and feel free to explore the **archeological site**, which since its excavation has been covered with earth again to protect the remains. The ancient city of Herdonia, located on the Via Traiana, was the site of the 212BC Battle of Herdonia in which the Carthaginians under Hannibal defeated the Roman army. Remains of a Roman theater, baths, market, and forum are just perceptible above ground.

Keep along the straight road and, after 1.5km, follow signs to turn left onto a gravel road. Pass the Lomaestro **agri-business office** and head back to fields scattered with massive wind turbines testament to the region's relentless wind. Ignore all sidetracks, pass a cattle paddock (where the cows drink from old bathtubs) in a shallow valley, and, after a swift ascent, descend more steeply into a deeper valley to a T-junction. Turn right onto the **SP86**, uphill around a **crenelated compound** and a watchtower. At the road beyond, turn left toward the compound but just before it, follow signs right onto a wider gravel road back into the vastness of the Tavoliere.

Stornarella starts to appear soon, followed by Stornara beyond. After a vineyard, and just before a **wind turbine**, zigzag along a path to **Stornarella**. Go straight at the first stop sign, turn right at the next one, then turn left in a block and a half. Turn right in three blocks onto Corso Garibaldi to the municipio and main piazza (**14.4km**, food, groceries, ATM, bus, pharmacy, clinic).

Stornarella, an agricultural town with a desolate feel, saw one of the bloodiest historical firefights of post-unification rebellion in Southern Italy in 1862, when 200 brigands on horseback, commanded by the gang leader Giuseppe Schiavone, faced II Squadron of the Lucca Cavalry Regiment, commanded by Lieutenant Leuci. The cavalrymen of the royal army received help from Stornarella's locals and, in a three-hour battle, defeated the bandits.

Turn left onto Corso Vittorio Emanuele III, leaving town. At a large fountain, fork left onto the **SP88**, where its pink bike lane makes a beeline for **Stornara**. In town, turn left at the intersection onto Via Regina Margherita then turn right onto Corso V. Emanuele III to find the Church of San Rocco, pilgrim saint (**4.9km**).

20.3KM STORNARA (ELEV 109M, POP 5772) (438.8KM)

Named after the many *storni* (starlings) that glide across the wheatfields in harvest season, the town sheltered many of the Arab population when they were driven out of Lucera by Charles of Anjou's troops. The remains of the tower served as a customs post on the drove road, and a peculiarity of its buildings is the lively street art that has developed since 2018.

- **Foresteria Parrocchia San Rocco** Do Via di Corato 3, tel 0885 431 302. Advance communication is difficult; check for services on arrival.
- **B&B Piazza Matteotti** O Pr R Cr S Z 2/4, €-/35/60-/-/-/-, Via Genovesi 11/B, tel 328 967 3240, valerio80@me.com.
- **B&B Antico Borgo** O Pr R Br Cr W S 10/20, €-/35/60/70/80/-, Via Regina Margherita 2, tel 328 550 8079.

One of Stornara's many murals

STAGE 26

Stornara to Cerignola

Start	Church of San Rocco, Stornara
Finish	Basilica Cathedral of San Pietro Apostolo, Cerignola
Duration	4½hr
Distance	17.9km
Total ascent	97m
Total descent	84m
Difficulty	Easy
Percentage paved	40%
Lodgings	Cerignola 17.9km

From extensive fields of crops, the scenery changes to vast olive groves, not to mention scattered vineyards and fruit orchards. This flat stage could be covered on a calm, direct road, the Via Don E. Tazzoli, in about 12km, but, at the cost of a few extra kilometers, the Francigena stewards have paid heed to your feet, guiding you onto soft paths first to the north then to the south of the road. There are no intermediate services, so carry all supplies.

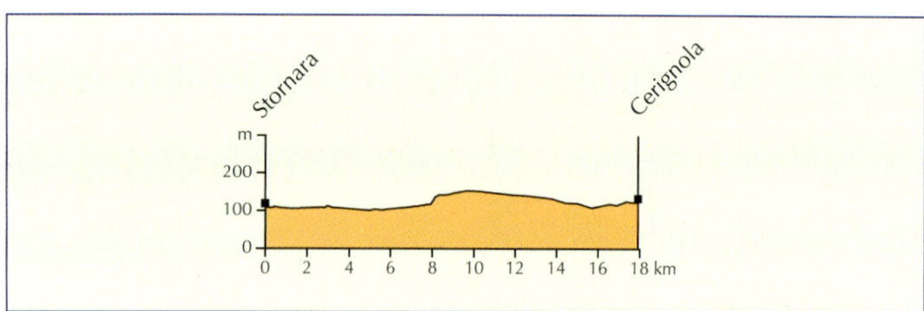

With the Church of San Rocco on your right, go straight for two blocks, turn left onto the SP83/**SP88**/Via Regina Margherita, and two blocks later, after the San Rocco statue, turn right onto the main arterial road connecting Stornara and Cerignola, **Via Don E. Tazzoli**.

Leave town, following bas-relief Stations of the Cross and Cyprus trees to pass the **cemetery**, where you are struck by the change of scenery, with large olive groves replacing wide-open fields. Just after a vineyard, and before the top of a low hill, turn left onto a gravel road between rows of olive trees then turn left at a T-junction by a

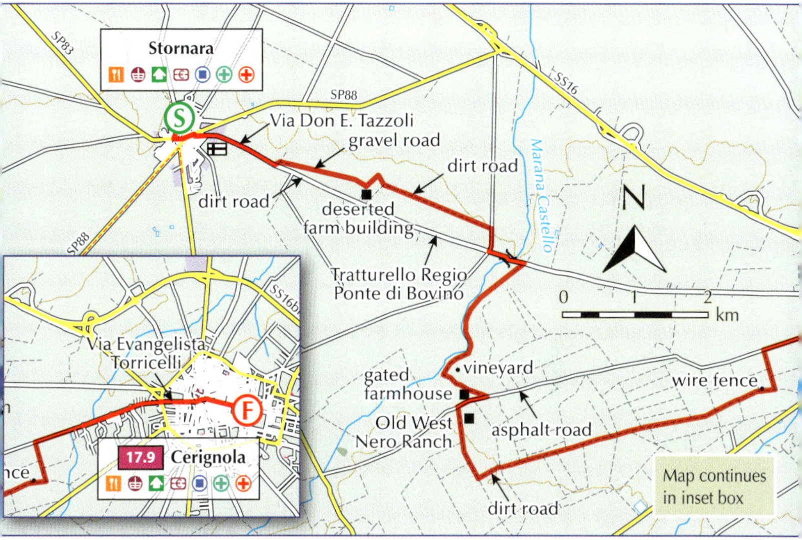
Stornara
SP83
SP88
Via Don E. Tazzoli
gravel road
dirt road
dirt road
deserted
farm building
Tratturello Regio
Ponte di Bovino
Marana Castello
SS16
N
0
1
2
km
vineyard
gated
farmhouse
Old West
Nero Ranch
asphalt road
wire fence
dirt road
Map continues
in inset box
SS16bis
Via Evangelista
Torricelli
17.9
Cerignola

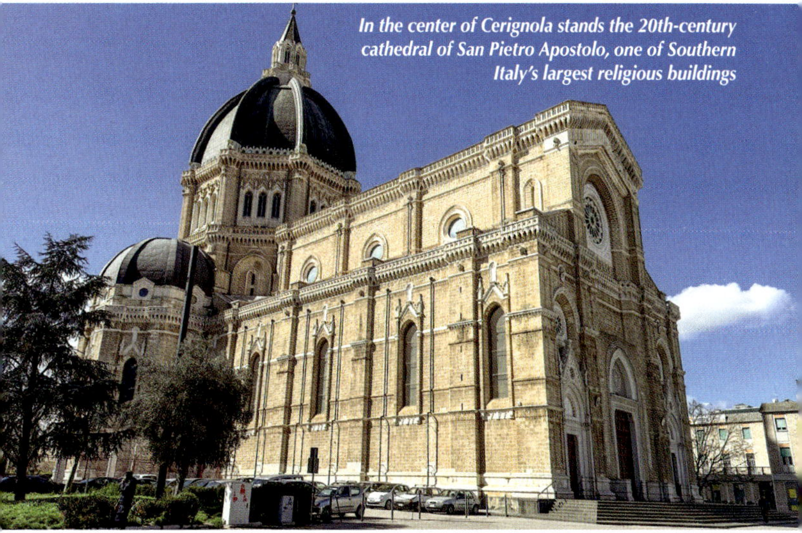
In the center of Cerignola stands the 20th-century cathedral of San Pietro Apostolo, one of Southern Italy's largest religious buildings

deserted farm building. Turn next right and soon veer left onto a wide dirt track under wind turbines, passing more olive trees, vineyards, and a solar farm. Turn left then turn right back onto the main road and take a **bridge** over the Marana Castello stream (**5.4km**) after which a right turn onto a dirt track leads back into orchards on the south side of the road.

Curve along the very same stream (which becomes a drainage channel), turn left uphill after a vineyard, pass a gated farmhouse, and, at a T-junction, turn right onto an asphalt road past a modern vineyard. Take a first left into a neighborhood of deserted homes marked '**Old West Nero Ranch**,' where fields predominate once again. Pass a cluster of homes and, before the asphalt ends, turn left onto a dirt road, with views to the Basilica Cattedrale of Cerignola ahead.

The **Basilica Cattedrale di San Pietro Apostolo** is known locally as the Duomo Tonti, named after Paolo Tonti, who, in the late 19th century, requested a neo-Gothic cathedral be built. Completed in 1934, the basilica earned the title of cathedral, replacing the 11th–13th-century Parrocchia di San Francesco d'Assisi – a church with six domes in Gothic, Romanesque, and Byzantine styles, which has retained most of its original features despite a destructive earthquake in 1731.

Leave the road, turn left after a wire fence, and, at the end of the road, turn right, arriving on the boulevard of **Via Evangelista Torricelli**, which leads directly to the grand Basilica Cattedrale (**12.4km**).

17.9KM CERIGNOLA (ELEV 127M, POP 56,978) (420.8KM)

Cerignola is a pretty city with a Roman mile marker in place: the inscribed number LXXXI positions it at approximately 81 Roman miles from Benevento. The 1503 Battle of Cerignola has gone down in history as the scene of a French and Spanish clash where the latter triumphed. Although little remains from the era due to the 1731 earthquake, the medieval fiefdom is evidenced in Cerignola's circular layout.

Parrocchia S. Trifone Martire Do R S Z 1/2, €10, Via dei Tigli, tel 0885 448550 or 349 074 7825. The parish is being restored (2024) so sleeping arrangements are in a sports hall with showers. Closed in August.

B&B La Casetta Pr Do R Br Cr S Z 4/7 & 4/13, €25/50/60/75/90/110, Vico I Melfi 1, tel 339 616 3315, dipilatomaurizio@gmail.com. Closed at Christmas and mid August.

STAGE 27

Cerignola to Canosa di Puglia

Start	Basilica Cathedral of San Pietro Apostolo, Cerignola
Finish	Basilica di San Sabino, Canosa di Puglia
Duration	5hr
Distance	19.3km
Total ascent	99m
Total descent	110m
Difficulty	Easy
Percentage paved	83%
Lodgings	Canosa di Puglia 19.3km

A quiet, pleasant rural route recalls yesterday's olive groves and vineyards while traveling to the day's best feature: a Roman bridge, part of the original Via Traiana. Although Canosa is half the size of Cerignola, its historic center has a similar charm. Plan on bringing food and water since there are no intermediate services.

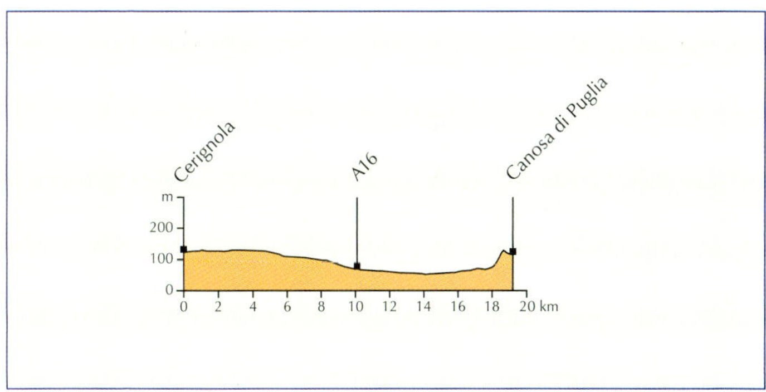

Continue on Via Roma, past the cathedral, and in a half-dozen blocks, turn right onto Viale Giuseppe Di Vittorio. At its end, turn right onto Viale di Levante and after two and a half blocks, turn left onto **Via Teano**, which heads directly out of town into open country where it becomes Via Scarafone and passes wineries then Tenuta Ripalta Alessandra Leone (**4.1km** **Tenuta Ripalta Alessandra Leone** Pr Do R Br Dr S 2/3, €Donation, Via Scarafone 17/A, tel 392 012 8783. Closes unpredictably).

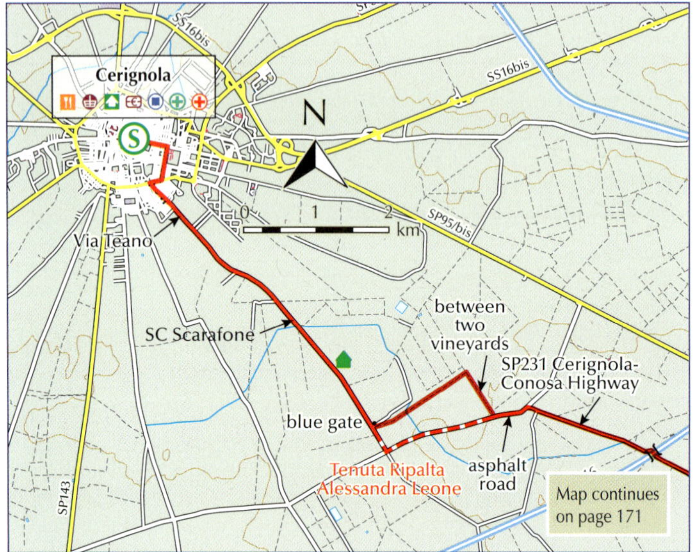

Soon Canosa appears to the left in the distance, and the route goes through a fenceless **blue gate** on the left after which turn left. An easier option is to simply continue to the next asphalt road and turn left there. Immediately fork right onto an asphalt road to pass houses as it turns to gravel then ends. Turn right between two vineyards without an obvious path then turn left onto a road and pass a seemingly abandoned church and tower (marked as 'Le Torri' on maps). After a curve, turn right with Canosa straight ahead. Catch a bridge over the **A16**/E842 motorway (**6km**), nicknamed the 'motorway of the two seas' ('Autostrada dei Due Mari') since it connects Naples on the Tyrrhenian and Bari on the Adriatic. Turn right onto the **SP231** Cerignola–Canosa highway then cross an interchange and after passing under the highway bridge, veer right toward 'Ponte Romano.' In 50m go left to the cobblestones of the **Roman bridge**.

The **Roman bridge** (1st–2nd century AD) spanning the Ofanto River connected the southern ports of Barium (Bari) and Brindisi with Rome. On the riverbanks, the notorious battle between the Romans and the Carthaginians, led by Hannibal, took place during the Second Punic War (216BC). It was rebuilt in the 18th century, reusing original materials and preserving the Roman isodomic squares, triangular spurs, and pyramidal cones, as well as the former five arches. The adjacent wooden tower offers a good vantage point for a complete view of this well-tended structure.

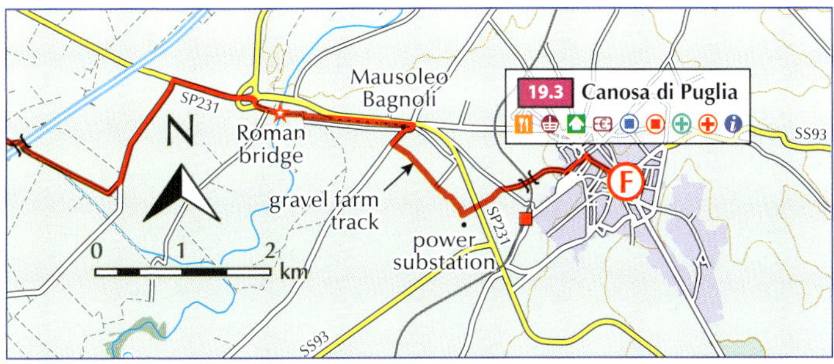

After crossing, turn right to cross a modern bridge then immediately go left onto a canal-side path toward town, passing the brick ruin of the Roman **Mauseoleo Bagnoli** after which turn right. The road curves right (counter-intuitively away from Canosa) and after 100m turn left onto a gravel farm track among vines and olives. Before a **power substation**, turn left then cross over the **SP231** as the road becomes the uphill Via Anfiteatro and passes under the railway to Canosa di Puglia's first streets. At the end of the road, turn left and cross the Piazza Umberto I, with its Padre Pio statue, then veer right downhill onto Via Gramsci. At the next piazza (statue of the Virgin Mary), turn right downhill through the charming historic district to the Basilica di San Sabino (**9.1km**).

The bridge across the Ofanto River was originally built by the Romans in the 1st–2nd century AD (photo: Lorenzo Scaraggi)

19.3KM CANOSA DI PUGLIA (ELEV 131M, POP 27,943) (401.6KM)

Canosa is rich with historical monuments celebrating its Daunian, Hellenistic, Roman, and medieval past. For those curious about Magna Graecia, head to the Palazzo Sinesi museum. To see treasures of Roman Canusium (Canosa di Puglia), visit the Ferrara and Lomuscio thermal baths, several hypogea, the temples to Minerva and Jupiter, and the complex at the Parco Archeologico di San Leucio, with the largest remaining 6th-century early Christian basilica in Puglia. The 11th-century Basilica di San Sabino honors the bishop of the same name, who made this cathedral the very first diocese in Puglia in the 6th century AD. The bishop's throne is beautifully preserved, the legs of which are carved into elephants. Beside the sanctuary recalling Jerusalem's Holy Sepulchre is the small 1111 Mausoleum of Boemondo d'Altavilla, Prince of Taranto and leader of the First Crusade. An excellent Via Francigena association offers assistance to pilgrims: tel 376 009 4395 or 347 481 3693, viafrancigenacanosadipuglia@gmail.com, www.viafrancigenacanosa.com.

Il Rifugio di Rick O Pr Do R Br Dr W S 1/2, €20/20/40/-/-/-, Via Ammiraglio Caracciolo 17, tel 347 823 3796, riccardoasselta01@gmail.com. Prices are €5 higher without the credenziale.

Parrocchia Santi Francesco e Biagio O Do K S €Donation, Via Matteotti 1, tel, 329 438 8999, doncarminecatalano@tiscali.it. No bedding provided. Advance communication is difficult; check for services on arrival.

Basilica – Concattedrale San Sabino O Do S €Donation, Piazza San Sabino 1, tel 0883 662 035, donfelicebacco@libero.it. Advance communication is difficult; check for services on arrival.

Casa di Nonna Lia O Pr Do Dr R K W S 3/7, €15–20/15–20/-/-/-/-, Via F. Rossi 56, tel 347 347 6119 or 327 682 5798, casadinonnalia@gmail.com. The communal dinner is held at the pilgrim community center nearby.

Domus Al Corso Guest House O Pr Do R K Br Cr W S Z 10/28 & 10/28, €35/50/65/90/106, Via Guglielmo Oberdan 134 and Via Ettore Carafa 11, tel 389 795 6788, canosa@domusalcorso.it, www.domusalcorso.it.

STAGE 28

Canosa di Puglia to Andria

Start	Basilica di San Sabino, Canosa di Puglia
Finish	Cattedrale di Santa Maria Assunta, Andria
Duration	6¼hr
Distance	24.1km
Total ascent	267m
Total descent	221m
Difficulty	Moderate due to length and several hills
Percentage paved	73%
Lodgings	Andria 24.1km

In this indisputably characteristic Puglian countryside of vast olive groves, this stage should dispel the notions of Puglia being both flat and asphalt underfoot and therefore an unenjoyable stage. The undulations today set the first idea to rest, and the quiet greenery of tranquil roads does the same to the second. The result is a surprisingly engaging and relaxed walk to the historic center of an interesting town. Bring sustenance since there are no intermediate services.

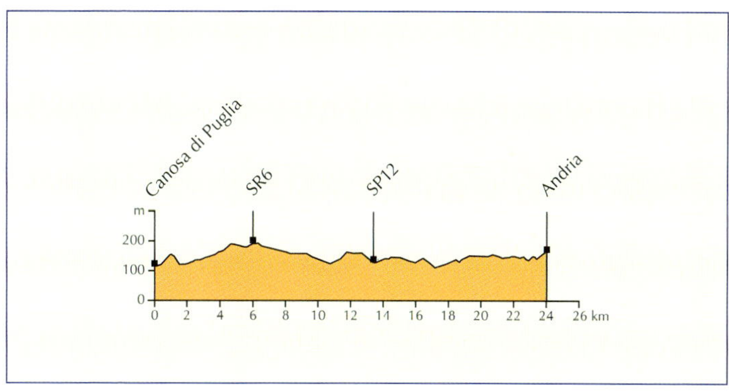

With the Basilica of San Sabino on your left, curve uphill with the SS93 then, in a few blocks and after an iron fence of the Scuola Media building, turn half right onto uphill **Via Roosevelt**, which eventually narrows into a lane leading back into the silver green quiet of olive groves.

Vast olive orchards like these between Canosa and Andria help the region of Puglia produce almost half of Italy's olive oil

Merge right with the next road uphill to turn left uphill just before the SR6 highway overpass (**4.4km**). Turn right at the SP181 between two yellowish walls. Cross over the highway on a **bridge**, looking back at the thin strip of Canosa's buildings, then turn left at the first intersection onto the straight **SP182**. At its end turn left onto a gravel track (still the SP182) winding gradually downhill. At the end, turn right onto asphalted Contrada Santa Brigida (the old highway to Andria), which also turns to gravel, for a splendid jaunt among olive trees, accompanied by the melodies of birdsong. Crossing a small **bridge**, pass a mile marker and soon Andria appears ahead.

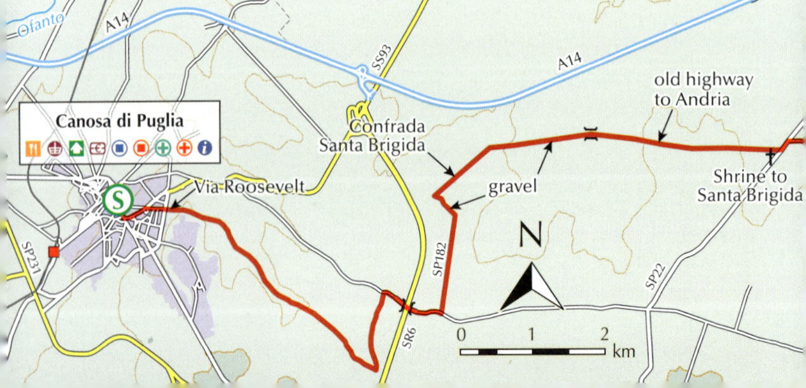

Reach the **road** where you ignore the road sign indicating 17km to Andria and instead turn left, heading toward Barletta. A scant 100m later, turn right onto a quiet road opposite a shrine to **Santa Brigida** (now following a sign for Andria), pass the **Tenuta Zagaria winery**, and climb up then down as Andria reveals itself to be surprisingly close. At the road's end take the second left at a sign for Castel del Monte (a 20km drive) then fork left uphill between dry-stone walls. Now a UNESCO World Heritage Site, Frederick II's Castel del Monte was built in an octagonal shape, which has perplexed historians, and the obsession with the number eight in mathematical precision fascinates visitors.

Arrive in a modern, residential area of town, making out the three-pointed white towers of Andria's churches. Fork left at the first **traffic circle** onto uphill Via Croci, pass through Porta Nuova into the medieval alleys, and pass the Church of San Domenico. Turn left at the road's end, by an imposing palazzo, and arrive at the Cattedrale di Santa Maria Assunta (**19.7km**) with the main piazza just behind it.

24.1KM ANDRIA (ELEV 161M, POP 97,146) (377.5KM)

Andria boasts the sublime Norman Cattedrale Santa Maria Assunta in Cielo within which lie relics of Saint Richard and, according to tradition, a thorn from Jesus's crown of thorns. The bell tower, the Chiesa di San Francesco, the Chiesa di San Domenico, the Chiesa di Sant'Agostino, and the Diocesan Museum within the Palazzo Vescovile (episcopal palace) are among the city's architectural and historic gems. Andria's culinary claim to fame is its Burrata di Andria cheese. In the 1920s, a farm near Andria, searching for a way to preserve its cheese, created a stretched cow's milk pouch which was then stuffed with shredded mozzarella and cream. Over time, the family perfected the art, and the traditional method is still used today much to everyone's delight.

B&B Palazzo Ducale O Pr R Br Cr W S Z 6/15, €-/40/60/80/90, 1° Vicolo Vaglio 10, tel 0883 884276 or 347 659 7431, archico@tiscali.it, www.bbpalazzoducale.com. Group offers available.

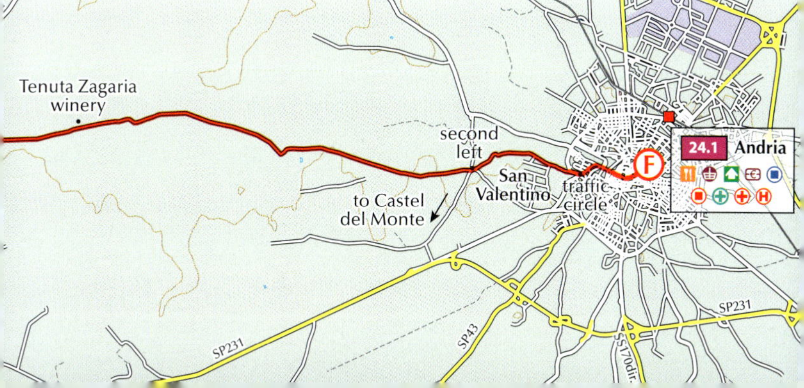

STAGE 29

Andria to Corato

Start	Cattedrale di Santa Maria Assunta, Andria
Finish	Chiesa Matrice di Santa Maria Maggiore, Corato
Duration	3½hr
Distance	13.9km
Total ascent	113m
Total descent	38m
Difficulty	Easy
Percentage paved	57%
Lodgings	Corato 13.9km, Ruvo di Puglia 26.1km

A short, quite flat stage among olives means you either have time to enjoy a slow morning in Andria or a long afternoon in Corato. Otherwise, if you continue on to Ruvo di Puglia, ensure you stock up in Andria.

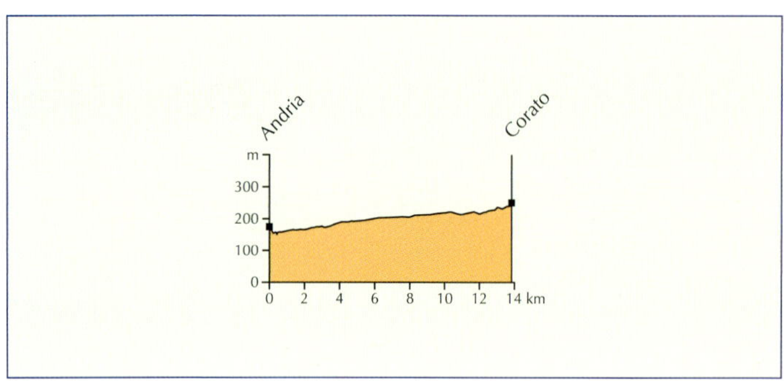

Keep the cathedral facade to your left and go straight, slightly downhill, passing the Palazzo Ducale after which turn right downhill and follow Francigena waymarking through the labyrinthine old town onto Via Sant'Angelo then Via M. Montessori. Pass **soccer pitches** and return to more olive groves set apart by tall but tippy dry-stone walls. When the road ends, turn left onto **Contrada Macchia di Rosa**, which veers right at the upcoming fork to narrow, and pass under the SP231 highway to end up at a highway entrance.

Turn right (sign for Bari) and after the slip road on the left, join a gravel road, which will mostly carry you to Corato. Pass an **abandoned farmhouse** then at a 2m stone wall

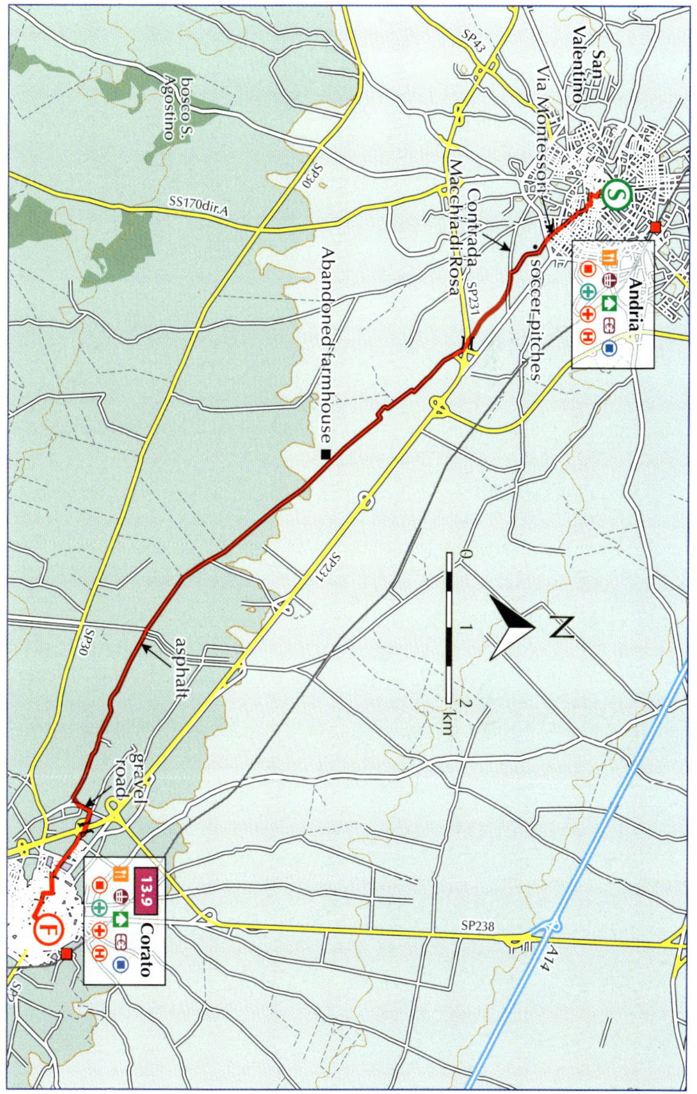

San Valentino
Via Montessori
SP43
bosco S. Agostino
SP30
SS170dir.A
Contrada Macchia di Rosa
SP231
soccer pitches
S
Andria
Abandoned farmhouse
SP231
0
1
2
km
N
asphalt
SP30
gravel road
13.9
Corato
F
SP238
A14

and gate marked 'Giuseppe Vendola,' turn left onto a gravel road to Corato's outskirts. After 100m, merge left onto a road then 200m later, turn right to cross the **SP231** on a bridge and turn left onto Via G. Gigante, in **Corato**. At the road end, jog right onto Via Carellario da Napoli then, at the T-junction, turn right onto Via Fanfulla da Lodi. After four blocks turn left. Cross Via Garibaldi into the old town, pass through Piazza di Vagno, and take a sidewalk half a dozen steps above it. Descend similar steps and, in 50m, turn left to the Chiesa Matrice di Santa Maria Maggiore and its squarish bell tower.

A narrow alley near Corato's duomo

13.9KM CORATO (ELEV 237M, POP 47,033) (363.6KM)

Corato's name derives from the Roman patrician Caius Oratus to whom the territory was ceded following the Second Punic War. Lombard influence is felt along the maze of lanes connected by overhanging arches and the many underground tunnels. The Palazzo Gioia is testament to the old Norman castle. Built in the 11th century, with very few original features remaining following the 1627 earthquake, the Chiesa di Santa Maria Maggiore managed to retain Romanesque flair in the bell tower, the main portal, and the 'Flight of Alexander' representation in the bas-relief of the facade. In Corato, the Knights Hospitaller of Jerusalem had two churches outside the city walls: the 12th-century Chiesa di San Vito and the Parrocchia Santa Maria Greca. The city's lovely municipal theater, inaugurated in 1874, hosts regular shows.

Parrocchia San Gerardo Maiella – Missionari Redentoristi Do Via Castel del Monte 115, tel 080 372 0048, corato@redentoristi.it. Advance communication is difficult; check for services on arrival.

B&B La Dimora O Pr R K Br Cr S Z 7/10, €-/40/50/60/70/-, Via Gisotti, 4, tel 350 023 2743.

STAGE 30

Corato to Ruvo di Puglia

Start	Chiesa Matrice di Santa Maria Maggiore, Corato
Finish	Concattedrale Santa Maria Assunta, Ruvo di Puglia
Distance	12.2km
Duration	3¼hr
Total ascent	126m
Total descent	96m
Difficulty	Easy
Percentage paved	70%
Lodgings	Ruvo di Puglia 12.2km, Bitonto 30.6km

A straight 7.5km by car becomes 12.1km on the pilgrim walking route, which is fine considering the quiet scenery of olive trees and the reward of the beauty of Ruvo's Romanesque *concattedrale* (co-cathedral) whose exterior contains fine medieval workmanship. With no services along the way, plan ahead.

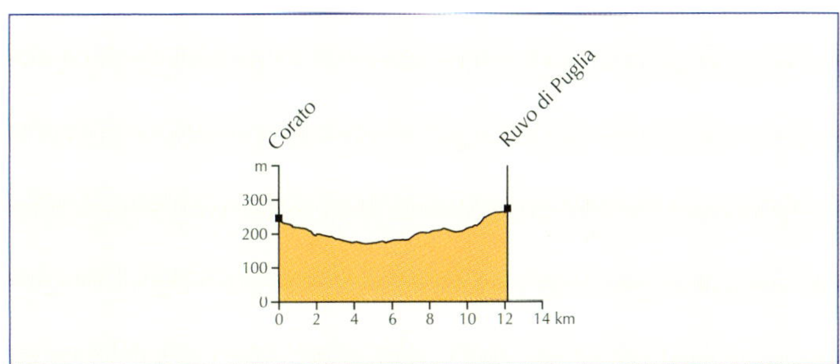

Continue downhill at the cathedral, cross Corso Cavour, and, after a few blocks, turn right onto Via Parini to pass through a park, cross a boulevard, and cross the railway at the **station**.

Turn left after the tracks onto a windy road that, after a **wastewater plant**, becomes gravel and snakes downhill between dry-stone walls to pass over a channelized stream. Climb up the other side, go straight at a crumbling shrine, join **Viale del Brigante** and gently descend to go through the **gate stanchions** of a one-time estate. In a section of orchards bounded by low concrete walls, watch carefully for an arrow to turn left onto another road. At its end turn right onto another asphalt road, cross the **SP23** onto a dirt track, and take the next left fork. Cross the **SP85** onto a wide dirt road and arrive at an intersection with the Corato–Terlizzi road as Ruvo di Puglia appears only a couple of kilometers away. Turn left downhill onto this road, turn first right, and, keeping the **Parrocchia Santa Famiglia** with its conical roof on your left, cross a boulevard. Turn left after a long block onto the very wide Via Palmiro Togliatti. At the play area in a shaded park, turn right to reach the center of town with a left turn onto

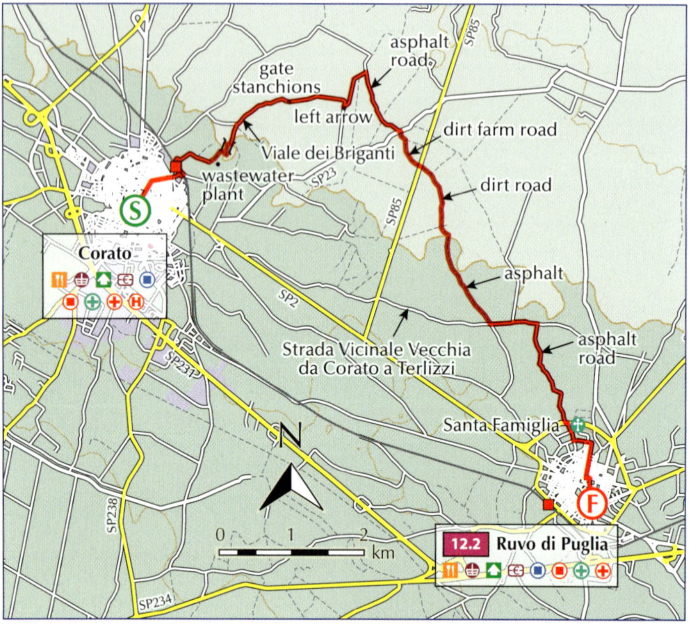

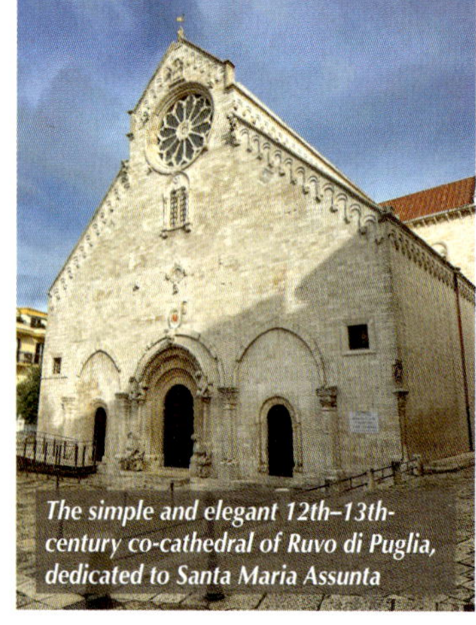

The simple and elegant 12th–13th-century co-cathedral of Ruvo di Puglia, dedicated to Santa Maria Assunta

Corso Giovanni Jatta. Turn right after one block and reach the beautiful Romanesque Concattedrale Santa Maria Assunta.

12.2KM RUVO DI PUGLIA (ELEV 257M, POP 24,347) (351.4KM)

An essential Roman *statio* (post station) along the Via Traiana, the ancient city of Rubi/Rubo is well documented in historical records, and the Jatta National Archeological Museum is a treasure trove of artifacts from as early as the 4th century BC. The magnificent 12th–13th century Concattedrale Santa Maria Assunta has withstood many earthquakes (1627 and 1628) and depopulation during the disastrous 1656 plague. Today, it remains an ornate masterpiece of Gothic and rural Romanesque, with a beautiful 12-spoke rose window. The 16th and 17th centuries saw the building of many palatial houses and religious buildings both in and beyond the city walls. Still appealing to the eye today are the Convento di San Domenico, the Chiesa del Purgatorio, and the Chiesa di San Michele Arcangelo.

Casa Fma Sacro Cuore Do R S 10/40, €Donation, Corso Antonio Jatta 19, tel 080 361 3506, direttrice.ruvo@fma-imr.it. €10 donation expected for dorms and €20 for single occupancy. Closed at Christmas, Easter, and for two weeks mid August.

Six successive archways frame the main portal of the concattedrale of Ruvo di Puglia, the inner five decorated with intricate Romanesque carvings as seen in photo detail on the right

STAGE 31

Ruvo di Puglia to Bitonto

Start	Duomo di Santa Maria Assunta, Ruvo di Puglia
Finish	Concattedrale di Santa Maria Assunta, Bitonto
Duration	4¾hr
Distance	18.4km
Total ascent	13m
Total descent	154m
Difficulty	Easy
Percentage paved	37%
Lodgings	18.4km Bitonto

After another day up close and personal with an olive-centric stage, it is no wonder that Bitonto is nicknamed 'City of the Olives.' Today, the flat route is mostly unpaved and has a few interesting monuments. Take the time to study Bitonto's co-cathedral of Santa Maria Assunta, a Romanesque treasure. There are no intermediate services, so plan ahead.

Keeping the co-cathedral on your left, follow plentiful Francigena waymarkers southward out of the confusing streets of the old town. At Piazza Giovanni Bovio (war memorial), fork left at the white baroque facade of the Church of San Domenico onto **Via Madonna delle Grazie SP22** then pick up a pink cycle path out of town.

Once the path ends, continue ahead anyway, cross the railway, and fork right at a pine-tree-shaded **stone chapel**. Cross over the **SP231**, pass the highway's slip roads,

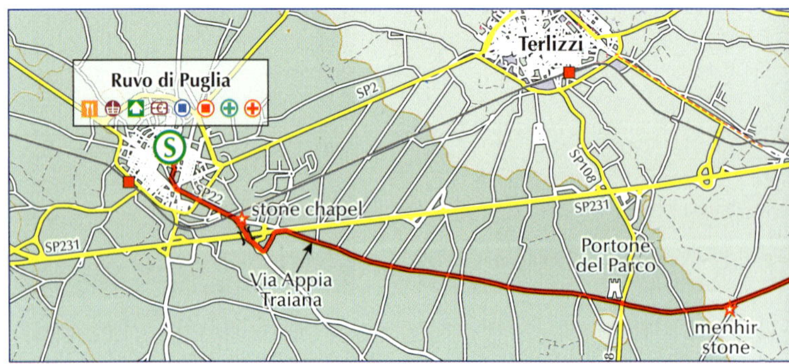

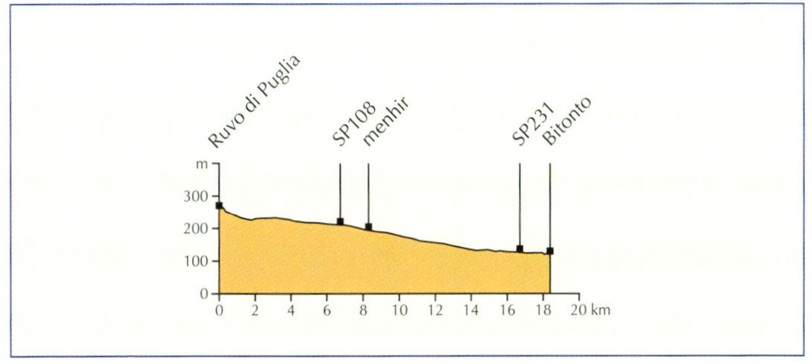

and turn left toward an industrial zone. Pass one of the properties and briefly snuggle next to the highway then fork right at the 'Via Appia Traiana' sign to head mostly parallel to the highway. Pass the freestanding **Portone del Parco** (**6.7km**), an 18th-century archway standing at the junction of the Via Appia Traiana and the access road to the town of Terlizzi, which lies just north. Cross the **SP108** and, enjoying the company of olive trees, cross highways, find shade under pine trees, pass small shrines, and reach a **menhir stone** by a park with local trails. The 16th-century menhir was an ancient territory border marker. After a sign proclaiming you are on an original portion of the Roman Via Traiana, pass the entry to Villa Ilderis (150m off route).

Villa Ilderis, an abandoned masseria comprising 90 hectares of agricultural plots, was first inaugurated in the 11th century by the Ilderis family. It was also a lodging for the Crusader Knights. Many renovations occurred in the 18th century. In 1848, while secretly hosting meetings with the aim of sabotaging the Kingdom of the Two Sicilies, Giovanni Antonio Ilderis was caught by Bourbon authorities and exiled, thus leaving the beautiful villa to its inevitable decline.

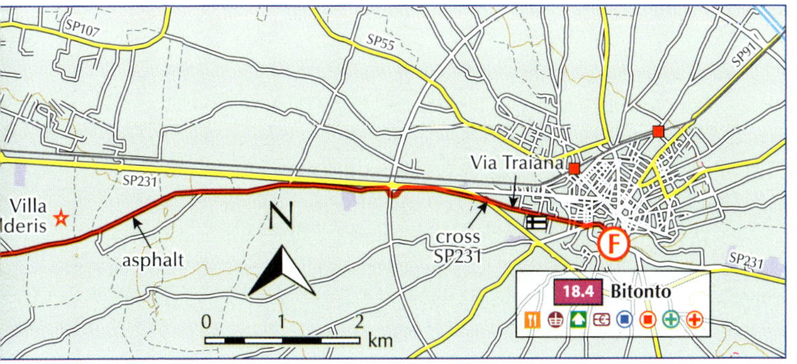

Domed, stone-built farm buildings like this are reminiscent of the trulli, *a building style unique to Puglia*

The road soon turns to asphalt and begins to nuzzle back up to the **SP231** before it turns left to cross the highway and pick up the **Via Traiana**, heading straight for Bitonto. At the end of the grand **cemetery**, turn left onto Via Palombaio into the historic center, finding the Piazza Cattedrale and prized Romanesque Concattedrale di Santa Maria Assunta (**11.7km**).

18.4KM BITONTO (ELEV 124M, POP 53,168) (333.1KM)
Bitonto's Concattedrale di Maria Assunta is a wondrous example of Puglian Romanesque, constructed on the foundations of a Christian shrine with the help of Benedictine monks in the 12th century and initially dedicated to San Valentino. Admire the old Angevin gate to the city at the intricate Porta Baresana. Scattered through town are remnants of the noble Renaissance palaces, such as Palazzo Sylos Calò on Via Giandonato Rogadeo with its pretty loggia and the location of the Galleria Nazionale della Puglia 'Girolamo e Rosaria Devanna,' distinguished by its collection of Italian and European artwork.

B&B Antico Monastero O Pr R Br S 3/9, €-/45/50/80/100/-, Via delle Marteri 35, tel 392 356 2889, anticomonasterobitonto@gmail.com, www.anticomonasterobitonto.it/it.

Palazzo Antica Via Appia O Pr R K Br Cr 7/20, €-/45/80/120/150/170, Via Porta Robustina 34, tel 351 986 7581, gaetanobrattoli60@gmail.com, www.palazzoanticaviappia.it. Group offers for €35 per person.

Arco Gentile B&B O Pr R K Br Cr S Z 4/18, €-/45/60/70/80/90, Vico Don Eustachio Gentile 11, tel 327 816 1054.

STAGE 32

Bitonto to Bari

Start	Concattedrale di Santa Maria Assunta, Bitonto
Finish	Basilica Pontificia San Nicola, Bari
Duration	6¼hr
Distance	23.7km
Total ascent	211m
Total descent	302m
Difficulty	Moderate due to hard surfaces and length
Percentage paved	99%
Lodgings	Bari 23.7km

On today's agenda is the Francigena's fourth sea (after the English Channel, the Ligurian, and the Tyrrhenian), and you experience it in the historically fascinating city of Bari, which is abuzz with street life. The Francigena stewards have altered the route (the old route is shown on the map for reference) to offer more enjoyable seaside walking. Some refreshment is available along the seaside promenade but come well-stocked for the first dozen or so kilometers. The train from Bitonto reaches Bari Centrale station in 30min.

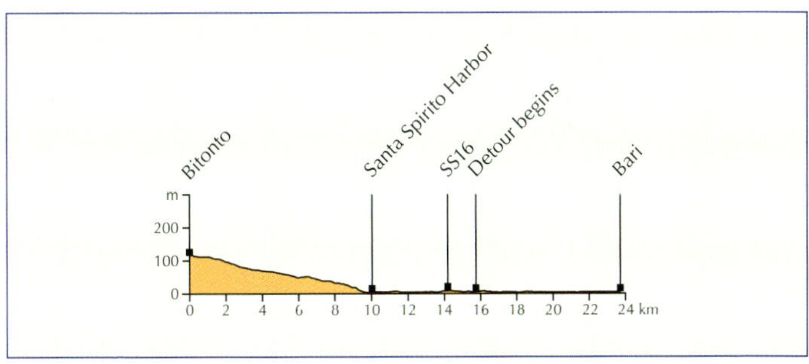

With your back to the co-cathedral, turn right onto a narrow lane and right again after one block to reach three of Bitonto's treasures on Piazza Cavour: Torrione Angioino, San Gaetano Church, and Porta Baresana. Head through the latter onto Corso Vittorio Emanuele II, which becomes **Viale Papa Giovanni XXIII**. keep Piazza Aldo Moro on the left, pass Villa Comunale Park, and, after four blocks, turn left onto Via Giacomo Saracina.

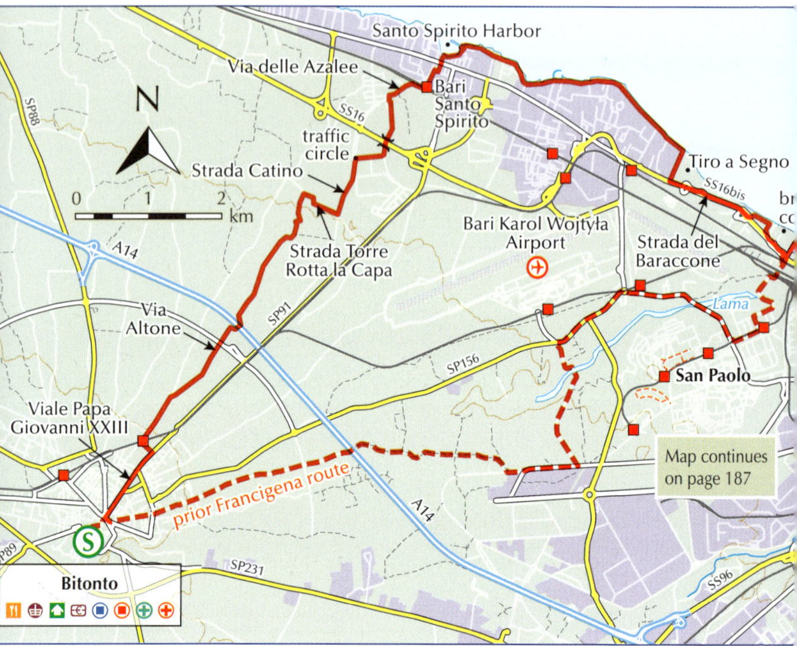

Pass under the railway of the **SS Medici train station**, turn right into a residential neighborhood with olive groves on the right, and be met with your first views of the distant sea. Fork right at the first option, among olive groves; cross onto the narrow lane of **Via Altone**; pass under the highway; and, at the end of the lane, by a vineyard, turn right onto **Strada Torre Rotta la Capa**. At its end, turn left onto Strada Catino, passing apartments which you keep on your right at a right-hand turn on the **traffic circle**. Turn left onto the next street, pass under the **SS16**, and cut through an arm of a park between two soccer pitches. Turn right onto **Via delle Azalee** and turn right before the railway onto a pink sidewalk. Take the tunnel under (train station) Bari Santo Spirito station's railway then keep straight downhill on Via Garibaldi toward the two towers of the Santo Spirito Church. Cross Via Napoli and greet the Adriatic Sea on the lungomare of **Santo Spirito Harbor**, joining the Via Litoranea Connection (**9.7km**). Here begin a 160km stretch of the Francigena that keeps on or near the Adriatic shoreline to Brindisi.

With the shore on your left, enjoy a lively walk along the promenade to Bari, accompanied by joggers and past cafés and restaurants. At the **Tiro a Segno Nazionale** shooting range, hug the edge of the **SS16bis** then return to the sea after a small park. Ahead is a usually dry riverbed crossing where a bridge is being built (writing in spring

2024). If complete, cross it back onto the lungomare; otherwise, detour by turning right onto Via Napoli, pass under the highway and four-arched stone railway bridge then cross the riverbed on a narrow dirt path and continue on what is now the **Lungomare IX Maggio**. At its end, turn right and cross over an inlet then follow the bike lane to another lungomare and pass the **Port of Bari**. As the series of 197 characteristic black streetlamps begin you are walking on the Lungomare di Bari, the longest seaside sidewalk in Europe. Pass a succession of imposing government buildings from the Fascist era (a large barracks, a high school, and the Guardia di Finanza) then arrive at the **Castello Svevo di Bari** where you turn right into the maze-like old town, following signs to the Basilica Cattedrale Metropolitana. Turn left and continue through narrow medieval streets to the Basilica Pontificia San Nicola (**14km**).

23.7KM BARI (ELEV 12M, POP 316,015) (309.3KM)

Origins

Bari came to prominence under the Romans. During Byzantine rule, it was inextricably linked to the Eastern Mediterranean (with oriental influences echoed in its lanes) when the port became a fulcrum of the slave trade and later a major departure point for the Crusades. In 1025, Bari came under the episcopal jurisdiction of the Patriarch of Constantinople.

San Nicola

It was in May 1087, under Norman rule, that the relics of San Nicola arrived, and the townsfolk hurried to host these within the city's now most important building: the Basilica di San Nicola. Completed in the 12th century, it is a fine example of Romanesque architecture and receives thousands of pilgrims yearly. The Festa di San Nicola is celebrated every May. Bari Vecchia (old town) is a delightful maze of alleyways with plenty of cafés and restaurants.

Architectural highlights

Other major architectural sites include the Cattedrale di San Sabino (12th century) and Frederick II's mighty Castello. Opera lovers should visit the Teatro

Petruzzelli; the fourth-largest opera house in Italy, it was built in the mid-19th century and reopened in 2009 following a fire in 1991.

Pilgrim assistance

For pilgrim assistance and a stamp, as well as help finding lodgings, contact the local volunteer group Itineranti, ideally via WhatsApp, tel 391 489 0721, www.facebook.com/itinerantibari. (Bari's description was contributed by Patrycja Bukaty.)

HaBari We Dorm O Pr Do R K Br Cr W S 2/12 & 2/3, €28/60/70/90/112/-, Via Calefati 249, tel 0808 170 525 or 327 423 5052, email info@habarihostel.com, www.habarihostel.com. Reservations required.

MovidaBlablabla O Do R K W S 5/20, €15–20, Piazza Luigi di Savoia 40, tel 351 249 8927. Reservations required through www.booking.com.

CConfortHotels O Pr Do R K Br Cr W S 5/42 & 60/171, €26/50/65/90120/150, Corso Cavour 204, tel 080 975 6863, reservation@cconforthotels.com, www.cconforthotels.com/bari/host-bari-centrale-bari. Kitchen only available to hostel users and not for private rooms. Rooms available at various locations around town; address provided is for the main office.

Comunità di camminatori ITINERANTI di Bari O reteaccoglienzapellegrinabari@gmail.com, your contact is Vito Mazzilli. For pilgrims who have the credenziale, this group of volunteers will help find accommodation in parishes and in other low-cost accommodation in Bari, based on availability. All advance communication is by email, and further information about their organized events is on their Facebook page: www.facebook.com/itinerantibari.

The Francigena's main route first meets the Adriatic at the Santo Spirito harbor

Bari

1 Habari We Dorm
2 MovidaBlablabla

STAGE 33

Bari to Mola di Bari

Start	Basilica Pontificia San Nicola, Bari
Finish	Piazza XX Settembre, Mola di Bari
Duration	6hr
Distance	23.6km
Total ascent	98m
Total descent	102m
Difficulty	Moderate due to length and hard surfaces
Percentage paved	91%
Lodgings	Torre a Mare 13.6km, Mola di Bari 23.6km

A blissful passage of 160km of Adriatic coastline begins, leading to Brindisi, the end point of the Roman Via Appia Traiana. This stage follows urban seaside sidewalks (lungomari), sandy beaches, and rocky coastline and also turns inland for hectares of olives and crops. Seasonal seaside restaurants and cafés offer plentiful food options but take enough snacks during quieter months.

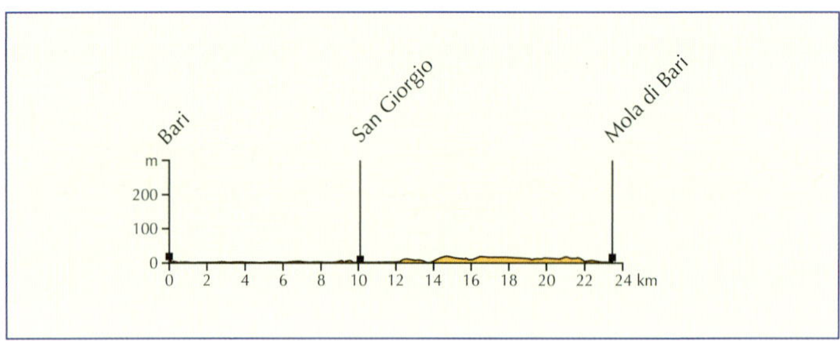

Follow the left side of the Basilica Pontificia San Nicola out to the **Lungomare di Bari** and pass the **marina**, noticing the newer part of the city on the right, with offices, government buildings, and apartments looking out over the beaches and parks. Pass the **Bari Torre Quetta train stop** and enjoy the quiet shoreline, with passing cars and crashing waves for company. After a time, come to the first houses of delightful **San Giorgio**, once only a small fishing village (**10km**, food, accommodation, bus). Cross a bridge and don't miss a left turn to zigzag then keep left to San Giorgio's shoreline where you bear right onto another lungomare first on a promenade and then by brown bedrock. Pass the Chapel San Domenico and, after a right uphill curve, take the second left among white stucco apartments before coming to the beach then harbor of **Torre a Mare** (**3.6km**).

13.6KM TORRE A MARE (ELEV 2M, POP 1498) (295.8KM)
At the site of this seaside town, an agricultural Neolithic civilization, the Peuceti, prospered in the 7th–3rd millennia BC and were some of the first farmers in the Western Mediterranean. They inhabited caves dotted along the coastline, such as Grotta della Regina and Grotta della Tartaruga. The current town was born in the 16th century around the Pelosa Tower, one of the many dominant defensive towers in the Kingdom of Naples, with many more further along the coast that will be discovered along the way. The names 'Pellosa' and 'Pellusa' were first documented in the 11th century, referring to the abundance of pelosa crabs in the coastline waters, the dialectal name of the *favollo* (*Eriphia verrucosa*) crab.

B&B Torre Pelosa Pr Do R Br Cr W S 2/5, €-/55–75/75/110/-/-, Via Pitagora 7/9, tel 347 703 2999. Closed from mid January to February.

After the town's piazza, head back to another lungomare among villas (water) and turn right uphill onto Via Fontana Nuova, passing the **Church of San Rocco** with its terracotta depiction of the saint. When the road ends, jog right one block on Via Morelli E.

The view from the route back toward central Bari

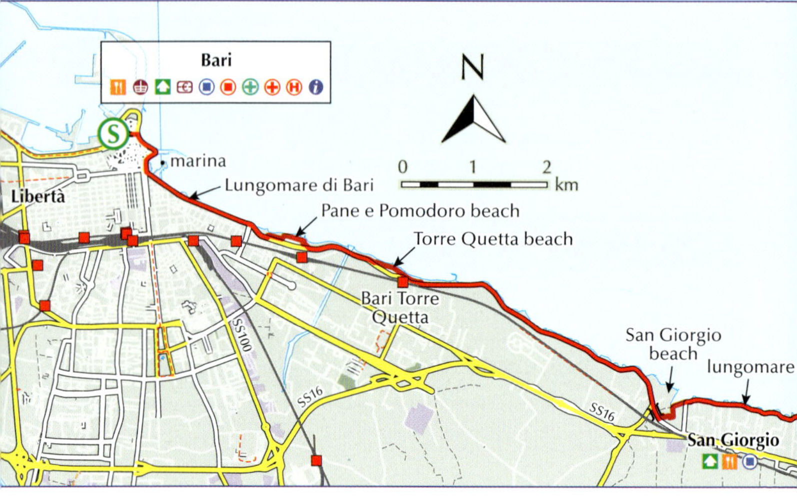

Silvati, turn left, pass under the busy **SS16 highway bridge** (which can take you straight to Mola di Bari), and turn left at the roundabout onto the highway frontage road. Pass a gas station, turn right (sign to Domus Familiae, a church ministry center), and 100m later, before raspberry greenhouses, turn left onto a more or less straight, quiet dirt farm road. Follow the tall wall of the **SS16** to the right and turn left under the highway. Curve left and right then soon see and reach apartments. At the end of the road, turn left then right at the T-junction, coming to a seaside road into **Mola di Bari**. Turn right before the **castle** and reach the large Piazza XX Settembre.

10KM MOLA DI BARI (ELEV 5M, POP 24,416) (285.8KM)

Mola boasts a lively rounded main square with a central fountain dedicated to sailors, and it holds over 100 fishing boats in the harbor. The tourist office is located in the sumptuous Palazzo Roberti. Nicknamed the 'palace of one hundred rooms,' it was built to block the sea views of a rival noble family. While heading down Via Vittorio Veneto to the eateries on the port, stop to admire the 16th-century Chiesa Matrice Parrocchia San Nicola di Bari, which exemplifies the blend of Romanesque origins and baroque interposition.

Accoglienza with Mariella Pr Do R Br Dr S 1/2, €-/30/60/-/-/-, Via Monsignor Tonino Bello, Traversa 19, n°12, tel 351 556 6669, mariella.brunetti4@gmail.com. Check ahead; price includes dinner and breakfast.

Hotel Gabbiano Pr R Br Cr S Z 48/75, €-/50/70/90/120/-, Viale Piero Delfino Pesce 24, tel 080 473 3441 or 080 473 2331 or 391 312 2581, info@hotelgabbiano.biz, www.hotelgabbiano.biz. Closed December 15 to December 31 inclusive.

A seaside walk between Bari and Torre a Mare

STAGE 34

Mola di Bari to Monopoli

Start	Piazza XX Settembre, Mola di Bari
Finish	Castello Carlo V, Monopoli
Duration	7½hr
Distance	29.1km
Total ascent	203m
Total descent	207m
Difficulty	Moderately hard due to length and uneven footing
Percentage paved	65%
Lodgings	Polignano a Mare 19.0km, Monopoli 29.1km

Easily one of the highlights of the entire Via Francigena, this unforgettable stage offers crashing waves, pristine beaches, shallow tide pools for splashing in the surf, salty sea air, and the beloved and atmospheric coastal towns of Polignano a Mare and Monopoli. In some cases, an asphalt road provides a shorter option. Since some long, remote stretches offer no services, bring plenty of snacks and water.

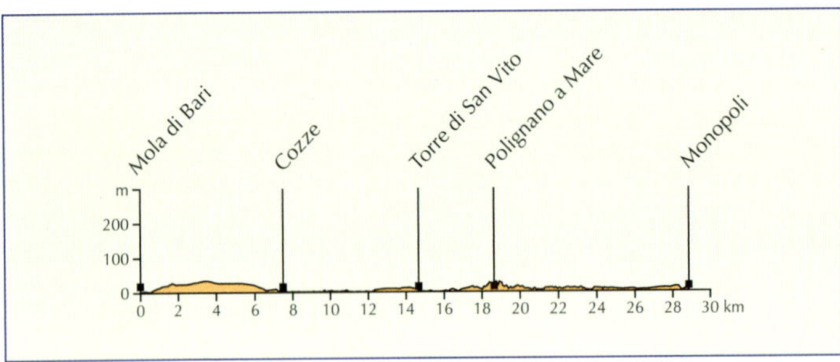

Go through the piazza and bear left at the bronze statue of Niccolo Van Westerhovt to the marina, picking up **Lungomare Dalmazia**. At the tower of the **Church of Loreto**, turn right uphill onto Via Madonna Loreto. Shortcut: stay on the lungomare, which becomes the old Mola–Cozze road with a sidewalk leading directly to Cozze in just 4km, 2.1km shorter than the main route. After that, keeping on the old highway to Polignano comes to 13.5km and all the way to Monopoli totals 23.1km, but it would result in you missing out on spectacular walking between Cozze and Monopoli.

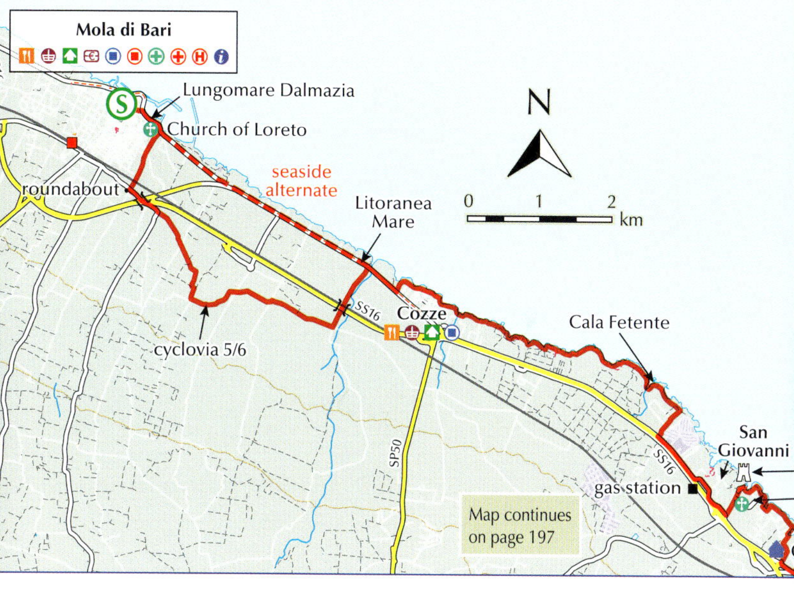

Pick up a bike lane, **Cyclovia 5/6**, downhill under the railway. Turn left at a roundabout, pass under the SS16 among farms and orchards, make a sharp left then right turn, and turn left immediately after. Jog left 15m, where the road seems to end, and then go right, in the same direction as before. Turn left over the **SS16** and turn left onto the old coastal highway that connects Mola and Cozze, soon arriving in the latter (**7.6km**, food, groceries, accommodation, bus).

Cozze, sometimes referred to as Spiaggia di Conversano, is closely linked to the town of Conversano, which lies 9km inland from the beach. According to legend, in 487, Simplicio, the first Bishop of Conversano, arrived on the beach, bringing the image of the Madonna della Fonte that is still venerated today in the Cattedrale Basilica Santa Maria Assunta in Cielo in Conversano.

Turn right onto the bike lane, with the sea and scattered houses, turn first left, and curve to follow the rugged and rocky shoreline. The road ends so continue on a path between the sea and the stone walls of private properties before enjoying the fabulous kilometers along a primitive coastline of narrow paths, splashing waves, and quiet inlets.

Several scattered old stone farmhouses called **casedde** appear. Similar in appearance to the well-known *trulli* houses, they were built between dry-stone walls along this wonderful unspoiled coastline of the Parco Regionale di Costa Ripagnola. This stretch has strongly resisted any resort construction and gained its regional park title for its protection in 2020. Among the Mediterranean scrub, you'll find wild olive, juniper, fig, and mastic trees and prickly pear bushes.

After a low, white building, skirt around **Cala Fetente** to find a gravel path between two low stone walls. A *cala* is a cove, and the rocky coastline of much of Puglia is dotted with them. They often collect sand, so many feature quiet beaches. At the wide sand road near the white buildings of the Pietra Blu Resort, watch for an uphill dirt road on the right then turn back onto the old highway, now cozied up against the SS16. Pass a **gas station** and the entrance to San Giovanni bay then turn next left and, at the sea, curve right toward the large Abbazia di San Vito Martire and imposing **Torre di San Vito**.

The 16th-century Arco Marchesale, or Porta Grande, at Polignano a Mare

The protective **Torre di San Vito** was built at the behest of the monks of the Abbazia di San Vito Martire in the 17th century, and the abbey is said to hold the relics of the eponymous Sicilian saint. Legend tells of Florenza, the Princess of Salerno, who when drowning in the Sele River (Salerno, Campania) was saved by Saint Vito. She later entrusted the Saint's relics to Basilian monks, who designed the 10th-century Romanesque abbey. The Lecce baroque features include the finely crafted bell tower and the external staircase, which leads to the spectacular loggia (outdoor corridor or gallery) with views to the horizon.

Keep along the beach, turn left on Via San Vito after the posh **Cala Ponte Hotel**, left again after a marsh onto **Contrada Santa Caterina** and turn right along Via San Vito, by the shore again. Watch for signs pointing left and either walk along the cliff trails above beaches and caves or simply head straight into Polignano a Mare. The two options converge at a statue of singer Domenico Modugno (1928–1994) on a viewpoint. Favorite son of his hometown, the singer/songwriter/actor/director co-wrote and recorded the 1959 Grammy-winning song 'Nel blu, dipinto di blu,' known also as 'Volare,' which is believed to have sold more than 19 million copies worldwide. Cross the bridge, turn left, and walk through the archway into the picturesque historic center (**11.3km**).

19KM POLIGNANO A MARE (ELEV 26M, POP 17,531) (266.8KM)

Protected by the walls of the Bastione di Santo Stefano and accessed over the old Roman bridge of the Via Traiana, the little medieval center of blinding white-washed houses set on the cliffs above the blue-green sea makes Polignano a Mare a photographer's dream. Important sites include the Chiesa Madre di Santa Maria Assunta sitting across the Palazzo dell'Orologio, but evidence of the town's Roman, Byzantine, Norman, and Aragonese construction is almost everywhere. Polignano also hosts the yearly Red Bull Cliff Diving World Series.

RomAntica O Pr R K W S Z 8/18, €-/60/60/-/-/-, Via Roma 208, tel 333 159 2848. Reservations required. Varied accommodation settings across the town in either double rooms or apartments for up to six people.

Wandering through the delightful maze, find any left-hand street leading back to the coast and turn right to catch the **Lungomare di Polignano**. At its end, by a tall wall of a **sports field**, use metal steps to cross onto a shoreline path of undeveloped coastline cliff walls and crashing surf. The coast here boasts an old calcarenite quarry, sea caves, snorkeling, and the Aragonese Torre Incina, which still retains its two floors following restoration work in 1966. Enter Monopoli on Via Marina del Mondo. Pass a **marina**, join a long bike lane along Via M. Sforza, and turn left upon reaching the lively Piazza Vittorio Emanuele II. Pass the Villa Comunale Park and follow the harbor road to the Castello Carlo V. For explorations in one of Puglia's most picturesque seaside towns, turn right into any of the labyrinthine streets.

10.1KM MONOPOLI (ELEV 17M, POP 47,996) (256.7KM)

Arriving in Monopoli is to be greeted by luxurious yachts, gigantic catamarans, and sublime coves beneath the precipitous, imposing pentagonal Aragonese castle that protects the labyrinthine old town. Within the fortress, an ancient Basilian church has withstood the test of time, its name, San Nicola de Pinna, referring to its position at the very tip of the headland. The baroque Duomo di Santa Maria Santissima della Madia preserves its Romanesque crypt, Byzantine icons, and *Last Supper* painted by Francesco de Mura (1696–1782). Along with Polignano a Mare, Monopoli's seaside charms make it quickly apparent why tourists flock here in season.

Convento di San Francesco da Paola O Do S Z 1/3, €Donation, Piazza San Francesco da Paola 13, tel 080 777 071. They do not tend to answer phone calls so do just show up, knock, and wait patiently. The monastery is situated 1.4km from the castle. Across the road, a supermarket with a café serves hot food.

Monopoli street at night

STAGE 35

Monopoli to Savelletri

Start	Castello Carlo V, Monopoli
Finish	Chiesa di San Francesco da Paola, Savelletri
Duration	5½hr
Distance	21.4km
Total ascent	137m
Total descent	136m
Difficulty	Moderate
Percentage paved	75%
Lodgings	Savelletri 21.4km, Torre Canne 30.3km

This stage is full of interesting sights: first a shoreline of beaches, cliffs, and caves then kilometers of twisted, gnarled monumental olive trees and the Egnazia archeological park. Skipping the upland portion by sticking to the SP90 Contrada Capitolo between Capitolo and Egnazia can shorten the day. Food might be available after the first 8km at Capitolo, but plan on plenty of water and snacks just in case.

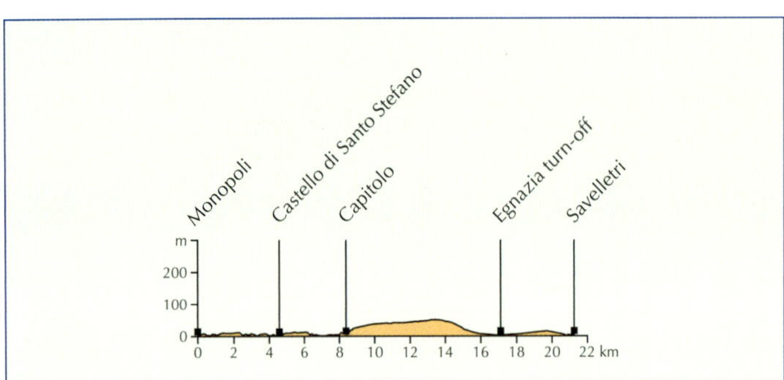

With the Castello Carlo V on your left, take the **Lungomare Santa Maria**, turn left at the end of the city wall, and take the lungomare at Cala Porta Vecchia. Continue on a street then a boardwalk and pass Porto Bianco beach. Take a red bike path to the sandy **Porto Rosso cove** and turn left onto the narrow gravel path after a sports field.

After 100m, at **Lido Colonia**, begin a seaside, clifftop walk into and back out of coves a total of nine times. Briefly take an asphalt road around a parking lot, turn right to gravel to Porto Marzano Piccolo beach, pass another inlet, and immediately turn right to the tall walls of **Castello di Santo Stefano**. Below the private castle, at Ghiacciolo beach, take the driveway up to Via Procaccia and turn left.

Founded in 1086 as part of a defensive system at the behest of the Count of Conversano, the Norman **Godefroi de Hauteville**, the Romanesque castle-abbey was inhabited by Benedictine monks between the 11th and 14th centuries, housing the relics of Saint Stephen and perhaps those of Saint Nicolas pilgrim before they were transferred to Bari. The Knights of Jerusalem closed it off with walls and a moat to protect travelers heading to the Holy Land.

Monumental olive trees like this can be hundreds of years old

Turn left when the road ends, go through the open gate (marked 'private property'), and turn immediately right. Go right around **Lido San Stefano caravan campground**, veer left before a home marked 'Verde,' pass secluded Cala Verde beach and **Torre Cinta Hotel** with its white domed cabins, then turn a corner, spotting the **Torre Cintola** ruin. After one block, follow Contrada Lamandia past the ruins of the rupestrian **Church of San Giorgio** then Porto Giardino and arrive in **Capitolo** (**8.6km**) on Contrada Capitolo along which lie **Residence Camping Atlantide**, an excavation area of the original Via Appia Traiana, a 16th-century defense tower, then the Ristorante Gran Pavese after which turn right uphill. The Contrada Capitolo becomes the SP90, a direct route to Egnazia and then Savelletri; the official route instead turns right uphill.

At the gate of a residential development, veer left uphill on **Contrada Lamandia**, cross the railway, and turn left. This bench of land above the sea houses centuries-old olive trees with massive trunks. The next few kilometers following the railway trajectory cross back and forth over the tracks four times. After the railway curves right, turn first left onto a dirt road and pass through a **farm complex**. Take a white gate, turn left onto the SP3, and in 100m turn right toward Egnazia. After 100m turn right then right again to the entrance and **ticket office of Egnazia** (**9km**).

The 4th-century **Acropoli di Egnazia** (also known as Gnathia) is one of the most important Greco-Roman archeological sites to have been discovered in Puglia, yet the first settlement arose in the 16th century BC. Remains include cobblestone of the original Via Traiana, ancient homes, the forum, and what was most likely an amphitheater. Most interesting are some of the best European examples of stone tombs of the Messapian necropolis and impressive 7m-high walls. The Christian Episcopal basilica with the baptistery and the southern basilica were built between the 4th and 6th centuries AD. After the collapse of the Roman Empire, the city faced Barbarian invasions and was majoritarily destroyed by Totila, the Gothic king, in AD545. The community sought refuge in the tombs, but the area was abandoned by the 10th century. The adjoining museum displays many items found in excavations, such as exquisite mosaics and prized vases.

Go back to the ticket office road, pass more giant, twisty olive trees then a **golf course** and the immense **Borgo Egnazia resort**. Before a soccer pitch, turn left toward Savelletri. At the road end, turn left onto a cycle lane in town, turn right by the sea, pass the small beach and harbor, and reach the Chiesa di San Francesco da Paola (**3.7km**).

21.3KM SAVELLETRI (ELEV 2M, POP 620) (235.3KM)

Savelletri and its coastline are popular with surfers, who enjoy the craggy shores that provide high waves on windy days. As a hamlet of the territory of nearby Fasano (train), and just like its neighboring villages, Savelletri was born of numerous masserie built in the 16th–18th centuries. As well as being devoted to agriculture and livestock production, they were capable of defending themselves from pirates and bandits. These farms lost their function with the abolition of feudalism in 1806.

Miramare O Pr R Br S 3/8, €-/25–35/50–70/75/105/-/-, Via Orazio Flacco 72, tel 348 520 9038.

Palm trees line Via Fiume which leads to the small boat harbor at Sevelletri

STAGE 36

Savelletri to Torre Canne

Start	Chiesa di San Francesco da Paola, Savelletri
Finish	Lighthouse, Torre Canne
Duration	2¼hr
Distance	8.9km
Total ascent	37m
Total descent	37m
Difficulty	Easy
Percentage paved	96%
Lodgings	Torre Canne 8.9km

Today is a very short and pleasant jaunt among farms and olive groves on a *cicloturismo* (cycle network) route in the hills above the shoreline. There are no intermediate services.

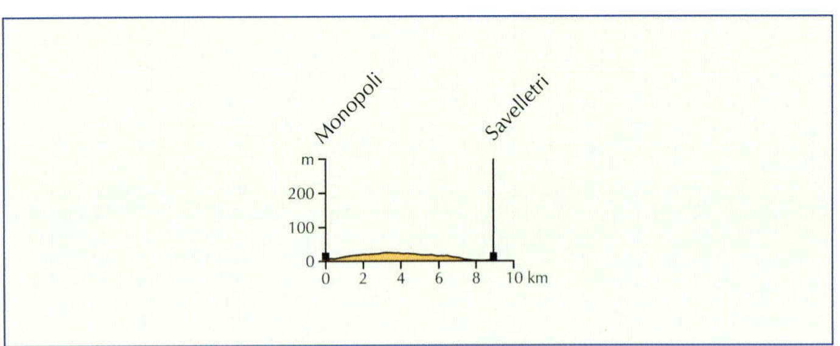

With your back to the Chiesa di San Francesco da Paola, go straight onto Via Ticino, turn right at the end of the road, left at the end of the next one then turn right and left onto yesterday's familiar cycle lane to a road out of town. After the soccer pitch, turn left onto **Strada Comunale Egnazia** and cross the SP4 to be met by 1m-high dry-stone walls separating olive groves and masserie.

Puglia's fortified **masserie** were built to withstand a siege. Some are still working farms, while others have been transformed into luxurious hotels with pools and fine-dining experiences with incredible local products.

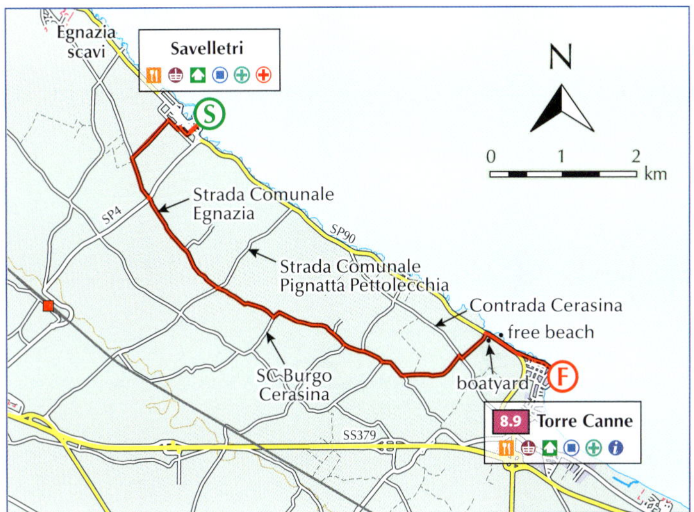

Cross **Strada Comunale Pignatta Pettolecchia** and at a T-junction turn left onto **Strada Comunale Burgo Cerasina**, which soon goes parallel to the shore. As it becomes a wide fork, go left toward Torre Spaccata. At the second fork go left then, at the road end, jog right on **Contrada Cerasina** for 40m and pick up a lane to the shoreline where you turn right, approaching **Torre Canne**. Fork left onto Via Eroi del Mare (services) and reach the prominent lighthouse (tourist information) on Via Marsala.

The shrine near the harbor at Torre Canne remembers those who risk their lives at sea

8.9KM TORRE CANNE (ELEV 2M, POP 306) (226.5KM)

The striking, 35m-high lighthouse of Torre Canne (1928) housed many keepers over the years within its ground-floor rooms, the last of whom humorously never learned to swim! Starting off as a garage owned by Gian Battista Punzi, the parish church (1940s) was built by the latter when he survived a train accident.

Francesco B&B O Pr R K Cr W S 2/8, €-/40/80/120/160/200, Via Portofino 15, tel 333 640 8246. Discounts for longer stays.

STAGE 37

Torre Canne to Torre Santa Sabina

Start	Lighthouse, Torre Canne
Finish	Tower, Torre Santa Sabina
Duration	7¾hr (6½hr beach)
Distance	30.1km (25.6km beach)
Total ascent	140m (112m beach)
Total descent	142m (114m beach)
Difficulty	Moderately hard due to distance (inland); hard due to distance and loose sand surface (beach)
Percentage paved	83% (21% beach)
Lodgings	Torre Santa Sabina 30.1km (25.6km beach), Specchiolla 34.1km (29.6km beach)

This stage and its beach variant both have their challenges and their beauties. The beach option is surely one of the most idyllic pilgrimage walks through rugged coastline, crystal-blue waters, and tranquil coves begging for a swim. Off season, Villanova di Ostuni is the only food stop, while in season there are many. The main inland option along a cycle route offers olive groves, masserie, a 4000-year-old dolmen, but no services so plan ahead.

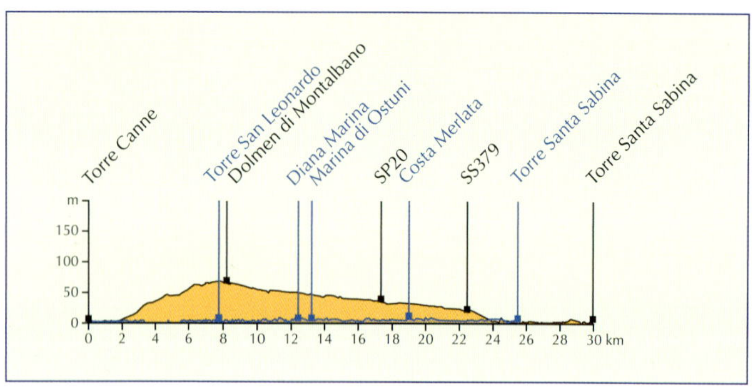

Past the lighthouse, continue on the lungomare and at its end, cross the sandy beach. In the mornings you may pass local fishermen selling their catch at the marina. On

Fortified masserie like this once sheltered farm families who served the farm owner

Torre Canne's wide bay, with sharp eyes you can see Torre Santa Sabina and beyond the tip of Brindisi's peninsula. At the porch of a weathered beachside villa, arrive at two options (**0.9km**).

Beachside option

Continue on the beach. All the way to Torre Santa Sabina, this option skips along the rocky coastline and around coves. After the first large hotel, the beach narrows and, depending on tides that can reach 30cm, shoes may need to come off to wade up to your calves. Afterward, ford a stream or take a bridge 10m inland then pass **Lido Verde**, a hexagonal pavilion with an orange roof, and enter a protected dune area now in Salento, the true 'heel of Italy's boot.' To protect endangered plants and wildlife, climbing the dunes in this area is prohibited by law. Rip-tide warnings are posted where swimming may be dangerous.

Pass many coves and beaches, seasonal bars and restaurants, the holiday village of **Il Pilone** (**7.8km**), and **Il Pilone campground** (**0.7km**). Then pass the village of **Cala Diana Marina** (**4.4km**) and Porto Villanova in Marina di Ostuni (**1km**) and veer away from the waterfront briefly onto a sidewalk leading to the main street in Villanova di

Ostuni (**0.9km**, food, groceries, pharmacy). After Sole In Me Resort, leave the road to cross a beach joining the main inland option at **La Dolce Vita beach** (**6.3km**).

Main inland option

Turn right away from the beach, take the first right then turn left onto **Via del Faro** out of Torre Canne. Take a hard left at the roundabout onto **Via Appia Antica**. Just before the tall GranSerena Hotel, fork right gradually uphill, pass under the SS379 highway bridge to olive trees and stone walls, and veer right at a tall **cell phone tower**, passing a steep ravine on the left. At a stop sign, turn right over the railway. Make a hairpin left bend onto an asphalt road along the railway then at the T-junction, turn left onto **Via**

delle Poste (marked as 'percorso cicloturistico') and pass the first masseria of the day, the ornate Masseria San Giovanni (**6.1km**, rest area), and cross the SP10. A swift 350m detour turning left along the highway leads to the Masseria Ottava Grande historical complex. Unfortunately, its underground church, crypt, and old oil mills cannot be visited, although the 1591 fortification walls and prominent square tower can be admired from outside.

Keeping straight, follow a sign leading you to the Dolmen di Montalbano (**1.4km**). The megalithic stone table dates back to the Chalcolithic period and was likely used for funerary purposes or sacrificial rites. The neighboring white stone building has a second-floor observation deck. Ensure to wind left with the road, pass under the railway (benches), continue alongside the tracks, pass the entrance to Masseria La Fonte (1.1km off route) across from the defunct **Fontevecchia station**, and enter an area of beautiful olive groves (rest area)

These monumental olive trees are part of the **Piana degli Ulivi** (Plain of Olives) that stretches between Monopoli and the inland town of Carovigno, near Torre Santa Sabina. Some are recorded as being up to 3000 years old, dating back to Messapian times, and they form the highest concentration of ancient trees in all of the Mediterranean. To classify as 'monumental,' the trunk of the tree must have a minimum circumference of 1m. They are protected by Puglian associations. As one of Puglia's oldest industries, more olive oil is produced in this region than anywhere else in Italy and accounts for more than 40% of Puglia's entire agricultural income.

Fork left at Masseria La Grave then fork right alongside the SP19 for 400m and fork left onto **Bicitalia 6 – Ciclovia Adriatica/Via Traiana**. Pass Masseria Sansone (**7.5km**), cross the SP20 at a shrine to the **Madonna and Child**, veer right onto the shoulder of the **SS379**, and, at the second interchange, pass under the highway ('Bari 75' sign). Turn right, head uphill briefly, and switchback left to circumnavigate a billboard for Grand Hotel Masseria Santa Lucia. Pass said hotel and, at the shoreline, turn right to join the beach option at **La Dolce Vita beach** (**8.1km**).

Route continues

Continue on gravel, through tall bushes, resuming the beach and cove pattern of walking. Pass the ruins of **Torre Pozzelle** (Camping Village Torre Pozzelle) and soon spot Torre Santa Sabina ahead. In town, stay to the left of a white dry-stone wall around another cove and, now on Via Socrate (with its luxury villas), reach **Spiaggia Mezzaluna** (**3.9km**). Veer right across the beach, aiming at the left side of a road in town, which turns to gravel and reaches the castle tower (**0.8km**).

30.1KM TORRE SANTA SABINA (ELEV 2M, POP 365) (196.4KM)

The octagonal coastal defense tower of Torre Santa Sabina reproduces, in plan, a four-pointed star topped with a crenelated crown. It is linked to the Torre Pozzella in the north and the Torre Guaceto further south, along Stage 38. The original tower was most likely built in the 14th century then rebuilt at the beginning of the 16th by the Spanish Viceroy of Naples, Pedro Afán de Ribera, adding to Puglia's coastal towers. It is now privately owned. In 1226 the Teutonic Knights, a Catholic religious and military order of the early 12th century in Acre, built a hospital and chapel here to aid devotees on their pilgrimages.

Donnosanto Residence Pr R Br Cr W S Z 25/85, €-/-/45–160/80–200/-/-, Via Monte Pollino, tel 0831 990 846, info@donnosantoresidence.com. Breakfast included; closed from November 4 until two weeks before Holy Week.

STAGE 38

Torre Santa Sabina to Brindisi

Start	Tower, Torre Santa Sabina
Finish	Via Appia Traiana Column, Brindisi
Distance	31km
Duration	8hr
Total ascent	148m
Total descent	143m
Difficulty	Moderately hard due to length and hard surfaces
Percentage paved	82%
Lodgings	Specchiolla 4km, Brindisi 31km

This stage to the Roman Via Appia Traiana's end has five parts. The first is similar to yesterday's beach option. To avoid a turtle sanctuary, the second chapter diverts to a monotonous cycle track next to the SS379 motorway. The third part follows the quiet and pleasant Via di Torre Testa until the last section, which switches to a busy access arterial into urban Brindisi. As a reward a finale composed of a boat ride into the old town makes for a charming change of pace. Some water is available along the way but plan food if walking out of season.

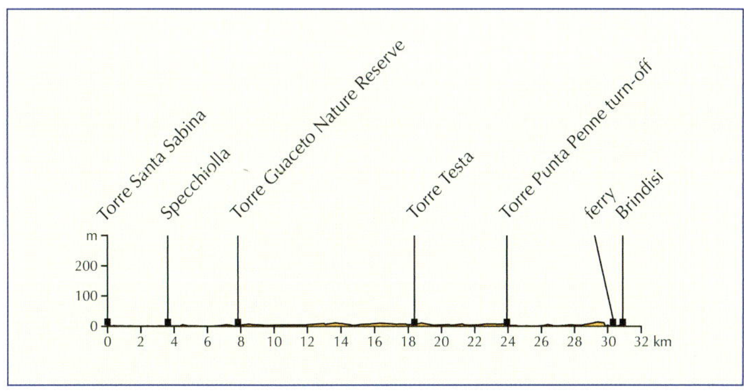

With your back to the tower, and keeping the cove on the left, go straight then turn left, cross the beach, aim for the cove's far side, and, at the last home, turn right alongside the seaside park (water). At the road end, keep on the gravel road, pass the white sand **Pantanagianni beach**, keep right of the dunes, pass a beachside restaurant, and turn left

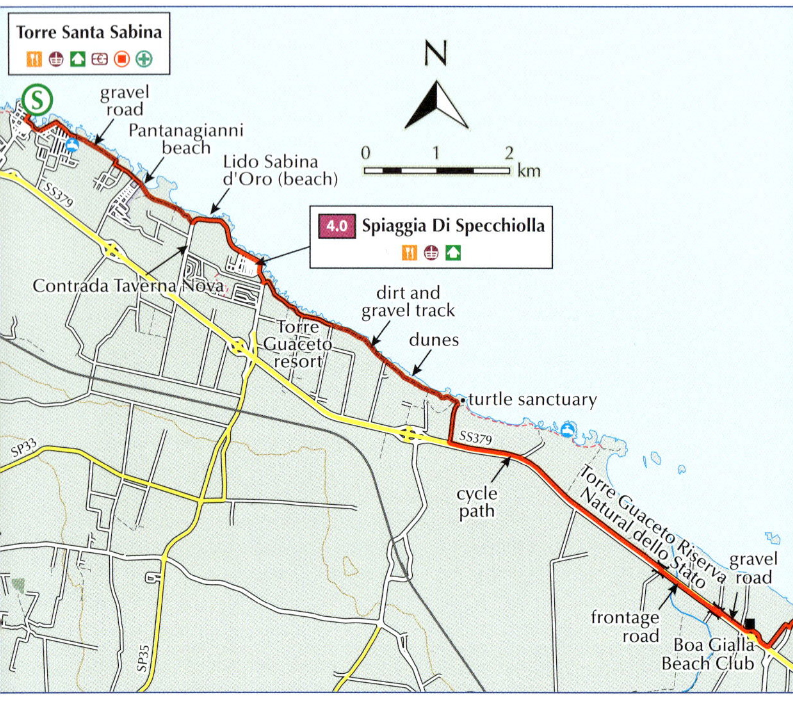

onto Contrada Taverna Nova. Pass **Lido di Sabina d'Oro** and arrive at sparsely placed restaurants and residences in **Specchiolla**.

4KM SPIAGGIA DI SPECCHIOLLA (ELEV 3M, POP UNKNOWN.) (192.4KM)

The entirety of this stretch of coastline is lovely for its maquis and olive groves, as well as for scuba diving and snorkeling among the small coral reefs and seagrass. There is also a seasonal campsite (food, groceries, www.campingpinetamare.com).

Hotel Il Timone O Pr R Br Dr Cr S Z 25/85, €-/-/45–160/80–200/-/-, Via Dei Tamerici, tel 0831 987 900 or 348 788 7503, email info@hoteltimone.it, www.hoteltimone.it.

Curve around the Marina di Specchiolla sign, pass the access to **Torre Guaceto Resort**, and leave the road onto a dirt and gravel track along an undeveloped shoreline. Head right by the low dunes onto a sandy path, pass derelict lido buildings, and arrive at the **green turtle sanctuary** building marking the start of the Torre Guaceto Nature Reserve (**4km**, water).

The impressive **Aragonese tower** is a symbol of the magnificent natural reserve of these shores, location of a 1200-hectare turtle sanctuary since 1991 that is home to a diverse population of aquatic life thanks to the combination of salt and freshwater. The tower is the largest of the square-base-style towers of the Kingdom of Naples territory, benefiting from the easy access to potable water; the name Guaceto stems from the Arabic 'Al Gawsit,' meaning 'a freshwater place.'

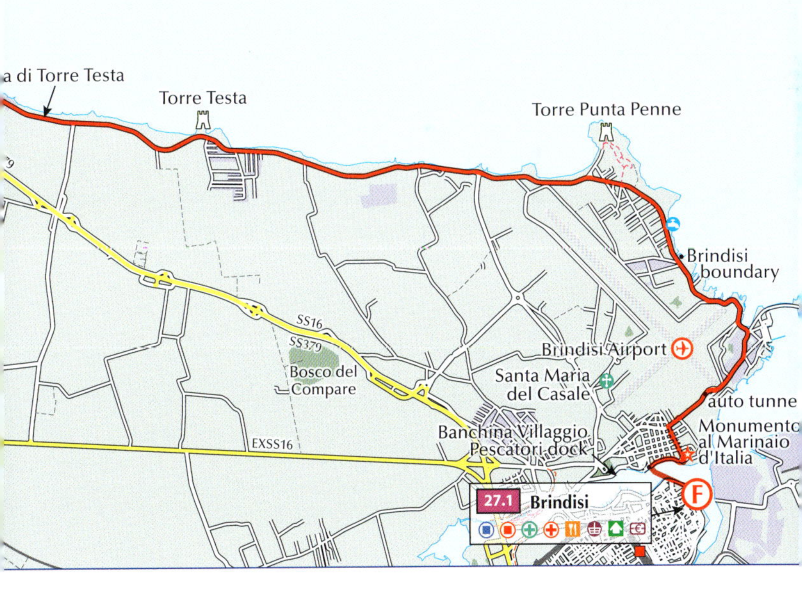

Bidding adieu to the sea for a time, turn right onto a gravel road after the first parking lot, and turn left onto a cycle path alongside the surprisingly quiet **SS379**. After 3.5km, turn right under the viaduct onto the SS379 slip road, and, after 1.5km, turn right to double back under the highway onto gravel. Pass the **Boa Gialla Beach Club**, and, after an interchange, take the first left to the sea (signs for Litoranea beach).

Palm trees line Corso Garibaldi, Brindisi's main shopping street

Now on Via di Torre Testa, pass beach clubs, farms, undeveloped shoreline, and the 16th-century **Torre Testa fortress** (**10.5km**). After **Lido Risorgimento**, signs lead left to the headland and the Torre Punta Penne ruin (**5.6km**), but instead, to shortcut, stay on the road, which soon offers views of Brindisi. Pass a shoreline park (water) and reach the city limits of **Brindisi**.

Head through an **auto tunnel** (**4.6km**) and at the first roundabout go straight and then turn left at the next traffic lights. To the north-west, 1.7km away, lies Santa Maria del Casale, one of Brindisi's most valued architectural and historic churches. In seven blocks come to the tall **Monumento al Marinaio d'Italia**. The 54m-high boat-rudder-shaped monument was inaugurated in 1933 to commemorate those fallen at sea during war. It is engraved with more than 36,000 names of deceased sailors. Visits cost €5. Climb onto the pedestal of the tower to find stairways down to a right-hand turn onto the lungomare, which leads to the second pedestrian ferry dock, **Banchina Villaggio Pescatori**. You can pay the €1.10 ferry ticket in cash or by card on board or follow the instructions on the sign to download the MooneyGo app. Ferries leave about every 20min, taking you across the harbor to **Banchina Montenegro** in the city center.

Dock, turn left onto the lungomare, and go up the wide right-hand steps to the Roman column marking the end of the Via Appia Traiana (**2.4km**). Keep straight past the monument for the pilgrim's office on **Via Giovanni Tarantini** in a weathered building called La Corte degli Artigiani. The main shopping street is on Corso Umberto I.

27.1KM BRINDISI (ELEV 19M, POP 87,820) (165.3KM)

Brindisi, with its Eastern Mediterranean flavor, has forever been a bridge between Italy and lands across the water. To this day, it is the favorite embarkation point for Greece. Throughout the late Middle Ages, pilgrims and crusading knights set sail from the docks, and the city has many stories to tell. Here ends the Via Appia Traiana. At the top of the Scalinata Virgiliana (Virgil's steps), two columns once stood, serving as navigation tools for incoming vessels. One 18.7m column remains with its ornate capital, while the other was moved to Lecce (Stage 40). Brindisi is also home to the remains of one of Frederick's beloved Norman-Swabian castles and the everlasting Cattedrale di San Giovanni Battista, built in the 11th century, which has survived seven earthquakes. The Museo Archeologico Francesco Ribezzo is cherished for its Punta del Serrone 3rd-century BC bronzes, discovered in Brindisi's waters. Two more stand-out churches are the 12th-century Chiesa di Santa Lucia and the Chiesa e Chiostro di San Benedetto (1090). Don't forget to pop into the Accademia degli Erranti (Academy of the Wanderers and now the Brindisi pilgrim office) for your Testimonium (see Introduction).

Parrocchia Cattedrale O Do €Donation, Piazza Duomo, tel 0831 521 157, cattedralebrindisi@gmail.com. Very basic sleeping arrangements on the floor; no mattress or bedding provided.

B&B Mare Nostrum Brindisi O Pr R K Br W S Z 5/18, €-/30–35/60/75/100/110, Via Armengol 47–49, tel 328 861 6413, bandbmarenostrum@libero.it, www.facebook.com/BBMareNostrumBrindisi/?locale=it_IT. Breakfast included; €25 per person for groups of five or more people.

A passenger ferry in Brindisi Harbor with the maritime monument in the background

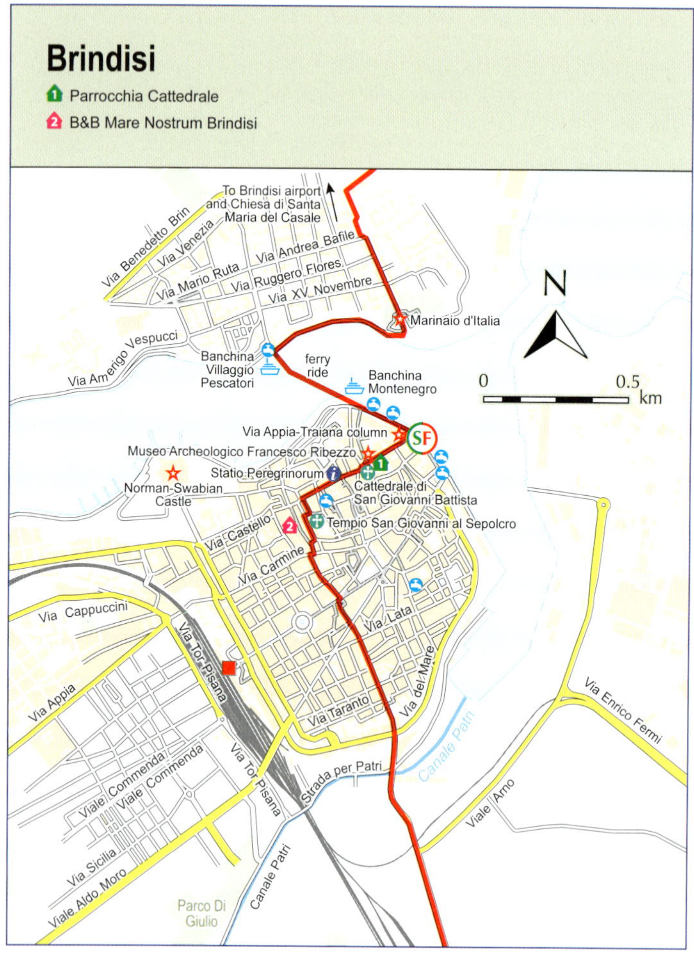
Brindisi
1 Parrocchia Cattedrale
2 B&B Mare Nostrum Brindisi
To Brindisi airport and Chiesa di Santa Maria del Casale
Via Benedetto Brin
Via Venezia
Via Andrea Bafile
Via Mario Ruta
Via Ruggero Flores
Via XV Novembre
Marinaio d'Italia
N
Via Amerigo Vespucci
Banchina Villaggio Pescatori
ferry ride
Banchina Montenegro
0
0.5
km
Via Appia-Traiana column
SF
Museo Archeologico Francesco Ribezzo
Statio Peregrinorum
Norman-Swabian Castle
Cattedrale di San Giovanni Battista
Tempio San Giovanni al Sepolcro
Via Castello
Via Carmine
Via Cappuccini
Via Tor Pisana
Via Lata
Via Appia
Via del Mare
Via Taranto
Via Enrico Fermi
Canale Patri
Strada per Patri
Viale Commenda
Viale Commenda
Via Tor Pisana
Viale Arno
Via Sicilia
Viale Aldo Moro
Canale Patri
Parco Di Giulio

SECTION 3A: PUGLIA – MONTE SANT'ANGELO VARIANT

Ruins of the Convento di Sant'Egidio after San Giovanni Rotondo (Stage MSA27)

Grain fields and wind turbines of the Tavoliere flatlands abruptly transition to narrow forest and shrubland paths in the remote limestone hills of the Gargano. Two of Italy's most important pilgrimage destinations, San Giovanni Rotondo and Monte Sant'Angelo, are framed by breathtaking views down to Manfredonia Bay on the Adriatic Sea.
N
0
20
40
km
CAMPOBASSO
San Severo
Stignano
MSA 25
MSA 26
MSA 27
Monte Sant'Angelo
San Giovanni Rotondo
Manfredonia
Via Litoranea Connection
Lucera
MSA 24
FOGGIA
Foggia FOG Airport
MSA 23
S
Troia
Margherita di Savoia
Barletta
Trani
Molfetta
Bari BRI Airport
F
BARI
BENEVENTO
Melfi
Venosa
AVELLINO
Avigliano
SALERNO
Matera
Tito
Bernalda
TARANTO
BRINDISI
LECCE

STAGE MSA23

Troia to Lucera

Start	Concattedrale, Troia
Finish	Basilica Cattedrale di Santa Maria Assunta, Lucera
Duration	5½hr
Distance	21.7km
Total ascent	122m
Total descent	340m
Difficulty	Easy
Percentage paved	48%
Lodgings	Lucera 21.7km

This tranquil, beautiful, and easy stage offers a wide horizon in every direction as the fields spread out around you. You see Lucera almost from the start, tantalizingly close, but it takes most of the day, walking among quiet fields, to arrive there. Be prepared to ford a stream if conditions are right and with nowhere to top up, bring plenty of water.

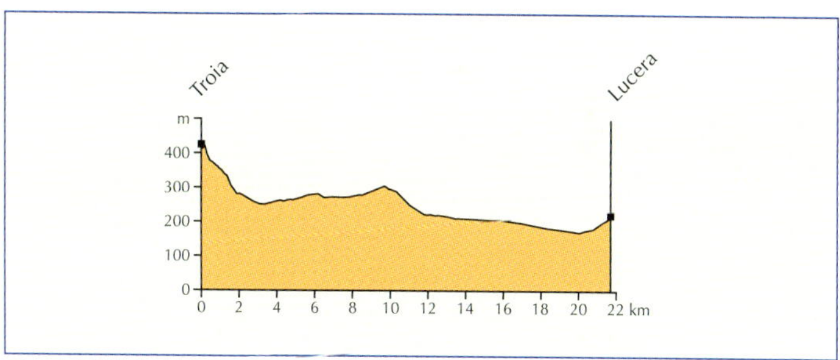

With the co-cathedral behind you, go straight onto the narrow alley, reaching, after one block, three streets crossing left to right. Take the third street going left steeply downhill and pass a caravan park, with sweeping views around you. The town toward the right is Lucera, and the hills to its right are the Gargano, sometimes called the 'spur on the boot of Italy,' which the route will take you over the next few days. Cross a road, continue ahead downhill, then follow signs to turn right onto a wider downhill road that gently traverses Troia's ridge.

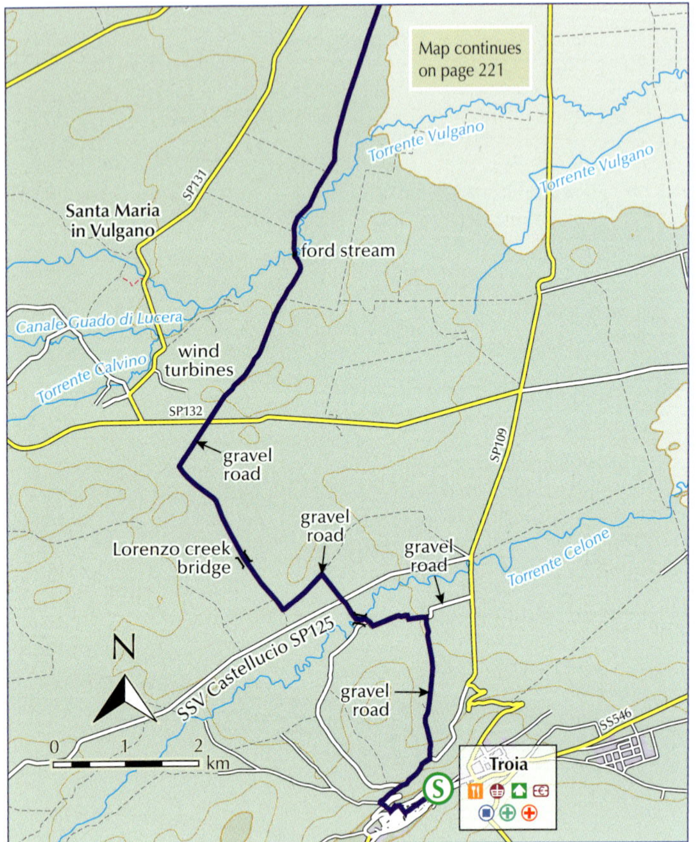

Soon signs point left onto a **gravel road** between fields down to the valley. Pass under power lines then among orchards, vineyards, homes, and isolated farm buildings to turn left at a T-junction onto another gravel road and then go right onto a lane. After 100m turn right onto a wider road between guardrails to cross over the Torrente Celone and the **SSV Castelluccio SP125** highway onto a gravel road that passes a crop-covered hillside and two farm complexes, reaching a T-junction. Turn left then bear right.

Cross the **Torrente Lorenzo** (muddy in wet weather) and immediately climb as the road dwindles to two tracks. After 2.5km, at the T-junction, turn right onto a gravel road that, 740m later, makes an arrow-straight trajectory across the **SP132** and up the hill, where views of Lucera are revealed between wind turbines. Keep ahead as other tracks merge and carefully ford the **Torrente Vulgano** to climb. Reach flatter ground and cross the SP18 and SP130 to pass a **farm headquarters** before entering a residential area of large houses. At a frontage road next to an arterial, turn right to Lucera, pass two highway slip roads, and carefully cross the **SS17** (leading to Foggia) to walk along it, slowly climbing to apartments. Continue on Via Pasubio, passing a gas station (food) and, at its end, turn right onto Via Appulo Sannitica,

The track follows a farm road that slices through the fields on its way from Troia to Lucera

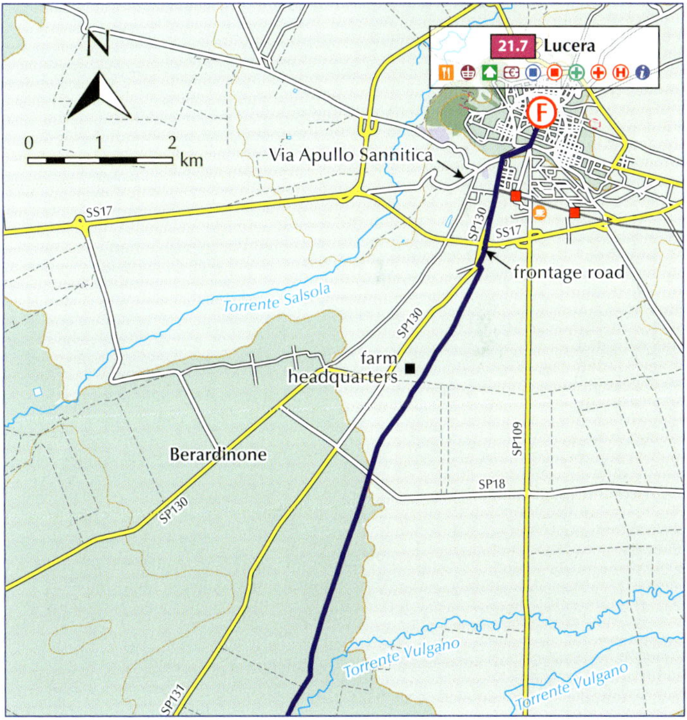

arriving at Piazza del Popolo. Go through the portal next to Hotel Federico II into the historic old town and head up to the south transept of the Basilica Cattedrale di Santa Maria Assunta. Turn left to its entrance on Piazza Duomo.

21.7KM LUCERA (ELEV 224M, POP 33,447) (541.7KM)

Built upon the ruins of a Roman amphitheater, Lucera arose in the 13th century when Frederick II repopulated the town with 20,000 Sicilian Muslims, having expelled the Arabs from Sicily. Allowing them freedom of faith, the town became a thriving hub and capital of the Tavoliere (tableland plains). Frederick ensured its fortification in 1233, and the tremendous castle walls were punctuated with 15 towers, taking military command over the open countryside. With the arrival and triumph of the Anjevins, the Arab population was once again shaken, their mosque replaced by the cathedral seen today. The Arabic influences can still be appreciated in courtyards and alleyways.

Hotel Federico II O Pr R Br Dr Cr W S 20/40, €-/50/70/90/100/-, Via G. Pizzuto 21, tel 0881 201 421, hotelfedericosecondolucera@gmail.com.

B&B Casa Cavalli Pr R Br Cr S Z 3/9, €-/45/75/95/120/150, Piazza Duomo 5, tel 347 193 5638, b_bcasacavalli@live.it, www.palazzocavalli.it. Closed at variable times, group offers available.

A street view toward Lucera's Duomo Santa Maria Assunta

STAGE MSA24

Lucera to San Severo

Start	Basilica Cattedrale di Santa Maria Assunta, Lucera
Finish	Chiesa della Santissima Trinità, San Severo
Duration	6¼hr
Distance	24.2km
Total ascent	115m
Total descent	246m
Difficulty	Moderate due to trail conditions and highway walking
Percentage paved	25%
Lodgings	San Severo 24.2km

Wide fields and distant views of the Gargano hills mark this fairly flat agricultural stage. Beware of a section of trail that sometimes disappears under the plowing of the crop rows. There are no intermediate services, so carry supplies for the full day.

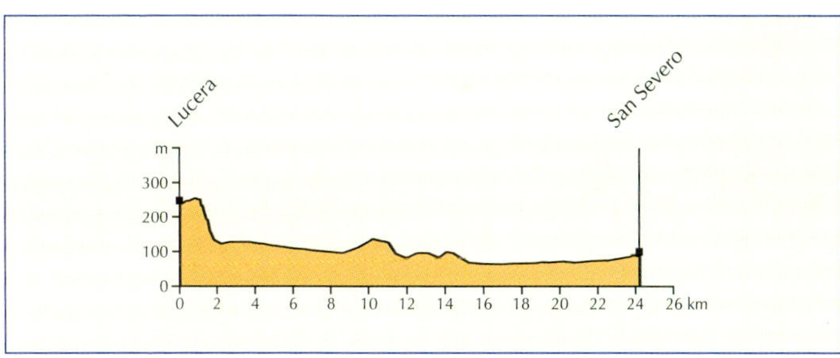

With your back to the cathedral facade, turn right, head through the piazza, turn left onto Via Giovanni Bovio, and, at its end, jog right onto Via Federico II, a charming retail promenade. Pass the 14th-century Church of Sant'Antonio Abate and go across into Piazza Matteotti. Veer toward the statue of Emperor Augustus and, keeping it on your right, take Viale Castello gently uphill toward the castle-fortress, spotting San Severo in the distance. Follow markings to fork downhill, arriving at the cylindrical tower of the **Fortezza**.

Fork right onto a gravel road and then onto a grassy track downhill. Watch carefully to take a steeper downhill path on the right marked 'A.I.B.19' and, at the bottom, turn right onto gravel to cross over the **Torrente Salsola**, entering fields and crops. Pass under the **SS692** and turn right onto the next gravel road, heading directly toward San Severo. Cross both the **SP8** and SP12 and zigzag among crops to turn left onto the wide shoulder of the **SP109**, the main Lucera–San Severo highway. After 1.2km, follow signs left onto a gravel road and then right onto another. Caution: this route is sometimes sown with crops, becoming a walk in the crops themselves, so the SP109 may be a better option. Pass a large **farm complex**, descend through vineyards, cross a gravel road, and reach a low hill.

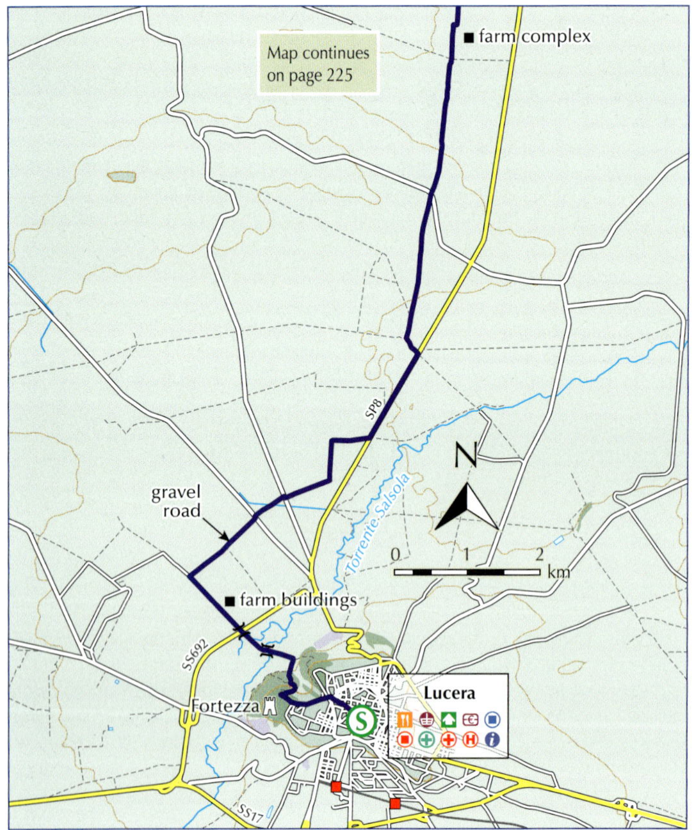

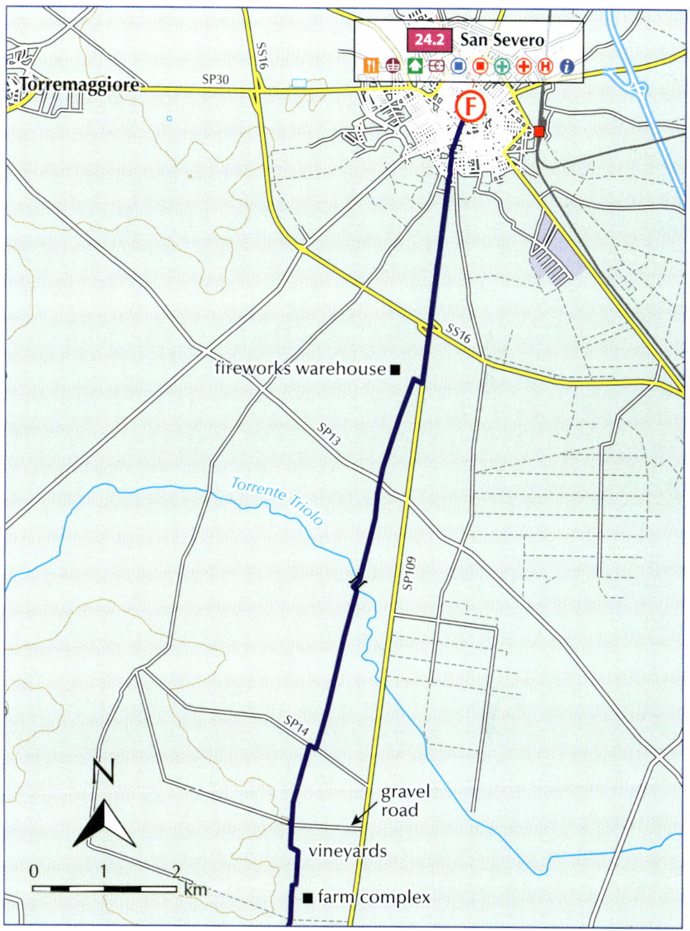

Jog right onto the **SP14** then pick up a white gravel road to cross over the **Torrente Triolo** and the SP13 as farm plots get smaller and San Severo nears. Pass a **fireworks warehouse** then turn left onto the SP109 (this time with no shoulder), which becomes Via Lucera. Cross straight over the roundabout and the road becomes Via Don Felice Canelli and then Via Daunia. At its end, turn left and arrive at the Chiesa della Santissima Trinità.

Farmworkers take a rain break from the broccoli harvest in the fields before San Severo

24.2KM SAN SEVERO (ELEV 96M, POP 53,434) (517.5KM)

As with many of the Tavoliere towns, legends attribute the foundation of San Severo to the Greek God Diomedes, and the town is internationally acclaimed for its sparkling white San Severo wine, the first wine in Puglia to be classified as DOP (protected designation of origin) in 1968. The old Castellum Sancti Severini stood around an 11th-century church, which became the San Severino Abate, devoted to Saint Severinus of Noricum, an evangelist during the 5th century in the modern-day Austrian/Slovakian area. Its few Romanesque features are concealed within baroque embellishments. The Museo dell'Alto Tavoliere holds a breadth of relics from prehistory through to the Middle Ages.

- **Parrocchia Maria SS. della Libera e San Sebastiano** O Do R K Br W S 1/4, €Donation, Via B. Moscatelli 2, tel 329 541 7883, madonnadellalibera@alice.it. Pilgrims are provided with an apartment for four people.
- **Enopolio Daunio | HUB Polifunzionale Culturale & Coworking** O Pr R Br Dr Cr S 3/10, €-/25/50/75/100/-, Via Soccorso 86, tel 347 353 8447, 349 260 5176, 377 082 8224 or 347 566 7173, info@enopoliodaunio.it, www.enopoliodaunio.it. Reservations recommended; check ahead for availability; sells the credenziale for €8.

STAGE MSA25

San Severo to Stignano

Start	Chiesa della Santissima Trinità, San Severo
Finish	Santa Maria di Stignano, Stignano
Duration	5¾hr
Distance	21.3km
Total ascent	447m
Total descent	283m
Difficulty	Moderately hard due to large, sharp gravel on the disused railway bed
Percentage paved	47%
Lodgings	Stignano 21.3km

This stage marks the transition from the flatlands of the Tavoliere to the beautiful, mountainous Gargano region. A full 40% of the stage is covered on a former railway bed, while the last quarter begins a climb up the mountains through scrubland, pastures, orchards, and fields. The target is Santa Maria di Stignano, a centuries-old monastery with no residents and no services, except the pilgrim quarters, by reservation. If you stay overnight there (no kitchen), bring food from the couple of grocery stores on the way out of San Severo. Ensure you carry enough water for the day because there is none along the way.

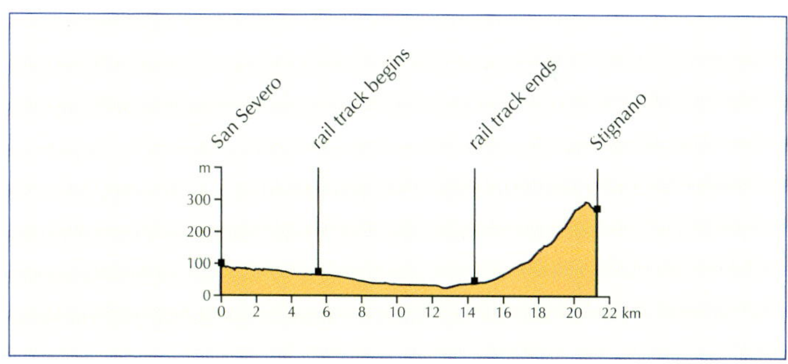

Facing the Church of the Holy Trinity, turn left. Turn right at the next block, heading toward the Palazzo di Città on the small Piazza Municipio. Pass through it toward the tower of San Severino Abate Church. Keep it on your left then pass San Nicola Church and admire its light-filled baroque interior, if it is open. This street becomes

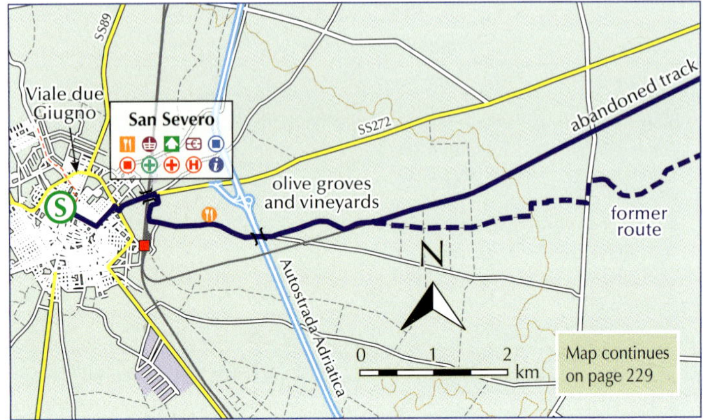

Via Zannotti and leaves the city through the retail district (groceries), coming to the major arterial **Viale due Giugno** at a roundabout. Cross over toward the tall wall with two pairs of twin brick columns, keeping them on the left. Cross over a **railway**, pass a car dealership, and follow signs to turn right onto a road that first follows the railway then curves left to the countryside. Pass a restaurant, cross under the **A14 Autostrada Adriatica**, and look to the range of intimidating Gargano hills ahead, our route for the next few days.

> The **Gargano headland** gained its national park designation in 1995 and is the only national park in Puglia, its name originating from the ancient Greek dialect word *gárgaros*, meaning 'mountain of stone.' Formerly an island, it became connected to the mainland by river sediment, and the national park peninsula karst landscape is marked by light shades of limestone, hollows, pastures, fruit orchards, and olive groves. Monte Calvo reaches an impressive 1065m, with drastic changes in weather patterns. This 'spur on the boot of Italy' is one of the largest protected natural areas in Italy and home to 2200 different species of plants, amounting to 35% of the entire national flora. The park is also the site of two UNESCO locations: the Umbra Forest, where centuries-old native pines have survived, and the Sanctuary of Monte Sant'Angelo.

Fork left onto a quiet, flat, gravel road and upon reaching the 1m-deep abandoned railway bed (**5.2km**), turn left on its large, sharp, crushed rocks. Note that the former route – marked with a dashed line on the map – wound along a complicated zig-zag route on farm roads. The direct and flat abandoned railway route is open and slated for future redevelopment as a pedestrian-bike path.

Continue for nearly 10km on this **abandoned track**, passing road crossings, abandoned buildings, including the San Matteo train station, and a stream channel to reach the **SS272**, which directs cars up to Monte Sant'Angelo. The northern ridges are dominated by a medieval fortress known as the Torrione di Castelpagano, which was enlarged by Frederick II and later occupied by his Arab soldiers. Continue on the railway bed, or take the parallel road on its right, to pass the San Marco in Lamis abandoned train station (**9.5km**). After a further 500m, you must exit the tracks onto a road before they are separated from the road by a drainage channel.

A wooden gate marked with blazes of the Via Francigena separates one pasture from the next in the Gargano

Heading up the valley on the road, cross the former tracks at a channel and end up at a barbed-wire fence. Turn left onto a gravel road, and, leaving the channel, pass a **farmhouse** and fork right uphill. Just after a tall, **yellow villa**,

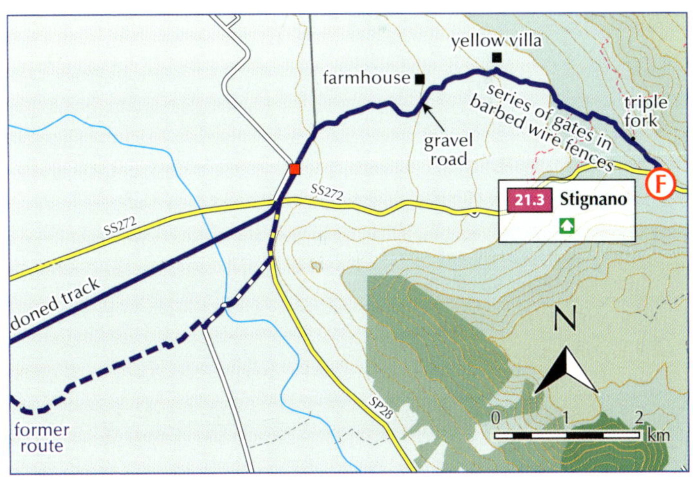

turn right to a right-hand uphill dirt road among scrub trees. At a timber-logging site, keep left and go through a first gate of a barbed-wire fence. You will pass through six similar gates (with diverse wiring connecting to fence posts) on this stage (ensure you secure each behind you). Cross a dry creek bed and keep on the left of the field, following ample red and white blazes uphill with no distinguishable path. Pass olive groves and a farm to arrive at a **triple fork**. The driveway to the farm is behind you on the right, and on the left behind you is tomorrow's route to San Giovanni Rotondo, so go straight downhill beside a reddish dry-stone wall, soon seeing the modern tower and tiled dome of Santa Maria di Stignano. Go through the parking lot to the entrance (**6.5km**).

The Sanctuary of Santa Maria di Stignano, from the 16th–17th century

21.3KM STIGNANO (ELEV 267M, POP<20) (496.2KM)

The arrival at the Sanctuary of Santa Maria di Stignano marks the gateway to the Gargano National Park from the old drove roads along the Tavoliere (tableland plains). This sacred place was the first shelter for political exiles and pilgrims upon reaching the Gargano Peninsula. Among its guests, the temple welcomed Saint Francis of Assisi on his way to Monte Sant'Angelo in 1216. His appreciation of the beauty of the place led him to give it his blessing. The current structure dates from the 16th century and was built on the chapel's foundations.

Santuario di Santa Maria di Stignano O Do €Donation, Via F. D'Alfonso, tel 347 680 9836, segreteria@santuaritaliani.it. Unmanned and very basic accommodation. Across the street, the Caselle Agriturismo serves food; tel 329 385 2885 or 327 153 6374, www.facebook.com/LeCaselleAgriturismo.

B&B Porta del Gargano Pr R Br Dr Cr S 4/14, €-/35/60/85/110/125, C. de Lancuglia SS272 km.12,5, tel 348 870 8898, info@bebportadelgargano.it, www.bebportadelgargano.it. Off route: pilgrims are picked up but must return on foot. Bus transport via Sita Sud, https://biglietteria.cotrap.it.

STAGE MSA26

Stignano to San Giovanni Rotondo

Start	Santa Maria di Stignano, Stignano
Finish	Santuario di San Pio da Pietrelcina, San Giovanni Rotondo
Distance	19.7km
Duration	6hr
Total ascent	885m
Total descent	503m
Difficulty	Hard due to uneven footing and climbs/descents
Percentage paved	11%
Lodgings	San Giovanni Rotondo 19.7km

This unforgettable stage ascends the Gargano hills to the top of breathtaking Monte Celano, where spectacular views down to Manfredonia Bay are one of the most beautiful sights of the entire Via Francigena. This challenging, athletic stage should not be attempted in adverse conditions, such as snow, heavy rain, or high winds. Although you are often crossing through gates of livestock pastures, the route feels remote, and your hiking skills will be tested. If this sounds too daunting, consider a bus ride (https://biglietteria.cotrap.it), although it would be a shame to miss the view from Monte Celano. An option for services at San Marco in Lamis adds 2.6km (one way) but also a significant descent and ascent (324m). The stage end, San Giovanni Rotondo, is a year-round pilgrimage destination for admirers of San Pio, whose remains are on display in the crypt of Renzo Piano's understated and beautifully modern Santuario di San Pio da Pietrelcina. Bring plenty of food and water for a strenuous day.

Retrace your steps from yesterday, following the uphill driveway behind the sanctuary. Take the gate to climb up on a red-dirt track, where San Severo appears in the valley. At yesterday's **triple fork**, go right uphill, pass a dairy farm set in a one-time quarry, and head through scrubland and meadows. At the fork take a right-hand grassy track, noticing the ridge above where you will soon be heading. A legitimate climb starts on crushed rocks, and combinations of red and white and/or yellow blazes lead the way. Pass through a **gate** and, 200m later, turn right, following waymarks up a steep earthen path of switchbacks on roots, rocks, and craggy outcrops. Near the top, take another gate and surmount the remnants of a wall into a pasture between two forests. Bear left, following waymarks along the ridge, with fabulous views to the Tavoliere below.

Keep uphill on a narrow path under low trees (muddy in wet weather) to turn left onto a gravel road under power lines at your first **summit**. A momentary comfortable

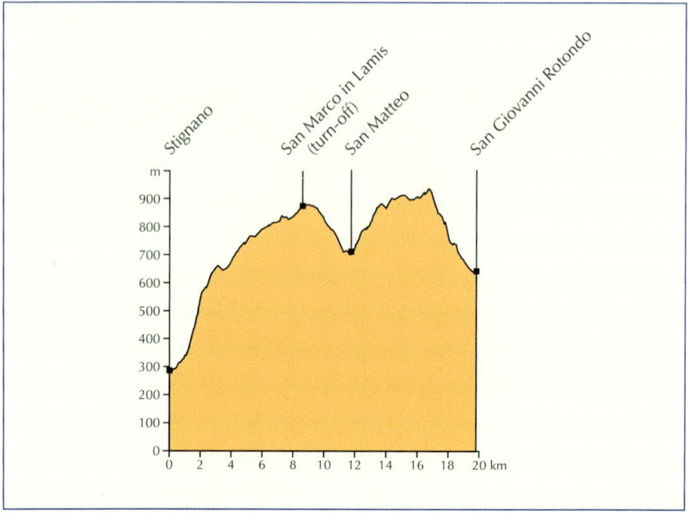

descent passes through a farmyard and gate (watch for dogs) to a road, where you turn left uphill. At its end turn right onto the **SP48** (**4.4km**) and, 50m later, follow signs onto an uphill gravel road among scrub trees and rocky meadows. Near a summit, go around a green **forestry gate** near a farm and, as the road turns sharp left, go right onto a narrow path to the right of an old stone wall, climbing gradually through the well-signed terrain of high, rocky meadows with plentiful wildflowers in season. At the stony ridge top, with spectacular vistas to the Adriatic Sea, turn left, following blazes further up and finding a well-trodden red-dirt path. Pass through a break in the barbed-wire fence into a moonscape of white rocks. Take another **gate** through barbed wire and follow blazes to turn right. As a barbed-wire fence joins, continue on a gravel road then go through a barbed-wire gate into a pine forest, arriving at two options at a **crossroads** (**4.3km**). Turn right to walk downhill to San Marco in Lamis (food, groceries, ATM, bus, pharmacy, clinic). A local highlight in San Marco in Lamis is the strong, mature *caciocavallo podolico* cheese, made from the milk of the hardy Podolica cattle, which were introduced in Italy during Barbarian invasions, originating from the Podolian steppe of Eastern Europe.

Alternatively, continue straight on the grassy gravel road by a fence line, re-entering the moonscape terrain. Pass a sign for Refugio Ciavarella (200m off route to the right) and descend gradually to merge with two left-hand tracks then immediately pass through a barbed-wire gate to descend on a grassy path. A sign indicates 2.2km to the Convento San Matteo so watch for blazes, descending through the forest on an **interpretive path**, where wooden staves marked 'Fajarama' describe the plants and

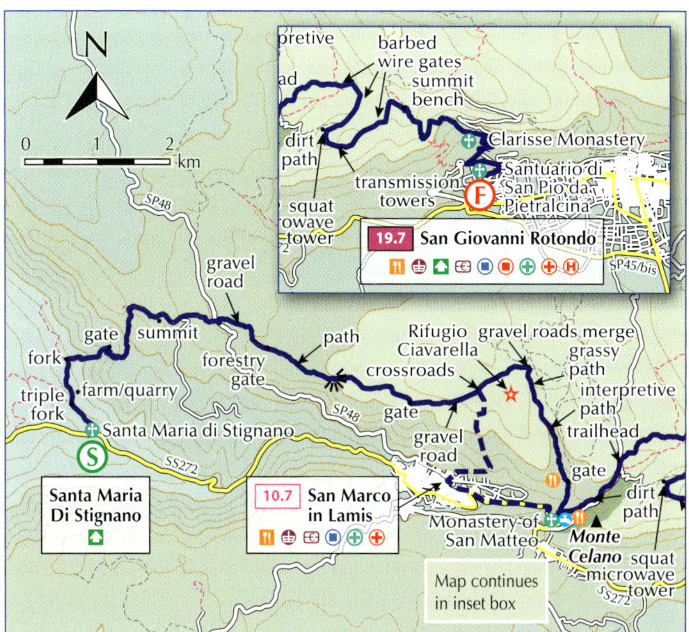

wildlife of the area. Follow the fall line of a shallow canyon with some supportive wooden barriers along the edge of the banks. At a **gate** take the gravel road ahead downhill onto asphalt and pass a pizzeria and steep limestone cliffs with occasional caves to reach the **Monastery of San Matteo** (**7.2km**, water).

Lore of the **monastery** includes tales of a 5th-century hospice for pilgrims and wayfarers, although the first documentation is dated 1007. It was initially dedicated to Saint John, but this changed when the Cathedral in Salerno donated one of Saint Matthew's teeth to the sanctuary. Inhabitants from Cerignola, on the main route, visit in his honor every September. Its splendid library stores over 60,000 books and documents.

After your visit, continue on the road and, at the next curve and before the restaurant, take a dirt path uphill into the forest. Cross a bridge over a channelized stream onto a **road** and, just after a road taking off to the right, take the well-marked Francigena trailhead on the right, noting the signed 7.5km remaining. Climb steeply on the path under deciduous trees, entering another pastoral area. The long dry-stone walls that form the enclosures on this stretch are called *jazzi*. They were used to shelter

Like a white ribbon, the SS272 highway makes its way up the valley toward San Giovanni Rotondo in the Gargano

livestock when shepherds moved their flocks downhill during colder months. Go through a **barbed-wire gate** downhill, at first along the far side of the fence then veering left uphill following blazes.

Leaving the forest, go through another gate onto a wide path that narrows through the pine forest and joins the road to the cluster of radio towers. Before a squat **microwave tower**, turn left onto gravel along the tower-filled mountaintop. After the Sentiero dei due Conventi joins from the right, take another gate, pass a shepherd's hut, and head uphill between two rows of white stones. The summit (**5km**, 932m, bench) is the highest point of the Via Francigena in the South (if you've taken the variant), and on a clear day you can see as far as Bari and make out the edge of San Giovanni Rotondo.

Waymarks lead downhill on a rocky path, followed by a smoother dirt path. Turn right downhill on the first asphalt road, pass the **Clarisse Monastery of the Resurrection**, and turn first left. Turn left onto Viale Padre Pio at the Santuario di San Pio da Pietrelcina's car park buildings and arrive at the large, sloping terrace of the sanctuary (**3.1km**), noting the pilgrim's office in the piazza. Turn left on Viale Cappuccini for restaurants and hotels.

19.7KM SAN GIOVANNI ROTONDO (ELEV 574M, POP 27,156) (476.5KM)

It is hard to travel through Puglia and not notice the wide array of posters depicting Saint Padre Pio, the most revered religious figure in Italy of the 20th century. What the town was like before his influence is indiscernible. Nearly the entirety of San Giovanni Rotondo is a shrine to the saint: the hospital (1956); the

Interior of the main chapel, designed by Renzo Piano, of the Sanctuary of San Pio of Pietrelcina

modern sanctuary that houses his relics (designed by Renzo Piano in 2004); the Monasterio di Santa Maria delle Grazie, where his monastic cell can be visited; and several museums, including a wax museum recounting his life. The town welcomes approximately seven million pilgrims annually, which makes it the world's most visited shrine after Lourdes. Born Francesco Forgione in 1887 in Pietrelcina (see Stage 20), the saint experienced his first calling in Foggia. Yet it was on September 20, 1918, on the Feast of the Stigmata of Saint Francis, that Pio was found wailing, blood coursing from his hands in the same position as Jesus's upon his crucifixion. Pio dedicated his life to miraculous healing and bled from his stigmata throughout his life. Unconvinced, Pope Pius XI barred him from preaching, and it wasn't until 24 years after his death that Pope John Paul II canonized him as St. Pio of Pietrelcina.

Ostello Torre Francigena O ⊕ Do R K W S Z 1/2 & 2/8, €15, Corso Matteotti 107, tel 393 175 3151, sgrfrancigena@gmail.com. Reservations preferred.

B&B Leggieri Villa Siria O Pr R K Br Cr W S 6/10, €-/20/40/60/-/-, Via Pietrelcina 6, tel 328 418 5785, leggieribb@gmail.com, www.villasiria.it/en.

Hotel Immagine O Pr R Br Cr S 11/36, €-/20–30/45–60/60–75/80–90/95–120, Viale Aldo Moro 150, tel 0882 412 065, info@hotelimmagine.it, www.hotelimmagine.it. Prices are for pilgrims with a credenziale; breakfast included.

The 13th-century bell tower at the Sanctuary of Monte Sant'Angelo, as seen from Via Castello

STAGE MSA27

San Giovanni Rotondo to Monte Sant'Angelo

Start	Santuario di San Pio da Pietrelcina, San Giovanni Rotondo
Finish	Santuario San Michele Arcangelo, Monte Sant'Angelo
Duration	6½hr
Distance	24.2km
Total ascent	533m
Total descent	342m
Difficulty	Moderately hard due to climbs and length
Percentage paved	35%
Lodgings	Monte Sant'Angelo 24.2km

In good weather this is a fabulous stage of countryside walking with wildflowers in season, spectacular views of the Gulf of Manfredonia, and a finish at one of the holiest shrines in Europe: the UNESCO World Heritage Sanctuary of San Michele Arcangelo. It is worth starting early to allow as much time as possible for the sanctuary and town. Better yet, stay an extra day to tour the castle, baptistery, church, holy grotto, and enchanting town center. Carry plenty of refreshments since there are no intermediate services. And congratulations on arriving at this historic and atmospheric pilgrimage destination.

With the Santuario di San Pio da Pietrelcina behind you, veer left toward the Church of Santa Maria della Grazie. From its steps, walk straight onto Viale Cappuccini, which leads downtown (past three piazzi: Europa, dei Martiri, and Padre Pio) and, upon reaching the Palazzo di Città, becomes **Viale Kennedy**, which guides you out of town (groceries).

After passing a **cemetery**, the street becomes the SS272 highway, which you follow on its shoulder uphill then down where signs fork off left onto an almost parallel downhill asphalt road that will be used in its many forms for the next 8km. The road was once a railway bed that extended from the now-abandoned San Marco in Lamis station (of two stages past) all the way to Monte Sant'Angelo. Arrive at orchards and fields on a hillside, glimpsing the highway below, and, after the road becomes a wide path between stones, come to a kiosk at the **Convento of Sant'Egidio di Pantano** (**4km**), a ruin 50m to the right, worthy of exploration.

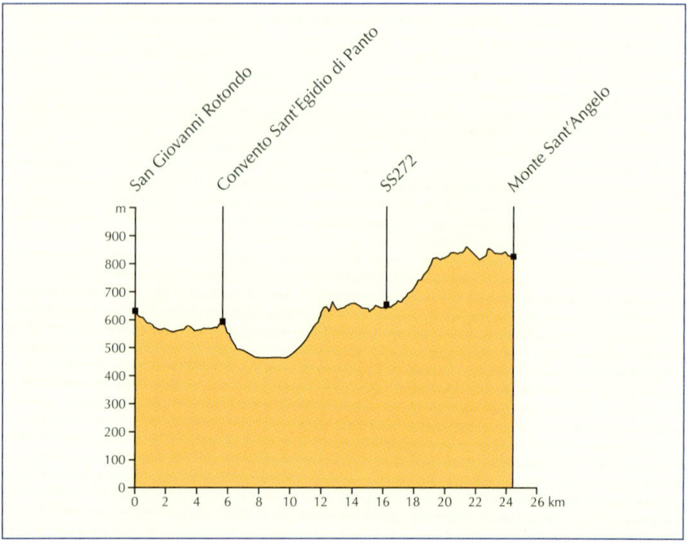

San Giovanni Rotondo
Convento Sant'Egidio di Panto
SS272
Monte Sant'Angelo
m
900
800
700
600
500
400
300
200
100
0
0 2 4 6 8 10 12 14 16 18 20 22 24 26 km

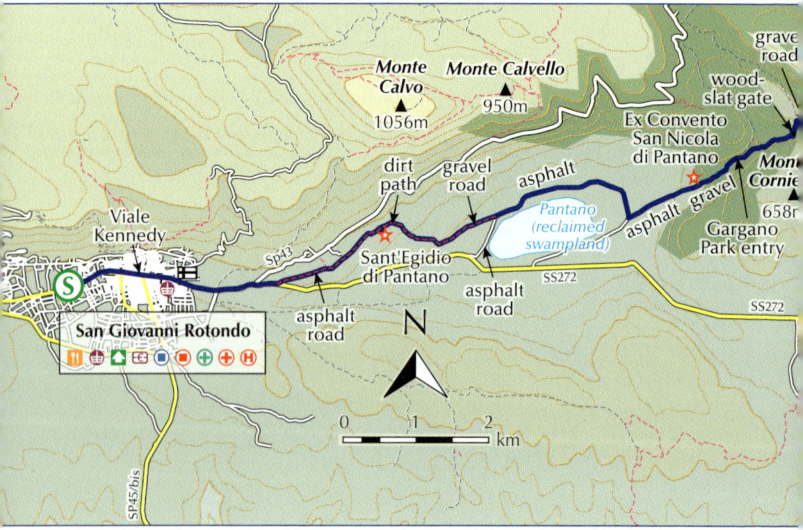

Monte Calvo
1056m
Monte Calvello
950m
grave road
wood-slat gate
Ex Convento San Nicola di Pantano
Mon Cornie
658r
dirt path
gravel road
asphalt
Pantano (reclaimed swampland)
asphalt
gravel
Gargano Park entry
Viale Kennedy
Sp43
Sant'Egidio di Pantano
SS272
asphalt road
asphalt road
SS272
San Giovanni Rotondo
N
0 1 2 km
SP45/bis

1086 donation by the **Norman Count Enrico** deeded this area to the Benedictines, who over the centuries would amass vast lands in the Gargano and establish a pilgrim hospital here to serve travelers to Monte Sant'Angelo. At one time, the now-drained Pantano (swamp) di Sant'Egidio, which gave the monastery its name, extended over the plain below.

Continue on the downhill path, which becomes a gravel road serving scattered farmhouses and is joined by a right-hand asphalt road at the valley floor with its row of pine trees. Once you are across the valley, a sign leads left onto another road uphill between two forested hills. The climb steepens as the road turns to gravel across Monte Corniello, reaching the ruins of the 11th–14th-century **Ex Convento San Nicola di Pantano** (**5.3km**). Pass through a wooden, auto-sized gate into the Parco Nazionale del Gargano, where the road becomes a delightful trail in a holm oak forest carpeted with more wildflowers. After a right fork, descend, cross a gully of a seasonal creek, climb (following red and white blazes), pass through a **wood-slat gate**, and head into the next field. Go uphill on the other side of the gully, pass two tumbledown stone walls (marked 'Private Property'), turn right before a paddock, and take a right-hand downhill gravel road through pastures to a metal gate. At the concrete switchback, go left then take another metal gate into more pastures. Pass an **old quarry**, turn right onto an asphalt (restaurant) drive then left onto the **SS272** highway (**5.2km**) we left in San Giovanni Rotondo. In 30m cross over to take a gravel road winding uphill and

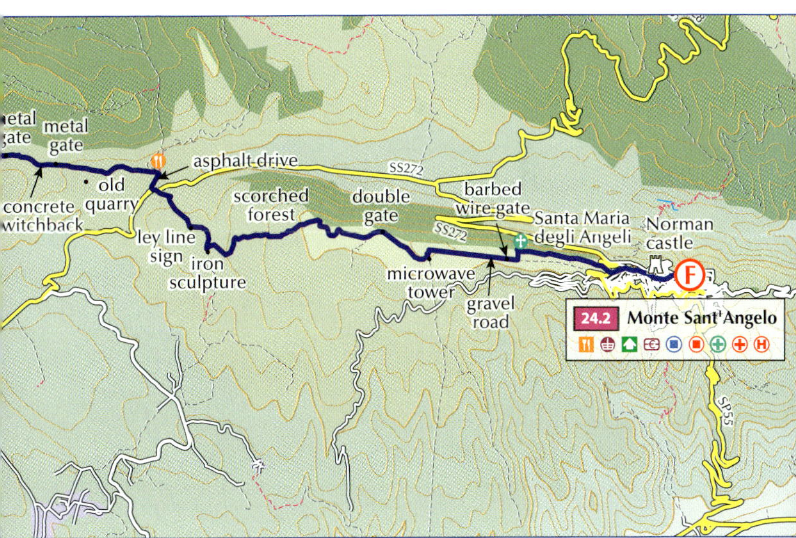

A nun approaches the twin-arched main entrance at the Sanctuary of Monte Sant'Angelo

A modern mural in the Byzantine style decorates the Chapel of Reconciliation at the Sanctuary of Monte Sant'Angelo

come to a sign that marks the passage of the ley line at this spot. Legends align several sites associated with St. Michael the Archangel between the Holy Land and Ireland as a single ley or perceived line between two or more locations. Pass an **iron sculpture** of three happy women and take a gate to circle uphill, back to a moonscape pasture waymarked with plentiful blazes.

Pass through a scorched forest as the path/road winds ever upward to reveal more views of the Adriatic. Pass through the easier pedestrian option of a double gate and, under a **microwave tower**, go left on a driveway. Turn right around the concrete fence and, part of the way around, turn right onto a gravel road leading into Monte Sant'Angelo. Go through a barbed-wire gate, take a left-hand path then a gravel road, pass the Franciscan Church of **Santa Maria degli Angeli**, and take your final pasture gate in the shadow of a radio tower. Join the uphill Via del Castello, pass a green military building then the **Norman castle**, and arrive at the hexagonal tower at the gate to the sanctuary (**8.1km**).

24.2KM MONTE SANT'ANGELO (ELEV 814M, POP 12,534) (452.3KM)

Most visitors enjoy the Gargano as an idyllic beach holiday or a mountain sports destination. You, on the other hand, have completed a pilgrimage to the shrine of the Archangel Michael, originally an act of devotion that started in the 5th century when, within a cave, the Bishop of Sipontum (near today's Manfredonia) witnessed one of the first apparitions of the Archangel ever recorded. The town has been a UNESCO World Heritage Site since 2011, and the rejoicing of pilgrims on their arrival is evidenced by inscriptions and runes on the walls of the temple. In the 7th century, the pilgrimage route became the Via Sacra Langobardorum when the Gargano area became part of the Lombard Duchy of Benevento. St. Michael became the Lombard patron saint, resembling their own warlike gods, and the basilica is listed among UNESCO's The Longobards in Italy, Places of Power. Access the shrine through the grand 11th-century bronze doors forged in Constantinople (another sign of close relationships between West and East) upon which past visitors knocked with vigor to wake the Saint. Descend the medieval staircase to the sacred grotto to attend the daily worship. Finally, receive the Testimonium at the entrance to the basilica. Other important sites include the 10th-century Norman castle, with its impressive Torre dei Giganti, and the basilica's 1274 octagonal bell tower.

Parrocchia S. M. del Carmine-Centro pellegrino O Do K Br S Z 4/6, €Donation, Via Umberto I 4, tel 340 862 7215, dondom95@libero.it. Maximum two nights' stay.

Foresteria per turisti Casa Del Pellegrino Do R Dr Cr Z 2/10, €8–10, Via Carlo d'Angiò, tel 0884 568 016, info@hotelcasadelpellegrino.it, www.hotelcasadelpellegrino.it. Usually open but check ahead in winter; priority is given to pilgrims on foot.

SECTION 3B: PUGLIA – VIA LITORANEA CONNECTION

Views of the Adriatic appear as pilgrims make their way down from Monte Sant'Angelo (photo: Nicole Bukaty)

Parco Nazionale del Gargano
Monte Sant'Angelo
Mattinata
S
Jazzo Ognissanti ruins
4.8 Madonna delle Grazie
Via Foggia
SS89
9.2 Manfredonia
Siponto
estuary
Torrente Candelaro
Lido Salpi
La Bussola
SP5
canal
Hotel African Beach
Ippocampo
Torre Rivoli
Foggiamare Village
27.4 Zapponeta
SP5
Chiesetta di San Michele
19.0 Margherita di Savoia
saltpans
Borgo Tressanti
Trinitapoli
local road
lungomare
can
San Ferdinando di Puglia
Ofanto River
Stornara
Cerignola
16.5 Barletta
Andria
La
Canosa di Puglia
San Valentino
Montegrosso
Loconia
Villaggio Moschella

After descending from the heights of the Gargano National Park, with splendid views across the Adriatic, this Via Francigena variant skips in and out of scenic harbors, with their colorful fishing boats and golden sand, and explores the enchanting historical towns of Barletta and Trani. Thereafter, the route flattens and continues along the menacing SP5 road, quiet local roads, beaches, and coastal promenades (*lungomari*). Apart from in towns with lodgings, refreshments are hard to come by, so plan ahead. It is strongly advised you take a bus between Manfredonia and Margherita di Savoia, or even Barletta, to avoid endless walking on the stressful SP5.

Note: points of interest and municipality descriptions on the Via Litoranea Connection were contributed by Patrycja Bukaty.

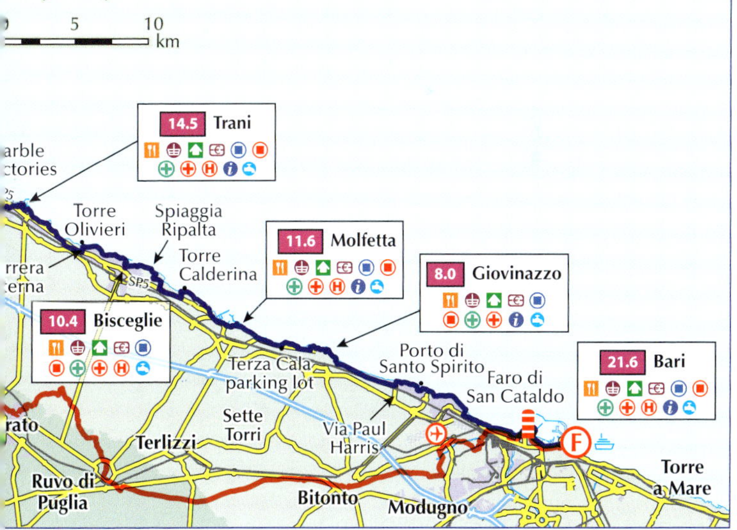

VIA LITORANEA CONNECTION

Monte Sant'Angelo to Bari

Start	Santuario San Michele Arcangelo, Monte Sant'Angelo
Finish	Basilica Pontificia San Nicola, Bari
Distance	143km
Total ascent	597m
Total descent	1344m
Difficulty	Moderate due to an initial steep descent and highway walking
Duration	33hr
Percentage paved	84%
Lodgings	Madonna delle Grazie 4.8km; Manfredonia 14km; Zapponeta 41.4km; Margherita di Savoia 60.4km; Barletta 76.9km; Trani 91.4km; Bisceglie 101.8km; Molfetta 113.4km; Giovinazzo 121.4km; Bari 143km

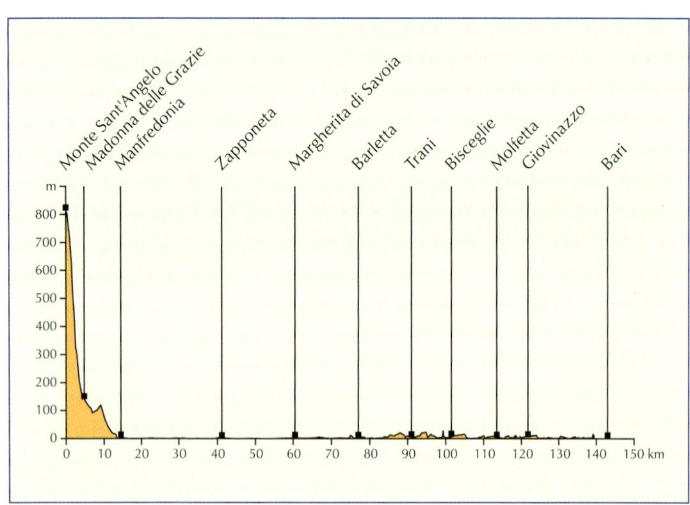

From the sanctuary, turn left down Via Reale Basilica, go through the arch, fork left onto Via Giuseppe Verdi, pass a tower, keep left past a chapel, then reach the information board at the head of the hill-walking trail (**1.1km**). Signs warn against walking in bad weather: the steep descent is on loose stones and overgrown paths, although without exposed edges. Brown signposts and red and white blazes indicate the way. Go through a gate on the left (ignoring the one ahead) and head left on a faint grassy path alongside the fence line, keeping the viewpoint and benches on the right. Pass buildings then the cave of Santa Lucia (**0.4km**), reaching two options at the signpost 160m later. The *sendero storico* (historical path) is preferred since the waymarking is clearer.

Sendero storico main route, 1.9km

Go right downhill on switchbacks then pass through two consecutive gates. Turn left and follow the red and white paint on a rock ahead. At the next gate, turn right toward an information board (**1.9km**). Go straight through the barbed-wire fence; it is not very obvious, but it does open! With some plots and houses scattered on the slopes, reach the union with the alternative route on a lane (**0.6km**).

Jazzo Ognissanti option, 1.7km

Rather than heading right downhill, keep ahead uphill then down. Veer slightly left and, in a switchback, reach the **Jazzo Ognissanti ruins** (**1.1km**). The church ruins hold residual 13th-century Puglian frescoes inspired by Byzantine iconography and testimonial inscriptions left by devoted pilgrims. Continue descending, passing a viewpoint 350m later, then go right and left, coming to the main route on the lane.

Main route continues

With both options united, bear left along the lane to **Madonna delle Grazie** then turn right onto the SP55.

4.8KM MADONNA DELLE GRAZIE (ELEV 166M, POP 25) (447.5KM)

Here lies the start of the Sentiero Scannamugliera, the ancient mule track leading to Monte Sant'Angelo. Along this historic pilgrim itinerary, footsteps creating a path within the rocks testify to many centuries of shared use by farmers, shepherds, and devotees, giving rise to the name of 'Scala Santa' (Holy Staircase).

Masseria Barone Gambadoro O Pr R Br S 6/10, €-/-/160/-/-, Via Madonna delle Grazie 2, tel 333 727 2868, info@masseriabaronegambadoro.it. Reservations required.

Upon leaving, waymarking is scant. Fork right off the SP55 onto **Via Foggia** by a dry-stone wall and olive groves (**1km**), soon to be met with sea views and a Gargano Park information board. Reach a **junction of lanes** and make a sharp left onto a lane with Manfredonia in sight below. Cross a bridge then the road and turn right then immediately left, following road signs for Manfredonia (**5.7km**). Go over the **SS89** then veer left by apartments onto Via Florio, passing a gas station, now in town. Cross the road and take the right-hand road ahead to keep on Via Florio. At the next crossroads, find Via Pulsano ahead (bakery) then cross over Via Gargano (services) and take the third right onto Via San Giovanni Bosco. Keep straight, passing a school, a stadium, the castle park (**2.2km**), and the Parrocchia Santa Maria Stella Maris (1100–1200) until the cobblestone street reaches Piazza del Popolo with its Chiesa di San Domenico and the town hall. Turn right onto Via Arcivescovado and arrive at the Piazza Papa Giovanni XXIII and Cattedrale di San Lorenzo.

9.2KM MANFREDONIA (ELEV 14M, POP 57,100) (438.3KM)

Founded by King Manfred in 1256, Manfredonia was built near the ruins of ancient Sipontum to respond to the economic expansion of Upper Puglia and to reinforce coastal defenses. The city endured much adversity. It was destroyed by the Turks in 1620 and hit by subsequent natural disasters. World War 1 reached Italy on the May 24, 1915, when Manfredonia was bombed by the Austrians and the torpedo boat *Turbine* was sunk. It is a classic Levantine city, currently engaged in industrial development characterized by agriculture, fishing, and tourism. The cathedral holds many noteworthy works of art, including an ancient wooden statue of the Madonna and Child, more commonly called the 'Madonna with wide eyes,' having witnessed an act of violence.

- **Residence del sole** O Pr R Br S Z 10/29, €-/50–80/60–110/70–110/80–140/90–200, Via Lungomare del Sole 34/A, tel 0884 543 377 or 371 3364711, info@residencedelsolemanfredonia.it. Breakfast included. American Express not accepted.
- **La maison B&B Manfredonia** O Pr R Br S 10/25, €-/50/50/65/80/-, Corso Manfredi 255, tel 329 425 5956.

Go back to Piazza del Popolo, cross the square diagonally to the far right-hand corner, and take the narrow Via Maddalena. Turn left onto Via Campanile, toward the sea, cross the road to the port, then turn right alongside the sea. At the end of the road, turn right then immediately left onto Viale Kennedy (water across the road). Pass a square with a fountain, the Parrocchia di Sant'Andrea apostolo e martire, and a restaurant, enjoying the promenade (water). Cross a stream and pass another restaurant, now in **Siponto** (**3.2km**).

The ancient Greek city of **Siponto** (Sepious), once a center of Daunia then conquered by Pyrrhus (330BC), prospered and became the largest port of northern Puglia following Roman colonization. Archeological remains expose vestiges of the Puglian-Romanesque style, particularly in the Basilica di Santa Maria Maggiore di Siponto. To its right are remains of an early Christian basilica, all encaptured within a fantastic mesh art installation by Edoardo Tresoldi, inaugurated in 2016.

At the end of a park, with a parking lot on your right (restaurant), turn left toward the beach. Shortcut: Keep on the main road out of town to link to the SP5. After the beach walk, turn right into pine woods and immediately left just before the **estuary** (**2.6km**). Follow the stream briefly then go right on the next track inland, which soon becomes asphalted by houses. At the end of the road, opposite fields, turn left onto the main road, leaving town. At the end of this road, turn left onto the SP141, which soon becomes the **SP5** (road signs for Bari). This busy, narrow highway with no pavement requires caution, so walk facing oncoming traffic. Cross the **Torrente Candelaro**, ignore the first track, then ignore the first road (sign for Sciale delle Rondinelle), but then take the next left toward abandoned white buildings among eucalyptus trees. Follow a path to turn right along the beach.

After 1.8km of beach walking, through the trees you can find **Lido Salpi** (**6.3km**). Then pass **La Bussola** and eventually turn left along a canal leading to a left turn onto the SP5. Cross a canal then turn right into the resort complex of **Ippocampo**. Pass an outdoor church then a grocery shop. Just after the road bends right, take a street on

A pilgrim walks the beaches between Manfredonia and Zapponeta (photo: Nicole Bukaty)

the left. This road also bends right after which take the first left again. Pass a pharmacy (unreliable) and turn left just before Hotel African Beach (food) (**7.5km**). The beach bar and hotel have a Via Francigena stamp for your credenziale. Follow the sandy path around the pond then turn right along the shore. Veer right between warehouses on the lane then turn left and right to continue between the canal and floodplain. Turn left onto the **SP5**, cross two canals, and take the entrance into **Foggiamare Village** beach resort (unreliable services). The big access gate is usually opened for you by a member of staff at the booth. If not, there are three options. Firstly, keep to the SP5 for another 1.6km then cross a canal and go over the road barriers onto a track on the left for 310m, leading to the beach. Secondly, take a track further along down to the beach at the next lido, Valentino. Thirdly, keep to the SP5 all the way to Zapponeta.

Keep straight among houses and after the road bends left, take the next track on the right, reaching the beach and spotting the 1568 **Torre Rivoli**, among the largest and best preserved of the Gargano watchtowers. Turn right along the coast, reaching a lido now in **Zapponeta** (**6.3km**). Veer right behind the lido and turn left. Turn first right onto Via Nettuno, pass a café, and reach the main street/SP5 (services) behind which lies the church.

27.4KM ZAPPONETA (ELEV 3M, POP 3422) (410.9KM)

Zapponeta developed around 1768 following encouragement from the local fiefdom master, Baron Michele Zezza, proprietor of Zapponeta's stone-built Posta Zezza Palace and Church of San Michele Arcangelo. Its local produce has attained a certain national popularity, particularly its onions, carrots, and potatoes, which have a distinctive flavor due to the sandy soil. The iron-rich black sands of Zapponeta beach have proven to be therapeutic for rheumatic diseases. Zapponeta is also the birthplace of the internationally renowned singer-songwriter Nicola di Bari.

Parrocchia S. Michele Arcangelo Do €Donation, Piazza Aldo Moro, tel 0884 520 275, sanmichele.zapponeta@tim.it. No bedding or showers provided. Advance communication is difficult; check for services on arrival.

B&B Il Fico O Pr R K W S Z 1/4, €-/55–65/60–65/70–75/80/85/-, Corso Manfredonia 80, tel 327 940 7957.

Turn left along the main street/**SP5**. Taking a bus to Margherita di Savoia from here is advised (see https://biglietteria.cotrap.it/#/ricerca for timetables, check local bus stops, and ask locals. The Google Maps route planner is also usually up to date). On this monotonous stretch, keep to the left side of the busy road, facing oncoming traffic. Although sometimes there is a walkable edge, you are forced back onto the road, including at dangerous bends. As a reward, views of the sublime **saltpans** emerge (**3.5km**).

Zapponeta's parish church is dedicated to St Michael Archangel (photo: Nicole Bukaty)

The red-tinted **saltpans** are the biggest in Europe and second largest globally, with an annual salt production of 500,000 tons. The important wetlands are home to many species of fish and birds, including pink flamingos.

Along the nerve-wracking road walk, pass the little **Chiesetta di San Michele chapel** on your left and enjoy the beauty of the sea and the exceptional birdlife. Pass the salt excavation point after which a blessed cycle path on the right-hand side can be used to finally step off the SP5. Take the bridge into **Margherita di Savoia** (**13.5km**), turn left onto Via Traiano (heading behind beach bars), and, at the next crossroads, turn left toward the beach then right onto the beachside promenade, arriving at Piazza Libertà.

19KM MARGHERITA DI SAVOIA (ELEV 4M, POP 11,855) (391.9KM)

Within a landscape of natural beauty, Margherita di Savoia's history is intertwined with that of the saltpans, the town having been known as Salinis (*saline* in Latin) since the 3rd century BC. Today, its name honors Margherita, Queen of Italy, who also had the ubiquitous pizza named after her. The salt museum portrays the local life, culture, and history. Within the Torre delle Saline, the Municipal Art Gallery Francesco Galante Civera exhibits over 150 Neapolitan works of art.

Parrocchia Maria SS. Addolorata Do €Donation, Corso Nunzio Ricco 49, tel 0883 652 831 or 349 723 6819, parr.m.addolorata@gmail.com. Advance communication is difficult; check for services on arrival.

Grand Hotel Terme O Pr R K Br Dr Cr S Z 70/130, €-/65/100/135/160, Corso Garibaldi 1, tel 0883 655 402, info@termemargherita.it, www.termemargherita.it/grand-hotel. Reservations required; 10% discount for bigger groups; closed November 1 to March 31 inclusive.

The impressive, intact 'Eraclio – Colossus of Barletta' statue towers at 4.5m (photo: Nicole Bukaty)

Keep to the promenade across another square then turn right between buildings to reach Margherita's main road, by apartments. Turn left then right along palm-tree-lined Via Polibio then turn left onto the **SP5** at a crossroads, passing a gas station (**1.3km**, food). At the next roundabout, take the first left onto a local road through crops and vineyards then go left again onto the SP5. Cross over the **Ofanto River**, take the next left (signs for Fiumara), ignore tracks either side, keep ahead at the junction, and soon take a sandy track on the left into fields. Keep right at the next fork, turn right onto the next road then immediately turn left to the sea. Turn right alongside the water, reaching **Barletta** on the city's very long lungomare and passing a drinking fountain (**12.7km**) then restaurants. After another drinking fountain on the other side of the road, cross the avenue, fork right, and take the narrow road on the right, following brown signs for historical monuments. Go through the Antica Porta Marina arch and head left behind the old well of Antico Pozzo di Piazza Marina onto a tree-lined avenue. Reach the cathedral opposite the castle (water by the castle grounds).

16.5KM BARLETTA (ELEV 17M, POP 94,673) (375.4KM)

Origins

Barletta, which dates back to the 4th century BC when the still-standing wharf was built, developed as a port during the Roman era and was an important crossroads for pilgrims and knights. The castle, although dating from 1202, has gone down in history as one of the Land of Bari castles built by Frederick II of Swabia, who announced the Sixth Crusade within its walls. Today, it stages events and exhibitions. The famous Disfida (challenge) di Barletta took place in February 1503, when 13 Italian cavaliers, commanded by Ettore Fieramosca, dueled and won against 13 French knights, captained by Guy de La Motte. The duel was the result of the French slandering the Italians. The 16th-century Cantina della Sfida, declared a National Monument in 1937, is evocative of the discord, with the 13 shields of the champions hanging on its walls.

Religious buildings

The 1458 coronation of Ferdinand I of Naples took place in the Cattedrale di Santa Maria Maggiore, which showcases many historical shifts: a Puglian-Romanesque style facade, a Renaissance portal, a Gothic presbytery, and an Eastern Mediterranean influence that can be seen in its 11th-century bell tower and sacred ornaments, such as the pulpit (1267) and ciborium. The underground crypt holds remains of a 10th–11th-century Christian basilica, while the Treasury contains jewelry, Islamic ivory, paintings, scrolls, and furnishings. Be sure to visit the incredibly intact 'Eraclio – Colossus of Barletta', a bronze statue from the Roman period depicting either the Emperor Valentinian I or the Emperor Marcian.

Modern-day Barletta

Barletta is the proud birthplace of Giuseppe De Nittis, a renowned 19th-century impressionist painter (the beautiful Palazzo della Marra displays some of his work), and Pietro Mennea, an Italian sprinter and 1980 Olympics 200m gold medalist and world-record holder for almost 17 years, the longest duration in the event's history. It is no wonder that it is the Sports Association in Barletta that welcomes pilgrims and stamps your credenziale (see Appendix B)!

B&B Il Campanile O Pr R S 3/6, €-/30/35/-/-/-, Via Abignenti 2, tel 349 512 4428. Bari airport and luggage transfers available. Your host is Gianni.

Continue up the road, turn left alongside the castle grounds, then turn left onto Via Trani. Turn left at the roundabout onto Viale Regina Elena and turn right by the sea. Pass a drinking fountain across the road and turn left onto a pavement and cycle path. Turn left down the second track (Contrada Le Paludi sign), following red and white waymarks. At the end of this track turn right onto another. As the track becomes a lane, veer right then left over a **canal** back to the shore. At the crossroads go straight across a **canal** toward buildings. Note that waymarking on the ground here differs from the EAVF GPX file (2024). Follow waymarks to continue straight, and at the end of the lane turn right. Along this next lane, and sprinkled across Puglia, seasonal fig and mulberry trees provide shade and welcoming refreshment.

Keep to the same road as it bends left, receiving your first glimpse of Trani's glowing cathedral. Ignore a left-hand path, veer right with the road, and, at the end of it, turn left, reaching the marble workshops in **Trani** (**10.1km**). At the end of the road, turn left onto the busy main road then turn right (road signs for Bari). Turn left and left again, following signs for 'centro' and 'cattedrale.' Pass the modern Parrocchia Santi Angeli Custodi and turn right onto Via Canonico Don Nicola Ragno. At the crossroads, take the third road and, at the junction, turn right, ensuring you fork left by the square (water), then keep left at the fork onto Via Mario Pagano. At the next crossroads, now in Trani's old town, turn left onto Via Fra'Diego Álvarez and pass Chiesa di San Giacomo

(**4.2km**), with views toward the sea (water on the right). At the castle, veer right along the coast, reaching the Basilica Cattedrale Beata Maria Vergine Assunta.

14.5KM TRANI (ELEV 12M, POP 56,076) (360.9KM)
Elegant buildings and monuments, the 11th-century cathedral (asserted as the 'Queen of Puglian Romanesque,' with a tower welcoming sailors), and the castle make for delightful sightseeing as you wander through the narrow streets and stunning port of Trani. The city's name derives from an ancient legend linked to Tyrrhenian, son of Diomedes, who founded Turenum in the 1st century. This picturesque town became an important bishopric during its trade with the East and, in the Middle Ages, its coastal access favored the passage of pilgrims and crusaders to the Holy Land. In August, the town commemorates the historical event of Manfred's wedding to Elena d'Oedipus as part of its vibrant Medieval Week.

HUB Portanova O Do R K Br Cr W S Z 2/15, €20/25/-/75/-/-, Via Nigrò 18, tel 327 824 0564 or 331 224 4407, turismo@hubportanova.it, www.hubportanova.it.

Trani Cathedral, an absolute queen of the Puglian Romanesque (photo: Nicole Bukaty)

Keeping the cathedral on your left, veer right on the square and go straight onto Via Archivio then turn right, fork left, and turn right at the port. At the Convento Madonna del Carmine piazza, almost at the end of the seafront, turn right. At a junction by a palm-tree-scattered park, cross straight over onto a road with a blue cycle path and keep ahead over all junctions along a lovely lungomare.

At the height of **Capo Colonna beach**, a 240m detour on the road on the left leads to the peninsula and the 1st-century Ex Monastero di Santa Maria di Colonna, which is glimpsed through the palm trees. No longer inhabited, it is now a beautiful cultural venue hosting exhibitions and concerts.

The cycle path ends but the route continues along the coast, past a drinking fountain on the left (**2.8km**). At the end of the road, continue ahead on a pedestrianized promenade, leaving town. After 700m, upon reaching a **statue of a boat**, turn right, away from the sea.

Turn left onto the **SP5** then 400m later, cross carefully and turn right onto Via Due Pozzi, among olive trees. Return to the SP5, cross back over, and turn right onto it. After 800m (restaurant), now on the edge of town, turn left onto Carrera Lama Paterna, with views of the 16th-century **Torre Olivieri** soon emerging to the left. At the end of the road, ignore steps that lead down to Spiaggia la Torretta beach, and, instead, turn right into an alley, which brings you onto Bisceglie's long lungomare. Pass the Teatro Mediterraneo, ice-cream parlors, bars, cafés, and a drinking fountain (**5.8km**) to arrive at the port.

10.4KM BISCEGLIE (ELEV 25M, POP 55,390) **(350.5KM)**

Bisceglie boasts a well-preserved medieval center, vast beaches, and a charming fishing harbor. Its rich architectural heritage includes the noble Palazzo Tupputi, the 12th-century Chiesa di Santa Margherita, and the splendid 11th-century Romanesque Concattedrale di San Pietro Apostolo.

B&B Agorà Bisceglie Pr R Br Cr 3/7, €-/50/65/90/-/-, Vico Conforti 7, tel 347 698 8793, www.facebook.com/agorabisceglie.

Continue along the promenade at the foot of the old town and head straight onto Via della Repubblica. Take the steps up on the left and continue above the beaches, still on the lungomare. Just as the road bends right, take the path along the coast, passing ruins and the **Spiaggia Ripalta**.

The **seagrass meadows** in the caves making up the Grotte di Ripalta are an important marine sanctuary for sea creatures escaping the otherwise quite industrial coastline. The caves are only accessible from the sea via a boat tour, or on a paddleboard for the more adventurous. Also, here you are treated to a sight of many *casedde*: round, stone huts used for farming and viticulture.

The path reaches a road. Turn right onto it and, at the end, turn left onto a new lane by a round stone building. Continue on the same lane, passing villas and plots and ignoring all sidetracks to turn left onto the **SP5**. After 100m, cross carefully to use the traffic lights and a pavement on the other side (road signs for Molfetta). At the next major junction, 600m later, cross carefully back over to use the pavement on the left, which soon ends, although a shoulder now keeps the cars at bay.

Pass the Nettuno tourist complex and restaurant (unreliable). After 600m, take the next track on the left (signed 'Private Entry'). Ignore all tracks from the left and find yourself back at the sea, where you turn right. Pass **Torre Calderina** and take the road ahead 300m later. At the next junction, as Molfetta appears, veer right to turn left onto the **SP5** and go straight over the roundabout. Now in town, pass warehouses and turn first left onto Via Salvatore Mininni. At the Basilica Santuario Madonna dei Martiri (**10.4km**), turn right along the coast. Pass a gas station, turn right, and, at the end of the road, turn right onto Molfetta's high street. Just after the square on the left, turn left onto Vico XV Madonna dei Martiri then turn first right onto Via Sant'Anna. After 100m, almost at the end of the road, turn right then turn left at the end of the alley (water on the square across the road). Take the next road on the left (signs for Porto) and arrive at the harbor.

11.6KM MOLFETTA (ELEV 16M, POP 59,623) (338.9KM)

Molfetta offers a leisurely atmosphere within its old town and traditional fishing harbor. Its seafront cathedral, in dazzling sandstone, has an octagonal dome and towers.

Seminario Vescovile O Pr Do R K Br Dr Cr W S Z Piazza Giuseppe Garibaldi 65, Italy, tel 080 397 1820, 080 337 4211 or 080 335 1919, segreteria@acmolfetta.it. Advance communication is difficult; check for services on arrival.

Oltre l'Arco O Pr R K Br Cr W S 2/4, €-/55/60/75/-/-, Via Trescine 4, tel 347 697 6747 or 347 822 2388, oltrelarco@gmail.com, www.facebook.com/oltrelarcomolfetta.

B&B Al Duomo O Pr R K Cr 2/7, €-/55/65/80/100/110, Via Chiesa Vecchia 15, tel 373 809 3289, infoalduomo@gmail.com, www.alduomomolfetta.it/en. One apartment with a kitchen for up to five people and one double room without kitchen access.

Continue along the promenade for 300m. At the junction with a left-hand road that leads to the cathedral, veer from the promenade to head through town. Keep the Chiesa del Purgatorio to your right and fork left onto a cobblestone road. Arrive on a new promenade, the Lungomare Marcantonio Colonna, and after 1.2km, at its end,

Fresh delicacies from the sea dominate coastal menus (photo: Nicole Bukaty)

turn right onto Via Don Grittani then turn first left. Pass a gas station and take the second road on the left to the coast.

Bend right (water on the right-hand side of the road) and 600m later, take the lane ahead, leaving Molfetta and spotting Giovinazzo in the distance. Turn right then left and left again onto the **SP5**. After 700m, turn left through the **Terza Cala parking lot** and, at the end, take the right-hand track by the sea. Fork right in front of a building and right again, following a coastal path to the walls of a beach complex. Here turn right then left onto the **SP5**. Pass a supermarket then a mini roundabout and take the next road on the left, passing Giovinazzo's cemetery. Turn right along the sea (**6.7km**), arriving at the Piazza Porto and harbor.

8KM GIOVINAZZO (ELEV 8M, POP 20,396) (330.9KM)

A town rich in history, Giovinazzo attracts many tourists, who gather with locals on the lively trapeze-shaped square, Piazza Vittorio Emanuele II. Among the most important monuments are the Chiesa di Santa Maria di Costantinopoli, built in 1528 and full of valuable paintings; the Trajan Arch; and the Concattedrale di Santa Maria Assunta, as well as the famous baroque palaces.

Casa di Accoglienza Frate Camillo Campanella Do Via Crocifisso, tel 342 321 4796, casapcamillo@gmail.com or accoglienzacappuccinipuglia@hotmail.com. Advance communication is difficult; check for services on arrival.

Cà de Mess O Pr R K Br Dr S Z 1/2, €-/-/70/-/-, Via Giordano Bruno 4, tel 329 606 4969. Two additional spaces for children.

Cross the port and bear left to reach the Concattedrale di Santa Maria Assunta. Turn right beside it, passing the main entrance, and soon take steps on your left to reach the coast (water in the square on the right), joining the lungomare. At the next mini roundabout go right then turn left onto the **SP5** (road signs for Bari), walking along its cycle path. At the exit for Foggia and Bitonto, turn left down **Via Paul Harris** and, once through the car park, turn right along the coast. Pass restaurants and reach **Porto di Santo Spirito** (train) (**8.2km**), part of **Bari**. Here connect with the main route and follow the walking directions as described in Stage 32 for the remaining 5.4km to the Basilica di San Nicola in Bari's old town.

21.6KM BARI (ELEV 12M, POP 316,015) (309.3KM)

See Stage 32 on the main route for municipality information, including lodgings, and city map.

A pilgrim explores Bari's maze of alleys (photo: Nicole Bukaty)

Bari's old city teems with shops and restaurants

SECTION 4: PUGLIA – BRINDISI TO SANTA MARIA DI LEUCA

Santa Maria di Leuca lighthouse at dusk (Stage 45)

Salento is the 'heel of the boot of Italy,' and as the route travels down to its tip, it heads inland to enjoy the cream-colored limestone treasures of baroque Lecce. The Greek influence becomes visible after the route touches the coast again at historic Otranto, before the Francigena ends on a white bluff over the glistening Ionian Sea.
BARI
Modugno
Casamassima
Turi
Crispiano
TARANTO
Puglia
BRINDISI
Brindisi BDS Airport
Adriatic Sea
Torchiarolo
LECCE
Martano
Otranto
Vignacastrisi
Tricase
Santa Maria di Leuca
Gulf of Taranto
Ionian Sea
N
0 20 40 km
Torretta di Crucoli
Isola di Capo Rizzuto

STAGE 39

Brindisi to Torchiarolo

Start	Via Appia Traiana Column, Brindisi
Finish	Piazza Castello, Torchiarolo
Duration	6½hr
Distance	25.2km
Total ascent	184m
Total descent	163m
Difficulty	Moderate due to distance
Percentage paved	55%
Lodgings	Torchiarolo 25.2km

The next four stages leave the sea until the route reaches Otranto, some 110km away. This stage returns to fields and olive groves (impacted by the Xylella plague), with the pleasant interlude of the first true woods since quite some time at Bosco di Cerano. Plan for an entire day's food and water since there are no intermediate services.

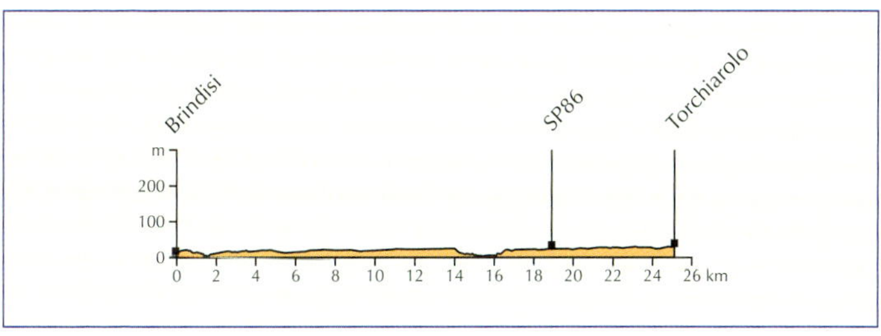

Keep the Via Appia Traiana column on your right and go straight onto Via Colonne. Here commences the Via Traiana Calabra, which linked Brindisi to Otranto where the Bordeaux Pilgrim docked upon their return from the Holy Land. In two blocks pass the cathedral's baroque bell tower then Piazza Duomo with the facade of the cathedral to your left. Now on Via Tarantini, pass Piazzetta della Zecca and, afterward, Brindisi's **Statio Peregrinorum** (pilgrim office). One street after passing Piazza Dante, turn left onto Via San Giovanni Al Sepolcro. Keep ahead to see another of Brindisi's most prized historic buildings, the 11th–12th-century somber, circular **Tempio di San Giovanni**

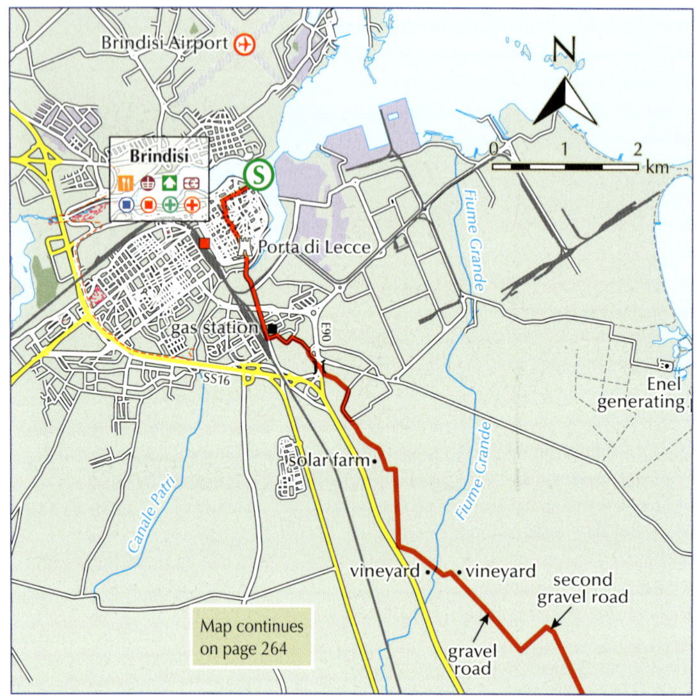

Map continues
on page 264

al Sepolcro, reminiscent of the Holy Sepulchre of Jerusalem, containing original 13th-century frescoes.

After your visit, turn right into an alleyway just before the church then turn left at the next street. Signs lead past the Chiesa di Santa Maria degli Angeli and to the palm-tree-lined high street Corso Umberto I. Go straight through Piazzetta Fornaro onto a narrow shopping lane, cross Corso Roma onto Via Porta Lecce, and go through the **Porta di Lecce**, leaving the center. Go straight at the next two roundabouts, turn first left after the **gas station** among apartments, zigzag to a right turn over a drainage channel, and head into an industrial and farming area.

After 300m, turn right onto a country lane, Strada per Formosa, and cross under the E90 highway. Pass a **solar farm**, fields, single rows of olive trees, and a vineyard. At the second vineyard, turn right onto a straight gravel road between two stone stanchions of a gate. Before the road curves right, turn left onto another gravel road (muddy in wet weather), which turns sharply right. Cross over a drainage channel and curve through countryside with the tall, cylindrical, striped tower of the Enel electrical

Francigena pilgrims leave town through Brindisi's Porta Lecce, which was built in 1464 by Ferdinand II of Aragon

generating plant to the left. Pass a **farm complex** and go straight at a stop sign onto the asphalted Strada per La Pigna. This very flat area of vast fields will lead to something quite different: a shallow valley of vineyards and woods. Cross the **SP88** and **SP87** (**12.7km**) and, at the road's end, turn left onto gravel. Upcoming trail conditions (and a small saving in distance) may make it wiser to turn left at the SP87 and skip the diversion through farmland and woods. Go first right downhill on rough stone into woods. At the bottom, turn left before a vineyard onto a dirt track and, at its end, keep ahead on a narrow path. Cross a ditch, join a dirt path skirting left around a vineyard, and turn right onto the **SP87**.

Cross over a drainage channel and immediately turn right onto a first track bordered by a dry-stone wall into the **Bosco di Cerano**.

The **Bosco di Cerano** comprises the last 126 hectares of forest that was once present along much of the Puglian coast, along the natural gully of Li Siedi. Among its elm holm oaks and black hornbeams are wandering badgers, foxes, and rodents as well as 60 species of birds, including the goldfinch, chaffinch, blackcap, warbler, and nightingale.

Head between log fences through the woods and onto a stone path. Curve right at another stone wall then curve left passing through a **masseria** farm complex surrounded by vineyards and orchards and reach fields on a wide gravel road. At a stop sign, cross the **SP86** to keep ahead to a substantial area of dead or dying olive trees, a result of the bacterium *Xylella fastidiosa* that invaded Southern Italy in 2013.

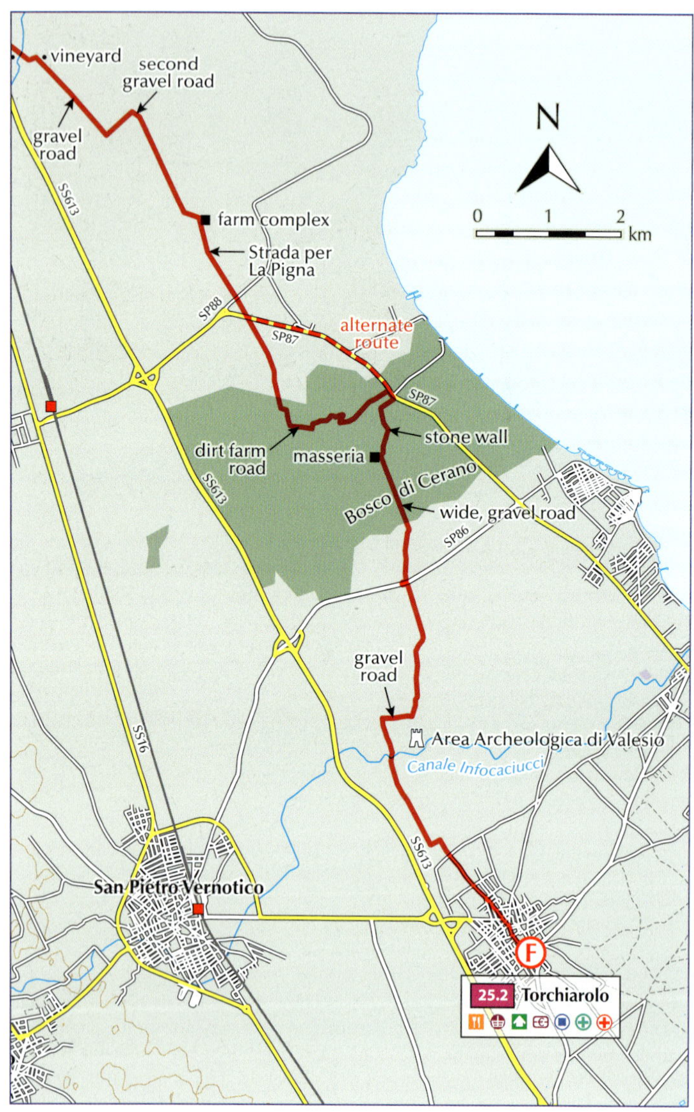
vineyard
second gravel road
gravel road
N
0 1 2 km
SS613
farm complex
Strada per La Pigna
SP88
SP87
alternate route
SP87
stone wall
dirt farm road
masseria
Bosco di Cerano
SS613
wide, gravel road
SP86
gravel road
Area Archeologica di Valesio
Canale Infocaciucci
SS16
SS613
San Pietro Vernotico
F
25.2 Torchiarolo

A white archway is the first sign of Easter preparations at Santa Maria Assunta in Torchiarolo

Take a gravel road on the right then turn left at its end to arrive at the **Area Archeologica di Valesio** (**9km**).

Built on Iron Age foundations and transformed into a city by the Messapians, **Valesio**, found along the Via Traiana Calabra, was mentioned by many known pilgrims. It included a spa complex and still displays traces of Messapian walls outlining the city's 84 hectares. In the 1st century AD, Pliny designated it an *oppidum*, as in a fortified city. After centuries of decline, the city was destroyed in 1157 by the Norman troops of William I of Sicily.

Pass a *casedda* (round, stone hut), which you can enter, make a zig left and a zag right then head directly into **Torchiarolo**, arriving at the long Piazza Castello and the Chiesa Madre di Maria Santissima Assunta (**3.5km**).

25.2KM TORCHIAROLO (ELEV 28M, POP 5459) (124.4KM)

Torchiarolo is the southernmost town of the Brindisi province and owes its modern foundation to the refugees from old Valesio, who built this town as a masseria in the 12th century following Norman invasion. Many of its monuments were constructed in reaction to the Saracen raids. The Palazzo Baronale of 1698 surrounds the pre-existing defense tower. The Chiesa Madre di Santa Maria Assunta was erected in the late 16th century, with further baroque modifications in the 18th century.

Foresteria Parrocchia Santissima Maria Assunta O Do R Br S Z 3/12, €17, Via Dante Aligheri 23, tel 347 060 4248 or 347 661 5213. Breakfast, snacks, and bottled water included.

STAGE 40

Torchiarolo to Lecce

Start	Piazza Castello, Torchiarolo
Finish	Piazza Duomo, Lecce
Duration	5¾hr
Distance	22.5km
Total ascent	144m
Total descent	117m
Difficulty	Moderate due to length
Percentage paved	69%
Lodgings	Surbo 15.7km, Lecce 22.5km, Merine 28.1km

The pinnacle of this flat, mostly tranquil stage is the beautiful Romanesque Abbazia di Santa Maria di Cerrate, truly a historic and artistic treasure. After Surbo a maze of hectic suburban roads lead to the cream-colored baroque city of Lecce, one of Italy's urban jewels. Intermediate services may be available at the Abbazia (depending on the time of day) and in Surbo, which offers bars and restaurants.

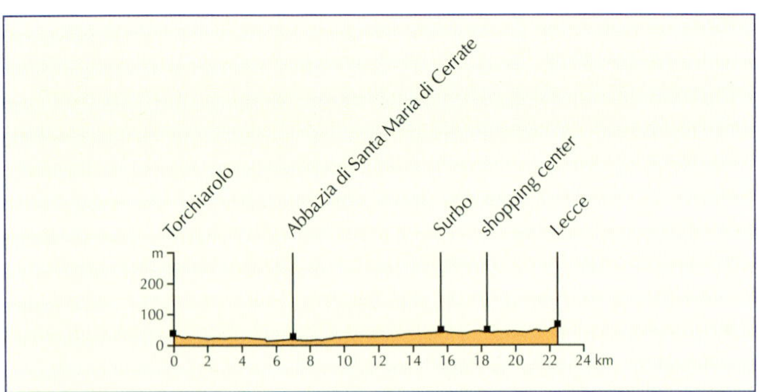

Facing the church, veer left onto Via Principe Amedeo for four blocks and turn left then right onto Viale dei Cipressi toward a lovely gauntlet of cypress trees surrounding the **cemetery**. Noting the poorly olive trees (writing in 2024), at a crossroads take the dirt track ahead then at a fork with a road, continue on the track along a dry-stone

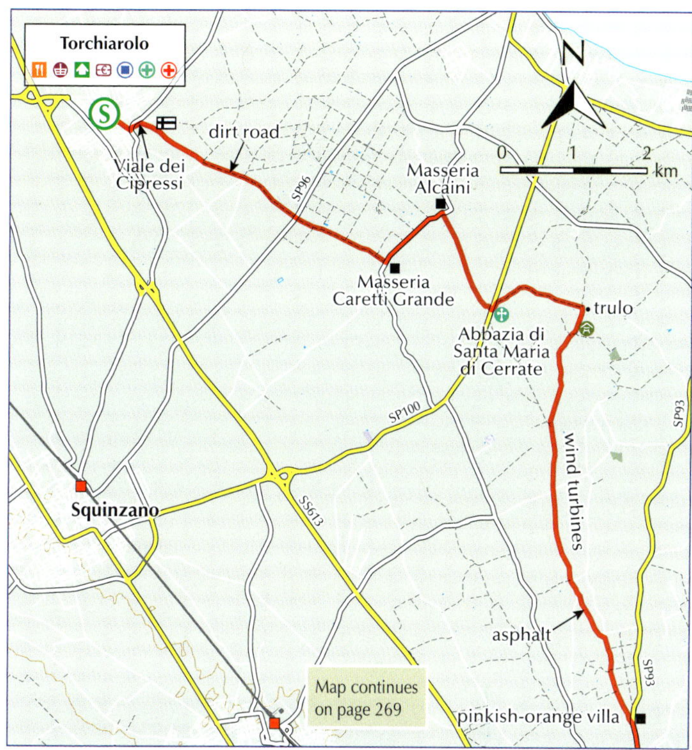

wall. Cross the **SP96** and at the entry gate to **Masseria Caretti Grande**, turn left onto a straight gravel road. Turn right at the gates of **Masseria Alcaini**, pass orchards, and, at the road end, cross the SP100 highway to the **Abbazia di Santa Maria di Cerrate** (**7km**, food, WC).

According to legend, King Tancredi and Count of Lecce, **Boemondo d'Altavilla** (son of Robert Guiscard) founded the monastery in the 12th century after the Madonna appeared to him between deer antlers in a cave (the word *cerrate* from *cervate*, meaning 'deer'). The abbey became one of the principal monastic shelters in Southern Italy but, following the Turkish sack of Otranto, was abandoned for over two centuries. The elegance of the Puglian Romanesque of the Abbey is embellished with 13th–14th-century frescoes, a lovely 13th-century portico, and a small rose window.

After your visit, continue on a gravel lane that begins near the highway. It turns into a dirt path through narrow woods then widens into a road and ends at a T-junction by a casedda. Turn right to views of wind turbines and dispersed casedde in a barren plain. After the third wind turbine, fork left then merge right onto another road. Merge again onto the SP93 to Surbo at a **pinkish-orange villa** that has weathered into a patina you would never be able to match at a paint store. Enter the town of **Surbo** on Via del Mare, which becomes Via San Giorgio in the colorful center (**8.7km**).

15.7KM SURBO (ELEV 41M, POP 15,135) (124.4KM)

It is believed that the town's name either derives from the Latin *surburbium*, referring to it being a suburb of Lecce, or from the Latin name for the rowan tree, which once was widespread in the area. The fun, colorful homes contrast with the uniformity of Lecce's cream-colored motifs. The oldest evidence of Surbo's existence dates back to the 12th century, when Boemondo d'Altavilla donated the farmhouse to Benedictine nuns. However, objects from the Mycenaean period have been unearthed in the vicinity.

Residenza del Sole O Pr R Br Cr W S Z 4/10, €-/30–35/60–70/-/-/-, Via Togliatti, 16, tel 328 616 0913 or 328 818 9978, info@bebresidenzadelsole.it. Group offers available.

Pass the Church of San Giuseppe, curve left with Via San Giorgio, and, at its end, turn right onto Via Vito Fazzi, which, leaving town, becomes Via Fratellio Trio then Via 1 Maggio to arrive at low apartments in **Giorgilorio** (**1.7km**, food, ATM, bus, pharmacy), a Lecce suburb. Pass the back of a **shopping mall** (gas station, fast-food restaurant, sports shop), head under the **Tangenziale Est di Lecce freeway**, come to the Brindisi–Lecce SS 613 highway frontage road, and begin a hectic walk into Lecce.

Porta Napoli was built in 1548 to honor Charles V of Habsburg. Its adjacent city walls were removed in the 19th century

Take the second or third left (either will do) onto Via Giovanni Falcone to the white and green **Church of San Nicola di Myra**. Once there, turn right onto Via Sinni and curve left to then take Via San Nicola, your key arterial into town. Pass a **Coop grocery store** and immediately make a left. After two blocks turn

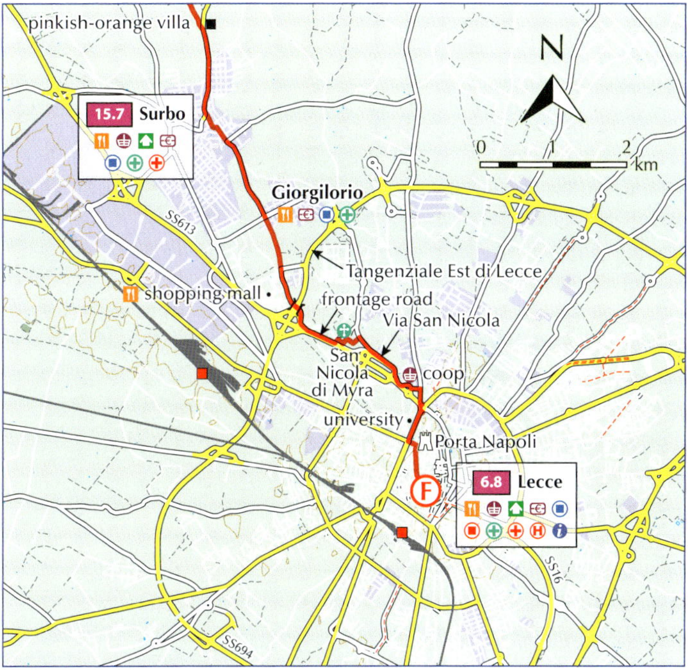

The Abbazia di Santa Maria in Cerata is a festival of Pugliese Romanesque architecture

right onto Via Adriatica, go straight through an enormous busy roundabout, pass the **Università degli Studi di Lecce**, and, at the next roundabout, turn left to breathe a sigh of relief at the city gate of Lecce.

Pass to the right of the monumental 16th-century **Porta Napoli** (or pass through and over the metal chain) and immediately turn right onto Via Giuseppe Palmieri. Walk a half-dozen butter-colored, historic blocks to arrive at the **Piazza Duomo** and the lovely baroque transept facade of the Duomo di Lecce (**5.2km**).

6.8KM LECCE (ELEV 51M, POP 94,989) (117.6KM)

Baroque extravaganza

Lecce is Italy's 'queen of the baroque.' It prizes its Barocco Leccese, a flamboyant style predominant in the 17th and 18th centuries across Italy that hailed the Roman Catholic Church and the end of Turkish raids (put to rest in the 1571 battle of Lepanto) while simultaneously jubilating the end of the 1656 plague. The mood, coupled with high taxes aimed at the nobility, transformed the city into something of a cream-colored fantasy world: intricate religious imagery combined with whimsical creatures, flora, and foliage all carved skillfully into the soft calcareous Lecce stone by key artists Giuseppe Zimbalo, Gabriele Riccardi, and Giuseppe Cino. Churches, palaces, monuments, and noble homes battled to show off their power and riches in a style that commands attention.

Lecce's churches

Lecce's prime baroque sites are its churches, including the lavish Cattedrale Maria Santissima Assunta e San Oronzo, rebuilt by Zimbalo in the 17th century, and its 72m-high bell tower (one of the highest in Europe), as well as Basilica di San Giovanni Battista, the Chiesa di Santa Chiara, and the Basilica di Santa Croce. The Palazzo Arcivescovile (Bishop's Palace) and seminary with its decorative loggia is another great stop on a tour of Lecce's baroque inventory, all of which can be seen with a single ticket (www.chieselecce.it/en/places).

Roman Lecce

For your Roman fix, Roman Lupiae's spectacular amphitheater has been preserved, while the town also sports a Greek amphitheater in its center. The Piazza Duomo is crowned by the 35m column that was brought from Brindisi, where two marked the end of the Via Appia; bishop and patron saint of Lecce, Sant'Oronzo, sits at the top, accredited with eliminating the plague.

- **Parrocchia San Giovanni Battista** O Do R S 2/6, €Donation, Via Novara, tel 349 777 3090, email dongerardoippolito@_alice.it. Reservations preferred; expected donation of €15; dinner sometimes available.

- **Parrocchia Santa Maria delle Grazie** Do Piazza Indipendenza, tel 349 469 3157, 389 637 0859 or 0832 240159, parrocchia.santarosa.lecce@gmail.com. Advance communication is difficult; check for services on arrival.

- **Urban Oasis Hostel** Pr Do R K Cr W S 5/18 & 9/24, €20–25/30–35/50–60/60–75/80/100, Via Nicola Cataldi 3, tel 328 571 9768, 0832 300 050 or 347 483 7341, info@urbanoasishostel.com, www.urbanoasishostel.com. Closed November 10 to January 31 inclusive.

Lecce

1. Parrocchia San Giovanni Battista
2. Parrocchia Santa Maria delle Grazie
3. Urban Oasis Hostel

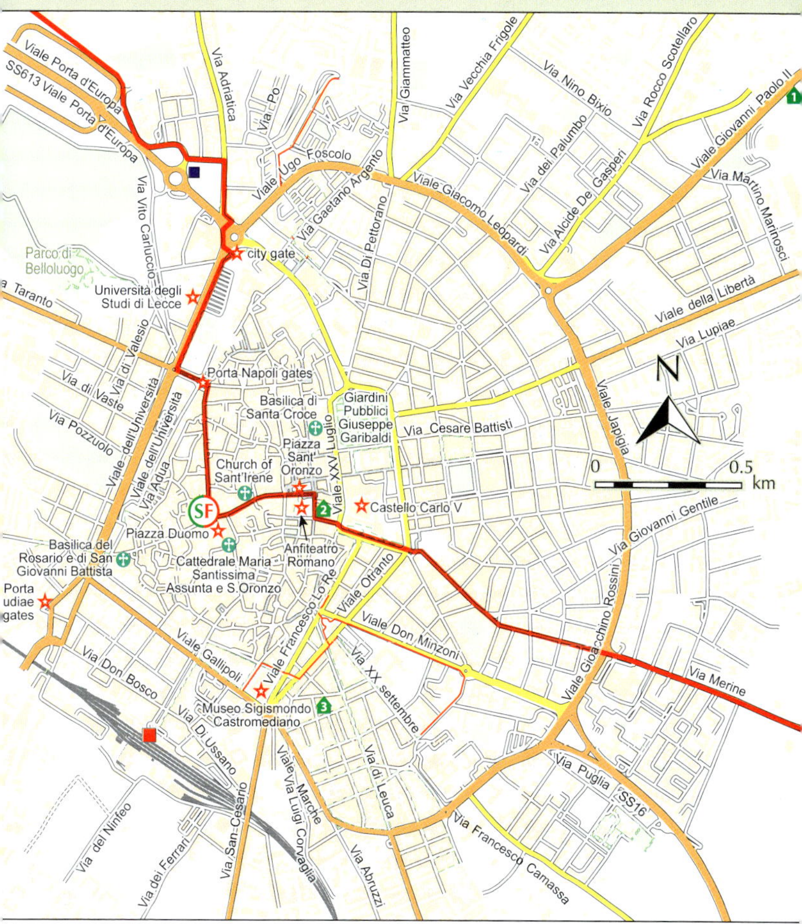

Afternoon sunlight emphasizes the lush, Baroque lines of Lecce's Chiesa di San Matteo

STAGE 41

Lecce to Martano

Start	Piazza Duomo, Lecce
Finish	Torre dell'Orologio, Martano
Duration	8hr
Distance	30.9km
Total ascent	194m
Total descent	174m
Difficulty	Moderately hard due to duration and hard surfaces
Percentage paved	77%
Lodgings	Merine 5.6km, Vernole 18.1km, Martano 30.9km

The mountains are long gone, peace has been made with the flat terrain of olive groves, and this delightful, long stage, mostly on cycle lanes, reveals several interesting and historic intermediate villages that offer services to ease the way.

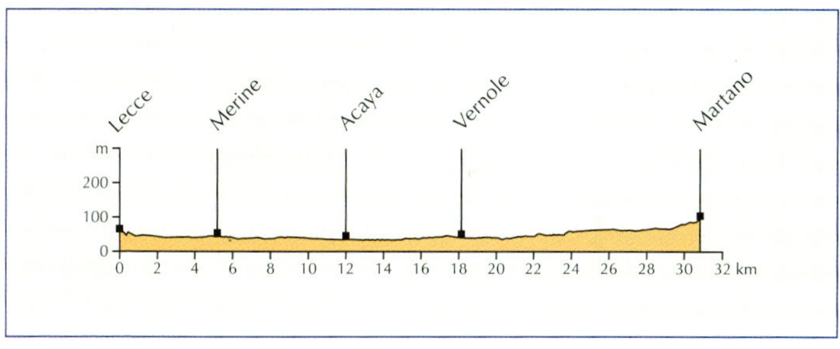

Leave Piazza Duomo with the cathedral behind you and turn first right onto Via Vittorio Emanuele II. Pass the **Church of Sant'Irene** and, on Piazza Oronzo, enjoy the Roman amphitheater to your right after which turn right to continue ahead onto Via G. Marconi, keeping the great walls of **Castello Carlo V** on your left. At the next roundabout, veer right toward Via del Balzo Orsini but jog immediately left onto Via San Lazzaro. Where it curves left, continue instead through a triangular park then head left onto Via Regina Elena, which crosses the SS16 arterial and becomes **Via Merine**. Pass two supermarkets, fork right after a **gas station** onto the quiet Ciclovia da Lecce al Mare, with homes on your left initially and fields on the right. Soon cross over the Tangenziale Est di Lecce motorway then enter **Merine**. Pass a grocery store, fork right at a **pizzeria**, and, in two blocks, reach the central Piazza Maria Santa Assunta.

5.6KM MERINE (ELEV 42M, POP CA. 4000) (112KM)
In the center stands a monolithic column on a square base known as 'Lu Sanna' (Hosanna) on which a statuette of Maria Santissima Assunta, protector of Merine, once stood, and after whom the square is named.

Casa di spiritualità Cuore Immacolato di Maria O Do R K Br Dr W S Z
15/40, €15, Via Montenegro 72, tel 328 893 8166, donlucalecce2002@libero.it. Reservations required.

Turn left on **Via Palmieri** to leave town then keep straight at the roundabout with the SP1 toward Acaya onto the narrow SP337 between tall property walls and into wide fields stretching to the horizon. Pass a **stone ruin** and merge left with the SP142 into **Acaya** (food, groceries, bus), arriving at its picturesque **Castello** (**6.3km**).

Along its narrow alleys and quaint squares, **Acaya** has many traditional buildings, arched doorways, and history dating back to the Messapians, the Greeks, and the Romans. The pentagonal Castello di Acaya was commissioned by Charles V of Spain in the 16th century and is flanked by its defensive wall and moat. Many consider it to be one of the finest examples of Renaissance defensive architecture in the lands surrounding Otranto. Turn left and go through Porta di Acaya to visit the castle.

After your visit go straight again to the stone chapel of San Paolo Apostolo, placed in the middle of the SP142.

This **18th-century chapel** is dedicated to St. Paul and was once a pilgrimage destination for people affected by spider bites that sent them into hysterical convulsions. The cure was an exorcism through an upbeat dance called

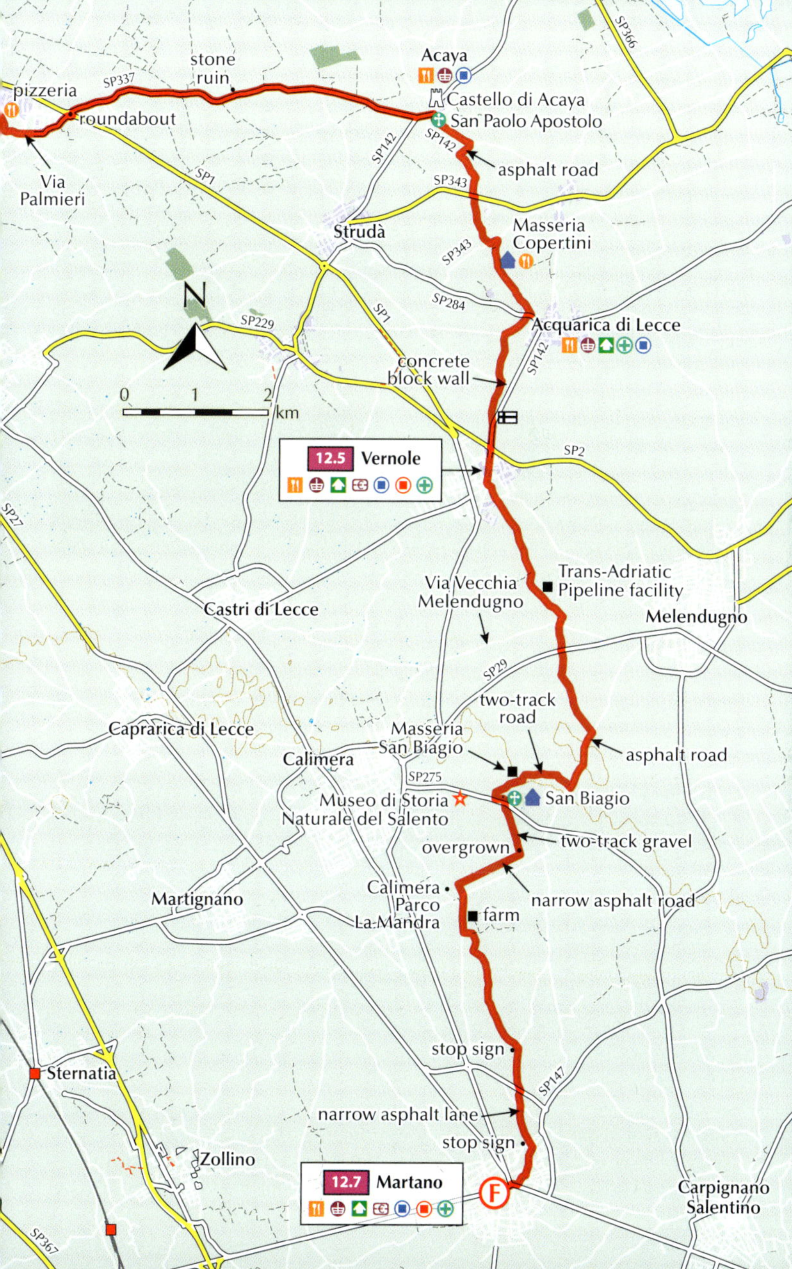

pizzeria
SP337
stone ruin
roundabout
Via Palmieri
Acaya
Castello di Acaya
San Paolo Apostolo
SP142
SP366
asphalt road
SP343
SP1
Strudà
Masseria Copertini
SP284
Acquarica di Lecce
SP229
N
0
1
2
km
concrete block wall
12.5 Vernole
SP2
SP27
Trans-Adriatic Pipeline facility
Via Vecchia Melendugno
Castri di Lecce
Melendugno
SP29
two-track road
Caprarica di Lecce
Masseria San Biagio
asphalt road
Calimera
SP275
Museo di Storia Naturale del Salento
San Biagio
two-track gravel
overgrown
Calimera Parco La Mandra
narrow asphalt road
Martignano
farm
stop sign
SP147
Sternatia
narrow asphalt lane
stop sign
Zollino
12.7 Martano
F
Carpignano Salentino
SP367

the Tarantella, now a traditional folk dance, where whirling around in manic circles would sweat out the poison from the body and mind. In this chapel, the dance was succeeded by hanging patients on a rope from the ceiling then making them drink holy water from an adjacent well.

Vernole's 18th-century Cathedral of Maria Santissima Assunta shows the rich detail of the baroque style

After the chapel, take the first road on the right, winding among olive groves. At the stop sign, jog left 30m on the SP343 to take another lane in the same direction. Pass Masseria Copertini (food) then small plots each with a casedda inside. Zigzag left and right and come to a road where a 390m detour left reaches **Acquarica di Lecce** (**3.7km**, food, groceries, accommodation, bus, pharmacy). The route instead skips this village, turns right onto the SP284 then immediately takes the next left onto a flat lane with more casedde. Fork left before a new, tall dry-stone wall, jog next left by a 3m block wall, and reach Vernole's **cemetery** (Note the all too true but jarringly somber cemetery inscription: 'Fui quel che tu sei sarai quel che io sono,' meaning 'I was what you are, you will be what I am.'). Merge with the **SP142** to the Church of Maria Santissima Assunta (**2.6km**).

12.5KM VERNOLE (ELEV 36M, POP 7135) (99.4KM)

The surprisingly cute town of Vernole, encompassed by millennial olive trees, has a quaint square and was a stopping place on the Via Traiana Calabra. Among its several churches, the Chiesa di Maria Santissima Incoronata and Chiesa di Maria Santissima Assunta stand out as extravagantly baroque. Yet, it was the little church that then became the Chiesa di San Lorenzo, which refreshed and sheltered pilgrims.

Piccolo Ulivo – Bed & Breakfast Pr R Br S 3/9, €-/171/172/178/184, Via Firenze 7, tel 338 507 7207, info@piccoloulivo.com, www.facebook.com/PiccoloUlivo. Only open July and August.

Pass through the square, fork right at the obelisk statue then fork left at the clock tower next to the church tower and leave town. At a stop sign jog left among more smallholdings, go along the metal fence of the **Trans-Adriatic Pipeline facility** then head onto a grassy track between stone walls alongside the plant's access road. Cross

Castello di Acaya

Via Vecchia Melendugno, join a gravel road, cross the **SP29** highway to a lane with some shade, and turn right at a T-junction onto a road that becomes a dirt track. Turn right at the next dirt road, passing Masseria San Biagio then the ruins of the **Church of San Biagio** below a square water tower. Make a left just before the SP275 highway then cross it onto a partially shaded two-track gravel ahead. A right turn along the highway leads to the Museo di Storia Naturale del Salento and wildlife protection center (870m off route), the largest museum in Southern Italy dedicated to nature and centered on butterflies.

After the track dwindles to an overgrown path, turn right onto a lane that joins another road from the right. Pass **Parco La Mandra** and, after a farm, turn left then fork right. At a **stop sign**, where you can make out Martano 1.5km away, turn right onto the road then, at a highway, jog slightly left onto a narrow lane. Left along the highway, 600m away, is the 17th-century Cistercian Monastero di Santa Maria della Consolazione. Go straight through the stop sign (café to the left) and turn next right to the Torre dell'Orologio and castle.

12.7KM MARTANO (ELEV 91M, POP 9151) (86.7KM)

Martano's origin is a combination of history and legend. Some attribute it to the ancestors of Minos, while others state it was founded by the Roman centurion Marcius to whom these lands were gifted following his successful battles for conquest in 267BC. After the fall of the Roman Empire, in 476, and the subsequent Hellenization of Salento, Martano became the capital of the 12 municipalities that formed this Greek Salento, and there are still traces of the Griko dialect here to this day, a minority language recognized by the Italian government. Of note is the Menhir di Santu Tòtaru, also known as the Menhir del Teofilo, which is the highest in Puglia at 4.7m and dates between the 9th and 7th centuries BC. The Parrocchia Maria Santissima Assunta was rebuilt in 1596, destroying the foundations and memories of the Greek church that once stood there.

B&B Ore Liete nel Salento O Pr R K Br Cr S 4/9, €-/40/60/75/100/-, Via Mameli 117, tel 329 669 1164, info@bboreliete.com, www.facebook.com/BBOreLietenelSalento. Breakfast included; reservations preferred; one bike maximum.

STAGE 42

Martano to Otranto

Start	Torre dell'Orologio, Martano
Finish	Castello Aragonese, Otranto
Duration	8hr
Distance	30.5km
Total ascent	205m
Total descent	266m
Difficulty	Hard, due to distance and hard surfaces
Percentage paved	68%
Lodgings	Carpignano Salentino 3.9km, Serrano 6.4km, Cannole 8.7km, Palmariggi 18km, Giurdignano 23.7km, Otranto 30.5km

This long stage on quiet Salentine roads returns you to the coast at historic and vibrant Otranto, stopping at several intriguing villages with refreshments where you will experience the Greek influence on local culture. Torcito Park, a Marian sanctuary, menhirs and dolmens, and the caves of the Val d'Idro hold your interest until the seaside offers its own rewards.

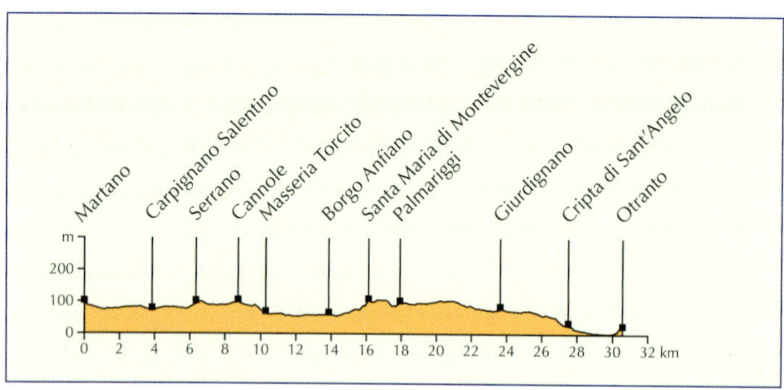

With the clock tower behind you, retrace yesterday's route but fork right onto **Via Constantino** (bakery) out of town. Pass a cell tower then, after a stop sign, cross the **Via Circonvallazaione**, curve left to a second stop sign, and turn right onto a road that soon turns to gravel. Before a field with ruins of a masseria, turn right then (ignoring the driveway on the right) hug the left side of a stone wall onto a grassy lawn, passing under power lines. Soon turn right onto a dirt road, directly on the location of the **Via Traiana Calabra**, but after 100m, turn left then next left before the arched ruins of the San Cosimo di Carbieno Church, now used by a farm. Arrive in **Carpignano Salentino**, double back on **Via S. Pasquale**, pass a roundabout, and curve to the central piazza.

3.9KM CARPIGNANO SALENTINO (ELEV 71M, POP 3783) (82.8KM)

Another town on the Via Traiana Calabra axis, Carpignano Salentino has held onto remains from the Byzantine domination. Most important is the Crypt of Santa Cristina with its 10th-century frescoes, the oldest in Puglia, and a tomb of a young Byzantine army officer.

Casina dei Nonni Pr R Br S Z 4/11, €-/40/45/66/88/-, Via Enrico Toti 6/8, tel 345 354 4145, info@casinadeinonni.com, www.casinadeinonni.com. Groups of eight or more people receive 10% discount; closed from July 15 to August 25 inclusive; two-night stays receive 10% discount.

From the piazza, follow **Via Roma/SP3**, cross straight over another piazza, leave town, go straight at the SP48 roundabout, and turn left onto **Via dei Carrubi**, passing gated properties, with views toward Serrano ahead. Cross a road onto a downhill, narrow, grassy lane and cut diagonally through an empty field, a second section of the Via Traiana Calabra, then head uphill on the **SP39** to Piazza Lubelli.

2.5KM SERRANO (ELEV 88M, POP 1334) (80.3KM)

Serrano is nicknamed the 'village of poetry' and hosts a yearly poetry event attended by writers from all over Italy. Notable monuments include the embellished 17th-century Palazzo Lubelli and the elegant and somber 18th-century churches of San Giorgio Martire and San Leonardo.

Sanlu Hotel Pr R Br Cr W S Z 30/69, €-/55/60/80/95/-, Via Provinciale Martano, tel 0836 586 010 or 349 790 7154, info@sanlu.it, www.sanlu.it. Open March to November.

Across the piazza, fork right onto Via Porta, cross Via Alcide de Gasperi, fork left onto narrow Strada Vicinale Serrano-Cannole, which curves to Cannole. At the road end, turn right onto Via Roma/SP39 and to Piazza San Vincenzo.

Fork left after the piazza's Chiesa Matrice onto Via Madonna down to a park. Turn right, hug a wall next to the open Festa della Municeddha piazza, turn left downhill onto Strada Vicinale Scopelle, and reach the **entry gate** of the Parco Naturale di Torcito. Enter the park (picnic tables) and veer left to the restored stone buildings of **Masseria Torcito**.

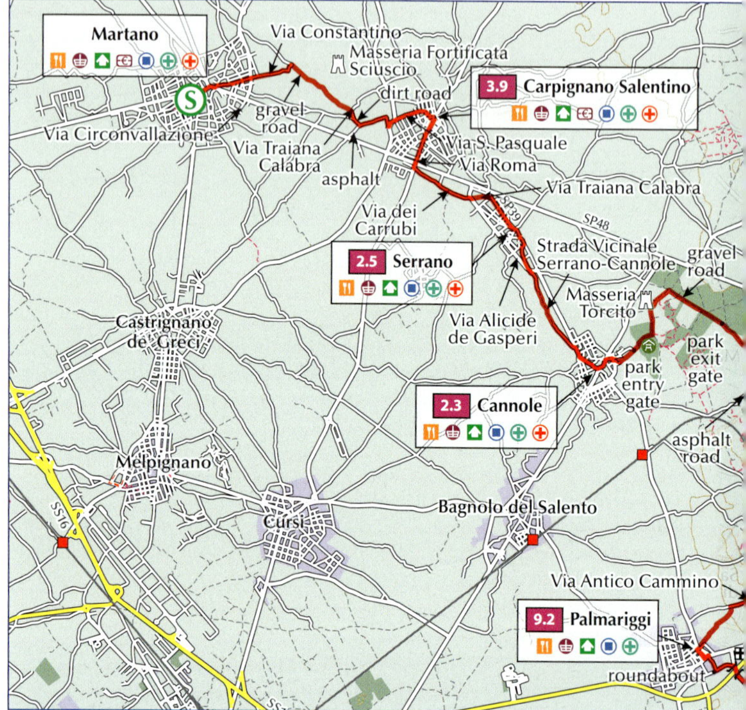

2.3KM CANNOLE (ELEV 98M, POP 1698) (78KM)

Legend has it that in 1480, in the aftermath of the Turkish invasion of Otranto, Saracen troops aimed to plunder the smaller surrounding villages. However, when they arrived in Cannole, the Madonna of Constantinople appeared to block their entrance, and the Turkish commander submitted to her and converted. Within the church, a papier-mâché statue depicts the Madonna with a Turk in chains at her feet.

- **Dimora 'Fabio & Lucia'** Pr R K Br Dr S 2/6, €Donation, Via Alcide de Gasperi 56/E, tel 388 633 4949 or 328 536 4538, stomaci.fabio@gmail.com. Fabio and Lucia, who are pilgrims themselves, welcome pilgrims into their own home. They ask for €3 for use of the shower, €3 for breakfast, and €10 for the communal dinner. Otherwise, the stay is donation based.

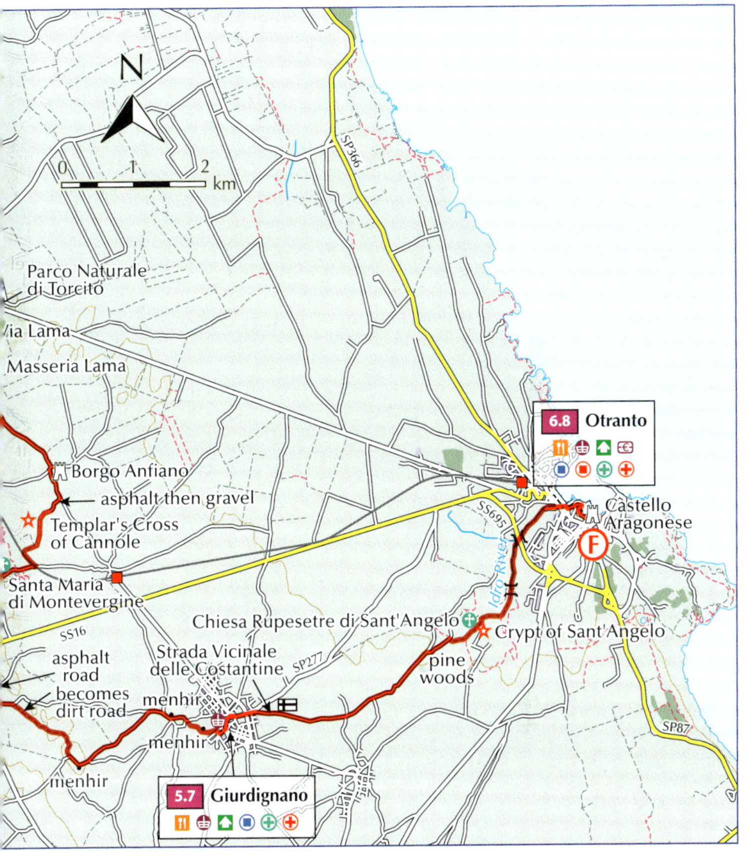

The splendid **Parco Naturale di Torcito** is an area of 203 floral hectares and the location of an unparalleled masseria of the same name. The farmstead dates back to the 12th century and was fortified in the 16th, ordered by the Spanish viceroys in response to the danger of Turkish attacks.

Follow arrows downhill between tall stone walls on a rough stone lane then turn right onto a gravel road to another outer boundary **park lift gate**. Go through it onto a dirt track through woods then olives then orchards and young olives. Jog left at a road and, at the staggered junction, keep ahead. At this location stood **Borgo Anfiano** (bench).

One of many painted benches welcoming pilgrims in the Cannole area

The historic **Borgo (village) and Masseria Anfiano** is one of three similar ancient sites in these surroundings. The word *anfiano*, which stems from the ancient Greek words *anfi*, meaning 'around,' and *ano*, meaning 'without,' translates as 'the place with nothing around it,' namely isolated and abandoned. It now appears in quite the state of abandon, perhaps as its name had always foreshadowed.

Turn next right and soon spot a far ridge with a monument on top, the Santuario Santissima Santa Maria Montevergine. Pass the Croce Templare di Cannole (**Templar's Cross**), where a devotional sign inspires: 'Traveler: before reaching the hill in front of the Madonna di Montevergine, leave your thoughts here.' The gravel road becomes a red-dirt track favored by motorcyclists on weekends (read: ruts and mud) then a narrow path along a stone wall that connects to another dirt track with a sign telling you that you are on the 'Percorso Classico' (classic/traditional route) to the hilltop sanctuary.

Continue along railroad tracks, turn right onto a road, cross the tracks on a railway bed, and head uphill arriving at a play area by the impressive statue pedestal of the unassuming **Santuario Santissima Santa Maria Montevergine** (**7.4km**). Christian pilgrimages to Montevergine commenced with the founding saint, William of Vercelli, San Guglielmo, in the first quarter of the 12th century. The 14th-century statue was struck by lightning and replaced in the 19th century. After the monument turn right onto **Via Antico Cammino** (marked 'Soli Giorni Festivi') and look out for a shrine to the Madonna and Child, at calf height in the wall on the left. Turn left after a tall stone wall, first downhill then up to **Palmariggi**. At the main square turn left to the Chiesa di San Luca Evangelista (**1.9km**).

9.2KM PALMARIGGI (ELEV 95M, POP 1497) (68.7KM)

Palmariggi was first documented in the 13th century, and some historians argue that it was built as a small fort just outside Otranto to defend the city. This municipality, as with many near the Montevergine sanctuary, maintains that it survived invasion by the Turks thanks to the Madonna who appeared with a palm leaf in her hand, frightening them away. The Aragonese castle stands mightily with its two cylindrical towers, and the Chiesa di San Luca Evangelista is in elegant Lecce baroque style.

Lu Palummaru B&B and B&B di Angela Scotellaro O Pr R K Br W S Z 6/18, €-/40/50/60/70/80, Via Vicinale Armine 5, tel 320 196 3475 or 0836 354 406, info@lupalummaru.com, www.lupalummaru.com.

Curve around the main square, keeping the church on your right, and turn left at the road end onto Via Roma then go next right onto Via Palma. Go left at the roundabout, turn right before the **cemetery**, pass under the SS16 on a pink bike lane, and fork left onto a narrow country road.

Pass a junction then fork right uphill onto a road that snakes between stone fences, revealing views of the sea and then Giurdignano. Continue ahead, pass a **menhir**, and where the road curves left, you can make a 300m detour on the left to a prehistoric dolmen. Keep straight and head downhill to a tall monolith: a prehistoric menhir common in this area, which was used as a navigational tool. Fork left at the **menhir**, pass through

Central piazza of Giurdignano, with its Chiesa di Trasfigurazione del Signore

A 20th-century statue, on Otranto's Lungo Eroi, remembers the martyrs and heroes of the 1480 Battle of Otranto

5.7KM GIURDIGNANO (ELEV 76M, POP 1970) (63KM)
The Giurdignano municipality is scattered with menhirs. Two almost identical menhirs stand together on Piazza Vico Nuovo, and fun can be had in trying to locate them and the other four in town; this is in addition to the three already scouted just before arriving here!

- Gli Archi Country Home Pr R Br W S 2/5, €-/40/50/60/-/-, Via Orto Nuovo 50, tel 340 163 1957. Open March to November.

a small park of pine trees (picnic tables), and cross a road at a second menhir. Turn left at the next two junctions, now in Giurdignano, passing a third menhir. Turn left toward the **Coop grocery** then turn right and left, winding toward the main piazza and Chiesa della Trasfigurazione del Signore.

Keep the church to your left and fork right off the **SP277** at the Villa Giovanni Paolo II park (benches) with its statue of Padre Pio. Now, on the gentle Strada Vicinale delle Constantine, pass the **cemetery** into the countryside, noting a radar building with its white sphere that you will see again tomorrow. Soon see the first of Otranto's houses and the sea and fork right, following signs for Cripta di Sant'Angelo, another shrine to the Archangel. Turn right, pass the **crypt**, and continue on a path in the valley of the Idro River (often dried up) from which Otranto's Roman name, Hydruntum, originated. While descending, see the stripes of limestone on the right, often with caves visible: an area that would feel spooky if not for Otranto's reassuring homes beyond. The caves (hypogea) were once dwelling places, temples, and tombs, particularly of the Messapians. Cross a **small bridge** over the river channel, pass the arched bridge across the channel, go under the highway, and soon emerge in central **Otranto** at the Church of San Antonio and San Francesco. Take the crossing over the river immediately after passing under the highway then turn right for 350m for **Orto dell'Idro** Pr Do R Br S 4/7, €15/15/40/50/60/-, Strada Comunale Idro, tel 340 848 3210, info@ortodellidro.com; www.ortodellidro.com. Head along the lungomare, veer right through the gates of the **Castello Aragonese**, and turn right onto Via Basilica. At the cathedral door, turn left and, in three blocks, come to the castle entrance.

6.8KM OTRANTO (ELEV 19M, POP 5742) (56.2KM)

This ancient town, mentioned in Virgil's *Aeneid* as 'Hydrontum,' saw two key figures dock here on their return from the Holy Land: first, the Bordeaux Pilgrim and later Saint Francis of Assisi in 1219. Otranto's strategic position between Adriatic nations provided the city with a rich heritage, including its charming Aragonese castle, subject of *The Castle of Otranto* by Horace Walpole. Written in 1764, and set during Frederick II's reign, it is the precursor to the Gothic novel.

The sack of Otranto

The lovely 9th-century Chiesa di San Pietro echoes a Hellenic past in its array of frescoes. With the prestige of its topographical location, the most eastern city in Italy also suffered great tragedy. The summer of 1480 saw the sack of Otranto by Ottoman Turks, who are said to have massacred the bishop and 800 inhabitants who refused to renounce their Christian faith. They became known as the Idruntine Martyrs and were canonized on May 12, 2013, by Pope Benedict XVI. A temple dedicated to Santa Maria dei Martiri ('of the martyrs') was built on Minerva Hill, where the massacre is said to have taken place, and the saints' relics are still venerated within the Cattedrale di Santa Maria Annunziata. The latter was consecrated in 1088, and the following century saw the completion of the beautiful mosaic floor by Pantaleone, a monk from nearby Abbazia di San Nicola di Casole (Stage 43).

Stanza di Tara O Pr Do R Br W S 1/2, €-/25/50/-/-/-, Via Pioppi 9, tel 329 124 7244, antonellascreti@gmail.com.

STAGE 43

Otranto to Vignacastrisi

Start	Castello Aragonese, Otranto
Finish	Piazza Umberto I, Vignacastrisi
Duration	6¼hr
Distance	23.9km
Total ascent	216m
Total descent	138m
Difficulty	Moderate due to length
Percentage paved	55%
Lodgings	Uggiano la Chiesa 11.8km, Cocumola 16.4km, Vignacastrisi 23.9km, Marittima 26.7km

Spectacular views of the Adriatic along the bluff just after Otranto are stars of this stage, and the more typical inland scenery of olive groves separated by dry-stone walls sets the scene for the last Roman road of the journey: the Via Sallentina. The Bauxite Lake adds a curiosity, and the interesting villages give options for supplies. It's worth dallying along the coastline as you begin to contemplate the approaching conclusion of the journey, now just 55km away.

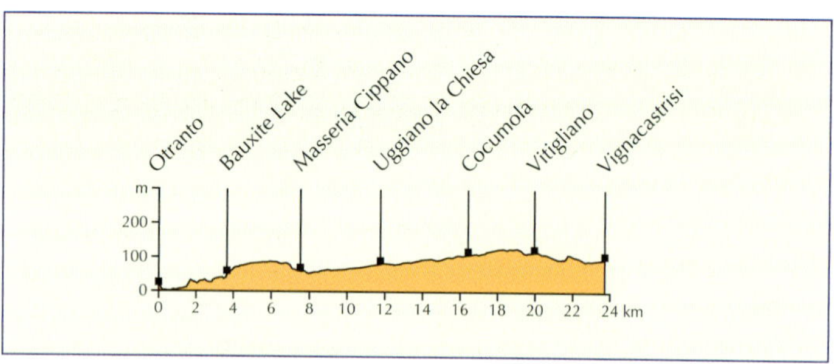

Facing the castle, head left and just after passing steps on the right-hand side, keep downhill on Via Costantino I, turn right through the walls at Porta Mare, and go down metal steps to join the lungomare at the small harbor. Keep ahead onto the panoramic gravel road, aiming for the 35m-high **Torre del Serpe** (**1.8km**) with 270-degree views of the coastline.

The **tower** is believed to have Roman origins but is said to have been used as a lighthouse in the Middle Ages. Its name derives from a legendary snake who would climb the tower each night to drink the oil used for the signal fires. The tower is a symbol of Otranto's antiquity, and it features in the city's coat of arms, along with the snake.

After your visit, head back toward the bluffs, keeping a dry-stone fence on your right, and head for the square stone bastion of **Torre dell'Orte** (**0.7km**). Turn inland, connecting with a path at Masseria Orte (if the gate is locked, continue on Via Orte, take the SP369 south then turn left at the first road). Turn left onto a red-dirt track then follow a right-hand path toward pine trees on a hill where you climb a bank overlooking the **Bauxite Lake**, a former quarry with dark, greenish-blue waters surrounded by deep red walls, although it may be closed off as it is private property. The red bauxite rock, rich in the aluminum, iron oxides, and hydroxides that produce the lake's mesmerizing emerald color, was mined in the early 20th century.

Keep on the path uphill toward power lines after which follow the **SP87** briefly then turn right onto a gravel road. Just before the turn-off, a dirt road leads to the entrance of **Masseria dei Monaci**. Pass the hotel and a dog sanctuary and arrive at the ruins of the **Abbazia di San Nicola di Casole**.

Lago di Bauxite's distinctive colors derive from the minerals contained in bauxite, mined in the Otranto region in the mid-20th century

The **monastery** is marked as private property, so seek the owner's permission to explore the ruin, where a remnant of what appears to have been an apse recalls its past glory. The abbey was once an outstanding Italian-Greek monastic cultural center, comparable to those of Chartres, Cluny, and York. It was also home to the artist monk Pantaleone, creator of the Tree of Life mosaic within Otranto's cathedral. By the 12th century the library and scriptorium had made the monastery the richest of all in Southern Italy and exemplified Puglia's ties with the East. The abbey was partially destroyed in the Turkish siege of 1480 and completely abandoned in the 17th century. Fortunately, many of the codes and scripts remain.

Pass a radar installation and a large spherical building (part of the Otranto military Air Force) and where the road seems to end at a field, continue on a smaller right-hand version of that road to head downhill. Soon pass between stone walls through wide fields with Uggiano la Chiesa ahead. Pass the ruins of **Masseria Cippano** (open for exploration and imagination), turn right between stands of an orchard, and join a town road at what was perhaps a medieval city wall. Veer right then right again at the **roundabout**, continuing on the **SP358** straight to Piazza Umberto I and the Chiesa di Santa Maria Maddalena (**9.4km**).

The ruins of the Masseria Cippano near Otranto

Otranto
alternate route
Torre del Serpe
Torre dell'Orte
Via Orte
red dirt road
Bauxite Lake
Masseria dei Monaci
dog sanctuary
N
0
1
2
km
SS16
SP369
SP87
Abbazia di San Nicola di Casale
radar installation
Giurdignano
11.8
Uggiano la Chiesa
Masseria Cippano
SP87
SP358
Via Santi Medici
roundabout
medievel city wall
SP56
Minervino di Lecce
Parco Santi Medici
Santi Medici
Via Appia-Calabra
Menhir of San Giovanni Malcantone
Porto Badisco
Strada Comunale Cocumola-Uggiano
4.6
Cocumola
Menhir Croce
Cerfignano
driveway gate
SP358
broken asphalt
asphalt
Via della Resistenza
Vitigliano
SP363
Santa Cesarea Terme
quarry
SS497dir
SP358
terraced hillside
SP84
asphalt road
Castro
7.5
Vignacastrisi

11.8KM UGGIANO LA CHIESA (ELEV 79M, POP 4409) (44.4KM)

The town gained its addendum, 'la chiesa' (the church), when it belonged to the Archbishop of Otranto. Byzantine frescoes can be found in the 12th–13th-century rupestrian Church Cripta di Sant'Elena, 800m out of town along the SP358. In the center, the 18th-century Chiesa di Santa Maria Maddalena displays simplicity while simultaneously expressing a typical Salento baroque style.

- **Casa Noemi Bed & Breakfast** O Pr R K Br Dr Cr S 4/11, €-/40/50/65/80/-, Via Nazario Sauro 3, tel 393 544 3644, casanoemiuggiano@gmail.com. Breakfast included; dinner available for €20.
- **Masseria Gattamora** O Pr R Br Cr W S Z 11/26, €-/38–45/-/-/-/-, Via Campo Sportivo 33, tel 0836 817 936 or 328 728 5913, info@gattamora.it, www.gattamora.it. Bed, breakfast, and dinner offer: €65–75.

At the church turn left against traffic onto Via Giuseppe Garibaldi and, at the next wide road, **Via Santi Medici**, turn left, leaving town. In the countryside, keep ahead, cross a road, and pass a play area of the Parco Santi Medici (water) and the **Church of Santi Medici** then fork left onto a gravel road, marked as 'Via Appia Calabro Salentina.' Turning left at the next crossroads of tracks brings you, in a 100m jaunt (one way), to the 4m-high Menhir di San Giovanni Malcantone. At the next crossroads, turn right gradually uphill onto the **Strada Comunale Cocumola-Uggiano**, spotting the town of Cerfignano with its domed church tower on your left. Continue along into **Cocumola**, coming to Piazza San Nicola.

4.6KM COCUMOLA (ELEV 108M, POP 943) (39.8KM)

Materials from a defense tower were repurposed to expand the Chiesa Parrocchiale di San Nicola Vescovo, which originates from the 18th century, with its facade of Lecce stone and bell tower with a Latin engraving of the date 1551.

- **Salento Terra Maris** Pr R Br Cr W S /5/13, €-/45/80/120/160/180, Via Giorgio La Pira 6, tel 335 820 8021, info@salentoterramaris.it, www.salentoterramaris.it. Closed in February.
- **B&B Cocuma** Pr R Br Cr W S Z 10/32, €-/38/39/72/92/98, Via Isonzo 62, tel 339 175 2289, info@cocumabb.it, www.cocumabb.it.

In Piazza San Nicola, fork left after one block against traffic then, two blocks later, fork left uphill at **Menhir Croce**, leaving town. At a fork, with a driveway gate in the middle, go right onto a country lane, soon seeing Vitigliano ahead. Once downhill, turn left onto **Via della Resistenza**, pass a war memorial, and arrive at Piazza Umberto I (**3.9km**, food).

The remains of what might have been an **underground place of worship** and the menhir both testify to Vitigliano's Bronze Age and Messapic past. The Messapians docked in Puglia from Greece and Illyria (modern-day Albania) around the 5th Century BC, living peacefully alongside the native residents. As supporters of Hannibal and Carthage, they were killed or enslaved when the Romans conquered the south of Italy.

Head straight through the Vitigliano then merge with the highway just before the **cemetery**. Fork next left, pass a quarry, and climb a terraced hillside that feels out of place in this flat terrain. Join another road with peekaboo views of Vignacastrisi to the right then Castro to your left. At the stoplight cross the **SP84** and, at the end of the road, now in the heart of town, turn left onto Via Umberto I then left again onto the SP83, coming to Piazza Umberto I and the church (**3.7km**).

7.5KM VIGNACASTRISI (ELEV 93M, POP 1350) (32.3KM)

Vignacastrisi's Chiesa Parrocchiale di Maria SS. Immacolata served as a refuge for the inhabitants of coastal Castro during 16th-century Turkish raids, and the two towns continue to be inextricably tied; Vignacastrisi roughly translates as the 'grapes of Castro' and was likely the location of Castro's vineyards. It was Castro that was the chosen landing place of Aeneas, the Trojan hero of Virgil's *Aeneid*, who is one of the supposed progenitors of the Romans.

- **Parrocchia 'Maria Ss.ma Immacolata' di Vignacastrisi** Do Via Umberto I, economato@diocesiotranto.it. Advance communication is difficult; check for services on arrival.
- **B&B L'Aia di San Giorgio** Pr Dr R Br Cr W S 7/20, €-/30/60/75/100/-, Via Vecchia Ortelle, tel 338 223 7722 or 340 220 5582, info@aiadisangiorgio.it.

STAGE 44

Vignacastrisi to Tricase

Start	Piazza Umberto I, Vignacastrisi
Finish	Piazza Giuseppe Pisanelli, Tricase
Duration	3¾hr
Distance	14.3km
Total ascent	127m
Total descent	119m
Difficulty	Easy
Percentage paved	74%
Lodgings	Marittima 2.8km, Tricase 14.3km, Tiggiano 17.9km, Corsano 20.1km, Gagliano del Capo 25.8km, Santa Maria di Leuca 32km

This short and easy stage, penultimate of the journey, includes two beautiful kilometers of trail along the Sentiero della Serra del Mito, whose bluff-top views surpass all prior beachside walks. The village of Marittima offers intermediate refreshment, and the day could be extended to Santa Maria di Leuca, totaling 32km.

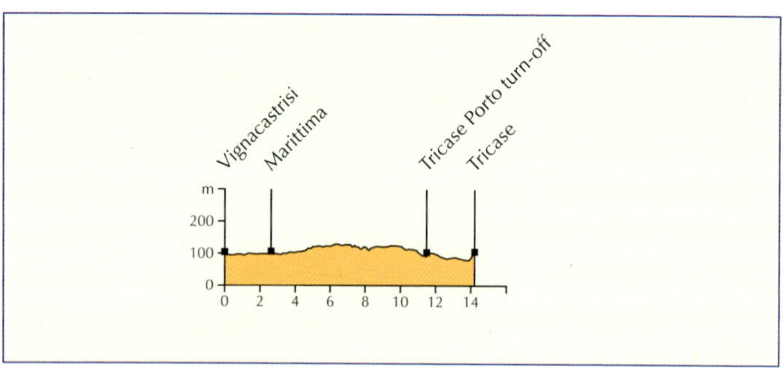

Keeping the front door of the Maria Santissima Immacolata Church on your left, pass the war monument on your right, fork right onto Via San Francesco out of town, and, at its end, turn left. Cross **Via Circonvallazione**, take the lane between stone walls marked 'Ciclopista 6,' and, in **Marittima**, immediately fork left onto Via Giuseppe Verdi.

Turn right onto Via San Antonio then left onto Via Roma, coming to Piazza Principe Umberto.

2.8KM MARITTIMA (ELEV 94M, POP 1796) (29.5KM)

The four remaining towers that were built in response to Turkish raids have gained this small village the local nickname of Town of Towers.

Trappitu dei Settimi O Pr R K Br Cr W S 9/18, €-/60/90/100/110/120, Via Convento 48, tel 0836 920 748 or 349 066 2199, info@trappitudeisettimi.it, www.trappitudeisettimi.it. Breakfast included; additional cost for only one night stays may apply.

Keep on Via Roma, passing a park (water) then, almost out of town, turn right uphill onto Via Aranisi. At the road end, turn left onto **Via Murtole** and as it turns uphill, fork left instead at a stone wall. At the end of the road, turn left briefly onto the **SP168** (which goes to Marina di Andrano on the coast) and fork next right. Fork left at a colorful Marian shrine in honor of Pantaleo Rocco (1990) then pass the 1960s **Capella Madonna dell'Attarico** (benches), where poorly conserved frescoes depict a cross, the Madonna breastfeeding the Child in a maternal gesture, and two saints.

Soon you are on a cliff above the sea. Head downhill, keep straight at an intersection, and be met with coastline views. Before the road ends, turn left onto a track on the grassy bluff, with unfettered views, to begin two of the most scenic kilometers of the Via Francigena. Turn left onto a narrow path before a stone wall and carefully

Clifftop paths of the Parco Regionale offer sweeping views of the Adriatic

Ortelle
SS497dir
Surano
Vignacastrisi
Spongano
Ciclopista 6
Via Circonvallazione
Diso
Castro
SP358
Via G. Verdi
2.8 Marittima
Via Murtole
Andrano
wet stone wall
SP168
SP358
Castiglione
Rocco shrine
Marina di Andrano
SP081
Madonna dell'Attarico
two-track gravel
Sentiero della Serra del Mito
Depressa
Torre del Sasso
Strada Comunale Arena
Madonna di Loreto
dirt path option
asphalt
Le Cupole hotel
Via Madonna di Loreto
SP335
Madonna di Costantinopoli
SP358
N
0
1
2
km
11.5 Tricase
Tiggiano

tread downhill along the beautiful, serene, and uninterrupted **Sentiero della Serra del Mito**. After a time follow a wooden fence on the left, sighting Tricase Porto and the ruins of the 110m-high Torre del Sasso ahead. Head inland, meet another gravel road, zigzag left and right, and soon glimpse Tricase itself as the road turns right as if on cue. Partway downhill go left onto a gravel road then, at a left turn, come to an option. Either turn right onto a slightly shorter, narrow dirt path and pass **Le Cupole** (shorter), or go left onto gravel (slightly longer, but less likely to be overgrown). Both routes end up on the same road, at the **Chiesa della Madonna di Costantinopoli**.

Also known as the **Chiesa dei Diavoli** (Church of the Devils), the octagonal rural church was built in 1684. One story tells of Marquis Gattinara, who ordered the construction of the church to seek God's grace for partaking in numerous bloody battles. Desperate for a swift blessing, he made a pact with the devil, who then erected the church overnight. The devil, in return, demanded offerings of several animals. Gattinara, frightened, did not pay up. In rage, the devil threw all the church bells into the Canale del Rio, a bay just south of Tricase port. To this day, locals can hear the bells on stormy nights, when the sea is in a frenzy.

Cross the SP313, pass the **Church of the Madonna di Loreto**, and go under the SP335. Now on Via Madonna di Loreto, climb to the base of a hulking building, the Church of the Nativity of the Blessed Virgin Mary. Turn right up then around it and go through the archway to the right of the facade to reach Piazza Giuseppe Pisanelli and the orange Chiesa di San Domenico.

11.5KM TRICASE (ELEV 103M, POP 17,621) (18KM)

Tricase was founded as a union of three masserie (*tri case* meaning 'three houses'), although the exact date remains disputed. The lovely monuments seen on the main piazza today are the Palazzo Gallone (17th century), with its original 15th-century tower named after its last feudal family, and the peach-colored Chiesa di San Domenico in gorgeous Salento baroque. The beloved local priest, bishop, and candidate for canonization, Don Tonino Bello, was ordained in the town's cathedral.

Accoglienza with Maria Grazia Bello O Do R K Br Dr W S 3/8, €Donation, Via Luigi Russolo 2, tel 339 644 8330, mariagraziabello@libero.it. Camping is possible and tents can be provided. Transfers from Santa Maria di Leuca to Tricase train station can be arranged with the host.

STAGE 45

Tricase to Santa Maria di Leuca

Start	Piazza Giuseppe Pisanelli, Tricase
Finish	Piazza Giovanni XXIII, Santa Maria di Leuca
Duration	4¾hr
Distance	18km
Total ascent	119m
Total descent	164m
Difficulty	Moderate due to hard surfaces
Percentage paved	97%
Lodgings	Tiggiano 3.6km, Corsano 5.8km, Gagliano del Capo 11.5km, Santa Maria di Leuca 18km

The Via Francigena finds its conclusion in this stage at the Finibus Terrae – the ends of the earth – facing the final sea of the Francigena, the Ionian. There is no more of eastern Italy south of Leuca, and what lies behind you are weeks, months, or years of dedication to arrive at this point, on a high promontory where both sunrise and sunset can be seen. Although the sunset may at first set the right mood, as this is the end of something, the sun will rise again in the morning, inspiring you to dream about which further adventure will answer the call of your heart.

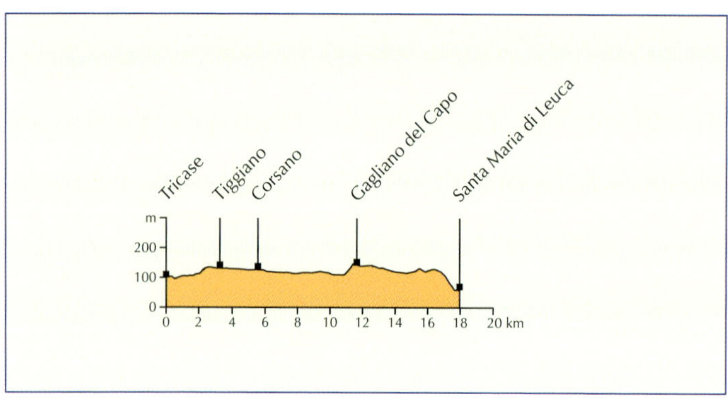

On the piazza, keep the Chiesa di San Domenico on your left and follow the light stone pavers slightly uphill against traffic coming to Via Domenic Caputo, Tricase's high street. Cross it onto narrow Via Liborio Romano against traffic, pass the boxy 17th-century Santa Lucia Church, and head downhill. Go through a stop sign and turn left onto the long, straight SP81. Pass two **grocery stores** then the Church of **Sant'Andrea Apostolo** and the Castello di Caprarica.

The **Castello di Caprarica** was constructed in response to the 1480 sack of Otranto and subsequent raids; thus it has a practical rectangular plan with four cylindrical towers and thick high walls. It has been restored into a sumptuous home.

Fork right onto Via Leuca then fork left onto **Via Salvio d'Acquisto** at a tile image of the Madonna and Child. Fork right onto gravel before the last homes, double back briefly on the SP81, and pick up a gravel road. Turn left onto an asphalt road and pass the play area in **Tiggiano**. Now on the SP81, turn right onto **Via Vittorio Veneto** and reach the tall tower of the Church of Sant'Ippazio.

3.6KM TIGGIANO (ELEV 131M, POP 2870) (14.4KM)

Sant'Ippazio Church in Tiggiano is dedicated to its patron Sant'Ippazio (Hypatius of Gangra), a 4th-century martyr and protector of male virility, from Turkey. A yearly fair on January 9 called Pestanaca di Sant'Ippazio celebrates a local yellow and purple carrot at a time coinciding with the peak period of the carrots' growth, also symbolically emphasizing the Saint's fertile virtues. These are also explained in the inscriptions on the 1601 altar within the 16th-century church.

Oratorio Luci Perti O Pr Do R Br S Z 1/4 & 7/56, €Donation/25/-/-/-/-, Via Chiuse Prima, tel 379 146 7915, oasidelbello@coopipad.it, www.coopipad.it.

Oratorio Sant'Ippazio presso Chiesa Cristo Redentore Pr Do Piazza Aldo Moro 9, tel 329 587 5964 or 0833 784 105, parrocchiasantippazio@gmail.com. Advance communication is difficult; check for services on arrival.

Pass the town hall on your right, fork left onto Via Calvario at the war memorial park, and go through two stop signs. Cross Via Cristoforo Colombo onto a winding lane and glimpse Corsano to the right. At a crossroads, aim for Via Tevere and, after one block, turn left onto **Via Giovanni Pascoli**. Follow signs right onto Via della Libertà and reach the modern Church of San Biagio and the municipio.

2.2KM CORSANO (ELEV 127M, POP 5500) (12.2KM)

Said to have been founded by the centurion Curzio, the hilltop town is nicknamed *cuore sano*, meaning 'healthy heart,' and its inhabitants *carcagni tosti*, meaning 'hardened heels.' The townsfolk used to walk barefoot on the sharp rocks when surveying the coast to protect their salt production, a key source of their livelihoods.

Mod Salento – Bed and Breakfast O Pr R K Cr S 7/24, €-/35/50/65/75/85, Via Rossini snc, tel 329 355 6989, modlovesalento@gmail.com, www.modsalento.it.

Keep through town, turn left at Piazza A. de Gaspari before the Church of Santa Sofia, and jog right one block at the stop sign. Fork left onto **Via Campo La Donna** and leave town to snake through the countryside. Cross the **SP210**, merge left onto a wider road, then immediately turn right, seeing Gagliano del Capo on a ridge ahead. At a stop sign at the **SP195**, go straight and begin the longest, hardest uphill you will have walked in Salento. When the road ends at the north wall of the **Chiesa di San Rocco**, turn right to Piazza San Rocco.

5.7KM GAGLIANO DEL CAPO (ELEV 139M, POP 5154) (6.5KM)

The town's Chiesa di San Rocco was built in 1574 and originally dedicated to Our Lady of the Assumption. The population requested the intercession of San Rocco and appointed him the town's patron saint following the 19th-century plague. Within are numerous canvases from the 17th, 18th, and 19th centuries by Salento painters. The Palazzo Ciardo, built in 1900 on the ruins of an old baronial castle, was the birthplace of the Italian painter Vincenzo Ciardo (1894–1970).

B&B Palazzo la Traja O Pr R K Br Cr W S Z 3/11, €-/45–50/80/90/100/-, Via Piave 32, tel 348 692 6342.

Continue through the piazza onto Corso Umberto I. After two blocks turn left before the Colonna dell'Immacolata and before the roundabout with the **SS275** turn left (groceries). Turn right onto Via San Giovanni de Mata/Ciclabile Percorso 4–5, following the far side of the **Collegio dei Padri Trinitari** complex, and when the road curves right, keep straight. At the next intersection, turn right gradually downhill as the road becomes **Contrada Chiani** (near the SS275) and, at a T-junction, turn right then fork right downhill. Merge left with another road downhill, finally pass the tall **microwave/cell tower** you've seen for some time, and start discerning the lighthouse of the Santa Maria di Leuca's cape to the right.

Tricase
Lucugnano
Castello di Caprarica
Sant'Andrea Apostolo
Via Salvio d'Acquisto
gravel
3.6 Tiggiano
Via Vittorio Veneto
Via Giovanni Pascoli
2.2 Corsano
Alessano
Via Campo La Donna
Montesardo
SP210
SP81
SS275
SP242
SP081
SP358
SP195
uphill
5.7 Gagliano del Capo
San Rocco
Padri dei Trinitari
Via San Giovanni de Mata/
Ciclabile Percorso 4-5
orciano
i Leuca
SP351
Patù
Castrignano
del Capo
SS274
Contrada
Chiani
cell tower
Via Foresta Forte
steps and
lungomare
roundabout
marina
SP214
6.5 Santa Maria di Leuca
N
0
1
2
km

Carefully follow waymarks right onto **Via Foresta Forte** and at a roundabout with the SS275 and SP124, turn left, following signs downhill to the headland. Once there, pass the **Albergo**, café, and a gift shop and arrive at the plain facade of the **Basilica Santa Maria de Finibus Terrae**, the Marian obelisk, and the tall lighthouse. To your right, and 284 steps downhill, is the lungomare and harbor of the town.

6.5KM SANTA MARIA DI LEUCA (ELEV 3M, POP CA. 1000) (0KM)

As we reach the Basilica di Santa Maria di Leuca by the cliffs and the 47m lighthouse (1864) that beams out to where the Adriatic Sea meets the Ionian (sometimes chromatically visible depending on gulf stream conditions), our gaze and thoughts turn toward the east: Albanian mountains, Greek shores, and the Holy Land. The promontory at *de finibus terrae* (at the ends of the earth) is perhaps where the Romans contemplated foreign domination. This site appears in ancient and classical literature by writers such as Herodotus, Varro, Ovid, Horace, Strabo, Virgil, and Galateo.

Pilgrimage

Pilgrims have flocked here since April 13, 343, when the Madonna is said to have miraculously saved the local fishermen by calming a terrifying storm ravaging the coastline. Yearly, on August 15, the Holy Mother is celebrated: her statue paraded through town from the Parrocchia Cristo Re then sent out to sea on a fishing boat and accompanying vessels. According to legend, St. Peter landed at the cape on the site of a pagan temple honoring Minerva, evidenced by relics preserved inside the sanctuary and the Ara a Minerva monolith, where he began evangelizing in Italy.

Myths

The origin of the addendum 'di Leuca' stems from the Greek *leukòs*, meaning 'white,' which could describe the setting sun illuminating the coast, as per Homeric geography, or perhaps refers to the spume crashing against the 100m cliffs, or even the color of the cliffs themselves. Two mystical interpretations also exist. Licofronte, in his 4th-century BC poem 'Alessandra' ('Αλεξάνδρα) mentions Leucasia. The three sirens defeated by Odysseus perished in the Tyrrhenian Sea and metamorphosed into cities: the siren Leucasia became Leuca. Another favorite myth, appearing recently in Carlo Stasi's *Leucàsia* (2022), recounts Leucasia's love for a mortal shepherd named Melisso, who was in love with another girl, Aristula. Leucasia took revenge by unleashing a storm that drowned the lovers. The goddess Minerva transformed their bodies into two immortal promontories facing each other across the bay: Punta Meliso (where the basilica stands) and Punta Ristola. The remorseful mermaid succumbed to the waves and became a sublime white cliff. When the skies and seas are storming, her song is still heard.

Your visit

The current sanctuary, following many destructions, was rebuilt in the 18th century, maintaining its perimeter walls but taking on the appearance of a home, to confound invaders.

Coming down to earth to Leuca's marina is spectacular, especially when lit up at night: a monumental double staircase frames a seasonal waterfall of the important Puglian Aqueduct, which ends at the sea in Leuca. At the bottom, a 1939 'Roman column' marks the arrival at the port.

Collect your stamp at either the gift shop or the basilica and ask for your Testimonium from one of the friendly nuns at the basilica (the Testimonia are filled in by hand, so it is best to reserve them in advance). Mass times are Mondays to Fridays at 19.00, and throughout the day on Sundays).

- **Albergo del Santuario** O Pr R Br Dr Cr S Z 40/80, €-/32/48/72/-/-, Piazza Giovanni 23, tel 0833 758 696, info@albergodelsantuario.it. Located at the sanctuary.

- **Hotel Terminal – Caroli Hotels** O Pr R Br Dr Cr W S Z 62/120, €-/50/80/105/130/-, Lungomare Colombo, 59, tel 0833 758 242, terminal@carolihotels.it, www.carolihotels.com/hotel-terminal.

The Basilica of Santa Maria de Finibus Terrae, at the tip of Italy, marks the ending of the Via Francigena in the South

Within 50m of the lighthouse, two poems by Salentine voices have been carved into the marble on display: one on the viewpoint overlooking town (easily missed), the other at the entrance to the basilica, bathed in light. With thoughts to ponder at sunset, perhaps they can begin to put into words what it feels like to have walked from Brindisi, or Bari, or Rome, or Canterbury, or home all the way here, to the Finibus Terrae (literally, 'at the ends of the earth'). The first is by the late poet, Cosimo Russo, who lived a few kilometers from here. The second is by the Venerable Bishop Antonino Bello (1935–1993) of Alessano, Lecce, who was proposed for sainthood ten years after his death.

Enchantment of Leuca

I try to breathe,
as if I were dying,
the blood pulses strongly.
I try to modulate
my voice, a thought comes out
by itself, but the enchantment
that I wanted to say remains
unexpressed.
It is here that the journey ends,
where for a moment
you feel at home
and that moment lasts
an eternity.
Cosimo Russo (1972–2017)

Santa Maria, Woman of the Last Hour

Holy Mary, woman of the last hour,
prepare us for the great journey.
Help us to loosen the moorings without fear.
You yourself take care of our passport paperwork.
If we have your visa, we will have nothing more to fear at the border.
Help us to settle, with signs of repentance and with the request for forgiveness,
the last pending issues with God's justice.
You yourself procure for us the benefits of amnesty,
which He lavishes with royal mercy.
Put our papers in order, in short, so that
when we reach the door of paradise,
it will open wide at our knock.
Don Antonio Bello, Bishop (1935–1993)

Sunset view of the town of Santa Maria di Leuca from the santuario above

APPENDIX A

Stage planning tables

Book stage	Location	Distance from start (km)	Distance from previous point (km)	Book stage distance (km)	My itinerary
1	Rome	0.0			
2	Castel Gandolfo	26.2	26.2	26.2	
	Albano Laziale	28.3	2.1		
	Nemi	36.7	8.4		
3	Velletri	47.7	11.0	21.5	
4	Cori	66.5	18.9	18.9	
	Norma	79.0	12.5		
5	Sermoneta	86.8	7.8	20.3	
6	Sezze	97.8	11.0	11.0	
	Priverno	111.1	13.3		
7	Abbazia di Fossanova	118.7	7.6	20.9	
8	Terracina	139.4	20.6	20.6	
	Monte San Biagio	152.5	13.1		
	Abbazia di San Magno	156.8	4.3		
9	Fondi	161.4	4.6	22.0	
10	Itri	176.5	15.1	15.1	
	Gaeta	190.8	14.3		
11	Formia	197.6	6.7	21.1	
	Gianola	202.9	5.3		
	Scauri	207.1	4.2		
12	Marina di Minturno	217.4	10.3	19.8	
	Castelforte	225.9	8.5		
13	Sessa Aurunca	241.6	15.7	24.2	
	Corbara	244.8	3.2		
14	Teano	257.0	12.2	15.4	
	Pietramelara	274.2	17.1		
15	Roccaromana	277.7	3.5	20.6	
	Dragoni	289.2	11.5		
16	Alife	299.0	9.8	21.4	
17	Faicchio	318.4	19.3	19.3	
18	Telese Terme	330.9	12.6	12.6	

Book stage	Location	Distance from start (km)	Distance from previous point (km)	Book stage distance (km)	My itinerary
	Solopaca	335.4	4.5		
19	Vitulano	347.5	12.1	16.6	
20	Benevento	364.7	17.1	17.1	
21	Buonalbergo	388.0	23.3	23.3	
	Casalbore	390.9	2.9		
22	Celle di San Vito	417.0	26.0	29.0	
23	Troia	434.3	17.4	17.4	
	Giardinetto	447.4	13.1		
24	Castelluccio dei Sauri	458.0	10.6	23.7	
25	Ordona	478.0	20.0	20.0	
26	Stornara	498.3	20.3	20.3	
27	Cerignola	516.2	17.9	17.9	
28	Canosa di Puglia	535.5	19.3	19.3	
29	Andria	559.6	24.1	24.1	
30	Corato	573.4	13.9	13.9	
31	Ruvo di Puglia	585.6	12.2	12.2	
32	Bitonto	604.0	18.4	18.4	
33	Bari	627.7	23.7	23.7	
	Torre a Mare	641.3	13.6		
34	Mola di Bari	651.3	10.0	23.6	
	Polignano a Mare	670.3	19.0		
35	Monopoli	680.3	10.1	29.1	
36	Savelletri	701.8	21.4	21.4	
37	Torre Canne	710.6	8.9	8.9	
38	Torre Santa Sabina	740.7	30.1	30.1	
	Spiaggia di Specchiolla	744.7	4.0		
39	Brindisi	771.7	27.1	31.0	
40	Torchiarolo	797.0	25.2	25.2	
	Surbo	812.6	15.7		
41	Lecce	819.4	6.8	22.5	
	Merine	825.1	5.6		
	Vernole	837.6	12.5		
42	Martano	850.4	12.7	30.9	
	Carpignano Salentino	854.2	3.9		

Book stage	Location	Distance from start (km)	Distance from previous point (km)	Book stage distance (km)	My itinerary
	Serrano	856.7	2.5		
	Cannole	859.1	2.3		
	Palmariggi	868.3	9.2		
	Giurdignano	874.0	5.7		
43	Otranto	880.8	6.8	30.5	
	Uggiano la Chiesa	892.7	11.8		
	Cocumola	897.3	4.6		
44	Vignacastrisi	904.8	7.5	23.9	
	Marittima	907.5	2.8		
45	Tricase	919.0	11.5	14.3	
	Tiggiano	922.6	3.6		
	Corsano	924.8	2.2		
	Gagliano del Capo	930.6	5.7		
	Santa Maria di Leuca	937.1	6.5	18.0	
			Total	937.1	
			Average distance/day	20.8	

Monte Sant'Angelo/Via Litoranea Connection

Book stage	Location	Distance from start (km)	Distance from previous point (km)	Book stage distance (km)	My itinerary
MSA23	Troia	434.3			
MSA24	Lucera	456	21.7	21.7	
MSA25	San Severo	480.2	24.2	24.2	
MSA26	Stignano	501.5	21.3	21.3	
MSA27	San Giovanni Rotondo	521.2	19.7	19.7	
	Monte Sant'Angelo	545.4	24.2	24.2	
			Total	111.1	

Via Litoranea Connection (assuming beginning at Troia)

Book stage	Location	Distance from start (km)	Distance from previous point (km)	My itinerary
	Monte Sant'Angelo	545.4	0	
	Madonna delle Grazie	550.2	4.8	
	Manfredonia	559.4	9.2	
	Zapponeta	586.8	27.4	
	Margherita di Savoia	605.8	19	
VLC	Barletta	622.3	16.5	
	Trani	636.8	14.5	
	Bisceglie	647.2	10.4	
	Molfetta	658.8	11.6	
	Giovinazzo	666.8	8	
	Bari	688.4	21.6	
		Total	143.0	

APPENDIX B

Useful contacts

To purchase the credenziale, contact/visit the following associations, which also advise pilgrims:

Rome

- Palazzo Merulana, Via Merulana 121, tel 06 6228 8768, segreteria@palazzomerulana.it. Open Wednesday to Sunday 09.00–20.00.
- Ciclofficina n.9 di Cristiano Michelazzi, Viale Angelico 297, tel 06 2539 8487, ciclofficina9@gmail.com. Open Tuesday to Friday 09.00–13.30 and 16.00–19.30, and Saturday 09.00–13.30.
- Bottega 10a di Barbara Medori, Via del Fiume 10/a, tel 380 515 4025, bottega10a@yahoo.it. Open Monday to Friday 10.00–13.00 and 15.00–19.00; call on Saturdays for requests.
- Bags Free by Bon Bags Srl, Via del Castro Pretorio 32, tel 06 445 5792, info@bags-free.com. Open 16 March to 31 October inclusive, Monday to Sunday 08.30–18.30.

Velletri

- PIT Velletri, Piazza Garibaldi, prolocovelitrae@libero.it. Open Monday to Sunday 10.00–12.30, also open Friday 17.00–19.00.
- Circolo ARCI R-Esistenza dopolavoro ferroviario, Piazza Martiri d'Ungheria 1, tel 338 579 7827, dopolavoroferroviario.velletri@gmail.com. Open Monday to Sunday 18.30–13.00.

Formia

- Spirit of Travel, Via Rotabile 115B, tel 0771 269 288, commercialelt@dmofrancigenasudlazio.it. Open Monday to Saturday 10.00–19.00.

San Severo

- Enopolio Daunio|HUB Polifunzionale Culturale & Coworking, Via Soccorso 86, tel 347 353 8447 or 349 260 5176 or 377 082 8224 or 347 566 7173, info@enopoliodaunio.it. Open Monday to Friday 10.00–13.00.

Monte Sant'Angelo

- Organizzazione di volontariato Monte Sant'Angelo Francigena, Via Reale Basilica 76, tel 349 528 5571, msafrancigena@gmail.com. Open daily 09.00–12.00 and 15.00–18.00 (20.00 in summer).

Canosa di Puglia

- Associazione Via Francigena Canosa di Puglia, Via Roma 10, tel 376 009 4395, viafrancigenacanosadipuglia@gmail.com. Contact name Rosa Anna Asselta; appointment required.

Barletta

- Barletta Sportiva ASD, Via Turbine 19/21, tel 389 182 0901, enzocascella@gmail.com. Contact name Pasquale Caputo; open daily 10.00–12.00 and 17.00–21.00.

- ASD Gli Amici del Cammino Barletta Running & Walking, Via Mulini 40, tel 338 812 6475, asd.amicidelcammino.barletta@gmail.com. Contact name Ruggiero Graniero; open daily 09.00–12.00 and 19.00–21.00.

Corato

- Comitato Via Francigena del Sud-Corato, Chiesa Santa Maria Greca, Corso Garibaldi 55, tel 347 304 4414, laviafrancigenadelsud@gmail.com. Open Monday to Sunday 14.00–16.00, also open Tuesday and Thursday 18.00–20.00.

Lecce

- Urban Oasis Hostel, Via Nicola Cataldi 3, tel 0832 300 050, info@urbanoasishostel.com. Open daily 10.00–20.00.
- Slow Active Tours, Via Corrado Alvaro 17/a, tel 0832 182 6868, info@slowactivetours.com. Open Monday to Saturday 09.00–13.00 and 15.00–18.00.

Santa Maria di Leuca

- Ciclofficina Fersini, Via Virgilio 57, tel 327 171 1583, ciclofficinafersini@gmail.com. Open daily 09.00–13.00 and 16.00–20.00

APPENDIX C

Bibliography

Attolico, Angelofabio; Focarazzo, Claudio; and Lozito, Lorenzo, *The Via Francigena in Southern Italy*, Terre di mezzo Editore, Milan, 2022

Beer, Eugene, *Italy: History and Landscape*, Barnes and Noble, New York, 2006

Belford, Ros, *The Rough Guide to Italy*, Rough Guides, 2022

Belloc, Hilaire, *The Path to Rome*, George Allen & Unwin Ltd, London, 1902

Black, Jeremy, *A Brief History of Italy*, Robinson, London, 2018

Brown, Sandy, *Walking the Via Francigena Pilgrim Route – Part 1, Canterbury to Lausanne*, Cicerone Press, Kendal, 2023

Brown, Sandy, *Walking the Via Francigena Pilgrim Route – Part 2, Lausanne and the Great St Bernard Pass to Lucca*, Cicerone Press, Kendal, 2021

Brown, Sandy, *Walking the Via Francigena Pilgrim Route – Part 3, Lucca to Rome*, Cicerone Press, Kendal, 2023

Butcher, Justin, *Walking to Jerusalem: Blisters, hope and other facts on the ground*, Hodder & Stoughton, London, 2018

Cardini, Franco, Il 'miraggio' della terrasanta tra pellegrinaggio e crociate, https://www.viefrancigene.org/wp-content/uploads/2021/03/storia_franco_cardini_-_il_miraggio_della_terrasanta_tra_pellegrinaggio_e_crociate.pdf

Caselli, Giovanni, 'La Via Appia Antica da Roma a Brindisi e la Via Traiana Nova da Brindisi a Benevento' in *Guida alle antiche strade romane*, Istituto geografico De Agostini, Milano, 1994

Caselli, Giovanni, 'Discovering the Via Francigena,' www.academia.edu/4354575/DISCOVERING_THE_VIA_FRANCIGENA

Collins, Michael, *The Vatican: Secrets and Treasures of the Holy City*, DK, Penguin, London, 2008

DeBella, Toni; Minoni, Cristina; and Pathe, Alex, *Italy 2024*, DK Penguin Random House, London, 2023

Drijvers, Jan Willem, 'Travel and Pilgrimage Literature' in *A Companion to Late Antique Literature*, John Wiley & Sons, New Jersey, 2018

Horace, *Satires, Epistles and Ars Poetica*, English and Latin Edition, English translation by H.R. Fairclough, Loeb Classical Library, No. 194, Harvard University Press and William Heinemann Ltd, 1926

Jacobs, Andrew S., 'The Bordeaux Pilgrim (c. 333 C.E.),' Translation by Andrew S. Jacobs, www.andrewjacobs.org/translations/bordeaux.html

Jepson, Tim, *Rome 25 Best*, Fodor's Travel, Basingstoke, 2021

Roberts, J.M., *Shorter Illustrated History of the World*, Helicon, Oxford, 1993

Ross, Zoë, *Puglia*, Thomas Cook Publishing, Peterborough, 2011

Stagg, Guy, *The Crossway*, Picador, London, 2018

Stopani, Renato, 'La Via Appia Traiana nel medioevo,' www.viefrancigene.org/wp-content/uploads/2021/03/storia_renato_stopani_-_la_via_appia_traiana_nel_medio-evo.pdf

Trono, Anna and Oliva, Luigi, 'Innovations in a Traditional Landscape of Pilgrimage: The Via Francigena del Sud toward Rome and Other Apulian Pilgrim's Routes,' https://www.viefrancigene.org/wp-content/uploads/2021/12/Innovations-in-a-Traditional-Landscape-of-Pilgrimage.pdf, 2021

Ure, John, *Pilgrimage: The Great Adventure of the Middle Ages*, Constable & Robinson, 2006

APPENDIX D

The route of the Bordeaux Pilgrim in Southern Italy

Crossing the sea, a thousand stadia, which makes a hundred miles, you come to Hydrontum (Hydruntum, Otranto), and halt a mile farther.

Change at the twelfth milestone Halt at Clipeae (Lupiae, Lecce) – miles xiii.

Change at Valentia (Baletium, Baleso) – miles xiii.

City of Brindisium (Brundisium, Brindisi) – miles xi.

Halt at Spilenees (Speluncae) – miles xiv.

Change at the tenth milestone (Pto. Villa Nova) – miles xi.

City of Leonatia (Gnatia, Egnatia, Agnazzo) – miles x.

Change at Turres Aurilianae (San Vito) – miles xv.

Change at Turres Julianae – miles ix.

City of Beroes (Barium, Bari) – miles xi.

Change at Butontones (Butuntum, Bitonto) – miles xi.

City of Rubi (Ruvo di Puglia) – miles xi.

Change at the fifteenth milestone – miles xv.

City of Canusium (Canosa di Puglia) – miles xv.

Change at the eleventh milestone – miles xi.

City of Serdonis (Herdonea, Ordona) – miles xv.

City of Aecae (Troja, Troia) – miles xviii.

Change at Aquilo (frontier of Puglia and Campania) – miles x.

Halt at Equus Magnus (Equus Tuticus, S. Eleuterio) – miles viii.

Change at the village of Fornum Novum (Forum Novum, Buonalbergo) – miles xii.

City of Beneventum (Benevento) – miles x.

City and halt at Claudii (Caudium, Casta Cauda) – miles xii.

Change at Novae – miles ix.

City of Capua (Capua) – miles xii.

Total from Aulon (Valona) to Capua 289 miles, 25 changes, 13 halts.

Change at the eighth milestone – miles viii.

Change at Pons Campanus (over the Savone River) – miles ix.

City of Sonuessa (Sinuessa, Mondragone) – miles ix.

City of Menturnae (Minturnae, on the Liris) – miles ix.

City of Formi (Mola di Gaeta) – miles ix.

City of Fundi (Fondi) – miles xii.

City of Tarracina (Terracina) – miles xiii.

Change at Mediae (Posta di Mesa) – miles x.

Change at Forum Appi (Foro Appio) – miles ix.

Change at Sponsae – miles vii.

City of Aricia (Ariccia) and Albona (Albanum, Albano) – miles xvi

Change at the ninth milestone – miles vii.

To the city of Rome – miles ix.

Total from Capua to the city of Rome 136 miles, 14 changes, 9 halts.

(source: Eugenio Alliata OFM, web.archive.org/web/20170208122825/http://www.christusrex.org/www1/ofm/pilgr/bord/10Bord01Bordeaux.html)

DOWNLOAD THE GPX FILES

All the routes in this guide are available for download from:

www.cicerone.co.uk/1249/GPX

as standard format GPX files. You should be able to load them into most online GPX systems and mobile devices, whether GPS or smartphone. You may need to convert the file into your preferred format using a conversion programme such as gpsvisualizer.com or one of the many other such websites and programmes.

When you follow this link, you will be asked for your email address and where you purchased the guidebook, and have the option to subscribe to the Cicerone e-newsletter.

www.cicerone.co.uk

LISTING OF CICERONE GUIDES

BRITISH ISLES CHALLENGES, COLLECTIONS AND ACTIVITIES

Great Walks on the England Coast Path
Map and Compass
The Big Rounds
The Book of the Bivvy
The Book of the Bothy
The Mountains of England and Wales:
Vol 1 Wales
Vol 2 England
The National Trails
Walking the End to End Trail
Cycling Land's End to John o' Groats

SHORT WALKS SERIES

15 Short Walks Hadrian's Wall
15 Short Walks in the Lake District: Keswick, Borrowdale and Buttermere
15 Short Walks in the Lake District: Windermere Ambleside and Grasmere
15 Short Walks Lake District: Coniston and Langdale
15 Short Walks in Arnside and Silverdale
15 Short Walks in the Ribble Valley
15 Short Walks in Nidderdale
15 Short Walks in Northumberland: Wooler, Rothbury, Alnwick and the coast
15 Short Walks in the Yorkshire Dales: Grassington, Skipton, Malham and Ilkley
15 Short Walks in the Peak District: Bakewell and the White Peak
15 Short Walks on the Malvern Hills
15 Short Walks in Cornwall: Falmouth and the Lizard
15 Short Walks in Cornwall: Land's End and Penzance
15 Short Walks in the South Downs: Brighton, Eastbourne and Arundel
15 Short Walks in the Surrey Hills
15 Short Walks on Dartmoor North: Okehampton and Chagford
15 Short Walks on Dartmoor South: Ivybridge and Princetown
15 Short Walks on Exmoor
15 Short Walks Winchester
15 Short Walks in Bannau Brycheiniog: Brecon Beacons
15 Short Walks in Pembrokeshire: Tenby and the south
15 Short Walks in Dumfries and Galloway
15 Short Walks in the Trossachs: Callander and Aberfoyle
15 Short Walks on the Isle of Mull
15 Short Walks on the Orkney Islands
15 Short Walks on the Shetland Islands

SCOTLAND

Ben Nevis and Glen Coe
Cycling in the Hebrides
Cycling the North Coast 500
Great Mountain Days in Scotland
Mountain Biking in Southern and Central Scotland
Mountain Biking in West and North West Scotland
Not the West Highland Way: A Mountain High Way
Scotland
Scotland's Best Small Mountains
Scotland's Mountain Ridges
Scottish Wild Country Backpacking
Skye's Cuillin Ridge Traverse
The Borders Abbeys Way
The Great Glen Way
The Great Glen Way Map Booklet
The Hebridean Way
The Hebrides
The Isle of Mull
The Isle of Skye
The Skye Trail
The Southern Upland Way
The West Highland Way
The West Highland Way Map Booklet
Walking Ben Lawers, Rannoch and Atholl
Walking in the Cairngorms
Walking in the Pentland Hills
Walking in the Scottish Borders
Walking in the Southern Uplands
Walking in Torridon, Fisherfield, Fannichs and An Teallach
Walking Loch Lomond and the Trossachs
Walking on Arran
Walking on Harris and Lewis
Walking on Jura, Islay and Colonsay
Walking on Mull, Coll and Tiree
Walking on Rum and the Small Isles
Walking on the Orkney and Shetland Isles
Walking on Uist and Barra
Walking the Cape Wrath Trail
Walking the Corbetts
Vol 1 South of the Great Glen
Vol 2 North of the Great Glen
Walking the Fife Pilgrim Way
Walking the Galloway Hills
Walking the John o' Groats Trail
Walking the Munros
Vol 1 Southern, Central and Western Highlands
Vol 2 Northern Highlands and the Cairngorms
Winter Climbs in the Cairngorms
Winter Climbs: Ben Nevis and Glen Coe

NORTHERN ENGLAND ROUTES

Cycling the Reivers Route
Cycling the Way of the Roses
Hadrian's Cycleway
Hadrian's Wall Path
Hadrian's Wall Path Map Booklet
The Coast to Coast Cycle Route
The Coast to Coast Map Booklet
The Coast to Coast Walk
Walking the Dales Way
The Dales Way Map Booklet
Walking the Pennine Way
Pennine Way Map Booklet

LAKE DISTRICT

Bikepacking in the Lake District
Cycling in the Lake District
Great Mountain Days in the Lake District
Joss Naylor's Lakes, Meres and Waters of the Lake District
Lake District Winter Climbs
Lake District:
High Level and Fell Walks
Low Level and Lake Walks
Mountain Biking in the Lake District
Outdoor Adventures with Children — Lake District
Scrambles in the Lake District —
North
South
Trail and Fell Running in the Lake District
Walking The Cumbria Way
Walking the Lake District Fells —
Borrowdale
Buttermere
Coniston
Keswick
Langdale
Mardale and the Far East
Patterdale
Wasdale
Walking the Tour of the Lake District

NORTH-WEST ENGLAND AND THE ISLE OF MAN

Cycling the Pennine Bridleway
Isle of Man Coastal Path
The Lancashire Cycleway
The Lune Valley and Howgills
Walking in Cumbria's Eden Valley
Walking in Lancashire
Walking in the Forest of Bowland and Pendle
Walking on the Isle of Man
Walking on the West Pennine Moors
Walking the Ribble Way
Walks in Silverdale and Arnside

NORTH-EAST ENGLAND, YORKSHIRE DALES AND PENNINES

Cycling in the Yorkshire Dales
Great Mountain Days in the Pennines
Mountain Biking in the Yorkshire Dales
The Cleveland Way and the Yorkshire Wolds Way
The Cleveland Way Map Booklet
The North York Moors
Trail and Fell Running in the Yorkshire Dales
Walking in County Durham
Walking in Northumberland
Walking in the North Pennines
Walking in the Yorkshire Dales:
North and East
South and West
Walking St Cuthbert's Way
Walking St Oswald's Way and Northumberland Coast Path

DERBYSHIRE, PEAK DISTRICT AND MIDLANDS

Cycling in the Peak District
Dark Peak Walks
Scrambles in the Dark Peak
Walking in Derbyshire
Walking in the Peak District -
White Peak East
White Peak West

WALES AND WELSH BORDERS

Cycle Touring in Wales
Cycling Lon Las Cymru
Great Mountain Days in Snowdonia
Hillwalking in Shropshire
Mountain Walking in Snowdonia
Offa's Dyke Path
Offa's Dyke Map Booklet
Scrambles in Snowdonia
Snowdonia: 30 Low-level and Easy Walks — North, South
The Cambrian Way
The Pembrokeshire Coast Path
The Pembrokeshire Coast Path Map Booklet
The Snowdonia Way
The Wye Valley Walk
Walking Glyndwr's Way
Walking in Carmarthenshire
Walking in Pembrokeshire
Walking in the Brecon Beacons
Walking in the Wye Valley
Walking on Gower
Walking the Severn Way
Walking the Shropshire Way
Walking the Wales Coast Path

SOUTHERN ENGLAND

20 Classic Sportive Rides
in South East England
in South West England
Cycling in the Cotswolds
Mountain Biking on the North Downs
Mountain Biking on the South Downs
The North Downs Way
The North Downs Way Map Booklet
The South Downs Way
The South Downs Way Map Booklet
The Cotswold Way
The Cotswold Way Map Booklet
The Ridgeway National Trail
The Ridgeway Map Booklet
The Thames Path
The Thames Path Map Booklet
The Two Moors Way
Two Moors Way Map Booklet
Walking the South West Coast Path
South West Coast Path Map Booklet
Vol 1: Minehead to St Ives
Vol 2: St Ives to Plymouth
Vol 2: St Ives to Plymouth
Vol 3: Plymouth to Poole
Suffolk Coast and Heath Walks
The Kennet and Avon Canal
The Lea Valley Walk
The Peddars Way and Norfolk Coast Path
The Pilgrims' Way
Walking Hampshire's Test Way
Walking in Essex
Walking in Kent
Walking in London
Walking in Norfolk
Walking in the Chilterns
Walking in the Cotswolds
Walking in the Isles of Scilly
Walking in the New Forest
Walking in the North Wessex Downs
Walking on Dartmoor
Walking on Guernsey
Walking on Jersey
Walking on the Isle of Wight
Walking the Dartmoor Way
Walking the Jurassic Coast
Walking the Sarsen Way
Walks in the South Downs National Park

ALPS CROSS-BORDER ROUTES

100 Hut Walks in the Alps
Alpine Ski Mountaineering Vol 1 — Western Alps
The Karnischer Hohenweg
The Tour of the Bernina
Trail Running — Chamonix and the Mont Blanc region
Trekking Chamonix to Zermatt
Trekking in the Alps
Trekking in the Silvretta and Ratikon Alps
Trekking Munich to Venice
Trekking the Tour du Mont Blanc
Tour du Mont Blanc Map Booklet
Walking in the Alps

FRANCE, BELGIUM, AND LUXEMBOURG

Camino de Santiago — Via Podiensis
Chamonix Mountain Adventures
Cycling London to Paris
Cycling the Canal de la Garonne
Cycling the Canal du Midi
Mont Blanc Walks
Mountain Adventures in the Maurienne
Short Treks on Corsica
The GR5 Trail
The GR5 Trail —
Vosges and Jura
Benelux and Lorraine
The Moselle Cycle Route
Trekking in the Vanoise
Trekking the Cathar Way
Trekking the GR10
Trekking the GR20 Corsica
Trekking the Robert Louis Stevenson Trail
Via Ferratas of the French Alps
Walking in Provence — East
Walking in Provence — West
Walking in the Auvergne
Walking in the Brianconnais
Walking in the Dordogne
Walking in the Haute Savoie: North
Walking in the Haute Savoie: South
Walking on Corsica
Walking the Brittany Coast Path
Walking in the Ardennes

PYRENEES AND FRANCE/SPAIN CROSS-BORDER ROUTES

Shorter Treks in the Pyrenees
The Pyrenean Haute Route
The Pyrenees
Trekking the Cami dels Bons Homes
Trekking the GR11 Trail
Walks and Climbs in the Pyrenees

SPAIN AND PORTUGAL

Camino de Santiago: Camino Frances
Coastal Walks in Andalucia
Costa Blanca Mountain Adventures
Cycling the Camino de Santiago
Mountain Walking in Mallorca
Mountain Walking in Southern Catalunya
Spain's Sendero Historico: The GR1
The Andalucian Coast to Coast Walk
The Camino del Norte and Camino Primitivo
The Camino Ingles and Ruta do Mar
The Mountains Around Nerja
The Mountains of Ronda and Grazalema
The Sierras of Extremadura
Trekking in Mallorca
Trekking in the Canary Islands
Trekking the GR7 in Andalucia
Walking and Trekking in the Sierra Nevada
Walking in Andalucia
Walking in Catalunya —
Barcelona
Girona Pyrenees
Walking in the Picos de Europa
Walking La Via de la Plata and Camino Sanabres
Walking on Gran Canaria
Walking on La Gomera and El Hierro

Walking on La Palma
Walking on Lanzarote and Fuerteventura
Walking on Tenerife
Walking on the Costa Blanca
Walking the Camino dos Faros
Portugal's Rota Vicentina
The Camino Portugues
Walking in Portugal
Walking in the Algarve
Walking on Madeira
Walking on the Azores

SWITZERLAND

Switzerland's Jura Crest Trail
The Swiss Alps
Tour of the Jungfrau Region
Trekking the Swiss Via Alpina
Walking in Arolla and Zinal
Walking in the Bernese Oberland — Jungfrau region
Walking in the Engadine — Switzerland
Walking in Ticino
Walking in Zermatt and Saas-Fee

GERMANY

Hiking and Cycling in the Black Forest
The Danube Cycleway Vol 1
The Rhine Cycle Route
The Westweg
Walking in the Bavarian Alps

POLAND, SLOVAKIA, ROMANIA, HUNGARY AND BULGARIA

The Danube Cycleway Vol 2
The High Tatras
The Mountains of Romania

SCANDINAVIA, ICELAND AND GREENLAND

Hiking in Norway —
North
South
Trekking the Kungsleden
Trekking in Greenland — The Arctic Circle Trail
Walking and Trekking in Iceland

SLOVENIA, CROATIA, SERBIA, MONTENEGRO AND ALBANIA

Hiking Slovenia's Juliana Trail
Mountain Biking in Slovenia
The Islands of Croatia
The Julian Alps of Slovenia
The Mountains of Montenegro
The Peaks of the Balkans Trail
The Peaks of the Balkans Trail
The Slovene Mountain Trail
Walking in Slovenia: The Karavanke
Walks and Treks in Croatia

ITALY

Alta Via
1 — Trekking in the Dolomites
2 — Trekking in the Dolomites
Day Walks in the Dolomites
Italy's Grande Traversata delle Alpi
Italy's Sibillini National Park
Ski Touring and Snowshoeing in the Dolomites
The Way of St Francis: Via di Francesco
Trekking Gran Paradiso: Alta Via 2
Trekking in the Apennines
Trekking the Giants' Trail: Alta Via 1 through the Italian Pennine Alps
Via Ferratas of the Italian Dolomites:
Vol 1
Vol 2
Walking in Abruzzo
Walking in Italy's Cinque Terre
Walking in Italy's Stelvio National Park
Walking in Sicily
Walking in the Aosta Valley
Walking in the Dolomites
Walking in Tuscany
Walking in Umbria
Walking Lake Como and Maggiore
Walking Lake Garda and Iseo
Walking on the Amalfi Coast
Walking the Via Francigena Pilgrim Route
Part 1
Part 2
Part 3
Part 4
Walks and Treks in the Maritime Alps

IRELAND

The Wild Atlantic Way and Western Ireland
Walking the Kerry Way
Walking the Wicklow Way

EUROPEAN CYCLING

Cycling the Route des Grandes Alpes
Cycling the Ruta Via de la Plata
The Elbe Cycle Route
The River Loire Cycle Route
The River Rhone Cycle Route

INTERNATIONAL CHALLENGES, COLLECTIONS AND ACTIVITIES

Europe's High Points
Pocket First Aid and Wilderness Medicine

AUSTRIA

Innsbruck Mountain Adventures
Trekking Austria's Adlerweg
Trekking in Austria's Hohe Tauern
Trekking in Austria's Stubai Alps
Trekking in Austria's Zillertal Alps
Walking in Austria
Walking in the Salzkammergut: the Austrian Lake District

MEDITERRANEAN

The High Mountains of Crete
Trekking in Greece
Walking and Trekking in Zagori
Walking and Trekking on Corfu
Walking on the Greek Islands — the Cyclades
Walking in Cyprus
Walking on Malta

HIMALAYA

8000 metres
Everest: A Trekker's Guide
Trekking in the Karakoram

NORTH AMERICA

Hiking and Cycling the California Missions Trail
Hiking the Pacific Crest Trail
The John Muir Trail

SOUTH AMERICA

Aconcagua and the Southern Andes
Hiking and Biking Peru's Inca Trails
Trekking in Torres del Paine

AFRICA

Climbing Toubkal
Kilimanjaro
Walking in the Drakensberg
Walks and Scrambles in the Moroccan Anti-Atlas

NEW ZEALANDAND AND AUSTRALIA

Hiking the Overland Track

CHINA, JAPAN AND ASIA

Annapurna
Hiking and Trekking in the Japan Alps and Mount Fuji
Hiking in Hong Kong
Japan's Kumano Kodo Pilgrimage
Japan's Kumano Kodo Pilgrimage
Trekking in Bhutan
Trekking in Ladakh
Trekking in Tajikistan
Trekking in the Himalaya

TECHNIQUES

Fastpacking
The Mountain Hut Book

MINI GUIDES

Alpine Flowers
Navigation

MOUNTAIN LITERATURE

A Walk in the Clouds
Abode of the Gods
Fifty Years of Adventure
The Pennine Way — the Path, the People, the Journey
Unjustifiable Risk?

For full information on all our guides, books and eBooks, visit our website:
www.cicerone.co.uk